P9-CEA-307

VALUES IN A BUSINESS SOCIETY | ISSUES AND ANALYSES

THE HARBRACE SERIES
IN BUSINESS AND ECONOMICS

VALUES IN A BUSINESS SOCIETY | ISSUES AND ANALYSES

JAMES W. KUHN

IVAR BERG

Columbia University

HARCOURT, BRACE & WORLD, INC.

New York / Chicago / San Francisco / Atlanta

to

Professor Ernest M. Fisher

a man of wisdom

Library of Congress Catalog Card Number: 68–11247
Printed in the United States of America

FOREWORD

Values in a Business Society is based on Columbia University Business School's core course on the Conceptual Foundations of Business. During the seven years in which that course has been offered, Professors Kuhn and Berg have collaborated with their colleagues in inviting graduate students to explore the problems faced by managers concerned with the corporation and its associated organizations.

This book, like the course out of which it grew, holds that business leadership requires "men who are literate, not just in the art of business management, but in understanding the changing and ever developing human condition." The role of consensus and consent is increasingly vital in the governing of corporations. Consequently the influence of a manager now depends less on the prerogatives of his position than on his professional competence and the respect he commands. If he is to maintain a profitable activity, and if he is to serve the long-range interests of a public that gives his organization its sanction, he must display initiative, creativity, and adaptability at all levels of authority.

Future business leaders must, in addition to learning about business functions and activities, prepare themselves to deal discerningly with the host of commitments that they and their corporate organizations will perforce be undertaking. They need to develop values that will give them true perspective as they make decisions affecting the conduct of business and the aspirations of men. The educated, disciplined businessman who knows the shortcomings of his perceptions and the limits of his perspectives is likely to act in ways that, though not always right and seldom totally right, will be sufficiently correct to generate confidence in his leadership.

In this book Professors Kuhn and Berg ask the reader to look at business as it relates to the many facets of society. In the spirit of the great liberating traditions of learning, they emphasize the analytical, historical, and comparative characteristics of those relationships. They urge the reader to search for understanding beyond specialized knowledge. They ask him to appraise the impact of business decisions on the intellectual and spiritual life of the individual and of society and to develop a measure of historical understanding, a sense of civic opportunity, and an appreciation of the enduring contributions of business to the well-being of mankind.

COURTNEY C. BROWN, *Dean*
Graduate School of Business, Columbia University

PREFACE

The large size of today's business corporations, the wide range of their activities at home and abroad, and the nation's dependence upon them for an amazing array of goods and services mean that the businessman is a highly influential American. His influence is increased even more by the fact that he is not only an administrator seeking to maximize profits but the head of a complex, little understood social system that has a profound impact on all its members. It is thus the lot of the business manager to face problems and make decisions for which training in finance, production, marketing, and the other functional specialties will only partly prepare him.

If a businessman today begins his career unskilled in analyzing intricate political and social issues of the kind that he will be called upon to resolve, he is in a position to be confounded and defeated. The cases in this book often illustrate what Dr. Henry Wriston called the "primacy of secondary consequences." A businessman who attacks his problems head-on and insists every time on reaching an uncomplicated common-sense solution is certain to provoke opposition and will be taken unawares by the forces he has indirectly and unintentionally set in motion.

The cases in this book present our analyses of principles and issues for those who want to understand better the involved, sometimes intractable, problems with which businessmen must grapple. We do not offer solutions to these problems, for no certain ones exist; the pairs of juxtaposed cases and the analyses raise more questions than they offer answers. Our hope is that the materials will alert the reader to some problems of which he was unaware and encourage him to re-examine his solutions to others. As James Thurber wryly advised, "It is better to ask some of the questions than to know all the answers."

A businessman needs to understand his own values and appreciate the force of the values of others. He cannot afford to be sentimentally romantic about the world or his problems; he must see them as they are, not as he wishes to see them. He must not only know his strengths and the resources available to him, but know also—and better than outsiders—his own weaknesses and the defects of the business institutions through which he works. He must be a professional with a sense of values that affords him a realistic perspective of where he has been and where he is going. The materials in this book will help those who examine it to gain insights into the nature of both the opportunities and the obstacles that businessmen face.

The cases and issues presented here have been strongly influenced by the graduate business students who have studied—and argued about—them in our classes in the Conceptual Foundations of Business over the past seven years. As we experimented with ways of analyzing the problems of management and approaching the issues of public policy that confront businessmen, we dropped many cases, added new ones, and revised others to keep them relevant and up to date. The use of paired cases dealing with the same basic issues in different situations has proved invaluable as a way to draw attention to the extent of complex and conflicting values in business decision-making. Our students have shown themselves deeply concerned with the issues, and their study of the paired cases has enabled them to write perceptive analyses and to engage in informative and stimulating classroom discussions.

We received valuable help in collecting materials and data for the cases from a number of research assistants, three of whom—Ross Weber, Alvin Puryear, and John Logan—wrote some of the early drafts. Our secretaries—Patricia Farley, Kathleen Fitzgerald, Joyce Phelan, and Patricia Emsworth—are due many thanks for the long hours they devoted to typing and putting the manuscript in order. We are also grateful to the Columbia University Business School for the opportunity to teach the course from which these cases and this book came.

James W. Kuhn
Ivar Berg
Columbia University

CONTENTS

section **1**

CORPORATIONS AND UNIONS

Business corporations and labor unions dominate the economy of the United States and exert a commanding influence on the lives and livelihood of most American citizens. Except for the government, no other institutions rival them in economic power or possess their capacity to direct the daily activities of millions of people. In a nation that celebrates personal independence, 85 per cent of the labor force now consists of employees who sell their services for wages and salaries. The greater part of the 62 million wage-and-salary employees depend upon corporations for their jobs. Some 3.6 million, or one-fifth of the total employed in manufacturing, are dependent on the 25 largest industrial corporations alone. Although Americans boast of their individuality, some 17 million workers—one out of every four persons in the labor force—have joined labor unions.

In the aggregate, business corporations have tremendous economic power, but even singly, some corporations are so vast that they exercise an influence over the whole of American society. Hundreds of corporations directly employ tens of thousands of people, and the largest number their employees by the hundreds of thousands. Indirectly, corporations provide income and support for a far larger number of people. In 1960 General Electric, a large but not the largest corporation, received parts and materials from more than 45,000 suppliers and sold or serviced its finished products through about 400,000 small companies.[1]

In the number of people directly affiliated with them, labor unions generally surpass even the largest corporations. Two unions, the Teamsters and the Auto Workers, claim memberships of over a million; and six enroll more than half a million workers. (Only one industrial corporation, General Motors, has as many employees—745,000—as some of the leading unions have members.) Unions have established over 71,000 locals throughout the United States, and they help administer some 150,000 collective agreements currently in force. While unions help set the wages, hours, and working conditions for only the 17 million employees covered by their agreements, indirectly they affect the terms of work for

[1] Statement by Ralph J. Cordiner, *New Views on Automation,* Subcommittee on Automation and Energy Resources, Joint Economic Committee (Washington: Government Printing Office, 1960), p. 129.

many unorganized employees, including managers, professionals, and white-collar workers. Unions are quite as concentrated as corporations; the three largest account for almost one-fifth of total union membership, and seven of them encompass over one-third of all locals. The unions' strength and influence in the nation rest upon their large membership, not upon their economic resources. All union assets—treasuries, buildings, investments, and pension and welfare funds, including those in which union officers have at least some voice—may total $4.5 billion; [2] but however impressive this sum is absolutely, it pales in comparison with the more than $12 billion in assets of Standard Oil of New Jersey or the $31 billion of American Telephone and Telegraph.

American corporations and unions have grown to gigantic size. We casually refer to "big business" and "big labor," and statistics confirm the aptness of these phrases. However, excessive familiarity with the "bigness" of corporations and unions can dull our perception of what this bigness means. The growth of corporations and unions has not simply enlarged them; it has changed their quality. A "big" corporation is not merely an owner-managed mill enlarged, nor is a "big" union simply a shop group of workers multiplied many times. Big corporations and unions alter the structure of the whole society, changing the role of the state and the liberties of individuals.

When measured against the government, business corporations and unions are put into a different perspective, one that not only reveals their size but also suggests the governmental role they have gradually assumed. They bulk so large, claim the loyalty or services of so many people, and spread so far the impact of the decisions made and the activities carried out under their imprimatur that they have become for many purposes substitute, if not rival, governments.

In 1965 General Motors' sales of $21 billion were over six times larger than the total tax revenues of the state of California and equal to about 18 per cent of federal tax revenues. Eleven other industrial corporations reported sales larger than the $3.1 billion in taxes levied by California. Another 59 industrial corporations made sales greater than $1 billion—a sum surpassed by the tax revenues of only seven states. Profits may be a more impressive dimension of corporate strength than sales; even these lesser figures stand out against the states' revenues. General Motors' net profits of $2.1 billion in 1965 were larger than the tax revenues of any state except California or New York. The profits of the American Telephone and Telegraph Company, $1.8 billion, were greater than the tax revenues of Illinois, Michigan, Ohio, Pennsylvania, or Texas. Standard Oil of New Jersey enjoyed profits of $1.04 billion, larger than the tax revenues of all but six states.[3]

Labor unions may occasionally cause the closing of a whole industry or major portions of one for as long as several months. The coal mining industry in the 1940's, the steel industry in 1959, and shipping on two coasts in the 1960's were brought to a standstill by unions, which had the power to stop production and so threaten the economy once they had mobilized their workers. Through lesser strikes affecting one or another of the large corporations in the automotive, electrical equipment, rubber, railroad, or similar industries, unions can sharply

[2] "Labor's Capitalists," *Fortune,* 66 (November, 1962), p. 153.

[3] *Fortune,* July 15, 1966, pp. 232–60; and U.S. Bureau of the Census, *Statistical Abstract of the United States: 1966* (Washington: Government Printing Office, 1966), table 590, p. 430.

affect the entire national economy by stopping production at crucial times. No other organization could so interfere with the nation's production except the government acting under emergency powers or a foreign invasionary force.

The great corporations and unions are conspicuous social institutions that directly or indirectly impinge upon the activities of the whole nation. Professor John P. Davis remarked 70 years ago, when corporations produced but two-thirds of all manufactured goods, compared with 95 per cent today, that Americans were beginning to "realize that they are governed more by corporations than by the state, that [corporate organizations] are the major part of the mechanism of government under which they live." [4] Legally, the men who command large corporate organizations possess only private power, but in truth they wield great public power. Their decisions about investments, pricing, buying, producing, and selling can defeat government policies and frustrate public programs as surely as any adverse vote by Congress or any Presidential veto. The power inherent in their ability to sway a whole industry and consequently to tilt the economy poses urgent problems of public as well as private policy.

As background to the further discussion of these problems, in Part I we must first consider how the large organizations originated. Why did a people who professed an individualistic social philosophy and affirmed a faith in a freely competitive market economy allow vast oligopolistic and monopolistic organizations to develop? Although the Founding Fathers spoke of factions and interests,[5] they hardly contemplated business corporations and unions of the importance and profusion of today. The political theory of John Locke and the economic theory of Adam Smith guided early American thinking, yet neither admitted combinations of capital and labor such as those that have flourished in the United States. It is as if the American people had aimed in one direction and hit a target in quite a different one.

[4] John P. Davis, *Corporations* (New York: Capricorn Books, 1961), p. 268.
[5] See *The Federalist* (New York: Modern Library, 1937), p. 56.

chapter **1**

CORPORATIONS AND UNIONS IN THE LIBERAL STATE

Americans in the eighteenth and nineteenth centuries recognized the liberal Lockean state as an appropriate model for government, having accepted the radical individualism on which it was based. They commonly maintained that each man was born naturally free, equal, and independent. No organization, rank, position, or class necessarily claimed his allegiance or ascribed his role in life. He sought his self-interest and made of himself what he would through work, which enabled any man to accumulate property. Though men had no natural ties with each other, they found one—and only one—inducement to join in the establishment of government: the protection of their property.

The relationship between the citizens and the government of the liberal state was direct and unmediated. The citizens granted the government limited powers; it, in turn, safeguarded their property. Since the government protected each man's use of his property and insured free competition for all, there was no proper place for combinations or monopolies; to have allowed them would have readmitted the special privileges, arbitrary royal favors, and exclusive rights against which the advocates of individualism had rebelled. Americans in particular viewed with distaste the remnants of feudal society—lordly families, guilds, chartered monopolies, established churches—that enjoyed legal immunities and governmental exemptions not allowed every citizen. Such groups and organizations limited the opportunities and threatened the liberties of free men.

English law had long denied business or labor the right to form private combinations, since these would interfere with wise state management of the economy. Tudor and Stuart political doctrines maintained that responsibility for the nation's welfare rested upon the king and his government, for only from the royal position of eminence could the common good be perceived. Thus men in their private pursuits were properly guided and directed by the king in the interests of the nation. The monarch might grant to a trusted lord or member of the court a monopoly—on the importing of wines, the sale of playing cards, or the export of cloth—to reward a deserving subject and to enable him to continue his services to the nation. From the time of Edward III in the fourteenth century, English kings regularly chartered guilds, such as those of goldsmiths, vintners (wine merchants), and drapers (cloth manufacturers), to regulate production methods, conditions of work, and apprenticeship in the trades, to be assured of quality production from which all might benefit. Kings also often granted an exclusive right of combination to businessmen who wanted to trade abroad. The traders would, of course, benefit; but they would at the same time, under the eye of the monarch, provide "good vent for the commodities of the realm . . . to the advancement of the honor and dignity [of the crown and to] the increase of royal revenue and the general wealth of the realm." [1]

Individuals could not be allowed to form combinations on their own, however, for such private persons would presume upon the royal prerogative and all too likely neglect the public good. To protect the nation, Parliament enacted many anti-combination statutes, and under common law monopolizing was illegal. There were, therefore, legal precedents and well-established traditions to buttress the antipathy to combinations and monopolies of the early nineteenth-century advocates of individualism and the liberal state. The purpose of the legal doctrine had subtly changed from protecting the authority of the king (and, later, Parliament) against presumptuous subjects to that of insuring the right of every man to compete freely in pursuit of his self-interest. The "general wealth" and the commonweal were still to be served but in a different fashion. No king or government need direct individuals, but rather each man could seek his own interest competitively with all others and in so doing be guided, as if by an invisible hand, to further the public good.

Colonial Americans were most concerned with monopoly in its political form, the privileges and special rights granted by or through the king. Suspicion of such favors ran so high that in 1714 some citizens of Boston argued against incorporation of the town, and throughout the colonies until the Revolution people tended to identify government charters, especially those for land companies, with monopoly.[2]

By 1776, however, the concept of monopoly had begun to broaden. The acceptance of the competitive market as the proper guide for buying and selling led Americans to recognize more clearly than they had earlier the economic aspects of monopoly. For example, the framers of the Maryland constitution of 1776 declared that monopolies are "odious, contrary to the spirit of a free government and the principles of commerce, and ought not to be suffered." In 1784 the New Hampshire constitution explicitly emphasized the economic threat of monopoly, stating: "Free and fair competition in the trades and industries is an inherent and essential right of the people and should be protected against all monopolies and conspiracies which tend to hinder or destroy it." The distinction between political monopoly as a special right granted by the government and economic monopoly as a conspiracy in restraint of trade is worth noting. It helps to illuminate, if not explain, the history of public policy toward business and labor combinations until the passage of the Sherman Act in 1890.

Whatever the devotion of Americans to competition in theory, they have tended to offer less than full homage to it in practice. The real problem with which they often wrestled was not how to maintain the competitive market of their ideal but, rather, how to fit to that ideal the combinations they organized.

[1] From a charter granted by Elizabeth I in 1581 to a group of businessmen desiring to trade with Turkey. Davis, *op. cit.*, p. 89.

[2] Shaw Livermore, *Early American Land Companies* (New York: The Commonwealth Fund, 1939), p. 67.

Legislatures or, more usually, the courts had to find some way to redefine and legitimize business combinations and unions. For many purposes they were exceedingly useful if not essential in an industrializing society. As commerce and industry grew, more and more people recognized that such combinations were convenient and necessary means for conducting business and protecting labor.

Business combinations took a variety of forms including partnerships and joint stock companies as well as the corporation. The latter form developed more quickly and spread more widely in the United States than abroad, but it was not a necessary nor even a more efficacious kind of business organization until after the middle of the nineteenth century. The importance and usefulness of business combinations lay in their bringing together more capital than a single individual usually possessed in order to exploit the efficiencies of scale. The state governments, as well as businessmen, found combinations of capital were required to provide the water systems, turnpikes, bridges, ferries, and canals needed by growing communities. Through special enactments the governments chartered companies to raise the capital for the various desired projects. They also granted incorporation rights to such service enterprises as banks and insurance companies. Between 1783 and 1801 the several states permitted the organization of almost 350 business corporations.[3] Workers, too, realized that in combination they could seek to improve their wages more effectively than they could individually. Concerted action promised them a return analogous to the businessmen's economies of scale.

By legal tradition the states had the right to grant charters for specific business ventures, but popular attitudes had begun to challenge it. Those who believed in democratic individualism questioned that right on the grounds that it was a manifestation of political privilege—a vestige of royal monopolies; the champions of the prevailing economic doctrine of competition contested it as a contribution to the monopolistic restraint of trade. Democracy demanded the end of political monopolies that benefited the few. To let competition serve the community interests, many businessmen argued, the states should grant charters of incorporation to any who wished them. The opportunity to enjoy whatever individual advantages these charters might provide should be equally available to all in a democracy; and as for the advantages and interests of the community, these would be served by competition among the corporations.

Businessmen pressed for general incorporation laws, and the states gradually provided them. In 1799 Massachusetts approved the first general incorporation law for firms to build aqueducts. In 1811 New York enacted the first general incorporation law for manufacturing companies. A quarter of a century later, in 1837, Connecticut went the full distance by approving a law that allowed any lawful business to incorporate. Other states followed, some going so far as to prohibit by constitutional provision incorporation by special charter. Arthur M. Schlesinger, Jr., observes that in making corporate charters freely available to every business combination the states "sprinkled holy water on corporations, cleansing them of the legal status of monopoly and sending them forth as the benevolent agencies of free competition. . . . Even the onetime 'monopoly' was thereby transmuted into a laissez-faire corporation and endowed with new prestige and virtue. Capitalism, in the end, gained a new moral force from the in-

[3] Oscar Handlin and Mary F. Handlin, "Origins of the American Business Corporation," *Journal of Economic History*, May, 1945, p. 4.

corporation laws." [4] The businessman's combination was accepted as democratic and legitimate, and so the form, if not the substance, of his practice was admirably fitted to accepted social and economic theory.

The early popularity of incorporation in the United States probably depended more on the ability of the general corporation charter to lift from business combination the odium of monopoly than on the benefits of limited liability, flexible structure, and perpetuity that finally accompanied it. Whereas Adam Smith declared that competition was insured by individuals seeking their self-interests in the marketplace, most Americans came to believe that the same competitive market still existed when corporate "persons" could enter the lists and contest with individuals—natural persons.

So complete became the identification of the business combination with the corporate person that even when business groups or associations failed to secure a charter from the state, the courts nevertheless considered them *de facto* corporations if they performed the objective functions of corporations.[5] Lockean political theory postulated that the state was the creation of men who made a compact for the protection of their property. In their own history—from the Mayflower Compact of 1620, through various state constitutions, to the Articles of Confederation in 1781 and the Constitution of 1789—Americans saw Locke's theory confirmed. It therefore seemed natural to ask, if men could join together to form a limited government, could they not join together again in other groups for other purposes not appropriate for the government to pursue? Many people thought they could, and in declaring business combinations without charters to be *de facto* corporations the courts appeared to agree. In such cases the courts apparently did not consider the states' grants of charters to be much more than a formality, the recognition of an action already taken. This view of incorporation suggests that the "person" of the corporation was created by those who joined together in the business combination and not by the state.

In other cases, however, the courts seemed to believe that the states performed the creative role and that the right of incorporation was acquired only from the state. This view was informed by the British theory that only the state can create corporations. In 1900 the great legal historian V. W. Maitland vividly described the relationship of state and corporation that British law had long maintained:

> The corporation is, and must be, the creature of the state. Into its nostrils the state must breathe the breath of a fictitious life, for otherwise it would be no animated body but individual dust.[6]

Probably few American jurists of the early nineteenth century would have chosen to use these words; elevation of the state to godship, even if only by analogy, would hardly have been in character for believers in Democratic Republicanism.

[4] Arthur M. Schlesinger, Jr., *The Age of Jackson* (Boston: Little, Brown, 1948), pp. 337–38.

[5] "There abound instances, in the history of corporations, where the 'associations' formed for a common purpose carried out this common purpose before the association became a corporation, in the legal sense. The corporation became *de facto,* as the legal brethren would say . . . and, provided no fraud was intended, the courts in this country and quite generally in England have viewed the *de facto* corporation as if it had complied with the statutes in all necessary particulars and had become a corporation *de jure* as well, through the acquisition of a charter." Arthur Stone Dewing, *The Financial Policy of Corporations,* I, 4th ed. (New York: Ronald Press, 1941), p. 6.

[6] Translator's Introduction, Otto Gierke, *Political Theories of the Middle Age* (Cambridge: Cambridge University Press, 1927), p. xxx.

Nevertheless, the American courts were unwilling to declare unequivocally that the state performed no role in the creation of corporations. Though they were not always clear whether the state was a contracting equal with the corporation, a physical or spiritual father of it, or simply a bestower of legal blessings, they usually insisted that the state did contribute something useful and probably necessary to an incorporation. Certainly combinations organized by individuals who possessed no property and received no grant from the state were viewed suspiciously. Workers' combinations were especially dubious. From the early 1800's until well into the 1900's combinations organized by businessmen were regarded by the courts as one thing and combinations organized by workers as quite another.

In forming combinations, businessmen were supposed to have infused the old, monopolistic corporation with the vigor of competition; but when workers organized to promote their interests, they were charged with violating the old common-law prohibition against forming a conspiracy to restrain trade. A Pennsylvania court first made the accusation in 1806 when it found 8 shoemakers "guilty of a combination to raise their wages." The indictment and findings in this case became precedents for other American courts until 1842, when the judgment was reversed. (See page 14.)

The shoemakers had organized their combination, the Society of Cordwainers, about 15 years earlier, for the sole purpose of improving their working conditions through mutual protection. They had bargained with the Masters' Society (an association of master shoemakers) over wages for many years, sometimes engaging in turnouts (strikes) and at other times suffering lockouts. In 1805 the masters had reduced wages and then refused the Cordwainers' request that their wages be made the same as the prevailing rate for shoemakers in New York and Baltimore. When the workers struck, the masters succeeded in having the Society's leaders arrested. The loss of their leaders undermined the morale of the strikers, and they soon gave up, returning to work at the same low wage as before.

Counsel for the defense argued that the freedom of laborers to combine to better their condition was a basic American right. To declare that the exercise of it by free men was a conspiracy under the common law would impair the natural, inalienable rights of men for which Americans had fought the Revolution of 1776. The presiding officer of the court was not impressed with the argument; he ruled that "a combination of workmen to raise their wages may be considered in a two-fold point of view: One is to benefit themselves . . . the other is to injure those who do not join their society. The Rule of law condemns both." [7]

Whether the law condemned them or not, the economic doctrine held by the court officials did. The shoemakers' concerted activities, they believed, interfered with the "natural" regulation of wages and prices by supply and demand. Interference with Nature's laws of the marketplace could not be the natural or inalienable right of any man. Had the court officials been able to perceive a tangible interest that the workers were trying to protect or enhance, they might have more favorably compared the shoemakers' combination with those of businessmen—even with the Masters' Society. Private combination might be justified in defense of property, even as the combination of property holders to

[7] Elias Lieberman, *Unions Before the Bar* (New York: Harper & Row, 1955), p. 13.

form a state was justified. Unfortunately, the workers owned no property at their place of work and thus had no claim that the court could recognize or protect. Since the workmen's combinations were not designed to protect property, they were judged to be an arbitrary, coercive means of exploiting those who had property. The Cordwainers were found guilty of threatening not only their employers but also the constitutional purpose and function of the state, which was the protection of property.

If organizations or groups within the state were to find legal favor, they had to justify themselves either as contributors to the public interest or as possessors of constitutional rights. If both justifications were available, their defense would be strong indeed. The following readings, excerpted from Supreme Court opinions, present the arguments and reasoning used by justices of the court to define the legal position of corporations and trade unions in four important decisions. The justices developed a strong defense for the corporation, but they were less adept in defending unions. By comparing the reasoning used to defend the one organization with that used to defend the other, and by contrasting the assumptions the justices made about the nature of the two organizations, the reader will gain an understanding of the sources of contemporary legal problems involving unions and corporations.

Legal Apologia for Organizations

DARTMOUTH COLLEGE V. WOODWARD

The Supreme Court's respect for property and the lengths to which the court would go in rationalizing arguments favoring property were made clear by Chief Justice Marshall in the Dartmouth College case. This decision provided business combinations with a mighty legal bulwark that kept them safe from effective attack for many years.

In 1816 the legislature of New Hampshire amended the charter of Dartmouth College to make it a public institution. The trustees of the college, who had not given their consent to the change, brought suit to regain the original charter. The state court found the legislature's action binding and valid *if* it were not repugnant to the Constitution of the United States. The trustees, of course, appealed to the Supreme Court for a decision on the constitutionality of the legislature's act. Chief Justice Marshall delivered the Court's decision; passages from his opinion follow.[1]

[1] The Trustees of Dartmouth College v. Woodward, 4 Wheaton 518 (1819).

I

The American people have said, in the constitution of the United States, that "no state shall pass any bill of attainder, *ex post facto* law, or law impairing the obligation of contracts." In the same instrument they have also said, "that the judicial power shall extend to all cases in law and equity arising under the constitution." On the judges of this court, then, is imposed the high and solemn duty of protecting, from even legislative violation those contracts which the constitution of our country has placed beyond legislative control; and, however irksome the task may be, this is a duty from which we dare not shrink.

The title of the plaintiffs originates in a charter dated the 13th day of December, in the year 1769, incorporating twelve persons therein mentioned, by the name of "The Trustees of Dartmouth College," granting to them and their successors the usual corporate privileges and powers, and authorizing the trustees who are to govern the college, to fill up all vacancies which may be created in their own body. . . . It can require no argument to prove that the circumstances of this case constitute a contract. An application is made to the crown for a charter to incorporate a religious and literary institution. In the application, it is stated that large contributions have been made for the object, which will be conferred on the corporation as soon as it shall be created. The charter is granted, and on its faith the property is conveyed. Surely in this transaction every ingredient of a complete and legitimate contract is to be found.

The points for consideration are:

1. Is this contract protected by the constitution of the United States?
2. Is it impaired by the acts under which the defendant holds? . . .

[It has been argued that] the term "contract" must be understood [to have been inserted in the Constitution in order] to guard against a power of at least doubtful utility, the abuse of which had been extensively felt; and to restrain the legislature in future from violating the right to property. That anterior to the formation of the constitution, a course of legislation had prevailed in many, if not in all, of the states, which weakened the confidence of man in man, and embarrassed all transactions between individuals, by dispensing with a faithful performance of engagements. To correct this mischief, by restraining the power which produced it, the state legislatures were forbidden "to pass any law impairing the obligation of contracts," that is, of contracts respecting property, under which some individual could claim a right to something beneficial to himself; and that since the clause in the constitution must in construction receive some limitation, it may be confined, and ought to be confined, to cases of this description; to cases within the mischief it was intended to remedy.

The general correctness of these observations cannot be controverted. . . .

If the act of incorporation be a grant of political power, if it creates a civil institution to be employed in the administration of the government, or if the funds of the college be public property, or if the state of New Hampshire, as a government, be alone interested in its transactions, the subject is one in which the legislature of the state may act according to its own judgment, unrestrained by any limitation of its power imposed by the constitution of the United States.

But if this be a private eleemosynary institution, endowed with a capacity to take property for objects unconnected with government, whose funds are bestowed by individuals on the faith of the charter; if the donors have stipulated for the future disposition and management of those funds in the manner prescribed by themselves, there may be more difficulty in the case, although neither the persons who have made these stipulations nor those for whose benefit they were made, should be parties to the cause. Those who are no longer interested in the property, may yet retain such an interest in the preservation of their own arrangements as to have a right to insist that those arrangements shall be held sacred. Or, if they have themselves disappeared, it becomes a subject of serious and anxious inquiry, whether those whom they have legally empowered to represent them forever may not assert all the rights which they possessed, while in being. . . . It becomes, then, the duty of the court most seriously to examine this charter, and to ascertain its true character.

II

From the instrument itself, it appears that about the year 1754, the Rev. Eleazar Wheelock established at his own expense, and on his own estate, a charity-school for the instruction of Indians in the Christian religion. The success of this institution inspired him with the design of soliciting contributions in England for carrying on, and extending, his undertaking. In this pious work he employed the Rev. Nathaniel Whitaker, who, by virtue of a power of attorney from Dr. Wheelock, appointed the Earl of Dartmouth and others, trustees of the money which had been, and should be, contributed; which appointment Dr. Wheelock confirmed by a deed of trust authorizing the trustees to fix on a site for the college. They determined to establish the school on the Connecticut River, in the western part of New Hampshire; that situation being supposed favorable for carrying on the original design among the Indians, and also for promoting learning among the English: and the proprietors in the neighborhood having made large offers of land, on condition that the college should there be placed. Dr. Wheelock then applied to the crown for an act of incorporation, and represented the expediency of appointing those whom he had, by his last will, named as trustees in America, to be members of the proposed corporation. "In consideration of the premises," "for the education and instruction of the youth of the Indian tribes," &c., "and also of English youth, and any others," the charter was granted, and the trustees of Dartmouth college were by that name created a body corporate, with power, for the use of the said college, to acquire real and personal property, and to pay the president, tutors, and other officers of the college, such salaries as they shall allow. . . . This charter was accepted, and the property, both real and personal, which had been contributed for the benefit of the college, was conveyed to, and vested in, the corporate body.

From this brief review of the most essential parts of the charter, it is apparent that the funds of the college consisted entirely of private donations. It is, perhaps, not very important who were the donors. The probability is, that the Earl of Dartmouth, and the other trustees in England, were, in fact, the largest contributors. Yet the legal conclusion, from the facts recited in the charter, would probably be, that Dr. Wheelock was the founder of the college.

The origin of the institution was, undoubtedly, the Indian charity-school, established by Dr. Wheelock, at his own expense. It was at his instance, and to enlarge this school, that contributions were solicited in England. . . . Dartmouth College is really endowed by private individuals, who have bestowed their funds for the propagation of the Christian religion among the Indians, and for the promotion of piety and learning generally. From these funds the salaries of the tutors are drawn; and these salaries lessen the expense of education to the students. It is, then, an eleemosynary, and, as far as respects its funds, a private corporation.

Do its objects stamp on it a different character? Are the trustees and professors public officers, invested with any portion of political power, partaking in any degree in the administration of civil government, and performing duties which flow from the sovereign authority?

That education is an object of national concern, and a proper subject of legislation, all admit. That there may be an institution founded by government, and placed entirely under its immediate control, the officers of which would be public officers, amenable exclusively to government, none will deny. But is Dartmouth College such an institution? Is education altogether in the hands of government? Does every teacher of youth become a public officer, and do donations for the purpose of education necessarily become public property, so far that the will of the legislature not the will of the donor, becomes the law of the donation? These questions are of serious moment to society, and deserve to be well considered.

Doctor Wheelock, as the keeper of his charity-school, instructing the Indians in the art of reading, and in our holy religion; sustaining them at his own expense, and on the voluntary contributions of the charitable, could scarcely be considered as a public officer, exercising any portion of those duties which belong to government; nor could the legislature have supposed that his private funds, or those given by others, were subject to legislative management, because they were applied to the purposes of education. When, afterwards, his school was enlarged, and the liberal contributions made in England, and in America, enabled him to extend his cares to the education of the youth of his own country, no change was wrought in his own character, or in the nature of his duties. Had he employed assistant tutors with the funds contributed by others, or had the trustees in England established a school with Dr. Wheelock at its head, and paid salaries to him and his assistants, they would still have been private tutors; and the fact that they were employed in the education of youth could not have converted them into public officers, concerned in the administration of public duties, or have given the legislature a right to interfere in the management of the fund. The trustees, in whose care that fund was placed by the contributors, would have been permitted to execute their trust uncontrolled by legislative authority.

Whence, then, can be derived the idea that Dartmouth College has become a public institution, and its trustees public officers, exercising powers conferred by the public for public objects? Not from the source whence its funds were drawn: for its foundation is purely private and eleemosynary. Not from the application of those funds; for money may be given for education, and the persons receiving it do not, by being employed in the education of youth, become members of the civil government. Is it from the act of incorporation? Let this subject be considered.

III

A corporation is an artificial being, invisible, intangible, and existing only in contemplation of law. Being the mere creature of law, it possesses only those properties which the charter of its creation confers upon it, either expressly or as incidental to its very existence. These are such as are supposed best calculated to effect the object for which it was created. Among the most important are immortality, and, if the expression may be allowed, individuality; properties by which a perpetual succession of many persons are considered as the same, and may act as a single individual. They enable a corporation to manage its own affairs and to hold property without the perplexing intricacies, the hazardous and endless necessity, of perpetual conveyances for the purpose of transmitting it from hand to hand. It is chiefly for the purpose of clothing bodies of men, in succession, with these qualities and capacities, that corporations were invented, and are in use. By these means, a perpetual succession of individuals are capable of acting for the promotion of the particular object, like one immortal being. But this being does not share in the civil government of the country, unless that be the purpose for which it was created. Its immortality no more confers on it political power, or a political character, than immortality would confer such power or character on a natural person. It is no more a state instrument than a natural person exercising the same powers would be. If, then, a natural person, employed by individuals in the education of youth, or for the government of a seminary in which youth is educated, would not become a public officer, or be considered as a member of the civil government, how is it that this artificial being, created by law, for the purpose of being employed by the same individuals for the same purposes, should become a part of the civil government of the country? Is it because its existence, its capacities, its powers, are given by law? Because the government has given it the power to take and to hold property in a particular form, and for particular purposes has the government a consequent right substantially to change that form, or to vary the purposes to which the property is to be applied? This principle has never been asserted or recognized, and is supported by no authority. Can it derive aid from reason?

The objects for which a corporation is created are universally such as the government wishes to promote. They are deemed beneficial to the country; and this benefit constitutes the consideration, and, in most cases, the sole consideration of the grant. In most eleemosynary institutions, the object would be difficult, perhaps unattainable, without the aid of a charter of incorporation. Charitable, or public-spirited individuals, desirous of making permanent appropriations for charitable or other useful purposes, find it impossible to effect their design securely, and certainly, without an incorporating act. They apply to the government, state their beneficent object, and offer to advance the money necessary for its accomplishment, provided the government will confer on the instrument which is to execute their designs the capacity to execute them. The proposition is considered and approved, the benefit to the public is considered as an ample compensation for the faculty it confers, and the corporation is created. If the advantages to the public constitute a full compensation for the faculty it gives, there can be no reason for exacting a further compensation, by claiming a right to exercise over this artificial being a power which changes its nature, and touches the fund, for the security and application of which it was created. There can be no reason for implying in a charter, given for a valuable consideration, a power which is not only not expressed, but is in direct contradiction to its express stipulations.

From the fact, then, that a charter of incorporation has been granted, nothing can be inferred which changes the character of the institution, or transfers to the government any new power over it. The character of civil institutions does not grow out of their incorporation, but out of the manner in which they are formed, and the objects for which they are created. The right to change them is not founded on their being incorporated but on their being the instruments of government, created for its purposes. The same institutions, created for the same objects, though not incorporated, would be public institutions, and, of course, be controllable by the legislature. The incorporating act neither gives nor prevents this control. Neither, in reason, can the incorporating act change the character of a private eleemosynary institution.

IV

From this review of the charter, it appears that Dartmouth College is an eleemosynary institution, incorporated for the purpose of perpetuating the application of the bounty of the donors, to the specified objects of that bounty; that its trustees or governors were originally named by the founder, and invested with the power of perpetuating themselves; that they are not public officers, nor is it a civil institution, participating in the administration of government; but a charity school, or a seminary of education, incorporated for the preservation of its property, and the perpetual application of that property to the objects of its creation. . . .

This is plainly a contract to which the donors, the trustees, and the crown (to whose rights and obligations New Hampshire succeeds) were the original parties. It is a contract made on a valuable consideration. It is a contract for the security and disposition of property. It is a contract, on the faith of which real and personal estate has been conveyed to the corporation. It is then a contract within the letter of the constitution, and within its spirit also unless the fact that the property is invested by the donors in trustees for the promotion of religion and education, for the benefit of persons who are perpetually changing, though the objects remain the same, shall create a particular exception, taking this case out of the prohibition contained in the constitution. . . .

The opinion of the court, after mature deliberation, is, that this is a contract, the obligation of which cannot be impaired without violating the constitution of the United States. This opinion appears to us to be equally supported by reason, and by the former decisions of this court.

COMMONWEALTH V. HUNT

In contrast to the strong legal foundations provided corporations in the Dartmouth case, labor unions enjoyed little legal protection against attack. With their legality questionable, they existed only on the sufferance of employers and the courts. Exist they did, nonetheless, disappearing in depressions or dissolving when their leaders were jailed but persistently reappearing in response to the need felt by American workers for better protection of their wages and working conditions than that afforded by the market.

In the late 1820's, workingmen's political parties began to appear in the large eastern seaboard cities of Pennsylvania, New York, and Massachusetts. In 1829 a workers' party won 28 per cent of the vote in New York City; the year before a labor party had gained the balance of power in Philadelphia. Inexperience kept the leaders of the new parties from exerting any practical influence, but unionists continued to lobby for favorable legislation, first in the state capitals and then, with the election of Andrew Jackson as President, in Washington. Some success was achieved. In 1836, Jackson responded to labor's appeals by ordering a 10-hour day at the Philadelphia Navy Yard. Early in 1840, President Martin Van Buren extended the 10-hour day to all government workers without a reduction in wages.

The unrest of laborers, who felt themselves at a disadvantage in a system that prosecuted them for trying to improve their unsatisfactory situation, expressed itself not only in such feeble, though occasionally effective, political efforts but also in direct action. Some of these actions were as dramatic and as impressive in their day as were the civil rights demonstrations in the 1960's. In 1835 and 1836, for example, the New York courts found a shoemakers' union and an organized group of tailors guilty of being illegal combinations. This was the culmination of thirty years of unfavorable court decisions, and the workers protested with a mass demonstration. Twenty-seven thousand workers marched on City Hall, and in the park in front of it they burned effigies of the judges who had presided at the recent trials. Judges undoubtedly were sensitive to the popular hostility towards their labor decisions. A few years later, in 1842, a learned but also politically perceptive judge, Chief Justice Lemuel Shaw of Massachusetts, appeared to have considered the outraged feelings of workers who were seeking to form and maintain unions. Expediency, or at best, common sense, guided Justice Shaw, not the high principles of constitutional law nor the honored political theory of John Locke. He reversed the precedent of the Cordwainers case of 1806, declaring workers' combinations, as such, to be lawful. His decision follows: [1]

I

The defendants and others formed themselves into a society, and agreed not to work for any person, who should employ any journeyman or other person, not a member of such society, after notice given him to discharge such workman. The manifest intent of the association is, to induce all those engaged in the same occupation to become members of it. Such a purpose is not unlawful. It would give them a power which might be exerted for useful and honorable purposes, or for dangerous and pernicious ones. If the latter were the real and actual object, and susceptible of proof, it should have been specially charged. Such an association might be used to afford each other assistance in times of poverty, sickness and distress; or to raise their intellectual, moral and social condition; or to make improvement in their art; or for other proper purposes. Or the association might be designed for the purposes of oppression and injustice.

But in order to charge all those, who become members of an association, with the guilt of a criminal conspiracy, it must be averred and proved that the actual, if not the avowed object of the association, was criminal. An association may be formed, the declared objects of which are innocent and laudable, and yet they may have secret articles, or an agreement communicated only to the members, by which they are banded together for purposes injurious to the peace of society or the rights of its members. Such would undoubtedly be a criminal conspiracy, on proof of the fact, however meritorious or praiseworthy the declared objects might be. The law is not to be hoodwinked by colorable pretences. It looks at truth and reality, through whatever disguise it may assume. But to make such an association, ostensibly innocent, the subject of prosecution as a criminal conspiracy, the secret agreement, which makes it so, is to be averred and proved as the gist of the offense. But when an association is formed for purposes actually innocent, and afterwards its powers are abused, by those who have the control and management of it, to purposes of oppression and injustice, it will be criminal in those who thus misuse it, or give consent thereto, but not in the other members of the association. In this case, no such secret agreement, varying the objects of the association from those avowed, is set forth in this count of the indictment.

Nor can we perceive that the objects of this association, whatever they may have been, were to be attained by criminal means. The means which they proposed to employ . . . were, that they would not work for a person, who, after due notice, should employ a journeyman not a member of their society. Supposing the object of the association to be laudable and lawful, or at least not unlawful, are these means criminal? The case supposes that these persons are not bound by contract, but free to work for whom

[1] Commonwealth v. Hunt, 4 Metcalf 111 (1842) Massachusetts.

they please, or not to work, if they so prefer. In this state of things, we cannot perceive, that it is criminal for men to agree together to exercise their own acknowledged rights, in such a manner as best to subserve their own interests. One way to test this is, to consider the effect of such an agreement, where the object of the association is acknowledged on all hands to be a laudable one. Suppose a class of workmen, impressed with the manifold evils of intemperance, should agree with each other not to work in a shop in which ardent spirit was furnished, or not to work in a shop with anyone who used it, or not to work for an employer, who should, after notice, employ a journeyman who habitually used it. The consequences might be the same. A workman, who should still persist in the use of ardent spirit would find it more difficult to get employment; a master employing such an one might, at times, experience inconvenience in his work, in losing the services of a skilful but intemperate workman. Still it seems to us, that as the object would be lawful, and the means not unlawful, such an agreement could not be pronounced a criminal conspiracy. . . .

We do not understand that the agreement was, that the defendants would refuse to work for an employer, to whom they were bound by contract for a certain time, in violation of that contract; nor that they would insist that an employer should discharge a workman engaged by contract for a certain time, in violation of such contract. It is perfectly consistent with everything stated in this court, that the effect of the agreement was, that when they were free to act, they would not engage with an employer, or continue in his employment, if such employer, when free to act, should engage with a workman, or continue a workman in his employment, not a member of the association. If a large number of men, engaged for a certain time, should combine together to violate their contract, and quit their employment together, it would present a very different question. Suppose a farmer, employing a large number of men, engaged for the year, at fair monthly wages, and suppose that just at the moment that his crops were ready to harvest, they should all combine to quit his service, unless he would advance their wages, at a time when other laborers could not be obtained. It would surely be a conspiracy to do an unlawful act, though of such a character, that if done by an individual, it would lay the foundation of a civil action only, and not of a criminal prosecution. It would be a case very different from [this one]. . . .

II

[It is alleged] that the defendants, with others unknown, did assemble, conspire, confederate and agree together, not to work for any master or person who should employ any workman not being a member of a certain club, society or combination, called the Boston Journeymen Bootmaker's Society, or who should break any of their by-laws, unless such workmen should pay to said club, such sum as should be agreed upon as a penalty for the breach of such unlawful rules, &c.; and that by means of said conspiracy they did compel one Isaac B. Wait, a master cordwainer, to turn out of his employ one Jeremiah Horne, a journeyman bootmaker, &c. in evil example, &c. So far as the averment of a conspiracy is concerned, all the remarks made in reference to the first count are equally applicable to this. It is simply an averment of an agreement amongst themselves not to work for a person, who should employ any person not a member of a certain association. It sets forth no illegal or criminal purpose to be accomplished, nor any illegal or criminal means to be adopted for the accomplishment of any purpose. It was an agreement, as to the manner in which they would exercise an acknowledged right to contract with others for their labor. It does not aver a conspiracy or even an intention to raise their wages; and it appears by the bill of exceptions, that the case was not put upon the footing of a conspiracy to raise their wages. . . .

[It is also alleged that] the defendants did compel one Wait to turn out of his employ one Jeremiah Horne. . . . [And] if this is to be considered as a substantive charge, it would depend altogether upon the force of the word "compel," which may be used in the sense of coercion, or duress, by force or fraud. It would therefore depend upon the context and the connection with other words, to determine the sense in which it was used in the indictment. If, for instance, the indictment had averred a conspiracy, by the defendants, to compel Wait to turn Horne out of his employment, and to accomplish that object by the use of force or fraud, it would have been a very different case; especially if it might be fairly construed, as perhaps in that case it might have been, that Wait was under obligation, by contract, for an unexpired term of time, to employ and pay Horne. As before remarked, it would have been a conspiracy to do an unlawful, though not a criminal act, to induce Wait to violate his engagement, to the actual injury of Horne. . . . [It is an] established principle, that every free man, whether skilled laborer, mechanic, farmer or domestic servant, may work or not work, or work or refuse to work with any company or individual, at his own option, except so far as he is bound by contract. But whatever might be the force of the word "compel," unexplained by its connection, it is disarmed and rendered harmless by the precise statement of the means, by which such compulsion was to be effected. It was the agreement not to work for him, by which they compelled Wait to decline employing Horne longer. . . .

III

[It is alleged that the members of the society], by wrongful and indirect means, [sought] to impoverish said Horne and to deprive and hinder him, from his said art and trade and getting his support thereby, and that . . . they did . . . greatly impoverish him. . . .

Suppose a baker in a small village had the exclusive custom of his neighborhood, and was making large profits by the sale of his bread. Supposing a number of those neighbors, believing the price of his bread too high, should propose to him to reduce his prices, or if he did not, they would introduce another baker; and on his refusal, such other baker should under their encouragement set up a rival establishment, and sell his bread at lower prices; the effect would be to diminish the profit of the former baker, and to the same extent to impoverish him. And it might be said and proved, that the purpose of the associates was to diminish his profits, and thus impoverish him, though the ultimate and laudable object of the combination was to reduce the cost of bread to themselves and their neighbors. The same thing may be said of all competition in every branch of trade and industry; and yet it is through that competition, that the best interests of trade and industry are promoted. It is scarcely necessary to allude to the familiar instances of opposition lines of conveyance, rival hotels, and the thousand other instances, where each strives to gain custom to himself, by ingenious improvements, by increased industry, and by all the means by which he may lessen the price of commodities, and thereby diminish the profits of others.

We think, therefore, that associations may be entered into, the object of which is to adopt measures that may have a tendency to impoverish another, that is, to diminish his gains and profits, and yet so far from being criminal or unlawful, the object may be highly meritorious and public spirited. The legality of such an association will therefore depend upon the means to be used for its accomplishment. If it is to be carried into effect by fair or honorable and lawful means, it is, to say the least, innocent; if by falsehood or force, it may be stamped with the character of conspiracy.

QUESTIONS

Legal Apologia for Organizations

1. What legal basis does Marshall present for the corporations? How does it differ from the legal basis of the union as given by Shaw?

2. The corporation and the union are both combinations or associations. In the eyes of the courts in the two cases, what is combined or associated to make each organization?

3. Why is the private nature of Dartmouth College important to Marshall's

argument? How do you evaluate the reasoning by which Marshall dismisses the claims that the college is a public institution?

4. A labor scholar once wrote: "Justice Shaw proclaimed for unions the doctrine of 'virtuous ends pursued by virtuous means.' If businessmen of the period had been held to such a standard, commerce and trade would have been seriously impaired." Give your reasons for agreeing or disagreeing with this characterization of Shaw's opinion. What would really have been the effect of imposing this standard on business? In the competitive marketplace where private business operated what, if any, measure of "virtuous" ends and means existed?

5. Contrast the two theories of the corporation offered by Marshall. Does a charter granted by the government provide the corporation with any benefit that increases the value of its property according to either theory?

6. Which of Marshall's theories of the corporation could be made to fit trade unions and how? What benefits would accrue to unions if either theory were applied to them? What social and economic implications would result if either theory were applied to unions?

7. If a charter is merely clothing for a corporation, as Marshall implies, what is the nature of the substance that is clothed? Where did the "substance" come from and what is its relationship to the state?

8. What is the "substance" of the union as described by Justice Shaw? How does it differ from that of the corporation?

Corporate Persons and Union Groups

SANTA CLARA COUNTY V. SOUTHERN PACIFIC

In 1868 the United States adopted the Fourteenth Amendment, which among other things forbids the states to abridge the privileges and immunities of citizens, to deprive any person of life, liberty, or property without due process of law, or to deny any person the equal protection of the law. The most obvious purpose of the Amendment was to protect the rights of former slaves, now citizens; soon, however, the Amendment was invoked in litigation involving the corporation, and its other uses tended to be forgotten.

I

The year following the adoption of the Fourteenth Amendment, the Louisiana legislature granted a 25-year monopoly to a slaughterhouse concern in New Orleans. It hoped thus to regulate the slaughtering of meat and better protect the health of the people in the city. Other slaughterhouse operators were unable to continue in business, and they complained that they had been wrongfully deprived of their rights under the Fourteenth Amendment. By 1872 their complaint reached the Supreme Court.[1] A majority of the Court held that the purpose of the Fourteenth Amendment was to establish freedom from slavery and personal servitude; its scope did not include the situation of the operators excluded from practicing their slaughtering trade in New Orleans. The dissenting minority strongly disputed the Court's limited interpretation of the Amendment, arguing that both "liberty" and "property" could and should be defined more broadly.

In the next dozen years after the Slaughter House cases were settled, the decisions

[1] Slaughter House Cases, 16 Wallace 36 (1873).

of the Supreme Court moved toward the minority opinion. The Court also began to reinterpret the words "due process" and "equal protection" in ways that were severely to limit the attempts of the states to regulate corporations and economic matters. In 1886 the Supreme Court discovered a powerful conceit to enhance the position of corporations—it brought them within the full protection of the federal Constitution and thereby under the guardianship of the laissez faire doctrines then subscribed to by a majority of the justices. The Court ruled unanimously and without listening to argument on the point that a corporation is a "person," thereby allowing the corporation to succeed to the rights that those who framed the Fourteenth Amendment thought they were bestowing upon the Negro.

The ruling that a corporation is a person arose out of a case involving Santa Clara County in California and the powerful Southern Pacific Railroad. The state of California had levied state and county taxes upon certain corporations using a special method of assessment that resulted in higher valuations for corporate than for individually owned property. The Southern Pacific Railroad refused to pay all its taxes for the fiscal year 1881–82, alleging that the state had exceeded its powers. The County brought suit to recover its share of the unpaid taxes. Justice Stephen J. Field delivered the majority opinion: [2]

II

The principle which justifies such a discrimination in assessment and taxation, where one of the owners is a railroad corporation and the other a natural person, would also sustain it where both owners are natural persons. A mere change in the state constitution would effect this if the federal constitution does not forbid it. Any difference between the owners, whether of age, color, race, or sex, which the state might designate, would be a sufficient reason for the discrimination.

[2] County of Santa Clara v. Southern Pacific Railroad Company, 118 U.S. 394 (1886).

It would be a singular comment upon the weakness and character of our republican institutions if the valuation and consequent taxation of property could vary according as the owner is white, or black, or yellow, or old, or young, or male, or female. A classification of values for taxation upon any such ground would be abhorrent to all notions of equality of right among men. Strangely, indeed, would the law sound in case it read that in the assessment and taxation of property a deduction should be made for mortgages thereon if the property be owned by white men or by old men, and not deducted if owned by black men or by young men; deducted if owned by landsmen, not deducted if owned by sailors; deducted if owned by married men, not deducted if owned by bachelors; deducted if owned by men doing business alone, not deducted if owned by men doing business in partnerships or other associations; deducted if owned by trading corporations, not deducted if owned by churches or universities; and so on, making a discrimination whenever there was any difference in the character or pursuit or condition of the owner. To levy taxes upon a valuation of property thus made is of the very essence of tyranny, and has never been done except by bad governments in evil times, exercising arbitrary and despotic power. . . .

The first section of the fourteenth amendment places a limit upon all the powers of the state, including, among others, that of taxation. After stating that all persons born or naturalized in the United States, and subject to the jurisdiction thereof, are citizens of the United States and of the state in which they reside, it declares that "no state shall make or enforce any law which shall abridge the privileges or immunities of citizens of the United States, nor shall any state deprive any *person* (dropping the designation 'citizen') of life, liberty, or property, without due process of law, nor deny to any person within its jurisdiction the equal protection of the laws." The amendment was adopted soon after the close of the civil war, and undoubtedly had its origin in a purpose to secure the newly-made citizens in the full enjoyment of their freedom. But it is in no respect limited in its operation to them. It is universal in its application, extending its protective force over all men, of every race and color, within the jurisdiction of the states throughout the broad domain of the republic. A constitutional provision is not to be restricted in its application because designed originally to prevent an existing wrong. Such a restricted interpretation was urged in the *Dartmouth College Case,* to prevent the application of the provision prohibiting legislation by states impairing the obligation of contracts to the charter of the college, it being contended that the charter was not such a contract as the prohibition contemplated. . . .

All history shows that a particular grievance suffered by an individual or a class, from a defective or oppressive law, or the absence of any law, touching the matter, is often the occasion and cause for enactments, constitutional or legislative, general in their character, designed to cover cases not merely of the same, but all cases of a similar, nature. The wrongs which were supposed to be inflicted upon or threatened to citizens of the enfranchised race, by special legislation directed against them, moved the framers of the amendment to place in the fundamental law of the nation provisions not merely for the security of those citizens, but to insure to all men, at all times, and at all places, due process of law, and the equal protection of the laws. Oppression of the person and spoliation of property by any state were thus forbidden, and equality before the law was secured to all. . . .

With the adoption of the amendment the power of the states to oppress any one under any pretense or in any form was forever ended; and henceforth all persons within their jurisdiction could claim equal protection under the laws. And by equal protection is meant equal security to everyone in his private rights—in his right to life, to liberty, to property, and to the pursuit of happiness. It implies not only that the means which the laws afford for such security shall be equally accessible to him, but that no one shall be subject to any greater burdens or charges than such as are imposed upon all others under like circumstances. This protection attends every one everywhere, whatever be his position in society or his association with others, either for profit, improvement, or pleasure. It does not leave him because of any social or official position which he may hold, nor because he may belong to a political body, or to a religious society, or be a member of a commercial, manufacturing, or transportation company. It is the shield which the arm of our blessed government holds at all times over every one, man, woman, and child, in all its broad domain, wherever they may go and in whatever relations they may be placed. No state—such is the sovereign command of the whole people of the United States—no state shall touch the life, the liberty, or the property of any person, however humble his lot or exalted his station, without due process of law; and no state, even with due process of law, shall deny to any one within its jurisdiction the equal protection of the laws. . . .

III

To justify these discriminating provisions [of the California constitution] and maintain the action in face of them, the plaintiffs have taken positions involving doctrines which sound strangely to those who have always supposed that the constitutional guaranties extend to all persons, whatever their relations, and protect from spoliation all property, by whomsoever held. These positions are substantially as follows: That persons cease to be within the protection of the fourteenth amendment, and as such entitled to the equal protection of the laws, when they become members of a corporation; that property, when held by persons associated together in a corporation, is subject to any disposition which the state may, at its will, see fit to make. . . .

Private corporations—and under this head, with the exception of sole corporations, with which we are not now dealing, all corporations other than those which are public are included—private corporations consist of an association of individuals united for some lawful purpose, and permitted to use a common name in their business and have succession of membership without dissolution. As said by Chief Justice Marshall: "The great object of an incorporation is to bestow the character and properties of individuality on a collective and changing body of men." . . . In this state they are formed under general laws. By complying with certain prescribed forms any five persons may thus associate themselves. In that sense corporations are creatures of the state; they could not exist independently of the law, and the law may, of course, prescribe any conditions, not prohibited by the constitution of the United States, upon which they may be formed and continued. But the members do not, because of such association, lose their rights to protection, and equality of protection. They continue, notwithstanding, to possess the same right to life and liberty as before, and also to their property, except as they may have stipulated otherwise. As members of the association—of the artificial body, the intangible thing, called by a name given by themselves—their interests, it is true, are undivided, and constitute only a right during the continuance of the corporation to participate in its dividends, and, on its dissolution, to a proportionate share of its assets; but it is property, nevertheless, and the courts will protect it, as they will any other property, from injury or spoliation.

Whatever affects the property of the corporation—that is, of all the members united by the common name—necessarily affects their interests. If all the members of the corporation die or withdraw from the association, the corporation is dead; it lives and can live only through its members. When they disappear the corporation disappears. Whatever confiscates or imposes burdens on its property, confiscates or imposes burdens on their property, otherwise nobody would be injured by the proceeding. Whatever advances the prosperity or wealth of the corporation, advances proportionately the prosperity and business of the corporators, otherwise no one would be benefited. It is impossible to conceive of a corporation suffering an injury or reaping a benefit except through its members. The legal entity, the metaphysical being, that is called a corporation, cannot feel either. So, therefore, whenever a provision of the constitution or of a law guaranties to persons protection in their property, or affords to them the means for its protection, or prohibits injurious legislation affecting it, the benefits of the provision or law are extended to corporations; not to the name under which different persons are united, but to the individuals composing the union. The courts will always look through the name to see and protect those whom the name represents. . . . [In other cases] the supreme court looked with undimmed vision through the legal entity, the artificial creation of the state, and saw the living human beings whom it represented, and protected them under their corporate name. . . .

The fifth amendment to the constitution declares that no person shall "be deprived of life, liberty, or property without due process of law." This is a limitation upon the federal government similar to that which exists in the constitution of several of the states against their own legislative bodies; and the term "person" thus used has always been held, either by tacit assent or express adjudication, whenever the question has arisen, to extend, so far as property is concerned, to corporations, because to protect them from spoliation is to protect the corporators also.

Now, the fourteenth amendment extends in this respect the same prohibition to the states that the fifth amendment did to the federal government: "Nor shall any state deprive any person of life, liberty, or property without due process of law;" and it adds to the inhibition, "nor deny to any person within its jurisdiction the equal protection of the laws." By every canon of construction known to the jurisprudence of the country, the same meaning must be given to the term "person" in the latter provision as in the former. Surely these great constitutional provisions, which have been, not inaptly, termed a new *Magna Charta,* cannot be made to read as counsel contend, "nor shall any state deprive any person of life, liberty, or property without due process of law, *unless he be associated with others in a corporation,* nor deny to any person within its jurisdiction the equal protection of the laws, *unless he be a member of a corporation.*" How petty and narrow would provisions thus limited appear in the fundamental law of a great people!

The constitutional guaranties of due process of law, and of equality before the law, would be dwarfed into comparative insignificance, and almost emasculated of their protective force, if restricted in their meaning and operation, as contended by counsel. A large proportion of our people are members of some corporation,—religious, educational, scientific, trading, manufacturing, or commercial,—and the amount of property held by them embraces the greater part of the wealth of the country. According to the report of the commissioner of railroads, made to the secretary of the interior, for the year ending June 30, 1882, the railroad companies operated that year 104,813 miles of railway, and transported 350,000,000 tons of freight, of the estimated value of $12,000,000,000. The value of these roads alone was $2,600,000,000, and they employed that year 1,200,000 persons in operating the roads, besides 400,000 in construction,—a total of 1,600,000 persons,—about one thirty-third part of our population, estimated at 53,000,000.

The value of the property of manufacturing companies is over $1,000,000,000; of national banks, over $700,000,000; of insurance companies, over $600,000,000; of mining companies, over $300,000,000; and of telegraph companies and shipping companies, each over $100,000,000. Indeed, the aggregate wealth of all the trading, commercial, manufacturing, mining, shipping, transportation, and other companies engaged in business, or formed for religious, educational, or scientific purposes, amounts to billions upon billions of dollars; and yet all this vast property which keeps our industries flourishing, and furnishes employment, comforts, and luxuries to all classes, and thus promotes civilization and progress, is lifted, according to the argument of counsel, out of the protection of the constitutional guaranties, by reason of the incorporation of the companies; that is, because the persons composing them—amounting in the aggregate to nearly half the entire population of the country—have united themselves in that form under the law for the convenience of business. If the property for that reason is exempted from the protection of one constitutional guaranty, it must be from all such guaranties. If, because of it, the property can be subjected to unequal and arbitrary impositions, it may for the same reason be taken from its owners without due process of law, and taken by the state for public use without just compensation. If the position be sound, it follows that corporations hold all their property, and the right to its use and enjoyment, at the will of the state; that it may be invaded, seized, and the companies despoiled at the state's pleasure. It need hardly be said that there would be little security in the possession of property held by such a tenure, and of course little incentive to its acquisition and improvement.

IV

But in truth the state possesses no such arbitrary power over the property of corporations. When allowed to acquire and own property, they must be treated as owners, with all the rights incident to ownership. They have a constitutional right to be so treated. Whatever power the state may possess in granting or in amending their charters, it cannot withdraw their property from the guaranties of the federal constitution. . . .

The doctrine of unlimited power of the state over corporations, their franchises and property, simply because they are created by the state, so frequently and positively affirmed by counsel, has no foundation whatever in the law of the country. By the decision of the supreme court of the United States in the *Dartmouth College Case,* it was settled, after great consideration, that the charter of a corporation, under which its franchise—its capacity to do business and hold property—is conferred, is a contract between the corporators and the state, and therefore within the protection of the federal constitution prohibiting legislation impairing the obligation of contracts. So far from the state having unlimited control over the franchises and property of corporations, because of its paternity to them, it has under that decision only such as it possesses over the contracts and property of individuals. It cannot, from that fact alone, alter, lessen, or revoke their franchises, although they be a free gift. It cannot, from that fact alone, interfere with or impose any burdens upon their property, except as it can interfere with and impose burdens upon the property of individuals.

Such is the doctrine not only of the *Dartmouth College Case,* but of an unbroken line of decisions of the supreme court of the United States, and of the supreme courts of the several states since that case. . . . The property acquired by corporations is held independently of any [power reserved by the state] in their charters. By force of the reservation the state may alter, amend, or revoke what it grants; nothing more. It does not grant the tangible and visible property of the companies, their roads, their roadways, road-beds, rails, or rolling stock. These are their creation or acquisition. Over them it can exercise only such power as may be exercised through its control of the franchises of the companies, and such as may be exercised over the property of natural persons engaged in similar business. . . .

NLRB V. JONES & LAUGHLIN

While the courts showed great ingenuity during the first 40 years after the Civil War in extending to corporations the protection of the Constitution and in restraining government regulation of business, they were unable to discover a legal basis for more than a reluctant toleration of trade unions until well into the 1930's.

I

The attitude of the courts toward unions was clearly manifested in the first great suit involving the Sherman Antitrust Act, passed by Congress in 1890. Ironically, the suit was not against a mammoth monopoly but against a union, the American Railway Union, and its president, Eugene V. Debs. The defendants had instituted a boycott of all Pullman-made cars in June, 1894, in support of striking Pullman workers. Charging the unions with conspiracy to restrain transportation and to obstruct the mails, the federal government successfully sought an injunction against further strike activities by all the labor leaders. Though the antitrust charge was finally never prosecuted, the strike was broken and Debs and several other leaders served jail terms for violating the injunction and thus putting themselves in contempt of court.

The government's effective use of the injunction made it a popular weapon against weak unions or workers trying to organize. The number of injunctions granted in labor-management disputes increased steadily for nearly 40 years; ridding themselves of the threat of this powerful legal device became a primary political goal of labor unions—a goal not won until 1932.

In addition to the restrictions of the injunction, unions had to contend with antitrust prosecutions, in the decision of which the Supreme Court could not find (and probably did not look for) a rule of reason to guide itself. In the second Coronado Coal case [1] Chief Justice Taft observed that if union leaders or strikers acted with intent to restrain or control either the supply of any good moving in interstate commerce or the price of it in interstate markets they would be in direct violation of the Antitrust Act. Since almost any strike will affect interstate commerce, and intent is either very difficult or very easy to prove, depending upon what a jury is predisposed to believe, almost any strike might lead to antitrust prosecution. In practice the antitrust remedy against unions was too cumbersome to apply in more than a few situations, but the ever present threat of it hindered union growth and union strength.

Despite its restrictions on union activities, the Supreme Court insisted that unions and strikes were lawful and indeed necessary in an industrial society. In 1921 Chief Justice Taft wrote in an opinion: [2]

> Labor unions . . . have long been thus recognized by the courts. They were organized out of the necessities of the situation. A single employee was helpless in dealing with an employer. He was dependent ordinarily on his daily wage for the maintenance of himself and family. If the employer refused to pay him the wages that he thought fair, he was nevertheless unable to leave the employ

[1] Coronado Coal Company v. United Mine Workers of America, 268 U.S. 295 (1925).
[2] American Steel Foundries v. Tri-City Central Trades Council, 257 U.S. 184,209 (1921).

and to resist arbitrary and unfair treatment. Union was essential to give laborers opportunity to deal on equality with their employer. They united to exert influence upon him and to leave him in a body in order by this inconvenience to induce him to make better terms with them. They were withholding their labor of economic value to make him pay what they thought it was worth. The right to combine for such a lawful purpose has in many years not been denied by any court. The strike became a lawful instrument in a lawful economic struggle or competition between employer and employees as to the share or division between them of the joint product of labor and capital. To render this combination at all effective, employees must make their combination extend beyond one shop. It is helpful to have as many as may be in the same trade in the same community united, because in the competition between employers they are bound to be affected by the standard of wages of their trade in the neighborhood. Therefore, they may use all lawful propaganda to enlarge their membership and especially among those whose labor at lower wages will injure their whole guild.

The court's approval of unionism in general and its continued disapproval of union activities in particular did not help unions. American managers, aided in their anti-union program by a powerful set of legal restraints on unions, succeeded in driving the labor movement into retreat. From a peak membership of over 5 million during World War I, labor union membership dwindled by half throughout the 1920's. The unemployment of the Great Depression in the early thirties decreased union numbers still further.

Even as union membership declined, many people were becoming convinced that the declaration of the Supreme Court in 1921 was correct: unions *were* necessary if industrial workers were to enjoy fair treatment. For unions to develop, a change would have to be made in the laws. This change came in 1932, when the Norris-LaGuardia Act freed unions of the injunction incubus and allowed them to confront employers on a more equal footing. The change in law had either come too late or at the wrong time, however, for the weakened unions and the millions of unorganized workers struggling to organize could not gather enough strength to meet their business opponents and win, even though the courts now remained neutral. If workers were to organize and unions were to develop into effective agents for collective bargaining, they would have to have the government help them.

After a brief period of experiment, during which unions and collective bargaining were encouraged under the National Industrial Recovery Act of 1933, Congress passed, and President Franklin D. Roosevelt approved, the National Labor Relations (or Wagner) Act in 1936. In a complete reversal of policy from just five years earlier, the federal government began to encourage workers to organize and legally to support collective bargaining. Under the new law employees could designate a union as their *exclusive* representative through majority vote. Once they had so chosen a union, management had to recognize the union and bargain with it over "rates of pay, wages, hours of employment, or other conditions of employment."

II

In the steel industry a number of the companies continued to fight unions after passage of the new laws as bitterly as they had ever done before. When managers of the Jones & Laughlin Steel Corporation discovered that a group of their employees had joined a union, they fired them. The discharged men complained to the newly established National Labor Relations Board, created to see that the provisions of the Wagner Act were carried out. After careful investigation, the Board issued a cease and desist order. The company was to stop interfering with the self-organization of its employees and to refrain from discriminating against union members. The Board also ordered the discharged men reinstated with back pay.

Jones & Laughlin refused to obey the NLRB order, and the Board appealed to the courts to enforce it. The case was appealed and finally reached the Supreme Court in 1937. The main issue facing the court was whether Congress had the constitutional power to regulate industrial relations between employer and employees. The company argued that it did not:

> The law has always been hesitant to interfere in questions of employer-employee relationships. From the standpoint of the employee, the law has recognized that he should not be forced into a relationship which may be distasteful, and from the employer's viewpoint, the courts have held that the right to judge the capabilities of employees is absolutely essential to the efficient management of the employer's business. The question of retaining or discharging an employee involves delicate considerations of discretion which the law is loath to attempt to weigh. The facts of the present case show the dangers of bureaucratic interference, in that each discharge involved some admitted fault on the part of the complaining employee, but the petitioner determined that it was better qualified to decide and that the respondent's action had been too drastic. This is clearly an interference with the normal right of the respondent to manage its own business, because it is a dictatorial usurpation of the respondent's discretion to determine the capabilities of its employees.
>
> Another dangerous implication of the law and of the petitioner's decision is that it confers a kind of civil service status upon union employees, which will inevitably encourage laziness, insolence, and inefficiency. This is confirmed by a notice which the petitioner, in its decision, has ordered the respondent to post in its plants, to the effect that it will not discharge members of the union. It would be the equivalent of informing the employees that if they become affiliated with the union, they will be thenceforth immune from discharge.
>
> We submit that the underlying philosophy of the National Labor Relations Act is a constant threat to the respondent's normal right to manage its own business. Not only does the Act provide, in effect, that an unqualified bureau will sit as a higher court over the respondent's employment office, but it also ordains that the respondent must deal with whatever union may be selected by a majority of its employees and refuse to negotiate with other employees or their representatives. The power which it delegates to a majority of the employees to bind the minority is arbitrary and unfair and will necessarily lead to the suffocation of minorities and to the closed shop, forcing the employer to herd his employees into an organization which is not of their own choice. This will in turn seriously disturb the discipline and morale of the respondent's employees, with obvious injury to them and to the respondent. . . .[3]

The court found against the company despite the arguments that the justices of an earlier day had found persuasive. The basis of the court's approval of the National Labor Relations Act and of unions was, however, in striking contrast to that used over half a century before in providing corporations a strong legal foundation. The case for unions was not founded on old and honored legal concepts, as was the case for corporations.

III

Chief Justice Hughes delivered the majority opinion: [4]

> The facts as to the nature and scope of the business of the Jones & Laughlin Steel Corporation have been found by the Labor Board and, so far as they are essential to the determination of this controversy, they are not in dispute. The Labor Board has found: The corporation is organized under the laws of Pennsylvania and has its principal office at Pittsburgh. It is engaged in the business of manufacturing iron and steel in plants situated in Pittsburgh and nearby Aliquippa,

[3] NLRB v. Jones & Laughlin Steel Corporation, Argument for Respondent, 301 U.S. 20–21 (1937).

[4] NLRB v. Jones & Laughlin Steel Corporation, 301 U.S. 1 (1937).

Pennsylvania. It manufactures and distributes a widely diversified line of steel and pig iron, being the fourth largest producer of steel in the United States. With its subsidiaries—nineteen in number—it is a completely integrated enterprise, owning and operating ore, coal and limestone properties, lake and river transportation facilities and terminal railroads located at its manufacturing plants. It owns or controls mines in Michigan and Minnesota. It operates four ore steamships on the Great Lakes, used in the transportation of ore to its factories. It owns coal mines in Pennsylvania. It operates towboats and steam barges used in carrying coal to its factories. It owns limestone properties in various places in Pennsylvania, and West Virginia. It owns the Monongahela connecting railroad which connects the plants of the Pittsburgh works and forms an interconnection with the Pennsylvania, New York Central and Baltimore and Ohio Railroad systems. It owns the Aliquippa and Southern Railroad Company which connects the Aliquippa works with the Pittsburgh and Lake Erie, part of the New York Central system. Much of its product is shipped to its warehouses in Chicago, Detroit, Cincinnati and Memphis, —to the last two places by means of its own barges and transportation equipment. In Long Island City, New York, and in New Orleans it operates structural steel fabricating shops in connection with the warehousing of semi-finished materials sent from its works. Through one of its wholly-owned subsidiaries it owns, leases and operates stores, warehouses and yards for the distribution of equipment and supplies for drilling and operating oil and gas wells and for pipe lines, refineries and pumping stations. It has sales offices in twenty cities in the United States and a wholly-owned subsidiary which is devoted exclusively to distributing its product in Canada. Approximately 75 per cent of its product is shipped out of Pennsylvania.

Summarizing these operations, the Labor Board concluded that the works in Pittsburgh and Aliquippa "might be likened to the heart of a self-contained, highly integrated body. They draw in the raw materials from Michigan, Minnesota, West Virginia, Pennsylvania in part through arteries and by means controlled by the respondent; they transform the materials and then pump them out to all parts of the nation through the vast mechanism which the respondent has elaborated.

To carry on the activities of the entire steel industry, 33,000 men mine ore, 44,000 men mine coal, . . . 16,000 men manufacture coke, 343,000 men manufacture steel, and 83,000 men transport its product. [The company] has about 10,000 employees in its Aliquippa plant, which is located in a community of about 30,000 persons. . . .

[The case is] concerned . . . with the employees in the Aliquippa plant whose discharge was the subject of the complaint. These employees were active leaders in the labor union. Several were officers and others were leaders of particular groups. Two of the employees were motor inspectors; one was a tractor driver; three were crane operators; one was a washer in the coke plant; and three were laborers. Three other employees were mentioned in the complaint but it was withdrawn as to one of them and no evidence was heard on the action taken with respect to the other two.

While [the company] criticizes the evidence and the attitude of the Board, which is described as being hostile toward employers and particularly toward those who insisted upon their constitutional rights, [the company] did not take advantage of its opportunity to present evidence to refute that which was offered to show discrimination and coercion. . . . Upon that point it is sufficient to say that the evidence supports the findings of the Board that [the company] discharged these men "because of their union activity and for the purpose of discouraging membership in the union." We turn to the questions of law which respondent urges in contesting the validity and application of the Act. . . .

The unfair labor practices found by the Board are those defined in § 8, subsections (1) and (3). These provide:

Sec. 8. It shall be an unfair labor practice for an employer—

"(1) To interfere with, restrain, or coerce employees in the exercise of the rights guaranteed in section 7."

"(3) By discrimination in regard to hire or tenure of employment or any term or condition of employment to encourage or discourage membership in any labor organization: . . ."

Section 8, subdivision (1), refers to § 7, which is as follows:

"Sec. 7. Employees shall have the right to self-organization, to form, to join or assist labor organizations, to bargain collectively through representatives of their own choosing, and to engage in concerted activities, for the purpose of collective bargaining or other mutual aid or protection."

Thus, in its present application, the statute goes no further than to safeguard the right of employees to self-organization and to select representatives of their own choosing for collective bargaining or other mutual protection without restraint or coercion by their employer.

That is a fundamental right. Employees have as clear a right to organize and select their representatives for lawful purposes as the respondent has to organize its business and select its own officers and agents. Discrimination and coercion to prevent the free exercise of the right of employees to self-organization and representation is a proper subject for condemnation by competent legislative authority. Long ago we stated the reason for labor organizations. We said that they were organized out of the necessities of the situation; that a single employee was helpless in dealing with an employer; that he was dependent ordinarily upon his daily wage for the maintenance of himself and family; that if the employer refused to pay him the wages that he thought fair, he was nevertheless unable to leave the employ and resist arbitrary and unfair treatment; that union was essential to give laborers opportunity to deal on an equality with their employer. . . . Fully recognizing the legality of collective action on the part of employees in order to safeguard their proper interests, we said that Congress was not required to ignore this right but could safeguard it. Congress could seek to make appropriate collective action of employees an instrument of peace rather than of strife. We said that such collective action would be a mockery if representation were made futile by interference with freedom of choice. Hence the prohibition by Congress of interference with the selection of representatives for the purpose of negotiation and conference between employers and employees, "instead of being an invasion of the constitutional rights of either was based on the recognition of the rights of both. . . ."

[The company] asserts its right to conduct its business in an orderly manner without being subjected to arbitrary restraints. What we have said points to the fallacy in the argument. Employees have their correlative right to organize for the purpose of securing the redress of grievances and to promote agreements with employer relating to rates of pay and conditions of work. . . . Restraint for the purpose of preventing an unjust interference with that right cannot be considered arbitrary or capricious. The provision of § 9 (a) [5] that representatives, for the purpose of collective bargaining, of the majority of the employees in an appropriate unit shall be the exclusive representatives of all the employees in that unit, imposes upon the respondent only the duty of conferring and negotiating with the authorized representatives of its employees for the purpose of settling a labor dispute. . . .

The Act does not compel agreements between employers and employees. It does not compel any agreement whatever. It does not prevent the employer "from refusing to make a collective contract and hiring individuals on whatever terms" the employer "may by unilateral action determine." The Act expressly provides in § 9 (a) that any individual employee or a group of employees shall have the right at any time to present grievances to their employer. The theory of the Act is that free opportunity for negotia-

[5] The provision is as follows: "Sec. 9 (a) Representatives designated or selected for the purposes of collective bargaining by the majority of the employees in a unit appropriate for such purposes, shall be the exclusive representatives of all the employees in such unit for the purposes of collective bargaining in respect to rates of pay, wages, hours of employment, or other conditions of employment: *Provided,* That any individual employee or a group of employees shall have the right at any time to present grievances to their employer."

tion with accredited representatives of employees is likely to promote industrial peace and may bring about the adjustments and agreements which the Act in itself does not attempt to compel. . . . The Act does not interfere with the normal exercise of the right of the employer to select its employees or to discharge them. The employer may not, under cover of that right, intimidate or coerce its employees with respect to their self-organization and representation, and, on the other hand, the Board is not entitled to make its authority a pretext for interference with the right of discharge when that right is exercised for other reasons than such intimidation and coercion. The true purpose is the subject of investigation with full opportunity to show the facts. It would seem that when employers freely recognize the right of their employees to their own organizations and their unrestricted right of representation there will be much less occasion for controversy in respect to the free and appropriate exercise of the right of selection and discharge.

IV

Mr. Justice McReynolds delivered the dissenting opinion:

[In the Standard Oil and the American Tobacco Company cases] a combination sought to monopolize and restrain interstate commerce through purchase and consequent control of many large competing concerns engaged both in manufacture and interstate commerce. The combination was sufficiently powerful and action by it so persistent that success became a dangerous probability. Here there is no such situation, and the cases are inapplicable in the circumstances. There is no conspiracy to interfere with commerce unless it can be said to exist among the employees who became members of the union. There is a single plant operated by its own management whose only offense, as alleged, was the discharge of a few employees in the production department because they belonged to a union, coming within the broad definition of "labor organization" prescribed by § 2 (5) of the Act. That definition includes any organization in which employees participate and which exists for the purpose in whole or in part of dealing with employers concerning grievances, wages, etc.

Section 13 of the Labor Act provides "Nothing in this Act shall be construed so as to interfere with or impede or diminish in any way the right to strike." And yet it is ruled that to discharge an employee in a factory because he is a member of a labor organization (any kind) may create discontent which may lead to a strike and this may cause a block in the "stream of commerce"; consequently the discharge may be inhibited. Thus the Act exempts from its ambit the very evil which counsel insist may result from discontent caused by a discharge of an association member, but permits coercion of a non-member to join one.

The things inhibited by the Labor Act relate to the management of a manufacturing plant—something distinct from commerce and subject to the authority of the state. And this may not be abridged because of some vague possibility of distant interference with commerce. . . . While . . . the rights of liberty and property guaranteed by the Constitution against deprivation without due process of law, are subject to such reasonable restraints as the common good or the general welfare may require, it is not within the functions of government—at least in the absence of contract between the parties—to compel any person in the course of his business and against his will to accept or retain the personal services of another, or to compel any person, against his will, to perform personal services for another. The right of a person to sell his labor upon such terms as he deems proper is, in its essence, the same as the right of the purchaser of labor to prescribe the conditions upon which he will accept such labor from the person offering to sell it. So the right of the employee to quit the service of the employer, for whatever reason, is the same as the right of the employer, for whatever reason, to dispense with the services of such employee. . . . The employer and the employee have equality of right [the one to discharge a worker for whatever reason he sees fit, and the other to quit the service in which he is engaged] and any legislation that disturbs that equality is an arbitrary interference with the liberty of contract which no government can legally justify in a free land. . . .

The right to contract is fundamental and includes the privilege of selecting those with whom one is willing to assume contractual relations. This right is unduly abridged by the Act now upheld. A private owner is deprived of power to manage his own property by freely selecting those to whom his manufacturing operations are to be entrusted. We think this cannot lawfully be done in circumstances like those here discussed.

It seems clear to us that Congress has transcended the powers granted.

QUESTIONS

Corporate Persons and Union Groups

1. In the Jones & Laughlin case the Supreme Court declared that it is as fundamental a right for employees to organize and select their representatives for lawful purposes as it is for a company to organize its business and select its own officers and agents. In what sense can this right be "fundamental"? Could Chief Justice Hughes have meant "constitutional" and, if so, why did he not say so?

2. Apply Justice Field's reasoning to a union and attempt to bring it under the protection of the Fourteenth Amendment as he did for corporations. What problems arise and what assumptions would you have to make about unions and workers to be successful?

3. Field sees through a corporation to the people whose rights are involved in it and thereby finds a constitutional basis for protecting the corporation; Hughes sees through the unions to the people whose interests and rights are involved in them. Unlike Field, however, Hughes makes no direct, explicit constitutional argument in support of unions. (He found that Congress had constitutional authority to encourage unions and collective bargaining, of course.) What is the difference between the people in corporations and the people in unions that makes it difficult to use Field's reasoning in the Jones & Laughlin case?

4. Do you agree with Field that when the state granted charters to corporations, it created no property? Did Congress create any "property" for unions when it passed the National Labor Relations Act? (Note how Field defines property.)

5. Compare the arguments of Hughes and Shaw in justifying unions, noting any similarities and differences.

6. Justice McReynolds declares that the National Labor Relations Act deprives an owner of the power to manage his own property. While ownership of property may give one the *power* to manage property and employees, does it give an owner the *right* to manage employees? (Consider carefully what the right of ownership entails and note what Chief Justice Shaw said about the way in which an owner secures the services of an employee.)

chapter **2**

WHAT IS PROPERTY?

Since 1842, American courts have found reasons to recognize the right of workers to associate together in unions, but these reasons have been quite different from and, in the context of American law, less convincing than those justifying the right of business incorporation. Constitutionally, unions are not as firmly based as corporations—at least as suggested by the cases in Chapter 1. While a majority of Americans have agreed that unions are necessary in an industrial society, many continued to be uneasy about them. Unions still seemed combinations tainted with the odor of monopoly even though they were encouraged by the Wagner Act of 1935 and later ratified again by the Taft-Hartley Act of 1947. They were unlike corporations, which had been found to be not combinations but democratic "persons" before the law. While acceptance of corporations could be squared with the ideal of the classical liberal state, the encouragement of unions seemingly could not.

Union combinations as such were suspect even though the public might excuse the concerted efforts of the workers in them to improve miserable working conditions. Conventional economic theory has provided no category for unions except that of monopoly, a group that pursues its own interests largely, if not entirely, at the economic expense of other groups and the public. Many people condemned unions as disruptive organizations that exercised power without any socially valid justification; in using concerted tactics to press their demands, the argument ran, union members are simply taking property away from others, not protecting or enhancing the value of any property of their own. And being propertyless, they were unlikely to further the interests of society or the purposes of the state, which were primarily the protection and preservation of property, the true source of man's life and liberty. This argument, as well as the arguments that contradict it, can be better understood in terms of the historical development of the concept of property.

In the seventeenth century, John Locke proclaimed the controlling significance of property ownership in the social order:

> Men unite into societies that they may have the united strength of the whole society to secure and defend their properties. . . . The preservation of property being the end of government, and that for which men enter into society, it necessarily supposes

> and requires that the people should have property, without which they must be supposed to lose that, by entering into society, which was the end for which they entered into it—too gross an absurdity for any man to own.[1]

Locke clearly believed that civil society had not created but merely recognized property; further, he implied that the ownership of property is basic and necessary to government and citizenship. A man without property might be within the community, but he could hardly be a part of it; he would be little more than a pariah, unable to participate in the activities of community life. Most Americans in the eighteenth and nineteenth centuries shared a Lockean attitude toward the socializing function of property and probably would have agreed with the British historian Macaulay when he proclaimed in 1832:

> [Property] is the great institution for the sake of which chiefly all other institutions exist, that great institution to which we owe all knowledge, all commerce, all industry, all civilization, all that makes us to differ from the savages of the Pacific Ocean.[2]

The property that Americans believed they had formed a government to protect and that Macaulay found to be civilizing was not, however, the same as Locke's. Locke's definition of property was more general and egalitarian:

> Every man has a "property" in his own "person." This nobody has any right to but himself. The "labour" of his body and the "work" of his hands, we may say, are properly his. Whatsoever he removes out of the state that Nature hath provided and left it in, he hath mixed his labour with it, and joined to it something that is his own, and thereby makes it his property.[3]

In Locke's time land was the most common kind of property and the most important and valuable. He recognized, however, that property might include other tangible goods, specifically money. Adam Smith's definition resembled Locke's but seemed to go beyond it in suggesting that property might include intangibles such as a person's service: "The property which every man has in his own labor, as it is the original foundation of all other property, so it is the most sacred and inviolate." [4]

Americans ignored or overlooked the opportunity to elaborate the concept of property offered by either Locke or Smith in such a way that a worker might claim a property right in his job or work. Rather, they intermingled the Lockean doctrine of private property with an agrarian emphasis upon the importance—indeed, the virtue—of land ownership. Thomas Jefferson, for example, stressed the necessity of each man owning land if a democratic nation and an economically secure, politically independent citizenry were to be maintained. "Those who labor in the earth are the chosen people of God, if ever He had a chosen people," he wrote. "While we have land to labor then, let us never wish to see our citizens occupied at a work-bench, or twirling a distaff." Should men leave their farms and property for the shops and mills of the cities, they would become propertyless—unable to help themselves and a danger to society. He warned that "the

[1] John Locke, *Of Civil Government,* Ernest Rhys, ed., Everyman Library (London: J. M. Dent & Sons, 1943), pp. 186–87.

[2] Lady Trevelyan, ed., "Miscellaneous Works," Part IX, *The Works of Lord Macaulay,* 19 (New York: George D. Sproul, 1908), 27–28.

[3] Locke, op. cit., p. 130.

[4] Adam Smith, *Wealth of Nations,* 1 (New York: Modern Library), 121–22.

mobs of great cities add just so much to the support of pure government, as sores do to the strength of the human body."[5] At another time he had forecast, "When we get piled up on one another in large cities, as in Europe, we shall become corrupt as in Europe, and go to eating one another as they do there."[6]

Though Jefferson's disdain and fear of city people and his praise of land-owning farmers were rooted in physiocratic economics and values, he showed insight in recognizing that the American economic and legal system would do well to serve and satisfy those who possessed land. In protecting land, the state protected life and liberty, too, in providing opportunities for exploiting land, the market offered opportunity for sustaining life and enjoying liberty. A farmer safe in the possession of his land could provide for himself and his family from the produce of his crops, consuming it directly to maintain life or, more likely, selling a portion of it for income with which to purchase tools, clothes, and other goods. Should the market fail him by offering an inadequate price, he was nevertheless buffered and protected by his land. He could eke out a living, continue his self-employment, and maintain his independence and liberty. He might be poor, but he would still be free. Thus, in a nation where most men farmed their own land, the law that upheld their property rights insured many of their social and economic rights at the same time.

The popular identification of property with land and ownership of land with liberty was supported throughout the nineteenth century by a compelling social fact, the rural character of American life. As late as 1880 almost three-fourths of the population dwelled in rural areas, for the most part living and working on their own farms. Three million of the 4 million farms were owner-operated, and most of the 8.6 million agricultural workers—half of the total American labor force—found employment on them.

Between 1880 and 1920, however, the nation changed rapidly and so did the occupations and conditions of its citizens. The proportion of workers who owned the property on which they toiled declined rapidly. Tenant farms increased almost twice as fast as owner-operated farms, and the number of industrial workers increased almost 10 times as fast as farm workers. The urban, industrial America of 1920, with three-fourths of its labor force engaged in non-agricultural pursuits and owning little or no economically significant property, was quite different from the rural, agricultural nation of 1880. It hardly resembled at all the seaboard agrarian nation of the early nineteenth century, when 72 per cent of the labor force had worked on farms.

Industrialism tended to separate men from the land; increasing numbers of workers—industrial and farm alike—owned no land and were unable to secure a claim to any kind of other property. They worked for wages, using the tools, machines, and land owned and supplied by others. The necessity of labor to seek employment and earn an income did not allow much personal liberty. Millions of workers had no reasonable alternative but to work at whatever jobs were available under whatever conditions an employer chose to offer. The continued identification of Jeffersonian property with the life and liberty of every individual citizen became more and more an anachronism in the twentieth century, though many eminent jurists steadfastly refused to realize it.

[5] Thomas Jefferson, "Notes on Virginia," *Writings,* Memorial Edition, II (Washington: Thomas Jefferson Memorial Association, 1907), 229–30.
[6] *Ibid.,* VI, 392–93.

However mistaken American jurists may have been to borrow uncritically the eighteenth- and even seventeenth-century ideas of political freedom for use in the twentieth century, they were not simply biased, prejudiced men who sought to defend the interests of one class at the expense of another by ignoring human rights and the dignity of men. They were concerned with personal liberty and the protection of life and the well-being of Americans, but they found the reasons for revising the concepts of property so as to apply them to business more compelling than the reasons for reinterpreting them to serve the needs of workers. Assuming that ownership of land—and therefore property—was the natural and common condition of Americans, twentieth-century judges were able to maintain, as had their predecessors, the thesis that if property were kept inviolate most of our cherished social rights and economic liberties would be insured as well.

In 1922, William Howard Taft, Chief Justice of the United States, revealed a traditionalist's faith in the right of property as a part of personal liberty as well as a more modern view of what property was when he wrote:

> Our Constitution . . . rests on personal liberty and the right of property. In the last analysis, personal liberty includes the right of property, as it includes the right of contract and the right of labor. Our primary conception of a free man is one who can enjoy what he earns, who can spend it for his comfort or pleasure if he would. . . . This is the right of property. . . . Personal liberty and the right of property are indispensable to any possible useful progress of society.[7]

Property had become a much different thing for Chief Justice Taft than it had been for Chief Justice Marshall. Gradually, in decision after decision, the courts had modified the definition of property. Those who possessed property now did indeed enjoy personal liberty, for the immunities of property reached further than ever before. Legislators could regulate it only with difficulty, and workers were swiftly enjoined from injuring it through strikes or picket lines.

The legal extension of the definition of property from the 1880's through the 1920's moved in a particular direction that greatly enhanced the rights of business but not of labor. The courts did not see fit during that time to define property rights in a way that would include the interests and activities of workers. On the other hand, the property rights of business were extended further and further; they impinged increasingly upon labor, restricting and limiting the workers' interests.

In the 1930's Congress removed many of the restrictions upon laborers' attempts to protect themselves at the expense of property rights of business. As unions grew large and powerful and assumed a regular, recognized role in our industrial society, the courts began to treat their interests and those of the workers with a consideration not previously given. They granted to unions and workers forms of legal protection that appeared to be establishing something like the property rights that had already been granted to business.

The cases in this chapter explore the development of property concepts for labor and business over the past century and examine the actual situations with which the courts had to deal and the contending arguments of those involved.

[7] William Howard Taft, *Liberty Under Law: An Interpretation of the Principles of Our Constitutional Government* (New Haven: Yale University Press, 1922), pp. 25–26.

Property for Some but Not for All

MUNN V. ILLINOIS

One of the first suggestions by the Supreme Court of how the traditional definition of property was to be extended and changed appears in the powerful dissent of Justice Stephen J. Field in Munn v. Illinois, 1876. The case arose as a result of an attempt by the state of Illinois to regulate the unscrupulous buccaneering business practices of grain warehousemen.

I

The Chicago Board of Trade had tried several times to commit the industry to self-regulation, but the warehousemen either defeated the proposals or weakened the agreed-upon rules to the point of uselessness. Several investigations and reports of fraud and shady practices, such as selling mixed grades of grain as the highest grade, had been hushed up. Talk was common that the firm of Munn & Scott had issued more warehouse receipts than it had grain. Munn & Scott was one of the four big firms that dominated grain storage in the area; it and the other three firms fixed storage fees and set the price of grain through pooling arrangements and market-sharing agreements.

As the 1860's came to an end, the double-dealing, profiteering, and defrauding by the major warehousemen was being conducted so openly and on such a scale that even businessmen finally called for state regulation. In a rare and temporary alliance, the grain merchants of Chicago and the farmers of Illinois persuaded the state's constitutional convention of 1869–70 to adopt a provision authorizing public regulation of warehouses and railroads. Shortly after the new constitution was approved, the legislature passed a regulating act that prescribed maximum charges (lower than those regularly fixed by the warehouse firms), required licensing and bonding, and established a commission to enforce its terms.

Munn & Scott refused to take out a license and denied state officials any access to their elevators. The state then sued the firm, and in July, 1872, won a judgment of $100. Munn & Scott appealed to the state Supreme Court. Before the court could hand down its decision, the firm was thoroughly discredited; the Chicago Board of Trade finally managed to inspect its elevators and discovered false bottoms in the bins and a shortage of 300,000 bushels of grain. At the same time, an unsuccessful attempt to corner the grain market drove the firm's partners, Ira Y. Munn and George L. Scott, into bankruptcy, and the surviving properties were bought by George Armour & Company. Nevertheless, despite the misadventures of the firm and its original partners, the new owners continued to defy the state Warehouse Act and carried on the case before the courts. Their principal argument was that the state was violating the Fourteenth Amendment, which forbids the states to "deprive any person of life, liberty, or property, without due process of law; nor deny any person within its jurisdiction the equal protection of the laws."

II

In 1873 Justice Breese delivered the majority opinion for the state court and upheld the right of the legislature to regulate business.[1] In so doing, he answered the argument of the firm's lawyers:

> Does the act of our General Assembly destroy any species of property, or deprive its owner of the use of it? It does not aim at the extinction of these warehouses or any of their attributes. The statute may affect them

[1] Munn et al. v. The People, 69 Illinois 80 (1873).

injuriously in a degree, but it does not say they shall not be allowed to exist at all. The constitutional provision is, no person shall be *deprived* of life, liberty or property, etc. This clause nowhere declares that, in the exercise of the admitted functions of government, private property may not receive remote and consequent injury. No person can claim that, in the exercise of the proper functions of government, his property shall not be diminished in value. The point is, the owner shall not be deprived of his property without due process of law. . . .

All regulations of trade with a view to the public interests, may more or less impair the value of property, but they do not come within the constitutional inhibitions unless they virtually take away and destroy those rights in which property consists. This destruction must be, for all substantial purposes, total.

The law must be held to be an honest effort on the part of the legislature to arrest a great and growing evil, by regulating the charges which these warehouses shall demand, and placing them under bonds that they will not violate its provisions. . . . This law in no respect affects the title, possession or use of this warehouse by the plaintiffs in error. It deprives them of nothing they owned and possessed at the time of its enactment. Anticipated profits are not, and can not, be held and regarded as property in the ownership or possession of him who owns the article out of which profits are expected to flow. The property is one thing, and remains untouched—the profits are not *in esse,* and cannot be claimed as property. When it is said one is deprived of his property, the understanding is, it has been taken away from him—he is divested of title and possession. This provision in the Bill of Rights has never been so construed by the courts of any State whose constitution has such a provision, as to deny to the legislature the power to make all needful rules and regulations respecting the use and enjoyment of property.

III

Sure in the belief that the state law would eventually be declared unconstitutional, the business interests of the day persuaded Armour to appeal the case to the federal courts. Munn v. Illinois reached the Supreme Court in 1876. Chief Justice Waite wrote the majority opinion, upholding the state court and declaring that the Constitution sanctioned economic regulation in the public interest. He pointed out that:

> When one becomes a member of society, he necessarily parts with some rights or privileges which, as an individual not affected by his relations to others, he might retain. "A body politic," as aptly defined in the preamble of the Constitution of Massachusetts, "is a social compact by which the whole people covenants with each citizen, and each citizen with the whole people, that all shall be governed by certain laws for the common good." This does not confer power upon the whole people to control rights which are purely and exclusively private, but it does authorize the establishment of laws requiring each citizen to so conduct himself, and so use his own property, as not unnecessarily to injure another. This is the very essence of government. . . . From this it is apparent that, down to the time of the adoption of the Fourteenth Amendment, it was not supposed that statutes regulating the use, or even the price of the use, of private property necessarily deprived an owner of his property without due process of law. . . . There is no attempt to compel these owners to grant the public an interest in their property, but to declare their obligations, if they use it in this particular manner. . . . We know that [the state's powers to regulate] may be abused; but that is no argument against its existence. For protection against abuses by legislatures the people must resort to the polls, not to the courts. . . .

IV

Justice Field wrote a dissent in which Justice Strong joined:

> I am compelled to dissent from the decision of the court in this case, and from the reasons upon which that decision is founded. The principle upon which the opinion of the majority proceeds is, in my

judgment, subversive of the rights of private property, heretofore believed to be protected by constitutional guaranties against legislative interference, and is in conflict with the authorities cited in its support. . . .

The question presented, therefore, is one of the greatest importance,—whether it is within the competency of a State to fix the compensation which an individual may receive for the use of his own property in his private business, and for his services in connection with it.

The declaration of the Constitution of 1870, that private buildings used for private purposes shall be deemed public institutions, does not make them so. The receipt and storage of grain in a building erected by private means for that purpose does not constitute the building a public warehouse. There is no magic in the language, though used by a constitutional convention, which can change a private business into a public one, or alter the character of the building in which the business is transacted. A tailor's or a shoemaker's shop would still retain its private character, even though the assembled wisdom of the State should declare, by organic act or legislative ordinance, that such a place was a public workshop, and that the workmen were public tailors or public shoemakers. One might as well attempt to change the nature of colors, by giving them a new designation. The defendants were no more public warehousemen, as justly observed by counsel, than the merchant who sells his merchandise to the public is a public merchant, or the blacksmith who shoes horses for the public is a public blacksmith; and it was a strange notion that by calling them so they would be brought under legislative control. . . .

The doctrine of the State court, that no one is deprived of his property, within the meaning of the constitutional inhibition, so long as he retains its title and possession, and the doctrine of this court, that, whenever one's property is used in such a manner as to affect the community at large, it becomes by that fact clothed with a public interest, and ceases to be *juris privati* only, appear to me to destroy, for all useful purposes, the efficacy of the constitutional guaranty. All that is beneficial in property arises from its use, and the fruits of that use; and whatever deprives a person of them deprives him of all that is desirable or valuable in the title and possession. If the constitutional guaranty extends no further than to prevent a deprivation of title and possession, and allows a deprivation of use, and the fruits of that use, it does not merit the encomiums it has received. Unless I have misread the history of the provision now incorporated into all our State constitutions, and by the Fifth and Fourteenth Amendments into our Federal Constitution, and have misunderstood the interpretation it has received, it is not thus limited in its scope, and thus impotent for good. It has a much more extended operation than either court, State or Federal, has given to it. The provision, it is to be observed, places property under the same protection as life and liberty. Except by due process of law, no State can deprive any person of either. The provision has been supposed to secure to every individual the essential conditions for the pursuit of happiness; and for that reason has not been heretofore, and should never be, construed in any narrow or restricted sense.

No State "shall deprive any person of life, liberty, or property without due process of law," says the Fourteenth Amendment to the Constitution. . . . [As liberal a construction] should be applied to the protection of private property [as is required for the protection of life and liberty]. If the legislature of a State, under pretence of providing for the public good, or for any other reason, can determine, against the consent of the owner, the uses to which private property shall be devoted, or the prices which the owner shall receive for its uses, it can deprive him of the property as completely as by a special act for its confiscation or destruction. If, for instance, the owner is prohibited from using his building for the purposes for which it was designed, it is of little consequence that he is permitted to retain the title and possession; or, if he is compelled to take as compensation for its use less than the expenses to which he is subjected by its ownership, he is, for all practical purposes, deprived of the property, as effectually as if the legislature had ordered his forcible dispossession. If it be admitted that the legislature has any control over the compensation, the extent of that compensation becomes a mere matter of legislative discretion. The amount fixed will operate as a partial destruction of the value of the property, if it fall below the amount which the owner would obtain by contract, and, practically, as a complete destruction, if it be less than the cost of retaining its possession. There is, indeed, no protection of any value under the constitutional provision, which does not extend to the use and income of the property, as well as to its title and possession.

This court has heretofore held in many instances that a constitutional provision intended for the protection of rights of private property should be liberally construed. It has so held in the numerous cases where it has been called upon to give effect to the provision prohibiting the States from legislation impairing the obligation of contracts; the provision being construed to secure from direct attack not only the contract itself, but all the essential incidents which give it value and enable its owner to enforce it. . . .

The power of the State over the property of the citizen under the constitutional guaranty is well defined. The State may take his property for public uses, upon just compensation being made therefor. It may take a portion of his property by way of taxation for the support of the government. It may control the use and possession of his property, so far as may be necessary for the protection of the rights of others, and to secure to them the equal use and enjoyment of their property. The doctrine that each one must so use his own as not to injure his neighbor—*sic utere tuo ut alienum non lædas*—is the rule by which every member of society must possess and enjoy his property; and all legislation essential to secure this common and equal enjoyment is a legitimate exercise of State authority. Except in cases where property may be destroyed to arrest a conflagration or the ravages of pestilence, or be taken under the pressure of an immediate and overwhelming necessity to prevent a public calamity, the power of the State over the property of the citizen does not extend beyond such limits. . . .

There is no end of regulations with respect to the use of property which may not be legitimately prescribed, having for their object the peace, good order, safety, and health of the community, thus securing to all the equal enjoyment of their property; but in establishing these regulations it is evident that compensation to the owner for the use of his property, or for his services in union with it, is not a matter of any importance: whether it be one sum or another does not affect the regulation, either in respect to its utility or mode of enforcement. One may go, in like manner, through the whole round of regulations authorized by legislation, State or municipal, under what is termed the police power, and in no instance will he find that the compensation of the owner for the use of his property has any influence in establishing them. It is only where some right or privilege is conferred by the government or municipality upon the owner, which he can use in connection with his property, or by means of which the use of his property is rendered more valuable to him, or he thereby enjoys an advantage over others, that the compensation to be received by him becomes a legitimate matter of regulation. Submission to the regulation of compensation in such cases is an implied condition of the grant, and the State, in exercising its power of prescribing the compensation, only determines the conditions upon which its concession shall be enjoyed. When the privilege ends, the power of regulation ceases. . . .

There is nothing in the character of the business of the defendants as warehousemen which called for the interference complained of in this case. Their buildings are not nuisances; their occupation of receiving and storing grain infringes upon no rights of others, disturbs no neighborhood, infects not the air, and in no respect prevents others from using and enjoying their property as to them may seem best. The legislation in question is nothing less than a bold assertion of absolute power by the State to control at its discretion the property and business of the citizen, and fix the compensation he shall receive. The will of the legislature is made the condition upon which the owner shall receive the fruits of his property and the just reward of his labor, industry, and enterprise. "That government," says Story, "can scarcely be deemed to be free where the rights of property are left solely dependent upon the will of a legislative body without any restraint. The fundamental

> maxims of a free government seem to require that the rights of personal liberty and private property should be held sacred." The decision of the court in this case gives unrestrained license to legislative will. . . . In the case of the warehousemen of Chicago, no right or privilege is conferred by the government upon them; and hence no assent of theirs can be alleged to justify any interference with their charges for the use of their property. . . .

V

The Supreme Court was not ready in 1876 to agree to Justice Field's argument that the expected earning power of things owned is property, just as are the physical things. However, as the Supreme Court continued to deal with the legal problems of business corporations in a rapidly industrializing market economy and attempted to interpret constitutional rights in the light of the new conditions, more and more jurists came to accept Field's logic. In the Minnesota Rate case of 1890,[2] a majority of the Supreme Court at last declared its acceptance also, maintaining that if a company "is deprived of the power of charging reasonable rates for the use of its property, and such deprivation takes place in the absence of an investigation by judicial machinery, it is deprived of the lawful use of its property, and thus, in substance and effect, of the property itself." The Court thus gave a constitutional imprimatur to the view that property was not merely physical goods but also the earnings of goods. By implication, therefore, it made the capitalized value of future expected returns a kind of property, worthy of all the legal protections offered by our government.

[2] Chicago, Milwaukee and St. Paul Railway Company v. Minnesota, 134 U.S. 418 (1890).

TRUAX V. CORRIGAN

If earnings are the "substance and effect" of property, as the Supreme Court ruled in the Minnesota Rate case of 1890, might not one contend that a worker possesses a property right in his job? It produces for him a livelihood and is thus something of value. Paraphrasing Justice Field, one might maintain that "all that is beneficial in a job arises from working in it and the wages of that work; and whatever deprives a person of them deprives him of all that is desirable or valuable in the title and possession of the job." Reasonable as this may seem, the Supreme Court would not soon discover a way to accept its substance as law.

I

Although the majority would not be convinced, a minority of the Supreme Court did argue in 1872 and again in 1884 that men possess property rights in their calling, occupation, trade, and labor.[1] In his dissent to the first Slaughter House decision, Justice Bradley wrote:

> [The] right to choose one's calling is an essential part of that liberty which is the object of government to protect; and a calling, when chosen, is a man's property and right. . . . Their right of choice is a portion of their liberty; their occupation is their property.

In a separate dissent, Justice Swayne declared:

> Property is everything which has exchangeable value, and the right of property includes the power to dispose of it according to the will of the owner. Labor is property, and as such merits protection. The right to make it available is next in importance to the rights of life and liberty.

[1] Slaughter House cases, 16 Wallace 36 (1873) and 111 U.S. 746 (1884).

The most radical stand of all appeared in a third dissent by Justice Field; not only did Field agree that men had a property right in a trade or calling, but he recognized that economic coercion might deny that right as effectively and surely as physical force used in outright enslavement. He even espoused an equality for all men to follow whatever employment they wished:

> A person allowed to pursue only one trade or calling, and only in one locality of the country would not be, in the strict sense of the term, in a condition of slavery; but probably none would deny that he would be in a condition of servitude. . . . The compulsion which would force him to labor even for his own benefit only in one direction, or in one place, would be almost as oppressive and nearly as great an invasion of his liberty as the compulsion which would force him to labor for the benefit or pleasure of another, and would equally constitute an element of servitude. . . . [The Fourteenth Amendment] was intended to give practical effect to the declaration of 1776 of inalienable rights which are the gift of the Creator, which the law does not confer but only recognizes. . . . It was supposed that there were no privileges or immunities of citizens more sacred than those which are involved in the right to the pursuit of happiness which is usually classed with life and liberty; and that in the pursuit of happiness, since that amendment became part of the fundamental law, every one was free to follow any lawful employment without other restraints than such as equally affect all other persons.

II

In the next half century the Supreme Court refused to accept the argument that a laborer's trade or calling might appropriately be defined as property, and as a result any worker or group of workers trying to protect their jobs or defend themselves against cuts in pay by striking could not be found to be legally engaged in anything more than malicious injury to other people's property.

So long as a person is using or protecting a property right, he may pursue his self-interest and seek benefits for himself even at the expense of another. A storeowner, for example, may drive another storekeeper out of business through competitive selling, depriving him of income and livelihood; or a landowner may place a building on his property that greatly reduces the view and thus the value of an adjoining plot owned by another person.

The ownership of property and the right to use it for the owner's self-interest justifies such injuries as its lawful use may inflict upon another's property. Should a person who owns no property inflict the same injury upon another, however, the action cannot be justified. Rather, the action is, or resembles, stealing or extortion. As long as the courts failed to perceive that workers possessed any property rights in their jobs, the workers found themselves severely restricted by law. When they struck an employer, the courts often enjoined their concerted activities to protect the employer's property rights in his business.

The restrictions upon union activities that were imposed by courts as a consequence of their definition of property were increasingly attacked after the turn of the century by men of progressive political views. In the new state of Arizona the progressives enacted a new legal code in 1913, one provision of which was designed to provide workers and unions with more freedom than they had heretofore enjoyed. It prohibited state courts from issuing injunctions in labor disputes as long as there were no disorders or violence.

Three years later the constitutionality of the prohibition was questioned by William and William A. Truax, the owners of the "English Kitchen" restaurant in Bisbee, employing about ten cooks and waiters. In early April, 1916, the Truaxes told their employees that wages were to be cut and working hours increased. The employees took the matter to their union, Local No. 5, Cooks and Waiters Union, of Bisbee. The local's officers asked the Truaxes not to change the working standards, but to no avail; the lower pay scale and new work schedule went into effect on April 9. The next day the employees went out on strike, hoping to induce the Truaxes to restore their pay to its former level.

The Warren District Trade Assembly supported the workers' efforts to protect their work standards and helped them run a well publicized campaign against the restaurant. The striking employees and other workers who supported them picketed the restaurant, warned passersby not to patronize it, and denounced those who did. In the sedate language of the court, the pickets were alleged to have attacked the character of patrons by "saying that their mental calibre and moral fibre fell far below the American average, and enquiring of the would-be patrons—Can you patronize such a place and look the world in the face?" The pickets called out to the people entering the restaurant such comments as "All ye who enter here leave all hope behind," and "Don't be a traitor to humanity."

The pickets also passed out handbills denouncing the Truaxes and the restaurant. The senior Truax was described as a tyrannical man—a "bad actor"—who chased his help down the street with a butcher knife in his hand; sometimes he was labeled "12-hour Bill Truax" and charged with having broken his contract and repudiating his pledged word. Some circulars declared that the restaurant's prices were higher and the food worse than any other in town and that assaults and sluggings were a regular part of the bill of fare. On several days, supporters of the workers publicized the strikers' cause by driving donkeys draped with banners about the town.

While the pickets were sometimes loud and made their feelings clear, the strike involved no violence and the picketing was peaceful. It had a decided effect upon the restaurant's business, however. Daily receipts, which had averaged over $156, dropped to $75. The Truaxes claimed that on a yearly basis their business had been reduced from more than $55,000 to a mere $12,000. To secure the constitutional protection of their property they believed was due them, they brought suit against the union, arguing that the state law restricting injunctions violated the Fourteenth Amendment. Their counsel maintained that they should not be denied legal protection from injury because of the "accidental and irrelevant fact that the property which [William Truax] seeks to protect is not of a tangible character, but consists merely of his business and of his right to conduct that business in such lawful manner as he sees fit."

In effect, the counsel asserted that any action by workers or a union that impaired business earnings destroyed the Truaxes' property; the restaurant possessed value for the Truaxes primarily as a means of producing revenue. For other men to diminish the usual and expected flow of revenue was to take property from the Truaxes as surely as a thief who made off with all the tableware or furniture. Moreover, the workers had no more right to take the Truaxes' property than a thief. In both cases the state had the duty to protect the owners.

Counsel for the picketing workers argued that whatever may have been injured by the publicity, it could not be called property. Admittedly the Truaxes' "good will" may have been infringed, but it was affected in a lawful manner. Since the law only protects "a man's fair right to obtain a livelihood," the employees had a right to publicize truthfully the fact that Truax was "unfair" to organized labor. Thus, according to the workers' counsel, the union's activities "did not constitute a gratuitous attempt to interfere with [the Truaxes'] business."

III

The Arizona Supreme Court upheld the union and the workers, pointing out that no man had a vested property in the esteem of the public and that the employees enjoyed the civil right of publicizing their dispute through peaceful picketing.

Truax (Senior) then appealed to the Supreme Court of the United States and received a sympathetic hearing from Chief Justice Taft who wrote the majority opinion: [2]

> [Truax's] business is a property right and free access for employees, owner and customers to his place of business is incident to such right. . . .
>
> It is argued that, while the right to conduct a lawful business is property, the conditions surrounding that business, such as regulations of the State for maintaining peace, good order, and protection against disorder, are matters in which no person has a vested right. The conclusion to which this inevitably leads in this case is that the State may withdraw all protection to a property right by civil or criminal action for its wrongful injury if the injury is not caused by violence. . . .
>
> The broad distinction between one's right to protection against a direct injury to one's fundamental property right by another who has no special relation to him, and one's liability to another with whom he establishes a voluntary relation under a statute is manifest upon its statement. It is true that no one has a vested right in any particular rule of the common law, but it is also true that the legislative power of a State can only be exerted in subordination to the fundamental principles of right and justice which the guaranty of due process in the Fourteenth Amendment is intended to preserve, and that a purely arbitrary or capricious exercise of that power whereby a wrongful and highly injurious invasion of property rights, as here, is practically sanctioned and the owner stripped of all real remedy, is wholly at variance with those principles.
>
> It is to be observed that this is not the mere case of a peaceful secondary boycott as to the illegality of which courts have differed and States have adopted different statutory provisions. A secondary boycott of this kind is where many combine to injure one in his business by coercing third persons against their will to cease patronizing him by threats of similar injury. In such a case the many have a legal right to withdraw their trade from the one, they have the legal right to withdraw their trade from third persons, and they have the right to advise third persons of their intention to do so when each act is considered singly. The question in such cases is whether the moral coercion exercised over a stranger to the original controversy by steps in themselves legal becomes a legal wrong. But here the illegality of the means used is without doubt and fundamental. The means used are the libelous and abusive attacks on the plaintiffs' reputation, like attacks on their employees and customers, threats of such attacks on would-be customers, picketing and patrolling of the entrance to their place of business, and the consequent obstruction of free access thereto —all with the purpose of depriving the plaintiffs of their business. To give operation to a statute whereby serious losses inflicted by such unlawful means are in effect made remediless, is, we think, to disregard fundamental rights of liberty and property and to deprive the person suffering the loss of due process of law. . . .

[2] Truax v. Corrigan, 257 U.S. 312 (1921).

IV

Four Justices dissented, and three wrote dissenting opinions. Justice Holmes took issue with Taft's definition of property:

> The dangers of a delusive exactness in the application of the Fourteenth Amendment have been adverted to before now [in earlier statements before this Court]. Delusive exactness is a source of fallacy throughout the law. By calling a business "property" you make it seem like land, and lead up to the conclusion that a statute cannot substantially cut down the advantages of ownership existing before the statute was passed. An established business no doubt may have pecuniary value and commonly is protected by law against various unjustified injuries. But you cannot give it definiteness of contours by calling it a thing. It is a course of conduct and like other conduct is subject to substantial modification according to time and circumstances both in itself and in regard to what shall justify doing it a harm.

Justice Brandeis wrote a longer dissent, exploring the meaning and effect of property rights in the industrial world of business and labor:

> The employer has, of course, a legal right to carry on his business for profit; and incidentally the subsidiary rights to secure and retain customers, to fix such prices for his product as he deems proper, and to buy merchandise and labor at such prices as he chooses to pay. This right to carry on business—be it called liberty or property—has value; and, he who interferes with the right without cause renders himself liable. But for cause the right may be interfered with and even be destroyed. Such cause exists when, in the pursuit of an equal right to further their several interests, his competitors make inroads upon his trade, or when suppliers of merchandise or of labor make inroads upon his profits. What methods and means are permissible in this struggle of contending forces is determined in part by decisions of the courts, in part by acts of the legislatures. The rules governing the contest necessarily change from time to time. For conditions change; and, furthermore, the rules evolved, being merely experiments in government, must be discarded when they prove to be failures.
>
> Practically every change in the law governing the relation of employer and employee must abridge, in some respect, the liberty or property of one of the parties—if liberty and property be measured by the standard of the law theretofore prevailing. If such changes are made by acts of the legislature, we call the modification an exercise of the police power. And, although the change may involve interference with existing liberty or property of individuals, the statute will not be declared a violation of the due process clause, unless the court finds that the interference is arbitrary or unreasonable or that, considered as a means, the measure has no real or substantial relation of cause to a permissible end. . . .
>
> The legal right of workingmen to combine and to strike in order to secure for themselves higher wages, shorter hours and better working conditions received early general recognition. But there developed great diversity of opinion as to the means by which, and also as to the persons through whom, and upon whom pressure might permissibly be exerted in order to induce the employer to yield to the demands of the workingmen. Courts were required, in the absence of legislation, to determine what the public welfare demanded;—whether it would not be best subserved by leaving the contestants free to resort to any means not involving a breach of the peace or injury to tangible property; whether it was consistent with the public interest that the contestants should be permitted to invoke the aid of others not directly interested in the matter in controversy; and to what extent incidental injury to persons not parties to the controversy should be held justifiable. . . .
>
> In America the injunction did not secure recognition as a possible remedy until 1888. When a few years later its use became extensive and conspicuous, the controversy over the remedy overshadowed in bitterness the question of the relative substantive rights of the parties. In the storms of protest against this use many thoughtful lawyers joined. The equitable remedy, although applied in accordance with established practice, involved incidents which, it was asserted, endangered the personal liberty of wage-earners. The acts enjoined were frequently, perhaps usually, acts which were already crimes at common law or had been made so by statutes. The issues in litigation arising out of trade disputes related largely to questions of fact. But in equity issues of fact as of law were tried by a single judge, sitting without a jury. Charges of violating an injunction were often heard on affidavits merely, without the opportunity of confronting or cross-examining witnesses. Men found guilty of contempt were committed in the judge's discretion, without either a statutory limit upon the length of the imprisonment, or the opportunity of effective review on appeal, or the right to release on bail pending possible revisory proceedings. The effect of the proceeding upon the individual was substantially the same as if he had been successfully prosecuted for a crime; but he was denied, in the course of the equity proceedings, those rights which by the Constitution are commonly secured to persons charged with a crime.
>
> It was asserted that in these proceedings

an alleged danger to property, always incidental and at times insignificant, was often laid hold of to enable the penalties of the criminal law to be enforced expeditiously without that protection to the liberty of the individual which the Bill of Rights was designed to afford; that through such proceedings a single judge often usurped the functions not only of the jury but of the police department; that, in prescribing the conditions under which strikes were permissible and how they might be carried out, he usurped also the powers of the legislature; and that incidentally he abridged the constitutional rights of individuals to free speech, to a free press and to peaceful assembly.

It was urged that the real motive in seeking the injunction was not ordinarily to prevent property from being injured nor to protect the owner in its use, but to endow property with active, militant power which would make it dominant over men. In other words, that, under the guise of protecting property rights, the employer was seeking sovereign power. And many disinterested men, solicitous only for the public welfare, believed that the law of property was not appropriate for dealing with the forces beneath social unrest; that in this vast struggle it was unwise to throw the power of the State on one side or the other according to principles deduced from that law; that the problem of the control and conduct of industry demanded a solution of its own; and that, pending the ascertainment of new principles to govern industry, it was wiser for the State not to interfere in industrial struggles by the issuance of an injunction. . . .

The Supreme Court of Arizona, having held as a rule of substantive law that the boycott as here practiced was legal at common law; and that the picketing was peaceful and, hence, legal under the [state] statute (whether or not it was legal at common law), necessarily denied the injunction, since, in its opinion, the defendants had committed no legal wrong and were threatening none. But even if this court should hold that an employer has a constitutional right to be free from interference by such a boycott or that the picketing practiced was not in fact peaceful, it does not follow that Arizona would lack the power to refuse to protect that right by injunction. For it is clear that the refusal of an equitable remedy for a tort is not necessarily a denial of due process of law. And it seems to be equally clear that such refusal is not necessarily arbitrary and unreasonable when applied to incidents of the relation of employer and employee. The considerations which show that the refusal is not arbitrary or unreasonable show likewise that such refusal does not necessarily constitute a denial of equal protection of the laws merely because some, or even the same, property rights which are excluded by this statute from protection by injunction, receive such protection under other circumstances, or between persons standing in different relations. The acknowledged legislative discretion exerted in classification, so frequently applied in defining rights, extends equally to the grant of remedies. It is for the legislature to say—within the broad limits of the discretion which it possesses—whether or not the remedy for a wrong shall be both criminal and civil and whether or not it shall be both at law and in equity. . . .

Nor is a State obliged to protect all property rights by injunction merely because it protects some, even if the attending circumstances are in some respects similar. The restraining power of equity might conceivably be applied to every intended violation of a legal right. On grounds of expediency its application is commonly denied in cases where there is a remedy at law which is deemed legally adequate. But an injunction has been denied on grounds of expediency in many cases where the remedy at law is confessedly not adequate. This occurs whenever a dominant public interest is deemed to require that the preventive remedy, otherwise available for the protection of private rights, be refused and the injured party left to such remedy as courts of law may afford. . . .

Instances are numerous where protection to property by way of injunction has been refused solely on the ground that serious public inconvenience would result from restraining the act complained of. Such, for example, was the case where a neighboring land owner sought to restrain a smelter from polluting the air, but that relief, if granted, would have necessitated shutting down the plant and this would have destroyed the business and impaired the means of livelihood of a large community. There are also numerous instances where the circumstances would, according to general equity practice, have justified the issue of an injunction, but it was refused solely because the right sought to be enforced was created by statute, and the courts, applying a familiar rule, held that the remedy provided by the statute was exclusive.

For these reasons, as well as for others . . . the judgment of the Supreme Court of Arizona should, in my opinion, be affirmed:—first, because in permitting damage to be inflicted by means of boycott and peaceful picketing Arizona did not deprive the plaintiffs of property without due process of law or deny them equal protection of the laws; and secondly, because, if Arizona was constitutionally prohibited from adopting this rule of substantive law, it was still free to restrict the extraordinary remedies of equity where it considered their exercise to be detrimental to the public welfare, since such restriction was not a denial to the employer either of due process of law or of equal protection of the laws.

QUESTIONS

Property for Some but Not for All

1. What are the implications of Field's declaration that "there is no magic in language [or law] which can change a private business into a public one"? What is the determinate of private business, then, according to Field?

2. Suppose the courts had defined a worker's expected earnings from a job as a property right, what effect would it have had upon workers' interests? What effect upon unions?

3. How would Field answer Brandeis' charge that businessmen sought to enjoin workers from striking and picketing not to protect property rights but to seek sovereign power? What was Field's understanding of the relationship of property and the government? How does it differ from that of Marshall?

4. Since Chief Justice Taft conceded that the picketing of the "English Kitchen" was peaceful and nonviolent, upon what grounds was he able to argue that it was illegal?

5. Examine Holmes's concept of property as presented in his dissent in the Truax case. How well does it fit the definition given in the Minnesota Rate case and that given by Chief Justice Taft in the majority opinion?

Intangible Property for All

NATIONAL TELEGRAPH V. WESTERN UNION

Twelve years after business income was declared to be the "substance and effect" of property in the Minnesota Rate case, the concept of property was elaborated and refined still further by the courts in a landmark case involving the Western Union Telegraph Company.[1]

[1] National Telegraph News Company v. Western Union Telegraph Company, 119 F. 294 and 56 CCA 198.

I

The service of Western Union being threatened consisted of the transmission of immediate, continuous news on a "ticker" to subscribers interested in receiving current reports on stock prices, the outcome of horse races, the play-by-play details of sports events, and the like. The company collected the news, transmitted it to central offices, and then redistributed it via wire to tickers located in the offices and places of business of its customers. The ticker printed the news upon strips of paper and was open to inspection of anyone who had access to the machine.

The National Telegraph News Company of Chicago also sold news via tickers. The two owners of this company, F. E. Crawford and A. K. Brown, subscribed to the Western Union ticker service and appropriated news that was reported through it for redistribution over their own company's wires. With the loss of only a few moments, items collected by Western Union reappeared on the National tickers. Crawford and Brown defended their use of the news from Western Union on the grounds that the widespread publication of the items on the tickers across the nation dedicated them to the public and deprived Western Union of any further claim to them.

Western Union pointed out that it went to great expense in gathering and transmitting the news. It had made a substantial investment in wires, instruments, and offices as well as a major effort in hiring and training employees to select and report the news it provided its customers. Since it could not secure a copyright on its printed tape, it was left with no protection of its business. National Telegraph News could charge a much lower price since it did not have to maintain Western Union's overhead staff and facilities. The result was that Western Union subsidized National Telegraph News, and it was possible that the parasitic company would eventually drive Western Union out of the ticker business by making it too unprofitable to maintain.

II

The matter came before the Court of Appeals for the Seventh Circuit and Judge Grosscup delivered the opinion of the court:

> The printed matter on the tape . . . is, at most the mere annal of events transpiring. . . . It is, in its totality, nothing more or less than the transmission by electricity, over long distances, of what a spectator of the event, occupying a fortunate position to see or hear, would have communicated, by word of mouth, to his less fortunate neighbor. It is an exchange merely, over wider area, of ordinary sightseeing; and the exchange is in the language of the ordinary sightseer. Matter of this character is not, within the meaning of the copyright law, the fruit of intellectual labor, and would not, if actually copyrighted, be protected by the courts.
>
> Indeed, the printed tape under consideration has no value at all as a book or article. It lasts literally for an hour, and is in the waste basket when the hour has passed. It is not desired by the patron for the intrinsic value of the happening recorded—the happening, as an happening, may have no value. The value of the tape to the patron is almost wholly in the fact that the knowledge thus communicated is earlier, in point of time, than knowledge communicated through other means, or to persons other than those having a like service. In just this quality—to coin a word, the precommunicatedness of the information—is the essence of appellee's service; the quality that wins from the patron his patronage.
>
> Now, in virtue of this quality, and of this quality alone, the printed tape has acquired a commercial value. It is, when thus looked at, a distinct commercial product, as much so as any other out-put relating to business, and brought about by the joint agency of capital and business ability. In no accurate view can appellee be said to be a publisher or author. Its place, in the classification of the law, is that of a carrier of news; the contents of the tape being an implement only, in the hands of such carrier, in its engagement for quick transmission. This is Service; not Authorship, nor the work of the Publisher. . . .
>
> The business involves . . . [however] the use of property. This consideration brings it at once, in a general way, within the protecting care of courts of equity. At first glance the immediate act restrained in the order below—the use of the information by a rival enterprise until after sixty minutes—may not appear as a trespass upon, or injury to, property, other than to the extent that there may

be property in the printed matter. But such a view falls short of looking far enough. Property, even as distinguished from property in intellectual production, is not, in its modern sense, confined to that which may be touched by the hand, or seen by the eye. What is called tangible property has come to be, in most great enterprises, but the embodiment, physically, of an underlying life—a life that, in its contribution to success, is immeasurably more effective than the mere physical embodiment. Such, for example, are properties built upon franchises, on grants of government, on good will, or on trade names, and the like. It is needless to say, that to every ingredient of property thus made up—the intangible as well as the tangible, that which is discernible to mind only, as well as that susceptible to physical touch—equity extends appropriate protection. Otherwise courts of equity would be unequal to their supposed great purposes; and every day, as business life grows more complicated, such inadequacy would be increasingly felt.

Nowhere is this recognition by courts of equity of the intangible side of property better exemplified, than in the remedies recently developed against unfair competition in trade. An unregistered trade name or mark is, in essence, nothing more than a symbol, conveying to eye and ear information respecting origin and identity; as if the manufacturer, present in person, and pointing to the article, were to say, "These are mine"; and the injunctive remedy applied is simply a command that this form of speech—this method of saying, These are mine—shall not be intruded upon unfairly by a like speech of another.

Standing apart, the symbol or speech is not property. Disconnected from the business in which it is utilized it cannot be monopolized. But used as a method of making an enterprise succeed, so that its appropriation by another would be a distinctive injury to the enterprise to which it is attached, the name, or mark, becomes at once the subject-matter of equitable protection. Here, as elsewhere, the eye of equity jurisdiction seeks out results, and though the immediate thing to be acted upon by the injunction is not itself, alone considered, property, it is enough that the act complained of will result, even though somewhat remotely, in injury to property.

Considering that in such case, equity, without question, lays its restraining hands upon the injurious appropriation of words that belong to the common language of mankind—than which nothing could be freer to the uses of men—there ought, it would seem, to be no difficulty, in the case under consideration, to find the power so manifestly needful. . . . Equity should see to it, that the one who is served, and the one who serves, each gets what the engagement between them calls for; and that neither, to the injury of the other shall appropriate more. . . .

Is the enterprise of the great news agencies, or the independent enterprise of the great newspapers, or of the great telegraph and cable lines, to be denied appeal to the courts, against the inroads of the parasite, for no other reason than that the law, fashioned hitherto to fit the relations of authors and the public, cannot be made to fit the relations of the public and this dissimilar class of servants? Are we to fail our plain duty for mere lack of precedent? We choose, rather, to make precedent—one from which is eliminated, as immaterial, the law grown up around authorship.

RAILROAD TELEGRAPHERS V. CHICAGO & NORTH WESTERN

Until recently a worker possessed only a fragile, transitory kind of right in his job. Once he was hired he might be said to possess a kind of property right but only in and through the terms of his work contract, which he and his employer were free to try to change—or to terminate—unilaterally at any time. Workers typically were hired by the hour and sometimes only by the minute; they accumulated no continuing claims to their jobs, although their contracts could be continually renewed so that they might count their employment in years. In such a situation the courts could find few "property" rights to protect for the worker. Whatever the worker "owned" in his individually bargained work contract, it had no more substance than a shadow as long as he was an ordinary individual and the employer was a vast corporation.

I

The ephemeral ties of the continually renewed work contract were not entirely satisfactory to either workers or corporate managers. The worker enjoyed little security in his job and was subject to the arbitrary whims of his foreman and supervisors. Managers, on their part, found that workers were not always dependable and would leave their work and job whenever an opportunity elsewhere beckoned. The resulting high turnover caused inefficiencies and waste in production and costly expenditures for hiring and training. Both parties thus found good reasons for creating job rules and work claims which could become—and may be now becoming—the basis of rights in and to jobs. The initiative came from the workers, through their unions, and from business management, not from legislators or jurists.

The craft unions that founded the American Federation of Labor in 1886 accepted the property-oriented legal and economic system and tried to find a place and role in it for themselves and their members. The unions of skilled craftsmen established rules to regularize the often chaotic labor market and to order the hiring, firing, and directing of employees at the place of work. While they benefitted their members by assuring recognition of job claims, they also helped employers by providing a more stable, often better trained work force than had previously been available. In gaining recognition for their work rules, American unions in both the nineteenth and twentieth centuries secured quasi-property rights for their members, as a kind of substitute for the real property of the farmer and the financial and contractual property of the businessman. They were adapting the old American ideal of "every citizen a property holder" to modern industrial society.

Corporate managers did not wait for unions to press for arrangements that would establish ties between the company and workers on a longer term than that of an unwritten work contract subject to cancelation at any time. In the 1920's American managers began to develop careful personnel selection processes, emphasize promotion from within the company, and recognize the value of investment in formal on-the-job training programs. These policies implied that workers were expected to stay with a company for some time. This expectation was even more explicit when managers began to introduce such programs as health services and pension plans. Managers and workers increasingly expected and tried to maintain an employment relationship lasting for years even though either could *legally* terminate the work contract at any time.

The spread of unions in the 1930's and 1940's and the threat of union organization encouraged managers to provide still more benefits that would accrue to long-term workers. By the mid-fifties such provisions as seniority in layoffs, rehiring, and promotion, vacation time based on length of service, unemployment pay, severance pay graded by length of service, and old-age retirement pay had become common benefits for industrial workers. Their widespread acceptance by both managers and workers suggested that neither any longer understood their relationship typically to be based on merely a continually renewed contract. Both were prepared to work together for an indefinite but long time.

By the end of the 1950's some union members were arguing that a further condition was inherent in the job relationship: if managers wish to end the relationship and the workers do not, the workers must be compensated in some way for their unrealized job expectations or for their cancelled job claims.

II

Congress and the courts have not yet accepted the unions' argument for the existence of this new condition of the job relationship, but they have begun to insist that management cannot unilaterally terminate a collectively bargained contract. It must first consult and bargain with the appropriate union negotiators, though it does not have to agree to any particular terms. In a number of cases involving railroad managers and railway workers the courts have declared that managers are not as free as they once were in changing and disposing of the contracts which define workers' job rights.

One of the most significant of these railroad cases arose when new management took over the Chicago and North Western Railway in the mid-fifties and began to modernize operations. The new management team found that efficiency required a substantial reduction in the work force. The company's outmoded and wasteful practices produced the highest ratio of wage and salary expense to the revenue dollar of all major American railroads. Its net revenues had declined so far that it lost $8 million in the first quarter of 1956, and this so reduced its cash position that its payrolls of $330,000 per day to its 18,000 employees were in jeopardy.

Alarmed by these conditions, North Western's new managers undertook in the spring of 1956 to improve the company's physical equipment and competitive position. When the railroad had begun operations about 100 years before, traffic patterns required stations every 7–10 miles, but freight and passenger traffic originating at most of the smaller stations had declined greatly since then. Despite this change several hundred "one-man" stations, principally on branch lines, were still in operation. Many of them served little purpose, and the employees who manned them did little or no work. Some of the stations, for example, were open and had agents on duty only during hours when no trains passed by at all. Company studies disclosed many instances where agents were drawing a full day's pay for as little as 15–30 minutes of work.

To cut out these wasteful practices North Western proposed to discontinue the employment of full-time agents at most of the little-used stations and provide instead a centrally located agent to perform the necessary services. The company filed petitions with the public utilities commissions of the states it served for approval of its reorganization. It asked first to close 69 "one-man" stations in South Dakota. At the state commission hearings in late 1957 and early 1958 the Order of Railroad Telegraphers opposed the company's plans. It contended, among other things, that its existing bargaining agreement with North Western prohibited abolishment of any agency jobs without its consent.

On May 9, 1958, however, the South Dakota Commission ordered the changes to be made in station operations where necessary in the public interest, directing North Western to establish 16 central agency stations and to abolish 53 full time agency positions immediately. In support of its order it pointed out that the workload of the agents at the stations involved varied from 12 minutes to 2 hours per day and averaged only 59 minutes per day. It declared:

> That the maintenance of full-time agency service at all of the subject stations, because of the lack of public need, constitutes mismanagement and a dissipation of carrier's revenues which has and will impair its capacity to render adequate railway service to the public at reasonable rates.[1]

[1] "The South Dakota Commission further found that the expenses of operating the 69 stations involved exceeded related revenues by $170,399 in 1956, and that if the Central Agency Plan had been in effect during that period there would have been a surplus of $58,884.

"Hearings were afterwards conducted upon the similar petitions before the Iowa, Minnesota and Wisconsin Commissions. The Union ap-

On December 23, 1957, the Telegraphers sent a letter to North Western asking for negotiations to discuss a proposed amendment to their bargaining agreement. They wanted to add the following provision:

> No position in existence on December 3, 1957, will be abolished or discontinued except by agreement between the carrier and the Organization.

North Western responded the next day by saying that it did not consider the request to be a proper subject of bargaining since it did not concern rules, rates of pay, or working conditions. It offered to meet with the union's officers and to discuss the matter further, though. The parties met, but they reached no agreement. The union then asked for mediation under the provisions of the Railway Labor Act. In the meetings arranged by the National Mediation Board the company suggested several means of cushioning the effects of the reduction in the work force. These included transferring agents affected to productive jobs, limiting job abolishments to an agreed number per year, and the payment of supplemental unemployment benefits to the employees affected. The union refused to discuss these proposals.

At one meeting North Western's chief executive asked if there was any possibility of "working out these station closing matters and the discontinuance of these station agents either on a South Dakota or a system basis." The union's general counsel replied, "I think we are too far apart"; the North Western official then said, "I want you to know that my door is always open." The president of the Telegraphers said later in court that "the only alternative which up to the present I have offered the North Western Railroad was to comply with this rule or strike." [2]

III

When the mediators were convinced that their efforts were to no avail they requested the parties to submit the controversy to arbitration under the provisions of Section 8 of the Railway Labor Act; both declined —the union on May 28 and North Western on June 12. On July 10, 1958, the union sent to its members a strike ballot under an accompanying letter that said in part:

> [It] became evident at an early date that to meet this [company] onslaught effectively would require strengthening of our agreements. . . . We must prevent a continuance of such a [work force reduction] program. While we hope the commissions in the other states will be more reasonable than the South Dakota commission, we have no assurance that we will not soon see a repetition in other states of what has happened in South Dakota. . . .

The vote was almost unanimous in favor of a strike, and on August 18, the union called a strike of its members to begin at 6 A.M. on August 21.

The National Mediation Board renewed its offer to mediate, and both parties accepted. Nothing came of the move, however, and on August 20 the Board advised the parties that it had terminated its serv-

---

peared in each of those proceedings and presented evidence, briefs and arguments in opposition to the petitions, but each was granted.

"The Iowa Commission found that the agents at the stations there involved worked an average of 1 hour and 14 minutes per day, a decrease of 28% since 1951, and that the estimated average workload under the Central Agency Plan would be 3 hours and 15 minutes per day. It said, *inter alia,* 'Savings must be made by reducing or eliminating service no longer needed. The case before us is a proposal to reduce agency service to the level of actual need.' And it found that such was necessary 'to insure efficiency, economy and adequate railway transportation.'

"The Union appealed from the orders of the respective Commissions to the courts of the respective States, but the Commission action was affirmed in each instance." Railroad Telegraphers v. Chicago & North Western Railway Company, 45 LRRM 3110 (1960).

[2] Railroad Telegraphers v. Chicago & North Western Railway Company, 45 LRRM 3111 (1960).

ices. On the same day North Western filed a complaint against the union and various of its officials in the United States District Court for the Northern District of Illinois, stating that the new provision the union wanted to add to the agreement was not a lawfully bargainable subject under the Railway Labor Act; that the impending strike called to force acceptance of that provision would be illegal; that the company had a right under the laws of the United States, particularly the Interstate Commerce Act and the Railway Labor Act, to be free of such an illegal strike; and that the union should be enjoined from striking.

The company argued that the union had no right to protest or to seek relief from managerial actions except by appearing before state public utilities commissions, which had power to determine whether station agencies could be discontinued. Private parties could not thwart the commissions' power. Furthermore, for the company to maintain unnecessary agencies was offensive to the national transportation policy Congress had adopted in the Interstate Commerce Act; the duties to obey the directives of state and national regulatory agencies to maintain and develop an economical and efficient railroad system were imposed on the rail companies and could not be contracted away.

The union contended that whether the commissions' rulings were mandatory or permissive, the states were without authority to order an abandonment of stations that would conflict with collective bargaining agreements made or to be made between the railroad and the union. The union also contended that the district court was without jurisdiction to grant injunctive relief under the provisions of the Norris-LaGuardia Act because this case involved a labor dispute; that the railroad had refused to negotiate in good faith on the proposed change in the agreement; that this was in violation of the Railway Labor Act, which requires every reasonable effort to make and maintain agreements concerning rates of pay, rules, and working conditions; and that an injunction could not be issued because Section 8 of the Norris-LaGuardia Act provides:

> No restraining order or injunctive relief shall be granted to any complainant who has failed to comply with any obligation imposed by by law which is involved in the labor dispute in question, or who has failed to make every reasonable effort to settle such dispute either by negotiation or with the aid of any available governmental machinery of mediation or voluntary arbitration.

The district court immediately issued a temporary restraining order and, after a full hearing, declared that since the provision the union wanted in the agreement related to rates of pay, rules, and working conditions it was a bargainable issue under the Railway Labor Act. A strike, therefore, would not be unlawful. North Western carried the case to the Court of Appeals, which reversed the lower court's decision, ruling that the union's provision was not a lawfully bargainable one and that its acceptance could not legally be forced by a strike. The Supreme Court then granted *certiorari.*

IV

Justice Black delivered the opinion of the Supreme Court, which upheld the union: [3]

> Unless the [language of the Norris-LaGuardia Act] is to be ignored, it squarely covers this controversy. Congress made the definition broad because it wanted it to be broad. There are few pieces of legislation where the congressional hearings, committee reports, and the language in the legislation itself more clearly point to the necessity for giving an Act a construction that will protect the congressional policy the Act adopted. Section 2 of this Act specifies the public policy to be taken into consideration in interpreting the Act's language and in determining the jurisdiction and authority of federal courts;

[3] Railroad Telegraphers v. Chicago and North Western Railway Company, 45 LRRM 3104 (1960).

it is one of freedom of association, organization, representation and negotiation on the part of workers. The hearings and committee reports reveal that Congress attempted to write its bill in unmistakable language because it believed previous measures looking toward the same policy against non-judicial intervention in labor disputes had been given unduly limited constructions by the courts.

Plainly the controversy here relates to an effort on the part of the union to change the "terms" of an existing collective bargaining agreement. The change desired just as plainly referred to "conditions of employment" of the railroad's employees who are represented by the union. The employment of many of these station agents inescapably hangs on the number of railroad stations that will either be completely abandoned or consolidated with other stations. And, in the collective bargaining world today, there is nothing strange about agreements that affect the permanency of employment. The District Court's finding that "collective bargaining as to the length or term of employment is commonplace," is not challenged.

We cannot agree with the Court of Appeals that the union's efforts to negotiate about the job security of its members "represents an attempt to usurp legitimate managerial prerogative in the exercise of business judgment with respect to the most economical and efficient conduct of its operations." The Railway Labor Act and the Interstate Commerce Act recognized that stable and fair terms and conditions of railroad employment are essential to a well-functioning national transportation system. The Railway Labor Act safeguards an opportunity for employees to obtain contracts through collective rather than individualistic bargaining. Where combinations and consolidations of railroads might adversely affect the interests of employees, Congress in the Interstate Commerce Act has expressly required that before approving such consolidations, the Interstate Commerce Commission "shall require a fair and equitable arrangement to protect the interests of the railroad employees affected." It requires the Commission to do this by including *"terms and conditions"* which provide that for a term of years after a consolidation employees shall not be "in a worse position with respect to their employment" than they would otherwise have been. (Emphasis supplied.)

In 1942 this Court held that when a railroad abandons a portion of its lines, the Interstate Commerce Commission has power to include conditions for the protection of displaced workers in deciding "what the public convenience and necessity may require." We so construed the Interstate Commerce Act specifically on the basis that imposition of such conditions "might strengthen the national system through their effect on the morale and stability of railway workers generally." . . . The brief for the railroad associations there called our attention to testimony previously given to Congress that as early as 1936 railroads representing 85% of the mileage of the country had made collective bargaining agreements with their employees to provide a schedule of benefits for workers who might be displaced or adversely affected by coordinations or mergers. In an effort to prevent a disruption and stoppage of interstate commerce, the trend of legislation affecting railroads and railroad employees has been to broaden, not narrow, the scope of subjects about which workers and railroads may or must negotiate and bargain collectively. Furthermore, the whole idea of what is bargainable has been greatly affected by the practices and customs of the railroads and their employees themselves. It is too late now to argue that employees can have no collective voice to influence railroads to act in a way that will preserve the interests of the employees as well as the interests of the railroad and the public at large.

The railroad has argued throughout the proceedings that the union's strike here may be enjoined, regardless of Norris-LaGuardia, because its effort to bargain about the consolidation and abandonment of railroad stations is unlawful. . . . Here, far from violating the Railway Labor Act, the union's effort to negotiate its controversy with the railroad was in obedience to the Act's command that employees as well as railroads exert every reasonable effort to settle all disputes "concerning rates of pay, rules, and working conditions." . . . Moreover, neither the respondent nor anyone else points to any other specific legal command that the union violated here by attempting to bring about a change in its collective bargaining agreement.

It would stretch credulity too far to say that the Railway Labor Act, designed to protect railroad workers, was somehow violated by the union acting precisely in accordance with that Act's purpose to obtain stability and permanence in employment for workers. There is no express provision of law, and certainly we can infer none from the Interstate Commerce Act, making it unlawful for unions to want to discuss with railroads actions that may vitally and adversely affect the security, seniority and stability of railroad jobs. And for a number of reasons the state public utility proceedings, invoked by the railroad to obtain approval of consolidation or abandonment of stations, could not stamp illegality on the union's effort to negotiate this whole question with the railroad. The union merely asked for a contractual right to bargain with the railroad about any voluntary steps it might take to abandon stations or to seek permission to abandon stations and thus abolish jobs. Nothing the union requested would require the railroad to violate any valid law or the valid order of any public agency. There is no testimony and there are no findings that this union has set itself up in defiance of any state mandatory order. In fact, there was no state order of any kind at the time the union first asked to negotiate about the proposed contractual change. Even if a Norris-LaGuardia "labor dispute" could not arise out of an unlawful bargaining demand . . . the union's proposal here was not unlawful.

The union contends that, whether the state rulings were mandatory or permissive, the States are without authority to order an abandonment of stations that would conflict with collective bargaining agreements made or to be made between the railroad and the union. Whether this contention is valid or not we need not decide since there is no such conflict before us. And the District Court expressly refused to find that the union's proposal was prompted by the railroad's action in seeking state authority to put its Central Agency Plan into effect. Instead, the District Court specifically found that the dispute grew out of the failure of the parties to reach an agreement on the contract change proposed by the union. . . .

In concluding that the injunction ordered by the Court of Appeals is forbidden by the Norris-LaGuardia Act, we have taken due account of the railroad's argument that the operation of unnecessary stations, services and lines is wasteful and thus runs counter to the congressional policy, expressed in the Interstate Commerce Act, to foster an efficient national railroad system. In other legislation, however, like the Railway Labor and Norris-LaGuardia Acts, Congress has acted on the assumption that collective bargaining by employees will also foster an efficient national railroad service. It passed such Acts with knowledge that collective bargaining might sometimes increase the expense of railroad operations because of increased wages and better working conditions. It goes without saying, therefore, that added railroad expenditures for employees cannot always be classified as "wasteful." It may be, as some people think, that Congress was unwise in curtailing the jurisdiction of federal courts in railroad disputes as it did in the Norris-LaGuardia Act. Arguments have even been presented here pointing to the financial debilitation of the respondent Chicago & North Western Railroad and to the absolute necessity for the abandonment of railroad stations. These arguments, however, are addressed to the wrong forum. If the scope of the Norris-LaGuardia Act is to be cut down in order to prevent "waste" by the railroads, Congress should be the body to do so. Such action is beyond the judicial province and we decline to take it. . . .

The Judgment of the Court of Appeals is reversed and that of the District Court is affirmed insofar as it held that the court was without jurisdiction under the Norris-LaGuardia Act to enter the injunction.

It is so ordered.

V

Justice Whittaker wrote a dissenting opinion:

Congress, in comprehensively providing for the regulation of railroads, their transportation services and their employer-employee relations, has declared its policies in several related Acts including Part 1 of the Interstate Commerce Act, the Railway Labor Act, and the Norris-LaGuardia Act, and, at least in cases such as this, none of them may meaningfully be read in isolation but only together as, for they are in fact, an integrated plan of railroad regulation. And if, as is frequently the case in such undertakings, there be overlappings, "[w]e must determine here how far Congress intended activities under one of these policies to neutralize the results envisioned by the other." . . .

By Part 1 of the Interstate Commerce Act, Congress has provided a pervasive scheme of regulation of all common carriers engaged in transportation by railroad in interstate commerce. The declared policy of that Act was to promote economical and efficient transportation services at reasonable charges and, as this Court has said, "It is a primary aim of that policy to secure the avoidance of waste. That avoidance, as well as the maintenance of service, is viewed as a direct concern of the public." . . . "Congress has long made the maintenance and development of an economical and efficient railroad system a matter of primary national concern. Its legislation must be read with this purpose in mind." . . .

To aid in effectuating that policy, Congress has contemplated the abandonment of railroad lines, stations, depots and other facilities and services when found by designated public regulatory bodies to be burdensome and no longer required to serve the public convenience and necessity. To this end, it has empowered the Interstate Commerce Commission, upon application and after notice and public hearing, to issue a certificate authorizing the abandonment of "all or any part of a line of railroad," and it has provided that "[f]rom and after issuance of such certificate . . . the carrier by railroad may, *without securing approval other than such certificate . . . proceed with the . . . abandonment covered thereby.*" (Emphasis added.) And in the Transportation Act of 1958 . . . Congress has empowered the Commission, under stated conditions, to authorize the abandonment of "any train or ferry." However, Congress has not sought completely to accomplish its abandonment policies through the Commission. Rather, it has sought to make use of state regulatory commissions, as additional instruments for the effectuation of its policies, in respect to the abandonment of some railroad facilities and services. Among others, it has long left to state regulatory commissions abandonments of railroad stations and station agency service; and, in 1958, after extensive review of that subject in the process of enacting the Transportation Act of 1958, it deliberately reaffirmed that policy. Moreover, in its report on S. 3778, which culminated in the Transportation Act of 1958, the Senate Subcommittee on Interstate and Foreign Commerce critically attributed a major part of the financial plight of the railroads to their failure to apply to regulatory bodies for permission to abandon burdensome and needless services in accordance with congressional policy, and strongly advocated that such be done.

For the fair and firm effectuation of these policies, Congress has provided that issues respecting the propriety of an abandonment shall be determined by a public regulatory body. It has contemplated that the carrier shall propose to the proper regulatory body the abandonment of particular facilities or services and that, after notice and hearing—at which all persons affected, including employees and their union representatives, may appear and be heard—the public regulatory body shall determine whether the proposal is in the public interest, and its order, unless reversed on judicial review, is binding upon all persons. These procedures plainly exclude any right or power of a carrier, at its will alone, to effectuate, or of a labor union representing its employees to veto, any proposed abandonment. Although both may be heard, neither of them, nor the two in agreement, even if their agreement be evidenced by an express contract, may usurp the Commission's decisional function by dictating the result or thwarting its effect. It is obvious that any abandonment, authorized by a proper regulatory body, will result in abolishment of the jobs that were involved in the abandoned service. And inasmuch as the maintenance of these jobs constituted at least a part of the wasteful burden that necessitated the abandonment, it is equally obvious that Congress intended their abolishment. Yet, here, the Union has demanded, and threatens to force by a strike, acceptance by the carrier of a covenant that no job in existence on December 3, 1957, will be abolished without its consent. Certainly that demand runs in the teeth of the recited provisions and policies of the Interstate Commerce Act. It plainly would destroy the public regulation of abandonments, provided and contemplated by Congress in the public interest, and render them subject to the Union's will alone. A demand for such a contractual power surely is an unlawful demand.

The Union argues, and the Court seems to find, that there is a basis for the claimed legality of the Union's demand in the provision . . . of the Interstate Commerce Act that the Commission in approving railroad mergers or consolidations "shall require a fair and equitable arrangement to protect the interests of the railroad employees affected." Instead of supporting legality of the Union's demand, I think the provisions of that section and its legislative history are further proof of its illegality. While that section authorizes the Commission to require temporary mitigation of hardships to employees displaced by such unifications, nothing in it authorizes the Commission to freeze existing jobs. . . .

There is no dispute in the record that the carrier sought to bargain and agree with the Union upon matters in mitigation of hardships to employees displaced by the station abandonments. It offered to bargain . . . [but] the Union refused even to discuss [the] proposals. . . .

This also answers the Court's argument that there is nothing in the Interstate Commerce Act "making it unlawful for unions to want to discuss with railroads actions that may vitally and adversely affect the security, seniority and stability of railroad jobs." . . . The Union's demand was not for a right "to discuss" such matters with the carrier, but was, rather, that the carrier agree that no jobs in existence on December 3, 1957, be abolished without the Union's consent. . . . Plainly the Union's demand was not for a right "to bargain with" the carrier about "abolish[ing] jobs," but was for a unilateral right to prohibit the abolishment of any job without its consent.

Justice Clark also wrote a dissenting opinion, adding to Justice Whittaker's argument the following:

Today the Court tells the railroad that it must bargain with the union or suffer a strike. The latter would be the death knell of the railroad. Hence, for all practical purposes, the Court is telling the railroad that it must secure the union's approval before severing the hundreds of surplus employees now carried on its payroll. Everyone knows what the answer of the union will be. It is like the suitor who, when seeking the hand of a young lady, was told by her to "go to father." But, as the parody goes, "She knew that he knew that her father was dead; she knew that he knew what a life he had led; and she knew that he knew what she meant when she said 'go to father.' "

I do not believe that the Congress intended to put the railroads in such a situation. In fact, its overall purpose has been to prevent the devastating effects of strikes from paralyzing our transportation systems, the efficient operation of which is so vital to the public welfare. As I read the Interstate Commerce Act—the provisions of which were reaffirmed as late as the Transportation Act of 1958—the Congress told the railroads to go to the States—not the union—before abandoning or consolidating its local stations. Respondent went to the States and obtained their approval. The Court today gives to the union a veto power over this action of the States. Until this power is removed, the railroads will continue to be plagued with this situation—so foreign to the concept of a fair day's pay for a fair day's work, which has been the basis of union labor's great achievements. . . .

VI

Two months after its decision in the Telegraphers' case, the Supreme Court emphasized the due consideration and legal regard now given to the interests of workers in their jobs and conditions of work in a new case. The Brotherhood of Locomotive Engineers had asked the courts to stop the Missouri-Kansas-Texas Railroad from eliminating a number of jobs on a branchline until it could bargain over the action, using the services of the government's mediation and adjustment boards. The company had originally operated the 302-mile line between Wichita Falls, Texas, and Forgan, Oklahoma, employing steam locomotives capable of only short runs and requiring five freight crews along the route. After the company purchased diesel locomotives it issued general orders that doubled the length of the freight runs, eliminated the jobs of two of the five-man crews, and changed the home or away-from-home terminals of the remaining crews.

The Engineers protested the orders and asked for the services of the National Mediation Board; nevertheless, the railroad put the change into effect. After the Board advised the parties that it did not consider the dispute subject to mediation, the union called a strike. The same day the railroad asked the federal district court for an order temporarily restraining the strike. After a hearing, the court granted the injunction pending a decision by the Railway Adjustment Board, but it forbade a strike and required that the railroad company either restore the situation that existed prior to the order eliminating the freight crews or pay the employees adversely affected by the orders the wages they would have received had the orders not been issued.

Both sides appealed the decision to the Supreme Court; the union objected to the injunction against the strike and the railroad objected to the conditions requiring preservation of the *status quo*.

Chief Justice Warren delivered the Court's opinion: [4]

> This case presents a . . . question as to nature of the relief which may be granted . . . specifically, whether the injunction granted the Railroad may be qualified by conditions imposed by the District Court under traditional equitable considerations.
>
> If the District Court is free to exercise the typical powers of a court of equity, it has the power to impose conditions requiring maintenance of the *status quo*. Conditions of this nature traditionally may be made the price of relief when the injunctive powers of the court are invoked and the conditions are necessary to do justice between the parties. "The award of an interlocutory injunction by courts of equity has never been regarded as strictly a matter of right, even though irreparable injury may otherwise result to the plaintiff. . . . [The court] will avoid . . . injury so far as may be, by attaching conditions to the award. . . ." Yakus v. United States. "[I]t is the duty of a court of equity granting injunctive relief to do so upon conditions that will protect all . . . whose interests the judgment may affect." Inland Steel Co. v. United States. . . . Since the power to condition relief is essential to ensure that extraordinary equitable remedies will not become the engines of injustice, it would require the clearest legislative direction to justify the truncation of that power. . . . The district judge was quite aware that it was not his function to construe the contractual provisions upon which the parties relied for their respective positions on the merits. . . . A District Court must make some examination of the nature of the dispute before conditioning relief since not all disputes coming before the Adjustment Board threaten irreparable injury and justify the attachment of a condition. To fulfill its function the District Court must also consider the hardships, if any, that would arise if the employees were required to await the Board's sometimes long-delayed decisions without recourse to a strike. But this examination of the nature of the dispute is so unlike that which the Adjustment Board will make of the merits of the same dispute, and is for such a dissimilar purpose, that it could not interfere with the later consideration of the grievance by the Adjustment Board.
>
> Moreover, such an examination is inherent in the grant of the injunction itself. . . . The dispute out of which the judicial controversy arose does not merely concern rates or pay or job assignments, but rather involves the discharge of employees from positions long held and the dislocation of others from their homes. From the point of view of these employees, the critical point

[4] Brotherhood of Locomotive Engineers *et al.* v. Missouri-Kansas-Texas Railroad Company *et al.*, 46 LRRM 2429 (1960).

in the dispute may be when the change is made, for, by the time of the frequently long-delayed Board decision, it might well be impossible to make them whole in any realistic sense. If this be so, the action of the district judge, rather than defeating the Board's jurisdiction, would operate to preserve that jurisdiction by preventing injury so irreparable that a decision of the Board in the unions' favor would be but an empty victory.

It is true that preventing the Railroad from instituting the change imposed upon it the burden of maintaining what may be a less efficient and more costly operation. The balancing of these competing claims of irreparable hardship is, however, the traditional function of the equity court, the exercise of which is reviewable only for abuse of discretion. And although respondents maintain that there has been such an abuse in this case, scrutiny of the record does not persuade us that the evidence was insufficient to support the judge's action. . . .

VII

Negotiators for the Telegraphers and the North Western resumed bargaining after the Supreme Court's decision, but by April, 1962, they were still far from an agreement despite the efforts of federal mediators. Since they had exhausted the bargaining procedures required under the Railway Labor Act, a strike seemed imminent. President Kennedy then appointed an emergency fact-finding board to report possible terms of a settlement. After the hearings, the board recommended that the Telegraphers drop its demand that the railroad abolish or discontinue jobs only after securing union approval; it also suggested that North Western liberalize its offer of severance pay to displaced employees and improve opportunities for transfers to other jobs for workers laid off.

The parties accepted most of the board's findings but ran into an impasse as they worked out the details. Since 1957, when the dispute first arose, the railroad had eliminated 600 telegraphers' jobs, and the union members were insistent that its members receive every possible job protection. Despite pleas from the Secretary of Labor and the President to continue negotiations, the Telegraphers finally began the first strike the North Western had experienced in its 114-year history. On August 30, 1962, North Western trains pulled into stations and sidings, leaving 10,500 miles of track throughout six midwestern states empty of traffic. The one thousand striking telegraphers immediately idled 15,000 other rail employees, and as the strike continued through September workers in other industries were forced to stop work as supplies and stocks dwindled. Competing railroads and trucking companies were able to transport most of the freight usually carried by the North Western, however. By the last week of September the burden of the strike weighed much more heavily on the contending parties than upon either the public or the railroad's usual customers.

On September 28 officials of the Telegraphers and North Western agreed to a request by Kennedy to submit their remaining differences to binding arbitration. With the ending of the strike arbitration, Sylvester Garrett heard the arguments of the parties; he ruled that the company should retain the initiative to maintain its competitive position through adjustments to changing conditions. He also agreed with the union that it should be given a 90-day advance warning of any cut in jobs. The company had not wanted to be held to a notice of more than 30 days for large job cuts or more than 10 days for small cuts.

Board chairman Ben Heineman said that the union had "obtained nothing from its senseless strike . . . nothing it could not have had at any time after the [April] emergency board report without a strike." A union official viewed the strike differently. "[We] came out of this dispute better than 50 per cent to the good. . . . [North Western was] adamant in refusing to give any notice at all except the 5 days required previously." [5]

On November 4, 1962, North Western announced it was about to eliminate a number of telegraphers' jobs; about 30 men would be retired, displaced, or transferred as a result.

[5] *Wall Street Journal,* October 10, 1962.

QUESTIONS

Intangible Property for All

1. Try to fit the arguments for a new definition of property in the Western Union case and the definition of property accepted by the court to the job claims of either the Telegraphers or the Locomotive Engineers. If you are successful, explain why the argument and definition give the workers more protection than the courts in fact offered? If you are unsuccessful, explain why a fit is not possible.

2. "The difficulty in the Telegraphers and Missouri-Kansas-Texas cases is not so much the conflict between business and labor as it is a conflict between two means of determining public policy." Explain your reasons for agreement or disagreement.

3. Has the court in the two railroad cases granted the workers a property right or only the liberty to seek a property right? Define what you mean by "property right."

4. What are managerial prerogatives? If managers gain the right to manage property through ownership, how do they gain the right to manage people—through ownership of the people? The property?

5. If workers were to receive clear legal recognition of a property right in their jobs, would technological change be adversely or favorably affected? State your arguments for both answers.

6. What are the various interests that the District Court probably considered in issuing the injunction in the Missouri-Kansas-Texas case? What groups or persons who were not parties to the case were affected by the decision?

7. Did the decision of court in the Missouri-Kansas-Texas case develop the concept of property rights for workers beyond that in the Telegraphers case and, if so, how?

section **2**

PUBLIC AND PRIVATE POLITIES

Although the largest American corporations rival our wealthiest states in revenues and financial strength, and some of our unions exercise powers beyond the authority of state governments when they close down whole industries or stop vital community services, we still call these organizations "private." The term is misleading to the extent that it suggests that these great combines of thousands and thousands of employees, many-layered bureaucracies, vast plants and properties scattered across the country, and multitudes of stockholders (or union members) exert only the influence of private individuals or behave like individuals at all. Rather, they are collective enterprises that require continuous cooperative efforts to maintain themselves and to operate. Some social commentators see in their widely distributed ownership and pervasive influence either a kind of non-governmental socialism or a reversion to the pluralistic, semi-autonomous baronies of medieval Europe.

Consider the American Telephone and Telegraph company. Although formally a private firm, it is actually regulated by the government. In 1966 the Federal Communications Commission began a detailed investigation of the company's rate structure; witness after witness stressed the fact that since so large a company affects the public in many other ways than through its service charges, the Commissioners ought to proceed carefully. The mere announcement of the Commission's probe brought about a decline in the price of AT&T shares, and each $2 of the decline meant the loss of $1 billion of capital values in the stock-market. A sizable portion of the public was immediately and directly affected, since nearly three million persons own shares in the company.

Quite apart from the question of stock ownership, the entire public is affected in other ways by what happens to AT&T and by the decisions of the managers of the Bell system. Almost 1 per cent of the employed, non-agricultural, civilian labor force of the United States works for this single system; the $3.89 billion these employees were paid in 1964 made up 1.17 per cent of the nation's wages and salaries. Paul W. McCracken, a former member of the President's Council of Economic Advisors, estimates that nearly 2 per cent of the GNP in 1965 originated in the Bell system and that its capital budget of almost $4 billion made up 7.5 per cent of total business spending for plants and equipment in the United

States. Its capital assets of $31 billion are about 4 per cent of the total productive facilities of American business, and its income taxes paid to the federal government in 1964 accounted for 7.42 per cent of all corporate income tax revenues.[1]

Little wonder that scholars argue that the big, modern corporation must be recognized as a political institution, a new instrument by which we order our economic and community life. While the effect of a single competitive firm was assumed in classical theory to be imperceptible and infinitesimal, economists now find that the impact of corporate giants upon our national life is noticeable, consequential, and measurable. Corporate influence spreads far afield; a decision that a board of directors imagines to be of concern only to those in the company may have repercussions in the highest councils of government as well as in the home of the ordinary citizen.

For example, during the 1950's the few large steel producing corporations invested in new open-hearth furnaces, enough to be able to produce 40 million tons of steel. For an industry that turned out an annual average of 102 million tons of iron and steel the new facilities were sizable. Unfortunately, they were also obsolete even as they were being built, producing steel at a cost of at least $5 a ton more than that of the newly available oxygen process.[2] Partly as a consequence of their continued investment in obsolete plant and the resulting cost and price structure the steel companies found an increasing flow of imports taking away their domestic markets in the late fifties and early sixties. Imports of iron and steel-mill products increased by almost 4.7 times in the seven years after 1957 and rose from $162 million to $714 million.

Had these companies been small producers in a perfectly competitive economy their questionable investment policy would have been of interest only to disgruntled stockholders; in fact, their commanding size in our oligopolistic economy made the policy a matter of public debate and concern. The nation faced a growing balance-of-payments problem even as imports of steel were rising, and the government's gold stock declined by nearly one-third between 1957 and 1964. To the extent that the steel companies would have been in a better competitive position in world markets had they invested more wisely, the American balance-of-payments problem would have been eased.

Similar to AT&T and the steel companies in the far-reaching effects of their managerial decisions are the four giant auto firms. In recent years they have spent billions of dollars upon styling and in developing bigger, higher-powered cars. In 1965 Chrysler expended a third of a billion dollars on retooling for new models. Simply for "souping up" and "jazzing up" the 1963 Thunderbird, as a company spokesman put it, Ford spent between $200,000 and $250,000. The total cost of model changes in the period 1956–59 has been estimated at over $5 billion.[3] During the same period, imports of automobiles and parts jumped

[1] Fred L. Zimmerman, "How Broad an Idea of Public Interest," *Wall Street Journal,* June 9, 1966.

[2] "Economic Concentration," *Hearings Before the Subcommittee on Antitrust and Monopoly of the Committee on the Judiciary* (Part I, "Overall and Conglomerate Aspects"), U.S. Senate, 88th Cong., 2nd Sess. (Washington: Government Printing Office, 1964), pp. 254–55.

[3] Franklin M. Fisher, Zvi Griliches, and Carl Kaysen, "The Costs of Automobile Model Changes Since 1949," *Papers and Proceedings,* American Economic Association, LII (May, 1962), 261.

from $144.6 million to a high of $843.8 million, a more than five-fold increase! [4]

As important to the public as how the managers of the automobile companies decided to engineer their products with the corporate resources available to them—money, engineers, scientists, research laboratories, and production plants —was what they decided *not* to do to the cars they produced. They did not choose to turn their efforts to any major program that would make cars less dangerous to those involved in automobile accidents nor did they take significant steps on their own to reduce air pollution from motor exhaust. Injuries in auto accidents and air pollution were both serious problems. Throughout the fifties and into the sixties deaths from automobile accidents mounted from about 35,000 to nearly 50,000 a year, and pollution became a major problem in most of our large cities. The decision of the managers to concentrate upon styling and to downgrade or ignore other emphases of design that could better have prevented injuries and pollution has had serious consequences for the community. It also redounded to the disadvantage of the companies when the state and federal governments began to impose safety and pollution standards on automobiles.

The decisions and activities of corporate officials also influence the arts, if in less obvious ways. Through their sponsorship of television or radio programs and their placement of advertisements, they favor some forms of art and encourage them over others. Insofar as they fail to sponsor philharmonic orchestras, grand operas, and ballets as part of their effort to build up good will, familiarize their trademarks, or peddle their wares, they make the widespread development and maintenance of these performing arts more difficult than the presentation of "soap operas," "horse operas," and situation comedies. They throw the immense weight of their vast resources toward one kind of art form, usually for reasons that have little to do with the art itself but that nonetheless significantly affect the relative success of the various kinds of art forms.

To point out the wide-ranging, indirect effects of the decisions made by corporate managers is not necessarily to blame them. Nor is it to say that they should act differently, although businessmen have themselves sometimes argued they should act more "responsibly," and various critics have denounced them for shortsightedness. Here we are simply illustrating the common lesson of everyday life that the exercise of economic power (like political or military power) produces unintended, unforeseen results; and the greater the power, the more far-reaching its effects. Any corporate official or union leader who is unaware that his decisions produce either beneficial or detrimental consequences beyond the limits of his organization will be rudely awakened by challenges to his authority, opposition to his proposals, and attacks upon his good faith. Managers of public utilities, for example, are discovering anew how failure to take into account unintended results can cause trouble for a business. In concentrating upon producing electric power cheaply according to the usual engineering standards they find themselves seriously questioned and sometimes blocked by conservationists intent upon preserving natural forests, pure air, clean rivers, and unpolluted seashores.

When men command large, prestigious organizations whose influence reaches

[4] Data for 1956 from U.S. Bureau of the Census, *Statistical Abstract of the United States: 1959* (Washington: Government Printing Office, 1959), table 1178, p. 894; data for 1959 from U.S. Bureau of the Census, *Statistical Abstract of the United States: 1960* (Washington: Government Printing Office, 1960), table 1191, pp. 892–93.

far, they become, by virtue of their position, consequential members of the national polity. They cannot escape membership by pretending that their decisions or views are of no consequence, nor can they avoid troublesome problems by not deciding—by not acting. In their situation, not deciding is a decision; by not acting, they act. Their involvement is not a matter of choice or will, but a matter of fact. It is understandable but not convincing for the president of United States Steel to say of the racial policies of Birmingham, Alabama (where a USS subsidiary, Tennessee Iron and Steel, is overwhelmingly the largest employer, purchaser, and taxpayer): "For a corporation to attempt to exert any kind of economic compulsion to achieve a particular end in the social area seems to be . . . quite beyond what a corporation can do." [5] If the Birmingham city council were to double property taxes, one cannot but wonder if the managers of the steel company would have no influential advice to offer. If the managers have had nothing to say for or against racial discrimination in the past, acquiescing in the status quo, they were in effect upholding that policy.

Many businessmen in recent years have felt uneasy about the power they wield and the unintended consequences they produce throughout the nation and the world. A few years ago, Gerard Swope, an outstanding president of General Electric for many years, called upon corporate managers to recognize the full extent of their social responsibility.[6] Later GE developed the slogan, "Do Right Voluntarily in the Balanced Best Interests of All." After the revelation in 1960 of the price-fixing conspiracy among electrical manufacturers, in which GE participated fully, many observers have doubted that the slogan has much content, but it expresses a sentiment other businessmen have repeated and sometimes tried to practice.

The general counsel for Ford Motor Company, William T. Gossett, declared a few years ago that the measure of the modern corporation's effectiveness in public affairs "is the degree to which its policy reflects the values, objectives, aspirations and reservations of society as a whole." [7] And Sol M. Linowitz, Chairman of the Board of Xerox Corporation, said in an address to the National Industrial Conference Board in 1966:

> To realize its full promise in the world of tomorrow, American business and industry —or, at least, the vast portion of it—will have to make social goals as central to its decisions as economic goals; and leadership in our corporations will increasingly recognize this responsibility and accept it.[8]

While businessmen, urged on by a chorus of critics within their own ranks, were trying to define their social responsibility, other critics spoke out against their doing anything of the sort. These scholars have taken alarm at managers trying to assume the burden of social responsibility or of being burdened with it. Professor Milton Friedman, for example, believes that business is injuring its own functions and the free market.

[5] *New York Times,* October 30, 1963.

[6] David Loth, *Swope of GE* (New York: Simon and Schuster, 1958), p. 129.

[7] Bernard D. Nossiter, *The Mythmakers: An Essay on Power and Wealth* (Boston: Houghton Mifflin, 1964), p. 100.

[8] "Public Affairs—The Demanding Seventies," Address before the NICB Public Affairs Conference, April 21, 1966, p. 3. (The passage quoted was italicized in the original.)

> The view has been gaining widespread acceptance that corporate officials and labor leaders have a "social responsibility" that goes beyond serving the interest of their stockholders or their members. This view shows a fundamental misconception of the character and nature of a free economy. In such an economy, there is one and only one social responsibility of business—to use its resources and engage in activities designed to increase its profits so long as it stays within the rules of the game, which is to say, engages in open and free competition, without deception or fraud. . . . Few trends could so thoroughly undermine the very foundations of our free society as the acceptance by corporate officials of a social responsibility other than to make as much money for their stockholders as possible.[9]

Professor Theodore Levitt does not fear for the business concern as much as he does for those who must live with—and under—the "socially responsible" decisions of businessmen.

> The danger is that all these things [that follow from having socially responsible businessmen] will turn the corporation into a twentieth century equivalent of the medieval church. . . . For while the corporation also transforms itself in the process, at bottom its outlook will always remain narrowly materialistic. What we have then, is the frightening spectacle of a powerful economic functional group whose future and perception are shaped in a tight materialistic context of money and things but which imposes its narrow ideas about a broad spectrum of unrelated noneconomic subjects on the mass of man and society. Even if its outlook were the purest kind of good will, that would not recommend the corporation as an arbiter of our lives.[10]

Reasonable men may disagree in what way businessmen and union leaders should be socially responsible; they may argue long and heatedly about whether or not we should devise new methods for calling to account those who exercise vast economic power. There has been little empirical study of the effects upon business operation of various forms of managerial accountability; therefore, each observer is free to stress whatever results he thinks most likely. Of course, both the businessmen and the scholars quoted above may be right. Corporate leaders may find that the explicit assumption of social responsibility is a necessity to avoid choking government regulations or restrictions on their business activities; consumers and the general public may have to bear new costs as business and unions begin to act "responsibly." As often happens in the affairs of men, we do not usually solve difficult problems, we only deal with them, again and again, in various forms.

Section 2 has three chapters. The first, "Private Power and Public Responsibilities," considers the nature of power exercised by businessmen and union leaders and highlights the problems caused by the exercise of that power; the next, Chapter 4, "When Are Private Interests Public?", explores in four cases some of the consequences of the intertwining of public and private interests; and Chapter 5, "When Is Government Concern Interference with Business?" examines the contradictory ways in which businessmen sometimes define a free market and denounce government interference with it.

[9] Milton Friedman, *Capitalism and Democracy* (Chicago: The University of Chicago Press, 1963), p. 133.

[10] Theodore Levitt, "The Dangers of Social Responsibility," *Harvard Business Review*, September–October, 1958, p. 44.

chapter **3**

PRIVATE POWER AND PUBLIC RESPONSIBILITIES

Men in high office and those who command large organizations often are more impressed with the limits of their position than with the breadth of the power they wield. As his months in the nation's highest office passed John F. Kennedy spoke increasingly of the limitations of Presidential power; he found that his words and commands did not alone produce the results he had hoped or had promised. Shortly before his death, he quoted an exchange from Shakespeare's *Henry IV* as an appropriate statement on the power of a President: [1]

Glendower: I can call spirits from the vasty deep.
Hotspur: Why, so can I, or so can any man;
But will they come when you do call for them?

As President he had mobilized the agencies of government and used his personal influence to rescind a price increase for steel in the spring of 1962; later that same year he had confronted the Soviet leaders with the might of our armed services in the showdown over missiles in Cuba. Yet he was as acutely aware of the limits of the power of his office as he was conscious of the scope of that power. Other Presidents, too, have discovered that the power of the man in the White House seemed far greater to those outside than to themselves. Their power has often appeared ephemeral and fragile when dealing with recalcitrant Senators, obstructionist house-committee chairmen, and revolts within the party ranks. Vociferously critical opponents and an unpredictable electorate seem to be the possessors of real power; the challenges of the first and the fluctuating support of the second appear to dictate the bounds within which the President's power is exercised.

American business and union leaders often regard their power in much the same way. They are most acutely conscious of the restrictions within which they act and the requirements they constantly meet. From their position, power seems to be putative rather than realized. When the public charges them with exercising power, they reply that they are but responding as they must to the demands of their responsibilities within the narrow range of opportunities afforded them.

[1] *1 Henry IV,* iii.1.53. Quoted in Theodore C. Sorensen, *Kennedy* (New York: Harper & Row, 1965), p. 392.

Consider the outlook that the leaders of the United Steelworkers might have had in 1959 as the union became involved in the longest strike the steel industry has ever suffered. With about 85 per cent of the steel-making capacity of the nation closed down for 116 days and half a million workers idled—and hundreds of thousands more being laid off each month the strike continued—the public generally attributed great power to the union officers who had recommended the strike and then conducted the negotiating efforts that failed to bring peaceful agreement. But the leaders may well have felt that they were pushed into the strike; to them the companies' adamant demands, the insistent pressures of technological change, and internal union difficulties conspired to provide no alternative.

Industry negotiators had offered a wage settlement of no more than a 2 per cent increase, and they demanded changes in the labor agreement to allow managers to get rid of obsolete, inefficient, featherbedding work rules. The wage increase was bargainable, and both parties believed that the other would settle for a bit more than 2 per cent—an addition of about 10¢ an hour to the average hourly wage of $3.11. It would have been a bit more than the company officials wanted to pay and somewhat less than the union leaders would have liked. No one believed that the differences between wages offered and demanded were worth a strike. The work-rule issue, though, was a more serious matter. It raised major problems for the workers and thus for the union leaders.

In 1959, the steel industry was in the midst of a recession, and unemployment was running high; in a few steel-producing centers as many as one out of five workers had been laid off. The 1958 unemployment rate among men represented by the Steelworkers had been 10.5 per cent in the consumer durables manufacturing industries. Since 1956–57 the number of production workers in basic steel had dropped 20 per cent, partly as a result of declining production and partly as a consequence of technological change. In 1958, 89,000 fewer workers were needed than in 1947 to produce about the same amount of steel, because the productivity rate had increased almost 25 per cent since 1948. In such circumstances workers were not willingly going to give management the opportunity to change work-rules that would eliminate more jobs and swell the rolls of those already laid off.

Without any severance pay, with no retraining programs to help the unemployed get new jobs, and with little likelihood of finding other jobs in or near steel-producing towns, steelworkers did not expect their leaders to give up any work-rules protecting their jobs that the union had secured through past negotiations. When David J. McDonald, their union president, vowed that the union would "never, I repeat, never yield" to the work-rule changes, he was undoubtedly expressing the strong sentiments of his members.

And McDonald had good reason to heed the feeling and opinions of his membership. Even had he found any merit in management's demands to change the work rules, he was in no position to accept them. In the last union election he had been reelected by a margin of only two to one over his challenger, an unknown shop steward of no particular qualifications for the office. For the leader of a major union, in control of the union organization and all the publicity media at its command, the large opposition vote was both surprising and sobering. McDonald needed to establish himself firmly as an effective union leader, one who fought for and protected the interests of his members. To have acceded to the work-rule changes would have ended his career. He must have felt that the companies were, indeed, trying to undermine or destroy the union or, at least, his already shaky hold on it.

Thus, McDonald and his lieutenants understandably felt they had no real choice in 1959. Without desiring a strike, they led the union into one because they saw no viable alternative. Recession, technological change, an inflexible management, and a weak political position were the conditions that forced them to act as they did. They hardly felt themselves to be men of power who could stop a basic industry and throttle down the economy of the wealthiest industrial nation in the world; they found themselves driven by circumstances beyond their control—other men more powerful than they limited their choices. The situation itself required them to act as they did.

We may not be convinced that McDonald and the other officials of the Steelworkers were simply responding to events and therefore not exercising power. We find the political pressures upon union leaders difficult to appreciate, since a common view of union leaders is one of "bosses" who order workers to strike at whim rather than one of more-or-less democratically elected officers sensitive to members' support or opposition. To many people, union leaders wield a kind of brute power, forcing their will upon an industry after having aroused the emotions and fears of the workers. However the leaders rationalize their decisions and justify their acts, the public is usually convinced that in any great strike union leaders are exercising power.

Like union leaders, American businessmen commonly deny their exercise of power; they, too, feel that they respond as they must, and have little room for initiative. Consider the position of the leaders of the steel industry in 1958, as they may have perceived it. Though there had been no strike in 1958, the industry produced eight million tons less steel than in 1959 when the strike shut down most mills for almost one-third of the year! If the union leaders were exercising power in the 1959 strike by reducing output, one might ask, were not the steel managers using a similar kind of power when they maintained an even lower level of output in 1958?

The managers, no doubt, would have denied it. They were responding to the market, the forces of competition, and the requirements of financial accounting. Automobile production had dropped 35 per cent since 1955, cutting deeply into a major market for steel. The oil industry's demand for steel products—well casings, tubing, and drill pipe—had slackened as domestic production of crude petroleum dropped off. Sales of durable household goods such as washers, dryers, and refrigerators had diminished as well. Faced with a declining market, the steel managers might argue that they did what any prudent businessman would do: they cut back production to fit the demand. To have continued producing at the rate they had maintained in 1955, almost 25 per cent higher, would have meant mounting inventories of unsold steel, continuing avoidable costs, and consequent financial losses. Such a policy would have jeopardized the positions of the managers by antagonizing shareholders and creditors.

That most of us accept the steel managers' arguments does not prove that they did not in fact exercise power, but rather demonstrates that we accept their right to exercise it, and agree that in this case they exercised it correctly. Like the union leaders the following year, they cut back production; they made decisions and gave orders that slowed a giant industry, throttling it back to barely 60 per cent of capacity. They wielded power as great as that of the union leaders, but they used it within a system that commands our acceptance. Since few in the public questioned their decisions or demanded that they justify their acts, one could argue they possess a power greater than that of the union leaders. Charles E. Merriam once perceptively noted that "power is not strongest when it uses violence, but weakest. It is strongest when it employs the instruments of substitution and counterattraction, of allurement, of participation rather than of exclusion, of education rather than of annihilation. Rape is not an evidence of irresistible power in politics or in sex." [2] Nor, one might add, in business.

Both union leaders and steel managers could have made other decisions. To have urged workers to accept changes in obsolete work rules and to bargain for aid to the workers consequently displaced might have been one possibility for the union officers. The managers in 1958 might have cut prices to stimulate the sale of steel. Both may have had good reasons for not acting in these ways, but they were hardly men who were forced by circumstances to act as they did. The decisions they chose were those that promised the greatest rewards for themselves and for the people to whom they were directly responsible.

Unfortunately, the decisions made by union and company leaders also affected many people indirectly. Cutting back employment and output was in many ways as serious as the four-month strike; both produced many adverse repercussions throughout the nation. Whether or not we find the decisions and acts of one group of leaders more acceptable than those of the other, we might wisely recognize that both occupy positions that allow considerable ranges of discretion in decision making and that have great influence upon the economy. Can they—should they—be made responsible to the various people affected by their power? If they are responsible only to a few of them, may they not be irresponsible to the others? Professor Walton Hamilton once warned us that "there is in a democracy no place for the exercise of irresponsible power. Where it exists it must be broken up or directed for the public good. Those who have power must, in the words of the Constitution, 'answer in another place' for their acts. If there is no other place in which to answer, the power itself must be denied." [3]

The following cases present situations in which men made decisions, in accordance with their immediate, official responsibilities, that had serious consequences for the employees and the communities involved. The responsibilities recognized by the decision makers and the reaction of elected government officials to the decisions were quite different in the two cases. As you read the cases, compare the circumstances of the one situation with those of the other, examining the nature of business power and social responsibility.

[2] *Political Power, Its Composition and Incidence* (New York: Whittlesey House, 1934), p. 180.

[3] "Forward: Legal Tolerance of Economic Power," *Georgetown Law Journal,* 46 (1958), 563.

Social Costs and Private Benefits

STUDEBAKER CLOSES A PLANT

When the Dow-Jones News Service ticker reported on December 9, 1963, that the Studebaker Corporation was halting auto production in South Bend, Indiana, the business community was hardly surprised. For months, rumors had suggested that Studebaker would abandon the manufacture of passenger cars; company officials fended off inquiring reporters with "no comment," but almost any taxicab driver in South Bend would assure fares that "the talk is they're gonna close."

I

Studebaker had been ailing since 1954, and its automotive division had shown no strength since 1959. In 1960 the Board of Directors appointed 40-year-old Sherwood H. Egbert as president; his job was to revive the company. Although he had had no experience with producing and selling automobiles, he had been an imaginative, able executive in the McCulloch Corporation, a producer of aircraft engines. His background in engineering and manufacturing seemed to fit him well for Studebaker, a company in need of a new car design to catch the consumer's eyes.

The Studebaker Lark, introduced in 1958, had done well and in 1959 had helped Studebaker to earn profits of over $28 million on sales of $387 million. With the compact Lark, the company captured about 5 per cent of the low-priced-auto market, but the Lark was competing only with American Motors' Rambler. When the big auto producers began to sell compact cars, too, Studebaker's sales fell. The number of cars it produced in 1960 was 31 per cent below that of 1959, and in 1961 the number dropped another 25 per cent. (See Table 1.)

Egbert sought to build up the company by introducing an advanced, radically designed car, the fiberglass Avanti, and promoting a broad program of diversification. The high priced Avanti ran into severe production problems that raised costs and delayed deliveries. And while it added prestige to the company's auto line, it did not contribute much to sales. By 1963 Studebaker was accounting for only nine-tenths of 1 per cent of the auto market; the new divisions in which Egbert had invested were more successful than his innovations in auto design. The company bought several small firms that made refrigerators and washing machines, plastics, and power tools, and it secured an interest in a non-scheduled air line. Its acquisitions also included facilities for producing floor-finishing machines, lawn equipment and farm implements, small generating plants, engine lubricants, superchargers, and heat shields and nose cones for space vehicles. These were managed through non-automotive divisions and accounted for almost half the company's sales and all of its profits.

In 1962 Studebaker showed a profit of $2.5 million, but only $489,000 was from operations. The rest was realized from the

TABLE 1 Studebaker Corporation: Sales, Earnings, and Production, 1957–63

	NET SALES (IN MILLIONS)	NET EARNINGS (IN MILLIONS)	CAR PRODUCTION (IN THOUSANDS)	TRUCK PRODUCTION (IN THOUSANDS)
1963	$303 [a]	−$9.8	64.6 [c]	12.2 [c]
1962	365 [b]	2.5	89.9	14.2
1961	298	2.5	78.6	7.6
1960	323	.071	105.9	12.3
1959	387	28.5	153.8	10.7
1958	181	−13.4	55.1	10.5
1957	213	−11.1	67.4	13.6

[a] For first 9 months.
[b] Sales for first 9 months were $251 million.
[c] For 11 months.
SOURCE: *Steel,* February 25, 1963, p. 94.

sale of a warehouse. "Standard volume" production—the output of cars that would allow the company to break even—was somewhere between 120,000 and 130,000. To reach that output in 1963, sales would have had to rise by almost 45 per cent. Unfortunately they continued to drop, even though the industry in general recorded the highest output since 1955. The company lost ground even faster financially than in its actual production. In the first nine months of 1963 the company recorded a deficit of $9.8 million, though the non-automotive divisions showed a $12 million profit.

II

The top managers at Studebaker disagreed about what should be done to save the company; those who favored severe retrenchment won out. Egbert took a medical leave of absence on November 11, and the company announced his resignation two weeks later. The board of directors then appointed a man with 25 years' experience in autos, first with Packard and then with Studebaker. He was Byers A. Burlingame, vice president of financial affairs, who already had assumed the duties of top executive in Egbert's absence. As soon as Egbert had left, Burlingame halted production "to let sales catch up." *Automotive News* reported that Studebaker dealers had a 96.5-day supply of cars. Production resumed, but only on the basis of a four-day a week schedule, interrupted by half a day for the funeral of President Kennedy and a week later by Thanksgiving. Studebaker seemed to be lurching to a shutdown.

The company's financial position was precarious not only because of the heavy losses but also because the first repayment of $7.5 million on a $25 million unsecured loan was coming due early in 1964. The loan had been used in 1962 to purchase the Franklin Manufacturing Company, a maker of refrigeration appliances. On December 3, Burlingame announced that he intended to cut costs enough to be able to support annual sales of less than 60,000 automotive units. He again shut down operations for a week to reduce inventories; then he laid off about 1,735 hourly workers and 325 salaried employees, 28 per cent of the work force. He also decided that the auto division would curtail bidding on defense contracts.

Whether company officials had any expectations that the drastic cost-cutting program could succeed or whether it was a stopgap measure to gain time to close down completely is not clear. Certainly before the program could have much effect, the company officers had decided to stop the production of cars in South Bend altogether. On December 10, Randolph H. Guthrie, the board chairman, and Burlingame met with the press in New York City to announce the decision. They explained the failure of the new 1964 model to sell in a prosperous auto year as a result of the fact that "everybody thought we were going out of business."

After noting that the closing would throw some 6,000 people out of work, Guthrie explained that "the economics of the situation leave no other course open. . . . We are sorry we find the necessity of putting all the people out of work in South Bend, but we were being bled to death." Burlingame echoed him, saying, "As a South Bend man, this is a sad day for me. But the action we're taking today would have taken place anyway . . . in a very short time." On the day the news of the closing broke Studebaker was the most active stock on the New York Stock Exchange; 296,000 shares were traded, closing at $7.125, up 37.5¢ from the close of the previous day. Investors undoubtedly approved the decision to abandon an unprofitable business and expected better returns from the corporation than they had been getting.

III

The workers and people of South Bend accepted, if they did not approve, the closing. It had been expected, but it was still a depressing blow to them and to the local economy. Studebaker had long been a part of the community. For 50 years as a successful wagon builder and then for another 61 years as a manufacturer of automobiles it had offered jobs to South Bend and contributed heavily to the income of the city. Although it was no longer the largest employer in the area, it still accounted for nearly 10 per cent of the 93,400 working people of St. Joseph County. The particular characteristics of Studebaker's employees made their sudden unemployment all the more painful. One-third of South Bend's Negroes worked at Studebaker, making up 20 per cent of all the employees; they would have a hard time finding new jobs because of discrimination. Many workers were third generation employees, for the company had delighted to advertise itself as one where fathers and sons worked together. Those who had worked for no other employer averaged 52 to 55 years in age. An estimated 3,000 of the 8,000 workers who would lose their jobs at Studebaker were over 50. Like the Negroes, the older workers could not expect to find reemployment quickly or easily.

Before the closing and the earlier layoff, unemployment in the South Bend area had dropped to 2.1 per cent, the lowest level in a decade. The recently improving economic climate was to make the Studebaker shutdown a less severe blow than it would have been a year or two earlier. The demand for skilled workers, evidenced in the five columns of help-wanted ads in the December 11 issue of the South Bend *Tribune,* seemed to promise plenty of new job opportunities. Unfortunately, most of the jobs were outside South Bend and the Labor Department estimated that no more than 1,000 to 1,500 of the laid-off workers would qualify as skilled. Since not all of them could, or would, want to leave their homes for jobs elsewhere, nearly 40 per cent of even the skilled men were expected to have some difficulty in finding new work. Unemployment in the area rose steeply and reached 9 per cent by March, 1964.

Many of the workers criticized former Studebaker managers for not modernizing plant and equipment when the company was making money. Some of the multi-storied brick buildings dated back to the early 1900's. *U.S. News & World Report* noted that one could still read the faded legend on the side of one building: "Studebaker, Vehicle and Harness Makers." On the other side of the same building was the name "Studebaker Electrics," reminiscent of the electric cars made in 1902! [1] Some workers complained that their loyalty to the company hardly deserved the scant reward they now received. Several years before, for example, the members of Local No. 5, United Automobile Workers, which represented 5,000 Studebaker production workers, had voted to require all its members to buy only Studebakers. The International Union had overruled the Local, but informal pressures were able to insure that Studebakers were in abundance in the company parking lots and on the city streets.

Moreover, union members complained, the union had "taken it easy" in recent negotiations with Studebaker, not pushing for settlements in accord with the industry pattern because of the company's poor financial position. As a result the workers could claim no severance pay,[2] and they had no transfer rights to other company plants under the labor agreement. Whatever seniority they enjoyed at Studebaker was of no use anywhere else, either. A 55-year-old assembly-line worker with 30 years on the job would begin at the bottom of any seniority ladder in a new company. The union's pension plan was not as liberal as those provided by General Motors, Ford, and Chrysler. The 800 workers old enough to retire received pensions of but $2.50 per month for each year of service.

[1] *U.S. News & World Report,* 55 (December 23, 1963), 76–78.

[2] The approximately 1,000 salaried white collar workers were eligible for severance pay under a unilaterally determined policy of the company. Those with up to five years of service were to receive one month's salary, and those with more than five years of service were to get three months' pay.

Most of the workers could look forward only to government unemployment payments to help them out in the lean months after closing. The union's Supplemental Unemployment Benefit fund had been nearly drained by earlier layoffs and short work weeks in 1963; the $60,000 left was to be used for individual emergencies and, in some cases, severance pay. Indiana law provided that full unemployment benefits be paid for a maximum of 26 weeks, after which most unemployed workers could qualify for lesser payments of $20–25 a week for from 15 to 20 weeks. Unfortunately, many workers were not eligible for the maximum rates since they had already drawn unemployment pay during the model changeover and other layoffs during the year.

IV

Community leaders were concerned with the shutdown for it meant an annual loss of $50 million in payrolls. Mayor Frank J. Bruggner immediately formed a committee to find ways to help bring in new industry to replace Studebaker. Representative John Brademas and Senators Vance Hartke and Birch Bayh in Washington expressed concern for the workers and their families. "We must," they said,

> turn our attention to the problem of these thousands of Studebaker employees who are out of work because of this decision. We are in touch with the Secretary of Labor, the Secretary of Commerce and other government officials, and they assure us of their complete cooperation in our efforts to help solve these problems. We share a great confidence in the people of the South Bend area. We are determined to work with them to meet this new challenge.[3]

Governor Matthew Welsh declared, "Every effort will be made by the state to ease this blow to the economy of South Bend and Indiana." No public official protested the closing or blamed the Studebaker managers for making the decision. It was accepted as necessary, and all that could be done was to try to ameliorate the impact upon the workers and the community.

President Johnson appointed an Interdepartmental Commission on the South Bend Shutdown to take such action as the federal government could and to recommend further action that might be found helpful. The deputy director for the Area Redevelopment Administration met immediately with representatives of other federal agencies; they decided to appoint at once a consultant and coordinator to work with local groups and to provide liaison among the concerned agencies. The day before Christmas President Johnson ordered a new program to establish training projects to help the former workers of Studebaker.

By March a 14-month retraining program had been set up, offering to 450 people courses ranging from chef's training to studies in computer operations. Some courses were as short as 16 weeks, while others lasted 50 weeks; costs per trainee ranged from $1,990 for a data processor, to $2,960 for a refrigeration mechanic, to a high of $7,487 for an entry programmer. Total costs ranged from $119,000 to $300,000 per course. The total costs for the 21 courses offered was estimated at $1.7 million, of which the federal government's share was about $1 million. Studebaker contributed facilities worth about $70,000.[4] Many of the workers required special help to improve their ability to read, write, and perform simple arithmetic. The Department of Labor estimated that without the retraining program South Bend would be left with a residue or hard core of unemployable workers whose relief costs would run to $2,750,000 a year.

The federal government took several other steps to help South Bend. The Labor Department reclassified the labor market in South Bend to make firms in the area eli-

[3] *Congressional Record,* 109 (December 9, 1963), 23882.

[4] *IUE News,* January 30, 1964, p. 9; *New York Times,* March 13, 1964.

gible to receive preference in government contracting; the Social Security Administration provided special counseling for older workers about retirement; the Federal Housing Administration and the Veterans Administration agreed to approve any forebearance agreements proposed by lenders if the home-owner was unemployed because of the Studebaker shutdown; the Small Business Administration agreed to consider the possibility of deferring payments on any small business loans in the area; the Department of Agriculture approved a request to increase the upper annual income limit of its food surplus program, thereby allowing unemployed workers in South Bend to receive surplus food without declaring themselves destitute; and the Defense Department pledged support and assured that Studebaker or whoever should take over its contracts with the government would be requested to do the work in South Bend.

The Kaiser Jeep Corporation purchased Studebaker's newest plant, the Chippewa plant in South Bend, in February, 1964, planning to produce in it five-ton military trucks for the Army. Kaiser announced that it would hire several hundred of the workers laid off by Studebaker. Emil Mazey, secretary-treasurer of the United Automobile Workers, believed that all the automobile firms ought to make a special effort to hire the laid-off workers. He argued that the automobile industry had a moral responsibility to Studebaker's former workers. In urging the Chrysler Corporation to locate in South Bend a new assembly plant that it had under study he said, "The automobile industry as a whole will produce and sell the cars that were formerly manufactured and sold by Studebaker Corporation. We believe, therefore, that every auto firm has an obligation to give employment opportunities to former Studebaker workers." [5] He noted that the location for the plant would give Chrysler the advantage of a skilled and experienced labor supply and close proximity to the Chicago and South Bend industrial complex and its thousands of suppliers. Mazey's suggestion received scant attention and no endorsement from businessmen or government officials.

Seven years earlier, the then Secretary of Defense, Charles E. Wilson, a former president of General Motors, had made a similar suggestion. He declared that industry leaders owed a special responsibility to others in the same industry. His proposal to help avert the threatened closing of Studebaker-Packard in 1956 had the same purpose as Mazey's in 1963: to maintain employment in and to sustain the economy of South Bend. The fierce competition between General Motors and Ford had even then nearly crushed the smaller company, and there was talk that it would have to get out of the car business. President Eisenhower had sent Wilson to Detroit to discuss with the managers of the big automobile companies ways in which they might help Studebaker-Packard and avoid a shutdown. Wilson urged General Motors officials to give the smaller company their 1957 styles to allow it a competitive advantage. The GM executives demurred, but they did agree to sell transmissions to Studebaker-Packard. Later, the government's interest in aiding the company helped persuade Curtiss-Wright to lend a hand, and Studebaker-Packard survived that crisis.

V

Almost five months after the closing, the United Automobile Workers sent a questionnaire to the more than 6,800 hourly workers who had been on the Studebaker payroll in November, 1963. Fifty-eight per cent (3,973) of the workers responded; of these, 62 per cent reported that they were unemployed and 61 per cent were over 50 years of age—23 per cent of the respondents were 60 or above. Though 42 per cent wanted to take retraining courses only 3.5 per cent had been able to, and another 11 per cent were scheduled for retraining. The survey also showed that many

[5] *U.S. News & World Report, op. cit.*, p. 77.

of the unemployed had almost exhausted their unemployment compensation and were unable to pay for their health insurance any longer.[6]

[6] "Five Months after the Studebaker Shutdown," *Monthly Labor Review,* 87 (August, 1964), 899.

Eight months after the shutdown Studebaker's President Burlingame was able to give to his stockholders a more encouraging report than the UAW to its members. The company had made a sharp recovery. It operated in the black in the first half of 1964 and showed a net profit of $3,455,611.

THE DEFENSE DEPARTMENT CLOSES AN AIR BASE

Not long after assuming his Cabinet post in 1961, Secretary of Defense Robert S. McNamara announced the closing of 52 military bases. Although the affected communities protested and their congressmen complained, the closings were carried out with few exceptions. The Secretary's arguments for his action won the respect, if not the enthusiastic approval, of Congress. He told the House Armed Services Committee:

> Technological progress causes obsolescence not only in systems but also in the often highly specialized facilities constructed for their deployment and maintenance. Just as we continually measure our weapon system development and procurement programs against the ever changing yardstick of military need, so too must we review our worldwide complex of installations in light of our present and future requirements. Facilities and installations which fail this test of true need only encumber the national security effort and waste resources.[1]

I

Critics had long accused the Defense Department of gross mismanagement, unbusinesslike dealings, and lavish spending of public funds. Attempts made from time to time by former Secretaries to cut waste and to tighten control of the million-man bureaucracy seemed to get nowhere; the department appeared to be too big to be managed effectively and too entrenched to change.

The Department of Defense is by far the largest agency of government. Since the Korean conflict its expenditures have accounted for 50–65 per cent of the federal budget, and the funds spent for military functions as a per cent of the gross national product have ranged from over 8 per cent to 11 per cent. In 1963 the budget expenditures for national defense were $52.8 billion, and the total value of property held by the Department amounted to $171.4 billion.

Secretary McNamara had decided to use the most advanced managerial techniques in a new effort to cut costs and to encourage tighter controls. The Department was so large and its expenditures so vast that the potential savings to taxpayers and to the whole economy could be substantial. On July 1, 1962, McNamara instituted a formal five-year cost-reduction program. Each management area in the Department was required to define cost-saving goals, stating in detail the objective to be sought and the methods and procedures to be followed. Each area was expected to report regularly on its progress, and the goals and results were to be audited by an independent group that would validate and substantiate the savings. Secretary McNamara expected the program to save about $1.9 billion annually in its first phase. By 1965, he hoped to be able to save $3.4 billion annually.

[1] *Background Material on Economic Impact of Federal Procurement, 1965,* Joint Economic Committee, 89th Cong., 1st Sess. (Washington: Government Printing Office, 1965), p. 52.

A major part of the program was based on increasing the efficiency of the Department's support activities—supply, maintenance, communications, transportation—by cutting operating costs. To this end the Secretary called for the closing of unneeded military bases and installations. He reported in March, 1963:

> To date, we have announced plans to close or reduce in scope 313 activities, of which 71 are located overseas and 242 in the United States. . . . Actions anticipated through the end of fiscal year 1963 should produce an annual saving of $292 million when completed. Our goal is to initiate actions by end fiscal year 1965 which will increase the annual rate of saving to $442 million.[2]

In the following months there was much speculation as to which air bases, army depots, and shipyards would be closed. Elected officials whose home districts included military installations of doubtful value sought arguments and found reasons for holding up any order for closing when it did come. Senator Kenneth B. Keating of New York, for example, heard through a source in the Pentagon that the Rome Air Materiel Area (ROAMA) in Rome, New York, would probably be on the December list of bases to be shut down. He immediately addressed himself to the problem, first by pointing out the excellent efficiency rating of the base and then by denouncing the proposed consolidation program:

> . . . it seems to me that the type of centralization which is taking place more and more in defense work is of dubious value. It does not always produce the desired economies, as the Comptroller General very ably points out. It puts small business at a serious disadvantage. And it gives rise again and again to questions of political influence that, whether proven or not, are damaging to the morale of all concerned.[3]

The day after this speech, the Department of Defense notified the Representatives and Senators of the 14 states in which military bases were to be closed. In the United States, 35 installations were affected, 7 of them in New York State. The New York bases included ROAMA, where 7,500 civilians were employed, the army depot at Schenectady that employed 1,700 civilians, and 5 smaller installations with a total of about 1,800 workers.

At a news conference on December 12, McNamara pointed out that the closings would be gradual, that they would be spread over more than three years, and that the Department would do all it could to help displaced workers to find new jobs. Eventually, he said, the 35 closings throughout the country would reduce the total of civilian jobs by 8,500 and allow the armed services to divert 7,800 soldiers to other assignments; the result would be savings of about $106 million. The Secretary's attempt to reassure the communities and people involved did nothing to soothe the feelings of New York's congressional delegation. Senator Jacob K. Javits called the closings a devastating blow to the state's economy and promised "we will fight the decision with every ounce of energy."[4] Representative Leo W. O'Brien, from Albany, complained that McNamara "would create a 120-mile belt of despair in upstate New York."[5]

The next week defense officials told the New York congressmen that not all of the 7,500 ROAMA employees would lose their jobs, since Griffiss Air Force Base, where ROAMA was located, was to be kept open. Thus only 4,238 civilians would become jobless, and they would be offered transfers to other bases. At the same time, 249 mili-

[2] *Background Material on Economic Aspects of Military Procurement and Supply,* Joint Economic Committee, 88th Cong., 1st Sess. (Washington: Government Printing Office, 1963), pp. 71–72.

[3] News release of remarks made by Senator Keating on the Senate floor, December 10, 1963.

[4] *New York Times,* December 12, 1963.

[5] *Wall Street Journal,* December 20, 1963.

tary personnel would be transferred. The total annual payroll that would be eliminated was estimated at $3 million.

II

Senator Keating, who was planning to run for reelection in 1964, was not satisfied with the official explanations. He found that the change in the estimate of the number of workers affected was

> a welcome one, insofar as it goes, of course, for that figure is about half the one we were originally given. But that change is indication of the fact that this entire matter was not thought through but, instead, was hurriedly concocted in order to give a great show of "economy" in a move which I intended to demonstrate is no economy at all.[6]

The Senator believed that the Defense officials were taking entirely too parochial a view of the effects of their decisions. While the Defense Department *might* realize the savings it claimed, he thought it more probable that the government would not realize any at all.

> When [we] . . . inquired how these great economies would result when the Defense Department was creating additional unemployment in areas that qualify for direct federal assistance under other programs [the Area Redevelopment Program and Accelerated Public Works Program], the reply of the Deputy Secretary of Defense and also of the Secretary of the Air Force was:
>
> "Yes, we know these activities in New York are in depressed areas. Yes, we know the work they're doing is not obsolete work. We know the facilities now in existence there are modern and up to date. We know the work being done is necessary and will have to keep right on being done wherever it's moved. But it's not our responsibility to give any consideration whatsoever to the fact that these parts of New York are depressed areas and that the other places that are going to get the jobs are areas of full employment. That's not our job."[7]

Senators Keating and Javits jointly introduced a bill that if passed would, they believed, help the situation where one government agency takes actions to save money only to impose an additional burden upon another agency. It was to require the Secretary of Defense to notify the Area Redevelopment Administration before he ordered the closing of any installation, major facility, or activity in an area of substantial unemployment when such action would involve the loss of more than 100 civilian jobs. The ARA was asked to furnish within 60 days a report on the estimated cost to the federal government of recreating the same number of jobs through other programs.

In defending the bill before the Senate, Keating explained why he thought it necessary:

> Mr. President, the purpose of this legislation should be clear. It is the express object and policy of the federal government to make particular efforts in areas of high unemployment to recreate jobs and business. This is based on the long-term recognition that depressed areas and areas of high unemployment are contrary to the national interest and result in long-term losses for the nation.
>
> Yet, Mr. President, incredible as it may seem, the Defense Department is actually prepared to close down installations in New York State and a number of others elsewhere that are in federal aid under the area redevelopment program or the public works program. . . . The Congress has just been asked to appropriate nearly $1 billion for accelerated public works projects. It costs on an average $4,230 to recreate a single job under this program. To recreate all the jobs that the Defense Department wants to take away from central New York, from areas that qualify for this type of assistance, would amount to $38 million. I cannot believe that any savings that the Defense Department might claim as a result of closing these in-

[6] *Congressional Record,* 109 (December 13, 1963), 23374.

[7] *Congressional Record,* 109 (December 16, 1963), 23476.

> stallations would compare in cost with the expense of recreating these jobs. The taxpayers are not saving money in the long run if the Defense Department budget is cut by a few million dollars, but the area redevelopment program then has to be increased by several hundred million dollars.
>
> . . .
>
> In the Schenectady area, as to which I have the figures, in order to save $1,500,000 it would cost $7,191,000 to recreate the same number of jobs. If that is economy, I think it will be necessary to rewrite the definition in the dictionary. If there is a desire to create another Appalachia in the nation, this is one of the best ways to go about doing so.[8]

In the following months many New York officials, in both the federal and state governments, came to the support of the Keating-Javits bill. Representative Samuel S. Stratton who had been mentioned as a possible Democratic gubernatorial candidate, commented in late December that he found Congress inconsistent in restricting the Defense Department in some actions but allowing it freedom in others. He declared that the Department cannot buy or sell an acre of land or switch a single contract dollar from one project to another without first coming to the appropriate congressional committee. Yet it can apparently add thousands of persons to the national unemployment rolls, often in areas already suffering from unemployment, without ever furnishing Congress with the figures on which such decisions have been based.[9]

The Speaker of the New York Assembly, Joseph F. Carlino, a Republican who was known to be interested in the governorship, denounced the way the Defense Department proceeded with cutbacks:

> Unfortunately, despite many promises of planning with the states to ease transitions following defense cutbacks, the thunderbolt technique continues to be employed by those in the Pentagon whose orientation seems to be one of regarding all levels of government outside of Washington as "enemy" rather than ally.
>
> There have been several instances of this guillotine method around New York State, with a community learning the day after the decision has been made that the props have been knocked out from under the key employer in its backyard.
>
> If we are to survive the transition and obtain the benefits of defense savings, it seems to me that there must be consultation and planning in advance which will involve not just area redevelopment administrators in distress regions, but local and state officials who are interested in preventing regions from developing.[10]

In Rome, local community leaders organized a Mayor's Committee on Griffiss AFB to fight the closings. Under the chairmanship of Fritz S. Updike, editor and general manager of the Rome *Daily Sentinel,* the committee was to investigate the impact of the base closings upon nearby communities and to persuade the Defense Department to rescind its order. "We believe that once Mr. McNamara knows all the facts," Updike said, "he will realize that it's false economy to rip up and split this centralized operation."

The committee presented its arguments in a "White Paper" dated January 8, 1964: [11]

> INTRODUCTION
>
> This nation is only as strong as its entire economy—civilian as well as military.
>
> Dispersal of ROAMA would deflate an already depressed labor market, discourage commercial investments and private manufacturing, disrupt a young electronics industry, and deplete retail sales by the loss of millions of payroll dollars in central New York.
>
> Dispersal of ROAMA would decrease the use of housing, schools, churches, and other

[8] *Congressional Record,* 109 (December 12, 1963), 23218.

[9] *New York Times,* December 23, 1963.

[10] Speech to the Greater Buffalo Advertising Club, January 14, 1964.

[11] Distributed by the Chamber of Commerce, Rome, New York.

public structures expanded on repeated Air Force assurances the ROAMA would stay. It would depreciate the value of expanded facilities and burden remaining property owners with upkeep costs of new facilities, which would not have been built except for ROAMA.

In short, the phaseout of ROAMA would irreparably harm the economy of central New York and materially weaken the economic (and military) posture of the country. . . .

IMPACT ON EMPLOYMENT

. . .

For years the Utica–Rome area's annual average rate of unemployment has been consistently higher than that of the nation and New York State. Data from the Bureau of Employment Security at Washington, D.C., shows this rate in 1963 was 11 per cent above the federal average and 13 per cent above the state average. . . .

Of the nation's 150 labor market areas, 106 now have better classifications than Utica–Rome.

This condition exists despite a post–World War II conversion of thousands of textile workers to hardgood employees, an effort accomplished with a minimum of government aid. . . .

IMPACT IN DOLLARS

. . .

Public and private expansion to keep pace with ROAMA's growth and the consequent overhead and debt retirement expenses have cost Rome, Utica, and vicinity an estimated $125 million in the past five years.

In 1963, payrolls and purchases by ROAMA and wholly dependent firms were estimated at *$189 million,* and payrolls and purchases by related trades and services were worth an estimated *$90 million.*

IMPACT ON GOVERNMENT ASSISTANCE

The Utica–Rome labor market area since 1951 has received state and federal unemployment benefits totalling $95 million. This includes an estimated $9.5 million for the entire year 1963. Of this total sum, $60 million has been received since January 1958.

ROAMA employees who do not move would be eligible for federal unemployment benefits and job retraining. The U.S. Department of Commerce estimates the average cost of recreating a single construction job, for example, in a depressed area at $4,230 for one year; and, if ROAMA moves, such costs could easily exceed $13 million a year in the Utica–Rome labor market area. . . .

This jobless situation is also evident in the fact that welfare assistance to employable residents of Oneida County (including Rome and Utica) has risen approximately 26 per cent from 1961 through 1963. The 1961 figure was $1.37 million; by the end of 1963, it was $1.74 million; and it is still going up. . . .

CONCLUSION

National security involves the national economy. The strength of the total economy is no greater than the strength of its component parts. . . .

Jobs as well as soldiers keep the nation strong, especially when the jobs are essential to defense and the persons performing them are skilled and efficient. . . .

III

The Defense Department proceeded with its program of base closings despite the criticism and blame it received. Congressmen whose districts and states were unaffected generally defended the action and commended Secretary McNamara for his political courage. Editors of several national publications condemned the politicians who fought the closings. The *Wall Street Journal* editorially attacked Senator Keating in particular for his "outrageous complaints about [the effects on] unemployment in New York." The Senator replied in a Senate speech:

> I wish to state, Mr. President, that I do not consider that [the complaints] are irrelevant. When there is unemployment in my state I intend to continue to "yelp" about it. I believe that is the duty of a Senator representing any state, particularly when the state is singled out for an increase in unemployment.[12]

[12] *Congressional Record,* 109 (December 13, 1963), 23374.

When members of the Joint Economic Committee later discussed with McNamara the economic problems and political difficulties of closing military bases, the Secretary explained his views:

> I think it is entirely appropriate that our citizens should question actions of this kind that so directly affect their lives and livelihood, and it is entirely appropriate that their representatives in Congress should question them, and it is incumbent upon us to be able to answer those questions. We recognize that responsibility, and I hope we can carry it out. So I expect, if not criticism, at least questions, in connection with base closings. But I do believe that our citizens must understand that when they advance their parochial interests at the cost of our nation that they are sowing the seeds of inefficiency which become frozen in our system, and which translate into declining rates of productivity, and which ultimately cause basic balance-of-payments problems of the kind that other nations have faced over time, and which ultimately will substantially reduce our standard of living and in the process of doing so affect our security. In any case, I consider it my responsibility, and I know the Congress considers it is theirs, to act in accordance with the national interest and not the interest of a particular citizen or geographic area, and it is the standard that we seek to apply in connection with the analysis of our base systems.[13]

Representative Thomas B. Curtis of Missouri added that he thought communities simply had to recognize that military bases might involve costs as well as benefits. McNamara agreed wholeheartedly:

> Obviously some of these base closures could have a serious impact on the employees and communities involved, at least in the short run. But it should be clear to all Americans that the continuing obsolescence of existing military facilities is one of the inescapable consequences of our efforts to keep our armed forces modern and equipped with the latest products of our extensive research and development program. No one would argue that we should retard the progress of military technology simply because it causes obsolescence. Yet, when technological progress makes facilities obsolete, there is frequently resistance to closing them, even though we have no further military requirement for them. Keeping unneeded facilities open not only results in inefficiency and unnecessarily increases the cost of national defense, but, even worse, it deprives our nation of the use of very valuable human and physical resources—without contributing one iota to our military strength.
>
> The dislocations created by the onrush of science and technology are not unique to the Defense program. Indeed, their effects on the economy as a whole are not much different, either in kind or degree, from those which periodically take place as a result of changes in civilian demand or technology or the exhaustion of natural resources in a particular geographic area. Under our free enterprise system, competition in the marketplace eventually forces the reallocation of resources from older, less efficient uses to new, more efficient uses, and no business firm can long survive unless it responds promptly to these market pressures. The ability of our system to adjust to such changes quickly is one of its greatest strengths and is one of the major factors contributing to the growth and efficiency of our economy. And I think this is the important point. But while the nation as a whole benefits from the prompt shift of resources from old to new uses, the employees and the communities directly involved may, temporarily, be adversely affected. From the viewpoint of both social equity and economic efficiency, these people should not be asked to bear by themselves the full burden of such adjustments unaided. The Defense Department, therefore, has adopted the policy of assisting in such adjustments to the extent that the law permits and its own capabilities allow.[14]

He went on to explain that he believed the Department of Defense had a special

[13] *Economic Impact of Federal Procurement,* Hearings Before the Subcommittee on Federal Procurement and Regulation of the Joint Economic Committee, 89th Cong., 2nd Sess. (Washington: Government Printing Office, 1966), pp. 26–28.

[14] *Idem.*

responsibility to its employees, since it was both an employer and an agency of government. To meet that responsibility the Department had adopted a program to guarantee a new job opportunity to each displaced employee. The several government agencies concerned operated a nationwide system for matching displaced employees with job vacancies. Restrictions on hiring new workers gave preference to displaced employees, whose placement was facilitated by the temporary waiver of job qualifications and by retraining programs. The agencies, he said, also protected the incomes of displaced employees during the period of transition, reimbursed them for the costs of moving to a new job in the Defense establishment, and made full use of the "job finding" resources of the U.S. Civil Service Commission and state employment offices.

McNamara concluded by saying that such an employment program not only minimized personal hardships but preserved the talents and experiences of our work force. More importantly, for the long run he thought that it would improve the climate for change itself.

QUESTIONS

Social Cost and Private Benefits

1. After reading these two cases a student said, "I think that Senator Keating's argument applies to the Studebaker closing as much as to the closing of the military base. It is no more desirable for us to allow the Studebaker plant to close than the military base." Why do you agree or disagree?
2. Secretary of Defense McNamara thinks it appropriate that citizens question the decision to close military bases because their lives and livelihood are affected. Would it be appropriate for citizens to question the closing of company plants? What might be the effect of such questioning?
3. Who gains and who loses in the closing of either a military base or a private company plant? Consider carefully the gains that accrue and the losses that fall upon the public at large.
4. What arguments would you advance to justify the actions taken by the federal government in South Bend after the Studebaker closing? How do they differ from or compare with those in the case of the ROAMA closing?
5. Charles E. Wilson declared in 1957 that industry leaders owe a special responsibility to others in the same industry—that the successful, profitable automobile companies should help out the failing firms. What would be the consequences if such a policy were followed?
6. In what way does the economy secure a better allocation of resources when unprofitable or inefficient plants close? (Carefully define "better.") How does the mobility of human and capital resources affect your answer?

chapter **4**

WHEN ARE PRIVATE INTERESTS PUBLIC?

Adam Smith declared nearly 200 years ago that "the wise and virtuous man is at all times willing that his own private interests should be sacrificed to the public interest." [1] Most businessmen and union leaders would probably agree in general. In the interest of maintaining full production during World War II unions willingly gave up the right to strike, and many corporations took on production assignments that benefited them little, if at all, and in some cases drained managerial effort and resources from profitable production. In peacetime, however, it is not always possible to distinguish the one interest from the other. If public and private interests are not well defined, it is doubtful when and under what conditions private interests should be sacrificed to public ones.

Milton Friedman has suggested, in pursuing private profit, businessmen are serving the public interest. (See page 63.) He thus avoids having to choose between the two interests, for they are identical. Many businessmen recognize some validity in his suggestion but do not believe that it is completely satisfactory. The views of several business leaders were quoted not long ago in an article for the *New York Times;* [2] Thomas J. Watson, chairman of International Business Machines Corporation said:

> How far . . . can [a company] go toward meeting its social responsibility if this effort detracts from or runs counter to what must be its primary mission—being successful and thereby providing jobs, goods or services and profits? . . . Ultimately . . . a businessman simply cannot ignore for long his primary mission to conduct a successful business enterprise. If he does, he will fail and end up serving no one.

And Henry Ford II has written, "To subordinate profit to broad social goals would be totally irresponsible. On the other hand, socially responsible behavior is essential to the long-term growth and profitability of the corporation." [3] These business leaders recognize what Professor Friedman is unwilling to admit: public and private interests tend to merge and diverge in a multitude of complex ways.

[1] Marquis W. Childs and Douglass Cater, *Ethics in a Business Society* (New York: New American Library, 1954), p. 121

[2] Robert A. Wright, "Beyond the Profits: Business Reaches for a Social Role," *New York Times,* July 3, 1966.

[3] *Idem.*

The free, competitive market does not operate so effectively that it necessarily bends all the decisions and activities of business firms to the service of the public.

Businessmen and union leaders would be helped if they had a standard or set of procedures that identified for them the private and public interests that they affect. Mr. Watson maintained that the businessman has no such help now. "There is," he said, "a wide range of choice between genuine self-interest and a concern for social responsibilities." Ford agreed: "Whether any particular cost is worth incurring can be decided only in the light of all particular circumstances." But how a businessman will choose within the "wide range" or among the "circumstances" neither said. They were assuming not only as Adam Smith did that one can distinguish conceptually between private and public interests but also that the interests of a large organization are practicably separable from public interests. Perhaps, however, the different interests are but two sides of a single coin, a coin that will have to be spent as a unit and whose worth is determined by both its faces.

Traditionally, Americans have looked to government (or more exactly, to the electorate as it is represented by elected officials in government forums) to define by a declaration or enactment of policy the public interest at any particular time. But if public and private interests are so entangled they cannot be completely separated, may not corporations and unions find themselves affecting public interest and making public policy, in fact though not in law, as they pursue their private interests? Some observers have proposed that the roles of government and private organizations must be clearly separated to keep public-policy making a governmental function and to avoid mixing private and public interests to the detriment of both. For example, Charles E. Eble, Chairman of New York's Consolidated Edison Company, has said, "Each has a different objective and rightfully so. Successful business creates, invents, develops, organizes, promotes, and administers. Government regulates, judges, and controls." [4] While one might argue that organizations *should* limit themselves to proper activities, they do not *in fact* respect such limitation. In developing uses for nuclear power, the federal government has performed functions that Mr. Eble believes are better suited to private business. The government furthered the public interest when it organized the nation's creative scientific talent for the Manhattan Engineering District and, through the Atomic Energy Commission, promoted the development of nuclear power for civilian use; but its policy also affected private interests—not by regulating, judging, or controlling them, but by opening opportunities for some firms and workers in the newly created industry and threatening others dependent upon coal markets and the production of coal-burning equipment.

One reason public and private interests are difficult to separate and their policies often overlap is that the government not infrequently uses "private" corporations and unions as agents for making as well as carrying out public policy. In both the National Labor Relations Act of 1935 (Wagner Act) and the Labor Management Relations Act of 1947 (Taft-Hartley Act), the federal government declared that the policy of the United States was to encourage the practice and procedures of collective bargaining and to protect the exercise by workers of full freedom of association, self-organization, and designation of

[4] *Idem.*

representatives of their own choosing, for the purpose of negotiating the terms and conditions of their employment. In organizing and representing workers, unions were expected to further the public interest by mitigating some of the industrial strife and unrest that could occur; unions would also serve the public interest by helping to maintain high levels of national employment and purchasing power.[5] In addition, the government charged unions with the responsibility of representing all workers within designated units whether or not they were members. Unions thus became, for the purposes mentioned, quasi-public organizations; the line separating the private interests of the unions and the interests of the public was easily blurred by both parties as the unions carried out the public policy of the basic labor laws and pursued their own policies at the same time.

In the last decade government and business have blurred the boundary between public and private interests as never before. Business firms are chosen to supply the technology for modern defense not on the basis of competitive bidding in the market but upon other, often vague or bewilderingly complex criteria such as their technical competence, contribution to the relief of a depressed area or to the development of a community, political lobbying, or importance to defense strategy. Moreover, in fulfilling its contracts a business may be asked not merely to provide missiles and radar for the armed services but may be expected to furnish a complete weapons system. In the process of designing the components, subcontracting work to specialty firms, developing new equipment, installing the "hardware," and operating the system, managers of private corporations find themselves modifying or extending public-policy making decisions about public interests and carrying out governmental functions that have nothing to do with profits or market standards of performance. A careful observer of recent government practices concludes that "contracting out is . . . a system that allows the government to farm out a complete range of administrative and executive responsibilities accompanied by money, authority, and responsibility." [6] Through contracting out, business firms have found themselves making or influencing public policy, a fact recognized within the government. In a 1962 report to the President a committee of Cabinet-level officers warned that "in recent years there have been instances—particularly in the Department of Defense—where we have come dangerously close to permitting contract employees to exercise functions which belong with top government management officials." [7]

One does not need to look to the dramatic example of defense contractors to find the mixing of public and private policies and the resulting blurring of interests. Large organizations have such a widespread, often crucial impact upon the nation through their normal functioning that they can affect public interest even as their managers and officers pursue private interests. Quite clearly, businessmen and union leaders affect public policy by using their positions and the resources of their organizations to lobby for favorable legislation, to exert politi-

[5] See Labor Management Relations Act, 1947, Title One, Section 1.

[6] Victor K. Heyman, "Government by Contract: Boon or Boner?" *Public Administration Review,* 21 (Spring, 1961), 61. See also J. Stefan Dupre and W. Eric Gustafson, "Contracting for Defense: Private Firms and the Public Interest," *Political Science Quarterly,* 77 (June, 1962), 161–77.

[7] U.S. Bureau of the Budget, *Report to the President on Government Contracting for Research and Development,* May, 1962 (Washington: Government Printing Office, 1962), p. 8.

cal influence, and to campaign for new laws or changes in old ones. This activity poses problems in a democracy, for corporations and unions may be all too successful in gaining positions of legal privilege. But at least their influence upon public policy is tempered by having to act through public forums and securing the support of men responsible to the voters.

The nation faces another and probably more serious problem when corporations and unions can frustrate or change public policy simply by carrying out their usual functions of buying, investing, producing, and selling. When organizations are large and their leaders effectively command vast amounts of material and numerous men, the pursuit of their private interests may cause them to refuse their services or products, thus undermining or thwarting government policy that has been established only after public debate and careful consideration. The following cases illustrate the conflict of private interests with public policy; the outstanding questions they pose are how this conflict can be resolved and how businessmen, labor leaders, and government officials might evaluate the private and public interests concerned.

A Choice Between Human and Business Values

THE RETURN OF ARMY DEPENDENTS

After World War II many European nations with whom the United States had long traded found themselves short of dollars. They needed to import considerable quantities of machinery and other goods from the U.S. as part of their effort to rebuild their shattered economies, yet they had few goods available for export to balance the accounts. To help meet the resulting dollar shortage, the American government approved the Marshall Plan and other forms of aid. These programs, together with large capital investments made privately by American citizens abroad, succeeded in reducing the dollar shortage caused by the unequal trade flows.

By 1958 a spectacular economic recovery in western Europe, coinciding with a period of relative stagnation in the U.S. economy, brought about a change in the monetary relations between the two areas. No longer were dollars in short supply; the European countries had earned more dollars than they needed, and they began to use their surplus to buy U.S. gold, thus building up their own reserves. During 1958, 1959, and 1960 the U.S. shipped abroad more than $12 billion in gold as a result of the deficit in its balance of payments.

I

From 1950 to 1960 American exports had grown by one-third, but this increase in current earnings was not large enough to finance the large capital outflow. An important cause of the outflow of dollars, and thus of the drain on the gold supply, was the high interest rate prevailing in many European countries. American interest rates throughout the 1950's remained considerably below those abroad, the gap growing as wide as 3 percentage points. The higher interest rates abroad, of course, tended to attract the funds of American investors.

By 1960 the United States government was faced with the problem of preventing a speculative assault on the dollar while pursuing a monetary policy appropriate for domestic needs. The total U.S. gold stock amounted to $17.8 billion, while the nation's short-term liabilities to foreigners came to $21.3 billion. Nearly $3.5 billion was owed to West Germans alone. The American payments deficit had to be reduced and the rapid gold drain halted. Raising the American interest rate to a level competitive with the rate in Europe would probably have succeeded in slowing the capital outflow, but it would also have cut back on funds available for investment within the U.S. at a time when the domestic economy was already in a recession. Accordingly, the government adopted a different strategy by seeking to control its dollar contributions to foreign economic aid and to reduce its military expenditures abroad. First the Eisenhower and then the Kennedy administration devoted careful attention to this problem in 1960 and 1961.

II

On November 16, 1960, President Eisenhower directed all federal agencies to cut their overseas spending in order to stem the increasing deficit in the United States balance of payments and the consequent drain on the nation's gold reserves. Included in his directive were the following specific instructions:

1) The State Department was to "place primary emphasis" on purchases of goods and services of United States origin in administering America's foreign aid programs.

2) The Defense Department was to cut "by a very substantial amount" all purchases of military equipment abroad during 1960.

3) Both the State and Defense departments were to discontinue the purchase of foreign goods for sale in military post exchanges (exceptions allowed only by special Secretarial permission).

4) All civilian agencies overseas were to reduce the number of their employees where this could be accomplished "without impairing the fulfillment of essential United States policy objectives."

5) There was to be a mandatory reduction in the total number of dependents of military personnel overseas.

The directive that received the most publicity was the last one, which required wives and children of servicemen to return home. The President estimated that the return of families would result in savings of about $1 billion a year, almost half of the expected total savings. At the President's directive, the Department of Defense was to reduce the number of dependents abroad from the then current level of 484,000 to 200,000 at the rate of 15,000 a month, beginning January 1, 1961.

Defense officials said that they hoped to soften the effects of the directive by requiring shorter tours of duty for men who went overseas without their families and longer tours for those who went with families. The reduction in dependents living abroad would be accomplished largely by stopping new movements of families overseas, rather than by shipping home dependents. When he was asked about the impact of this order on the morale of the soldiers, the Secretary of Defense, Thomas S. Gates, Jr., said: "Our people are accustomed to sacrifice. Our people have lived abroad and been separated from their families. This is traditional in the military service."

On December 15, 1960, the Army, whose personnel accounted for about two-thirds of the 484,000 dependents overseas, announced that most of its married men who were sent abroad would be permitted to have their families with them at least part of the time. Officers and enlisted men would not be able to bring their families over during the first year of their three-year tours of duty; during the last two years, however, their dependents could join them.

On January 5, 1961, the Army ordered its major overseas military commands to send home by June, 1962, about one-half of the 16,000 dependents of civilian employees residing on military bases. Only the dependents of men performing essential services would be allowed to stay.

III

In October, 1961, President Kennedy's Secretary of Defense, Robert S. McNamara, announced that the government would no longer provide transportation and housing for dependents of United States servicemen going overseas. The reason given was that the shipping space normally assigned to wives and children of servicemen going on overseas duty was needed to accommodate the movement of 40,000 troop reinforcements and of supplies needed in Berlin.

At a Presidential news conference on February 21, 1962, reporters asked President Kennedy about the contents of a memorandum from the Secretary of Defense concerning the restriction of travel overseas by military dependents and about the moral implications of separating men serving overseas from their families.

> QUESTION: Mr. President, concern has been voiced by church leaders that wives and children of servicemen cannot accompany them to Europe and live with them. They are worried about moral implications, breakup of homes. Since the logistics requirements are no longer so urgent, it seems, is there a chance that this order may be changed soon?
>
> THE PRESIDENT: Well, as you know, most of the servicemen in Europe have their—who are married—have their families with them. There may be some who may be there for a more limited time who do not. In addition, of course, we're concerned about the gold flow which comes because of our troop commitments to Europe. I've said before that we spend $3 billion a year in maintaining our military forces around the world, and our bases. So if we are able to cut that somewhat, we should do so. But to be more specific, most of the servicemen now in Europe have their families with them. There are some who do not, and the purpose of it, of course, is to limit this drain.
>
> QUESTION: Mr. President, may I ask, was there not a memorandum on September 6 by the Defense Secretary forbidding the travel, though, for wives and children?
>
> THE PRESIDENT: We have attempted in recent weeks and months to limit the number of families going overseas, and the only reason for it has been that we are losing dollars and gold, and we have to attempt to bring it into balance, and this has been one of the ways which we've considered. We have left the families over there which were already there, but we're attempting to limit those that may go. This presents a hazard and a difficulty. But we're also very concerned about attempting to bring this flow into balance. . . . And one of the ways in which we can do this is to attempt to limit family travel, even though, quite rightly, it does present burdens to those involved.[1]

In a news conference on April 11, the matter was raised again:

> QUESTION: Don't you think that service wives have borne the brunt of our gold shortage long enough, and should be permitted to join their soldier husbands in Europe? After all you could almost say that service couples have had to bear a cross of gold alone, and in a very lonely way. . . .
>
> THE PRESIDENT: I agree. . . . As I've said it costs us $3 billion to maintain our forces and bases overseas. . . . I've asked Secretary McNamara to try to reduce that in the next 12 to 18 months by $1 billion in order to try to bring this gold flow into balance. And that means taking a third out of the Defense Department without reducing its strength. So that's why these women are bearing hardships—and these families. . . . Because the fact of the matter is, if we're not able to compete, this results in a larger increase of imports from foreign markets, and therefore lowers our dollar values—and those wives are going to have to stay home.[2]

IV

Apparently because of the pressure to permit families to accompany servicemen over-

[1] Harold W. Chase and Allen H. Lerman, eds., *Kennedy and the Press* (New York: Thomas Y. Crowell, 1965), pp. 190–91.
[2] *Ibid.*, pp. 225–26.

seas, on April 25 the Defense Department lifted its ban on government-paid travel by military dependents. In announcing the resumption of the dependents' travel allowance, Secretary McNamara said that by the end of May about 6,000 wives and children would be going abroad each month. He added, however, that they would merely be replacing about the same number who would be coming home with military men returning to this country. Before the travel ban about 9,000 dependents per month had accompanied servicemen overseas. During the half year that the government had refused to transport dependents overseas, about 20,000 dependents had moved to Europe at their own expense and had paid for their own housing on arrival. McNamara announced that while servicemen would not be reimbursed for the expense of bringing their families over on their own, the families' return trips would be paid for by the government.

On May 31 the Defense Department announced that it was considering rotating troops overseas on short tours of duty without their families. The announced purpose of this proposal was to reduce dollar expenditures overseas.

On July 16 McNamara announced the opening of a drive to reduce the dollar drain by $900 million without cutting down on United States fighting power overseas. He said that about one-half of this reduction was to come through reduction of American expenditures in Europe but that the government was not "thinking of stopping the flow of dependents overseas." He added, "We are hopeful we can expand the experimental rotation of 1,500 man Army battle groups to Europe without wives and children." McNamara went on to estimate the yearly savings of such a short-term rotation without dependents at between $1,000 and $3,000 a year per soldier.[3]

[3] *New York Times,* July 12, 1962.

FORD BUYS A SUBSIDIARY

On November 14, 1960, the officers of the Ford Motor Company announced their intention of buying for the company the shares of the minority interests in Ford of England. The business and financial communities of both the United States and Great Britain were surprised; since Ford already owned 54.6 per cent of its subsidiary's stock, the purchase of the rest seemed to be an unnecessary, if not unlikely, investment. In a public statement Henry Ford II explained the proposed course of action:

> One of our major objectives in proposing to acquire the minority shares of Ford of England is to achieve greater operational efficiency and greater marketing effectiveness in both countries. If we are successful in attaining this objective, we shall have a product position and a cost position which should enable us to compete more effectively throughout the world. This should benefit not only both companies, but also their employees, their suppliers, their dealers, and the public.

A similar letter to his managers for Ford of England was released to the British press:

> Our objective is to obtain greater operational flexibility and enable us better to coordinate our European and American manufacturing facilities and integrate further product lines and operations on a worldwide basis. We would like to add that, so far as we are concerned, we intend that your company's operations shall continue under your direction without change in its employment policy or in its development program.

I

Ford proposed to buy, at $20.50 each, the approximately 17.5 million shares outstanding for a sum of $358,400,000. Between 1955 and 1959 Ford of England had done well. Sales had increased by almost 54 per cent, from £152 million to £233 million, and profits after taxes had more than doubled from £10.5 million to £23 million.[1] Further, the subsidiary was in the midst of a $216 million expansion program, financed out of retained earnings. Established in 1911, it was Ford's largest affiliate and second largest automobile manufacturer in Great Britain. In 1959 it produced 27 per cent of all automobiles made in Great Britain.

In analyzing the purchase, a writer for the *Economist* pointed out that although Ford officials may have had several motives for proposing the purchase, no one could deny that it seemed to be a good investment.[2] He also explored other explanations for the decision. Because of antitrust legislation there might be advantages in having the foreign units wholly owned by the American company. Of most importance, however, was the reason given by the company: The resultant increase in corporate flexibility would help sales in a world market becoming increasingly competitive. The market for automobiles in western Europe had been expanding, and market researchers predicted that it would continue to expand over the next decade. It was growing relatively faster than the North American market, and its absolute size was great enough to be extremely attractive.

In the United States, auto companies had been operating below capacity for several years. Increasing imports of small foreign cars and the success of the new compact cars had led to uncertainty about the kinds of design and product to which the companies should give their attention. New model designs, hastily following one another, had not always been elegant or particularly attractive to buyers, and production runs had shortened. Thus the usual advantages of producing in Detroit had been somewhat diminished, accentuating the high costs of American labor. At the same time the growth of output and the lengthening of manufacturing runs overseas, including Britain, had reduced the disparity between unit overhead costs in Ford's American plants and those in England.

If observers of the business scene were puzzled by Ford's proposal, so was the British government. The Chancellor of the Exchequer, Selwyn Lloyd, told Parliament that he had tried to find out what Mr. Henry Ford's statements meant. That Mr. Lloyd be satisfied about their meaning was important, for under the Exchange Control Act of 1947 Treasury approval of the Ford transaction was required. Lloyd reported that he had talked with representatives of both the American and the British firms; from what he was told he had "formed the view that full American ownership would lead to more vigorous development of British Ford and even greater efforts in export markets. Without full ownership of the United Kingdom company, there might be a greater incentive for the United States company to concentrate efforts on the development of the German company which is nearly 100 per cent owned."

The *Economist* speculated that Ford officials might have suggested to Mr. Lloyd their hope of producing a car in either the English plant or the one in Cologne, Germany, to compete in the small- to medium-sized car market of western Europe. Or, given the uncertainties of the American market at the time, the Ford managers may have been looking forward to production runs of relatively low volume on certain models, which would favor the use of the company's European facilities for reasons of cost structure. The British company would be the most efficient because it was larger than the Ford company in Germany.

Though a number of explanations had been offered by Ford spokesmen, and others

[1] At this time, the pound sterling (£1) was worth approximately $2.80.

[2] "Ford Buys Ford," *Economist,* November 19, 1960, p. 803.

were suggested in the newspapers, observers still could not find a wholly satisfying reason for the purchase. On November 17, 1960, Sir Patrick Hennessy, chairman of British Ford, explained that if the deal were consummated British motorists would in the long run get a better article for their money. British Ford would, of course, continue to follow its own line of design but would have more access to American engineering and production techniques. Sir Patrick did not go further into details, and he did not make clear why more information would be available under 100 per cent ownership than under 55 per cent. A month later he offered the argument used to satisfy Mr. Lloyd. In writing to the stockholders he said:

> With the more intense competition in world markets, particularly in Europe, the Ford group will have to pay even more attention in the future to questions of competitive cost profitability. Other things being equal, greater support is likely to be given to the expansion and development of companies in the Ford group which are wholly owned rather than to that of companies in which minority interests are held outside the group.[3]

The *New York Times* pointed out that although Ford owned a majority of the stock, it actually had only minority representation on the board of directors of Ford in England. As a consequence the subsidiary sometimes had gone off on its own, as in planning for a huge plant near Liverpool, which the Detroit managers had opposed as not fitting in well with the overall strategy for expanding European production.

II

A look at the financial statements of the two companies provides many reasons for the decision of the Ford officials to buy out the British minority interests. (See Tables 1 and 2.) American Ford had the money, and the investment was sound. Any other benefits to be gained would be welcome extras. In the United States, Ford had spent heavily for plants in the mid-1950's, investing $487 million in 1956 and $329 million in 1957. By 1959 it had to spend only $75 million on plants; in 1960, its capital expenditures amounted to only $128 million. In the meantime Ford's cash flow—retained profits and depreciation—was becoming a torrent. In 1959 it amounted to $471 million, and by November 1960 it was running at an annual rate of over $400 million. (The final figure was $427 million for the year.) Cash and marketable securities had increased rapidly. In 1956 they amounted to $215 million; after gaining modestly—about 25 per cent—the next year, they jumped in 1958 to over 70 per cent, from $265 million to $452 million. The following year, 1959, they spurted another 47 per cent to $666 million! *Fortune* later observed that one might look at these figures and say that "the company is making more money out of the United States automobile business than it can profitably reemploy in the United States automobile business." A less kindly critic remarked, "Excess cash and near cash was burning holes in Ford's pockets." [4]

If Ford of America was an investor with ready cash, Ford of England was a likely investment. It was certainly more profitable than the Ford Motor Company in the United States, earning nearly 40 per cent more on its assets than the corporation as a whole. Moreover, its sales of cars and trucks through the fifties had increased much faster than the sales of American Ford; between 1954 and 1959 British Ford's sales rose by 83 per cent while American Ford's increased by only 7 per cent.

Whatever the reason for the transaction, the British government approved it. The Chancellor of the Exchequer gave his consent, and Parliament supported him. The government requested that Ford pay for the

[3] *New York Times,* December 13, 1960.

[4] Bernard D. Nossiter, *The Mythmakers: An Essay on Power and Wealth* (Boston: Houghton Mifflin, 1964), p. 98.

TABLE 1 Ford Motor Company, United States (in millions of dollars)

	1954	1955	1956	1957	1958	1959	1960
Sales	4,062	5,594	4,647	5,771	4,130	4,356	5,238
Income Before Taxes	511	986	490	581	183	843	775
Income After Taxes	243	454	248	294	116	451	428
Year-end Position							
Cash and Marketable Securities	328	568	215	265	452	666	454

SOURCE: Annual Reports, 1954–60.

minority interest in dollars and that the whole sum of the purchase price be placed on deposit with the British Treasury before proceeding with the formal offer to the stockholders of Ford of England.

III

After the announcement and during the preliminary discussions of the purchase, American government officials found reason to take an interest in the proceedings. In a television address on November 1, 1960, just two weeks before Ford's original statement, President Eisenhower and Secretary of the Treasury Robert Anderson had discussed the critical balance-of-payments problem facing the nation. The President said, "Let us make no mistake about it, the preservation of the soundness of the dollar, as well as the preservation of the confidence that the dollar will remain sound, is absolutely essential, both for the welfare of our citizens at home, and the rest of the free world." The Secretary had warned that all Americans "ought to be profoundly concerned" about the recent disturbance in the gold market.

Two days after Ford announced its purchase plans Secretary Anderson again warned the nation of our balance-of-payments problem. He feared that the deficit in the balance for 1960 would be greater than the $4 billion for 1959. "Obviously," he said, "improvement in our balance-of-payments position is vital not only for the economic well being and the military security of the United States but also for the free world." He went on to show that the deficit was growing at an accelerating rate. During the July–September quarter, the value of U.S. exports topped the value of imports by about $3.9 billion, computed on an annual basis. This was over 20 per cent larger than in the April–June quarter. The balance-of-payments deficit had risen in the July–September quarter from the preceding three months' $2.7 billion to an annual rate of about $4.5 billion.

The Secretary apparently talked to Henry Ford a number of times by telephone about the proposed transaction. When the news of these conversations first came out, a spokesman for the Ford Motor Company said that the reports that Secretary Anderson had approached Mr. Ford were "absolutely not true." The next day, however, Ford issued a statement explaining that Anderson had talked with Ford officials in mid-November about the projected purchase of the minority holdings in Ford of England. Ford denied that Anderson had then or at any time thereafter requested the company to hold up the transaction.

IV

Apparently the Secretary had urged Mr. Ford to consider buying out the minority holders with pounds sterling, since the Brit-

TABLE 2 Ford Motor Company, Ltd., England (in millions of dollars)

	1954	1955	1956	1957	1958	1959
Sales	356.4	424.5	408.0	464.8	578.5	653.0
Income Before Taxes	54.0	46.8	28.8	54.3	73.9	95.2
Income After Taxes	31.6	29.4	21.8	35.3	41.2	64.1
Year-end Position						
Cash and Marketable Securities	126.3	131.9	89.0	104.7	139.4	191.0

SOURCE: Annual Reports, 1954–59.

ish company held enough to complete the transaction. When the British government required the purchase to be in dollars, however, Anderson made no objection. He had no legal power to block Ford's transaction, and he did not try to enforce a greater sense of public responsibility upon the company by appealing to public opinion. Mr. Ford later remarked to a writer for *Fortune,* "Secretary of the Treasury Anderson was a gem about the whole thing. He just wanted to know what we were doing, and we kept him fully informed." The *Fortune* article continues: "It was unfortunately inopportune, Ford agrees, that the deal had to be closed just when the rumble over the U.S. gold flow was at its height." [5]

The United States Treasury assured the Chancellor of the Exchequer on December 6 that it had "no intention of intervening in the transaction," though the Secretary had directed the attention of Ford "to the impact of the proposed sale on the U.S. balance-of-payments position." In the middle of December the Ford Motor Company deposited with the British Treasury the required sum, which added $204 million to the pressure on the United States monetary gold stock in the week ending December 14 and brought the total loss of gold since the first of the year to $1.483 billion.

By January 11, 1961, more than 90 per cent of the shareholders of Ford of England had accepted the offer to buy their stock. On January 23, a Bank of England check for $334,867,807.68 drawn by the Ford Motor Company of the United States was handed over to the National Provisional Bank, and the next day this bank mailed out more than 19,000 checks to stockholders. This, in effect, completed the deal for turning over the British stock to the Ford Motor Company.

[5] Robert Sheehan, "It's a New Kind of Ford Motor Company," *Fortune,* 66 (February, 1962), 116.

QUESTIONS

A Choice Between Human and Business Values

1. What values do you think influenced the Eisenhower administration as it dealt with the gold crisis and the Ford purchase?

2. Suppose you are an advisor to a President who always wants to consider carefully the pros and cons of his decisions, and who has just received advice to discourage the flow of servicemen's families overseas and not to interfere with Ford's purchase of its British subsidiary. Prepare a brief argument countering this advice.

3. If you were the president of a large company contemplating a major purchase like that made by Ford, what lesson, if any, would you draw from Ford's experience? If you would not proceed as Ford did, explain how you would want to handle your purchase.

4. Since Secretary of Defense Gates argued that the presidential order reducing the number of dependents of military personnel living abroad would not cause a morale problem, what objections could churchmen and other groups make to the order?

5. Appraise the policy of the two administrations toward reducing the number of dependents of military personnel living abroad—and that of the Eisenhower Administration toward the Ford purchase—from both a short and a long run perspective. How does your appraisal differ for each time perspective?

The Private Right to Frustrate Public Policy

UNIONS AND THE ARAB NATIONALISTS

A few pickets parading in front of a pier on New York's waterfront usually indicate nothing more than a local dispute or a wildcat strike. The issues at stake usually concern only a few men or, at most, a single local of one of the several maritime unions. The six pickets in front of Pier 16 at the foot of Fulton Street on April 13, 1960, however, were concerned with an issue that affected all the maritime unions around the world. The boycott that they were enforcing upon the Egyptian cargo and passenger ship *Cleopatra,* moored at an East River berth, was to have international repercussions and disturb diplomats and government officials in a dozen national capitals.

I

The roots of the issue lay in the interminable conflict between Israel and the Arab nations. The armistice agreement following the Israeli-Arab war of 1948–49 did not lead to a peace settlement; the Arabs, led by the Egyptians, promised to continue the war through boycott and blockade. Egypt argued that since a state of war still existed with Israel it had the right under articles 9 and 10 of the Constantinople Convention of 1888 [1] to bar Israeli ships from the Suez Canal in its own self-defense. Attempts were made to work out a system of international control after President Nasser nationalized the Canal in 1956, but the debacle of the Anglo-French invasion later that year left unchallenged Egypt's control of the Canal.

Throughout 1957 and 1958 Israel shipped goods through the Suez Canal by putting them on foreign flag ships. Then, unexpectedly and without warning, Egypt began stopping ships that carried Israeli goods, often confiscating the cargoes and detaining the vessels for periods of a few days to several weeks. In March, 1959, it held up the Liberian ship *Kapitan Manolis* and the West German ship *Läloth* and took their cargoes. In May a Danish freighter, the *Inge Toft,* suffered the same treatment.

Dag Hammarskjöld, Secretary General of the United Nations, conferred with President Nasser, trying to work out a way in

[1] All the major European powers had agreed to the Convention, which declared the Suez Canal neutral and supposedly guaranteed free passage to all ships in both peace and war. Egyptian diplomats maintained that the Convention allowed an exception to free passage if their country acted in self-defense.

which the ban on Israeli cargoes might be eased with no loss of face to Egypt. He was not successful, for in December Egypt stopped the Greek ship *Astypalea* and removed the cargo that had been loaded in Israeli ports. In the following months other ships of several countries were held up and their cargoes confiscated. Among the blockaded ships was at least one that employed American sailors who were also members of the Seafarers International Union. After the Egyptian authorities stopped this ship and took the cargo, the operators had been bankrupted and had left the ship stranded. The ship's crew felt that the Egyptians had harassed and mistreated them, punishing them even though they were neutral in the dispute with Israel. They arrived back in New York early in April, 1960, and complained to their union president, Paul Hall.

In the meantime Egypt continued to stop ships, confiscate cargoes, and blacklist ships carrying goods to Israel. On March 3 authorities in Port Said stopped the *Caribbean Wave,* a 10,700-ton tanker of Liberian registration. They had earlier blacklisted the ship, and they now suspected it of being under Israeli charter. They found that though it was coming from the Jordanian port of Elath, bound for Venezuela, it carried only ballast; Egypt released the ship on March 5. A month later attention was again focused on the Egyptian boycott when the *Astypalea* was released after five months, her 400 tons of Israeli cement having been unloaded and sold at auction.

II

The American maritime unions had long been annoyed by the Egyptian blockade of the Suez Canal and the Arab blacklisting of ships trading with Israel. Early in February, 1960, the executive board of the Maritime Trades Department, AFL–CIO, adopted a resolution condemning the "Hitlerite boycott." Concerned with the interests of the 250,000 workers they represented, the board members charged that the U.S. government was, in effect, joining the boycott by allowing the Navy to bar any U.S. tanker that used Israeli ports from carrying oil purchased for the Navy in the Middle East. Furthermore, American jobs were being sacrificed by the government policy that allowed "American ships, manned by American seafarers and built by American shipyard workers, to be blacklisted because they were owned in whole or in part by persons of the Jewish religion." [2] The board called upon the government to uphold the principle of freedom of the seas and asked Congress to investigate thoroughly the government's "disgraceful and un-American contacts with the Arab states."

After passage of the resolution, neither the State Department nor Congress took any action that satisfied the maritime unions. Because of continued Egyptian harassment of American ships and sailors, the leaders of two unions, the Seafarers International Union and the International Longshoremen's Association, decided to act. Following the precedent of the maritime unions in Finland and Sweden, they decided to institute their own boycott and refused to load or unload any ship from the United Arab Republic.

When the 8,193-ton *Cleopatra* arrived in New York on April 13, 1960, with 400 tons of general cargo to be unloaded and nine passengers, it was met by a picket line. The pickets handed out leaflets asking the U.S. Navy to stop buying oil in any port where American ships were blacklisted and demanding a halt to shipments of farm surpluses to nations that blacklisted American ships. Paul Hall of the Seafarers told reporters that the SIU and the ILA "will keep up the steam until this situation is corrected" and promised to continue the picketing indefinitely and possibly to extend it to other Atlantic coast ports. Thomas W.

[2] *New York Times,* February 10, 1960.

Gleason, general organizer for the ILA, said that his union supported the boycott to help restore full freedom of the seas for the benefit of maritime workers around the world. Both union leaders urged the United States to notify the United Arab Republic that it would use all the resources at its command to restore international law and freedom of the seas.[3]

The day after the picketing began, attorneys acting for the Khedivial Mail Line of Alexandria, owner of the *Cleopatra,* petitioned the federal courts for an order restraining the picketing. Ten days later the district court refused to grant an injunction on the grounds that the picketing was protected under the provisions of the Norris-LaGuardia Act of 1932. The shipping company then petitioned the Court of Appeals, but three weeks later it was turned down there, too. The judges disagreed with the lower court's reasoning, however, declaring instead:

> The case falls upon a ground older and more fundamental than the Norris-LaGuardia Act, namely, that the complaint does not state a claim that would warrant the grant of an injunction by a Federal court.

They suggested that the owners of the ship might be able to seek injunctive relief or damages in a state court. The attorneys acted upon the suggestion, applying in the New York Supreme Court for an injunction and suing for $100,000 in damages and costs because of the delay and idleness of the *Cleopatra.*

While the case proceeded deliberately through the courts, it was stirring up an international furor. Arabs throughout the Middle East interpreted the picketing as the result of Zionist pressures and reacted with anger. The leaders of the 32,000-member General Union of Stevedores in the United Arab Republic prepared to boycott all American ships. Within a week after the picketing of the *Cleopatra* began, Syrian dockworkers had idled four ships; they refused to unload two U.S. cargo vessels in Latakia harbor and to load two American tankers at Baniyas. Gravely concerned with the spread of the boycott and counter action, U.S. Ambassador G. Frederick Reinhart met twice with officials of the U.A.R. foreign office in Cairo on April 19 but no agreement was reached. President Nasser evidently intended to encourage reprisals upon American shipping until the picketing in New York ceased.

On April 20, Paul Hall sent to President Nasser a long telegram vigorously denying that Zionists had anything to do with the unions' picketing. The action was designed, he insisted, to protect the welfare and security of union members and to enforce observance of international law guaranteeing freedom of the seas. No action was taken against Arab seamen, and as proof he noted that the 103-man crew of the *Cleopatra* had full freedom to come and go and that the unions were allowing food and medical supplies to be taken aboard. In contrast, SIU members had been mistreated when their ships had been stopped in Egypt. Mr. Hall concluded by saying that Omer Bercu, secretary general of the International Transport Workers Federation in Brussels, had commended the American unions and called their picketing justified.[4]

The International Federation of Arab Workers answered Hall by threatening to boycott all American ships in Arab ports. The Confederation also sent a message to President Eisenhower denouncing Zionist attempts to destroy friendly American-Arab relations. "The boycott of American longshoremen of a United Arab Republic vessel is a flagrant intrusion in political affairs and a new method of international Zionism to settle the Palestine problem at the expense of the rights of 1,000,000 Arab refugees forced out of Palestine." [5]

[3] *New York Times,* April 14, 1960.

[4] *New York Times,* April 21, 1960.

[5] *New York Times,* April 28, 1960.

III

Alarmed that the United States and the Arab countries would soon be involved in a major crisis, the Department of State issued a statement asking the American unions to consider the implications of their actions. The Department recognized the right of free speech as well as "the special status of labor unions to picket in labor disputes," and it understood the unions' concern with the Arab boycott.

> From the foreign policy standpoint, however, it should be made clear that the picketing is regarded abroad as a political demonstration related to the United Arab restrictions against Israel. . . . With such complex questions involved, an effort by a private group to apply pressure publicly with a view to bring about shifts in the policies of foreign governments is, of course, embarrrassing to the conduct of our government's foreign relations and may have unfortunate consequences.[6]

Senator J. William Fulbright of Arkansas brought the situation to the attention of the Senate in a speech on April 25:

> I hold no brief for U.A.R. interference with international traffic passing through the Suez Canal. The point is, however, that the U.S. government is proceeding through diplomatic channels to promote free passage through the Canal. The Israeli government, which complains that the U.A.R. stops its ships, has available to it the procedures of the United Nations as well as other diplomatic devices for urging its views on the government of the U.A.R. Yet, despite the official actions of the United States, we find private groups proceeding by coercive devices of their own to interfere with the official activities of our government in the field of foreign policy.
>
> These maritime unions do not seek an economic result related to wages or working conditions. Rather, they seek to force political action in an area of most delicate international negotiation. . . .
>
> It is my position that the President is the constitutional vehicle through which the American people engage in the day-to-day conduct of their foreign policy. There are constitutional channels through which citizens can legitimately and effectively petition their government and thus bring about changes in the conduct of foreign policy. Actions on the part of individuals or organizations which interfere directly or indirectly with the constitutional exercise of governmental authority or activity in the conduct of foreign policy, however, should be avoided as inimical to the total national interest. And finally, our constitutional system is designed to give free expression to the will of citizens of the United States. It must not be corrupted by calculated influence and pressure from any other source.[7]

The debate was joined by Seymour W. Miller, general counsel to the SIU. In a letter to the *New York Times* he wrote:

> The facts are that many of SIU's contracted companies have suffered a severe loss of business as a result of the policy all of us, including the State Department . . . appear to decry. As a consequence, job opportunities for its members have decreased substantially.
>
> Moreover, its seamen have been subject to personal abuse and harassment in U.A.R. ports. This situation has existed for years and constitutes a flagrant affront to our flag, to our country, to American shipping companies and merchant mariners.
>
> The State Department has accomplished nothing in the way of a remedy. It has mostly confined itself to the issuance of sporadic, ineffectual, general statements. In the meantime, the union's losses continue, as does, indeed, the threat to its very existence. It grows with each Arab League conference called for the purpose of enlarging upon this blacklist and in making increased use of Nasser's physical control of the Suez Canal, notwithstanding the U.A.R.'s contravention of numerous United Nations resolutions and open violation of international law. . . .

[6] *New York Times,* April 22, 1960.

[7] Statement by J. William Fulbright, Chairman, Committee on Foreign Relations, United States Senate, *Public and Private Responsibility in the Conduct of Foreign Relations,* July 26, 1960, p. 6.

> It is incumbent upon [those opposed to the action taken by the SIU] to suggest an alternative procedure which would offer the union some hope of eventual surcease from the threat which hangs over its contracted companies and available job opportunities. Certainly [they] cannot be suggesting it sit by and do nothing.[8]

At a news conference on April 27 President Eisenhower was asked to comment on the Arab boycott of Israeli shipping. He replied:

> Now, I don't know what you can do unless you want to resort to force in such affairs, and I'm certain that we're not trying to settle international problems with force. We have done everything we could to make it clear that we stand by our commitments and we think that other nations should do the same. Particularly when it comes to the free use of the Suez Canal. But I do not know that there is any idea whatsoever of making a new step in this direction or new arguments because I think it's all been said.[9]

Not everyone in government agreed with the President that it all had been said or that no new step could be taken. Senator Paul H. Douglas of Illinois introduced the following amendment to the policy statement of the Mutual Security Act to provide:

> That the United States favors freedom of navigation in international waterways and economic cooperation between nations. The peace of the world is endangered when nations which receive Mutual Security aid wage economic warfare against each other. These principles shall be applied in administering the Mutual Security Program as the President may determine.

The Senate approved the amendment 45 to 25 on April 29; the House of Representatives already had approved it without significant debate. By its action Congress indirectly but clearly supported the purposes —if not the picketing by—of the SIU and the ILA. The House Committee on Foreign Affairs had already declared that "the United States has not done as effective a job as it should have in urging the removal of the restrictions on the free movement of commerce through the Canal." In giving the President discretionary authority to withhold aid from the United Arab Republic if it did not lift the ban on Israeli shipping in the Suez Canal, Congress expressed its belief that the U.S. government could do more than it had.

Among the government officials who opposed the amendment were Undersecretary of State C. Douglas Dillon, Senator Sherman Cooper of Kentucky, and Senator Fulbright. Senator Fulbright maintained that the amendment was most unwise and was not offered for "the overwhelming good" of the United States,

> but because of the existence of a pressure group in the United States which seeks to inject the Arab-Israeli dispute into domestic politics. . . . This amendment and recent economic coercion to prevent the loading of an Arab ship in New York are part of a pattern which I find disastrous in the functioning of our constitutional system. . . . One-hundred-eighty million Americans find their foreign policy being whipsawed by an irresponsible maritime union and by a minority pressure group. . . . [These actions are attempts to involve American politics in] the feuds and emotions that are part of the political conflicts of foreign nations. This is one of the things our Founding Fathers came here to avoid when they created this nation. . . . [Foreign policy is] too important to our total national security for it to become the instrument of minorities whose lobbyists stand outside the Chambers of the Congress to persuade the members to follow courses of action beneficial to special interests but with potentially catastrophic consequences for the Nation as a whole.[10]

For this speech, Senator Fulbright was attacked by Zionists and by a number of Jewish organizations. Dr. Emmanuel Neu-

[8] May 3, 1960.

[9] *New York Times,* April 28, 1960.

[10] *Congressional Record,* 106 (April 29, 1960), 8977.

mann, a member of the Jewish Agency executive council, said:

> No one questions the right of Senator Fulbright or anyone else to advocate all-out American aid and support [of the U.A.R.]. . . . It is also the inalienable right of American citizens to advocate a firmer policy toward a dictator who is daily violating international law." [11]

In Washington, the national executive committee of the Jewish War Veterans called Senator Fulbright's remarks "an outrageous insult to the democratic way of life."

IV

Stung by the Congressional support for the two maritime unions and angered by the Zionist and Israeli delight with the picketing of the *Cleopatra,* the Arabs initiated a formal boycott of American ships. On April 30 President Nasser told a conference of 30 African-Asian nations in Cairo that the Arab boycott would continue until the New York dock workers abandoned their picket line. The International Confederation of Arab Trade Unions called upon all Arab workers "from the Persian Gulf to the Atlantic Ocean to tighten their boycott to foil the aims of Zionism, which is behind the American picketing of Arab vessels." [12]

The same day more than 3,000 students in Beirut marched through the streets shouting anti-American slogans and carrying signs supporting an Arab boycott of American ships. The first American freighter to reach Port Said after the boycott was the *Sir John Franklin;* dock workers circled the ship in small boats and waved signs reading, "Arab workers can strongly counter American picketing of Arab ships," "No canal for Israel," and "Long live Nasser." Dock workers in Tripoli, Libya, began boycotting American ships, and ships loaded with surplus food bound for the Syrian port of Latakia and for Alexandria were diverted to other, non-Arab ports. A U.S. tanker under Navy charter was refused handling at a Persian Gulf port, and two ships of the Military Sea Transportation Service had to bypass Tripoli. Other military ships were refused service, too, and the MSTS commander, whose organization each month transshipped about 300,000 tons of Middle Eastern petroleum products to the U.S. Far Eastern forces, became seriously concerned.

Saudi Arabia and Iraq joined the boycott on May 2 and banned the loading and unloading of American ships. The Bombay General Workers Union threatened to join the boycott, and the Tunisian Labor Federation, while not an active participant, announced its support of the other Arab states. By May 3 more than 28 ships had been affected, and the executive committee of the Arab Labor Confederation began to hint it might extend the boycott to include American aircraft.

V

President Eisenhower feared that the boycott and counter-boycott would soon be out of hand. Through his Secretary of Labor, James P. Mitchell, he appealed on May 3 to George Meany, president of the AFL–CIO, to help find a solution to the diplomatically explosive issue. This request received a hearing, but the next day the Executive Council of the AFL–CIO pledged its support of the maritime unions' protests against the Arab boycott and blacklisting. It also called upon the State Department to take all appropriate diplomatic action to safeguard American shipping and seamen against discriminatory treatment.

Seeing an opening for a settlement in the AFL–CIO Council's statement, acting Secretary of State Dillon conferred with Arthur J. Goldberg, special counsel for the labor federation. In two days of discussions, Secretaries Mitchell and Dillon on one side and Mr. Meany and Mr. Goldberg on the other drafted a declaration of the basic principles "which actuate United States for-

[11] *New York Times,* May 2, 1960.
[12] *New York Times,* May 1, 1960.

eign policy affecting the American Merchant Marine." The State Department for the first time publicly acknowledged that American seamen had been harassed in Arab ports. Of most importance to the Seafarers was the assurance that the Department would "undertake to investigate fully the grievances of the Seafarers International Union and, through appropriate diplomatic action with the foreign countries involved, to renew its efforts to assure freedom to the seas and to protect the interests of our shipping and seamen now being discriminated against by the Arab boycott and blacklisting policy." [13]

Mr. Meany then urged the SIU and the ILA to withdraw their picket line on the strength of the assurance of good faith given by the government. By this time the unions were maintaining a patrol of only two men at Pier 16. Paul Hall dismissed the pickets at 5 P.M., May 6, 24 days after they had begun the boycott of the *Cleopatra.* He warned, however, that the union would resume the picketing if the State Department failed to give practical implementation to its pledge.

The International Confederation of Arab Trade Unions ended its boycott of American ships on May 9, and it issued a statement expressing the hope that American workers realized they had been the victims of a Zionist plot when picketing the *Cleopatra.*

[13] *New York Times,* May 7, 1960.

RUBBER COMPANIES AND THE COMMUNISTS

The Firestone Tire and Rubber Company tersely announced on April 20, 1965, that it had "terminated negotiations for a contract to design and equip a synthetic rubber plant in Rumania." There was nothing more in the announcement, and a casual reader of the newspapers would probably have passed it by without realizing its significance. To a number of officials in the State Department, however, the announcement brought keen disappointment; to the Young Americans for Freedom it came as cheering news; to Senators Stephen M. Young of Ohio, and J. William Fulbright, chairman of the influential Committee on Foreign Relations, it represented the deplorable end to one part of a critical experiment in foreign trade.

I

The experiment had begun 11 months earlier when State Department experts and a Rumanian delegation met in Washington to discuss trade and related matters. The Rumanian government had been seeking improved relations with the United States for some time as part of a program to lessen its economic and political dependence on the U.S.S.R. The U.S. government's policy of cautiously building bridges to the eastern European nations through increased trade encouraged Rumanian hopes of establishing the basis for some businesslike, mutually profitable transactions.

A communiqué issued on June 1, 1964, after two weeks of negotiations, recommended that "further steps should be taken to carry forward the improvement in mutual relations" and reported that "the U.S. Government agreed to establish a general license procedure under which most commodities may be exported to Rumania without the necessity for individual export licenses. In addition the U.S. Government agreed to grant licenses for a number of particular industrial facilities in which the Rumanian delegation expressed special interest." [1] The United States was not prepared to extend long term credits to Rumania, but the President authorized the

[1] *Congressional Record,* 111 (July 26, 1965), 18227.

Export-Import Bank to issue guarantees of private short- and medium-term credit for financing the sale of American goods and services to Rumania.

The Rumanians particularly wanted to buy two synthetic rubber plants and were most pleased that the U.S. had agreed to issue the necessary export licenses. In 1960 Rumanian officials had indicated they were ready to spend more than $100 million on such a purchase, but the Defense Department had disapproved selling any advanced technology to Communist countries. By 1964, however, the processes and machinery for producing synthetic rubber were widely available in Europe. Recognizing this fact and the desirability of a more independent Rumania, defense officials agreed with officials in both the State and Commerce departments that the sale would be in the public interest.

The synthetic rubber plants were a significant, even vital, investment for Rumania. Petroleum is its major industrial resource, and since such plants use petrochemicals, they would help profitably exploit this resource and greatly strengthen the country's economic development. Rumanian officials wasted no time after the communiqué was issued. They immediately approached a number of American firms and arranged to send trade delegations to discuss the possible purchase of rubber plants and other manufacturing facilities.

A delegation visited the Goodyear plant at Beaumont, Texas, on June 9. Its members got a casual look at activities, but the Goodyear management did not permit them to observe the details of the processes involved in making polyisoprene rubber—a product that exactly duplicates natural rubber. The Rumanians asked for some samples of the synthetic; Goodyear agreed to supply it, and applied to the government for an export license.

II

The required export license was granted six months later, but Goodyear never used it. By that time the Rumanians had decided that they preferred a process used by Firestone; certain legal problems also made a sale of the Goodyear process almost impossible. For their part, Goodyear's managers were said to doubt that a synthetic rubber plant should be sold in any case. On October 1, Goodyear wrote Secretary of State Dean Rusk that "the company did not desire to build such a plant because the company did not believe such information should be sent behind the Iron Curtain because of its strategic value and because we felt the Communists could use the synthetic natural rubber to disrupt natural rubber prices, if they so desired." [2] The State Department replied that the Rumanians had assured the United States that they would not divulge any secret processes obtained here to other Communist nations. The Goodyear managers were not convinced.

Russell DeYoung, Goodyear's chairman of the board, later explained his and his colleagues' attitudes:

> Goodyear, like other companies in the rubber industry, was called upon by our government in World War II to help solve the rubber shortage which was threatening the success of our military effort; we have recently lost a rubber plant in Cuba to the Communists and plantations in Indonesia to a regime friendly to the Communists. For these reasons, we are perhaps more reluctant than some to turn over secret processes to a Communist nation.[3]

Goodyear did not make any public announcement of its decision not to sell the plant, since the matter was confidential and had not gone beyond discussions. Three weeks later, however, a Washington newsman reported Goodyear's refusal, apparently having learned of it from government sources. The story was printed in newspapers throughout the country and received attention from a number of public commentators. Walter H. Judd, former congressman from Minnesota, praised the

[2] *Wingfoot Clan,* August 5, 1965, p. 1.
[3] Letter to the author, August 10, 1965.

company's decision on his "Washington Report of the Air," broadcast over 700 radio stations. He declared that the proposed sale would not be in the best interests of the United States.

The New York *Daily News,* the newspaper with the country's largest daily circulation, commended Goodyear in an editorial condemning trade with any Communist nation.

> Meanwhile, there is one honorable exception—and there may well be many more that we haven't heard of—to the list of U.S. firms now yearning to do business with the Communists. The Goodyear Tire & Rubber Co. recently refused pointblank to sell a synthetic rubber plant to Red Rumania, despite a Commerce Department OK on such sales and the Administration's desire to cozy up to Rumania. Goodyear considers such deals unpatriotic and injurious to our side . . . [H]ow about fixing the patriotism of this company in your memory? [4]

On December 3, 1964, Goodyear published in its house organ, *Wingfoot Clan,* a lengthy explanation of why it had turned down the Rumanian sale that Firestone seemed about to make; it also noted the praise the company had received for its action. The *Wingfoot Clan* is distributed to all employees and is read throughout the industry. Under the headline, "An Order Goodyear Didn't Take," the article read:

> Even to a dedicated profit-making organization, some things are more important than dollars. Take the best interests of the United States and the Free World, for example. You can't put a price tag on freedom. And when you believe in something you may be called upon to back up your belief with action. That goes for a company such as Goodyear, just as it does an individual. Recently, Goodyear did just that—it stood firmly on the side of freedom, as a foe of aggression. Goodyear did this even though the company stood to lose financially . . . Goodyear elected not to seek the business—which could amount to some $50 million—even though the State Department had sanctioned such traffic with Rumania. This in itself was something of a paradox, as one newspaper writer observed: "In this case of East-West Trade, the positions of the government and a big corporation are the reverse of a traditional pattern. Usually, business is pictured as favoring such sales to bolster profits and the government as opposed on grounds of not bolstering a communist economy." . . . Goodyear feels that the dangers far outweigh the possible benefits in the proposed deal. For that reason Goodyear has no intention of being a party to it. . . .

[4] Quoted in *Wingfoot Clan,* December 3, 1964, p. 2.

After noting the praise and commendation the company had received, the article closed by noting that:

> [T]here is every indication that in addition to the warmth that this decision brings, Goodyear may benefit from a sales standpoint—a benefit that couldn't have been further from the company's mind when the decision was made not to sell to Rumania.

Even before Goodyear had decided to drop the sale, the Rumanians had begun negotiating with officials of Firestone for a plant using Firestone processes and techniques. By late November the final details of the $40 million to $50 million purchase of equipment and machinery were being discussed.

III

On January 5, 1965, a month after Goodyear's explanation of its position in the *Wingfoot Clan,* it was announced in Washington that Firestone and Rumania had signed a preliminary contract for a plant to produce polybutadiene rubber. The manufacturing processes were all public knowledge and involved no patented techniques or unpublished data. Final arrangements were expected to be completed by spring. A first important step towards regular trade between Rumania and the United States seemed to have been taken.

Several conservative journalists and commentators reported the Firestone-Rumanian agreement and attacked the company for entering it. The controversy soon came to the attention of John LaMothe, head of the Philadelphia County Chapter of Young Americans for Freedom. The YAF is an organization of political conservatives that in 1965 claimed a membership of about 25,000. Although Senator Fulbright had once referred to it as "an extremist political organization," in 1964 its National Advisory Board listed as members 4 U.S. Senators and 34 members of the House of Representatives, along with at least 5 other board members alleged to belong to the very conservative John Birch Society. LaMothe believed that a public boycott of Firestone products was in order, and he drew up plans for demonstrations in front of the company's offices and stores.

The Philadelphia County chapter began its demonstrations March 20 outside Firestone retail outlets. The pickets handed out flyers that said in part:

> In South Vietnam, Americans are being killed daily by Communist bullets. It would be disastrous for American companies to supply the atheistic Communist governments with valuable materials, especially rubber, which the Reds must have to wage their war on free nations. In the past month, Communist Rumania shipped 500 heavy-duty trucks of military value to Red China, the principal supplier of the North Vietnam Communists. The synthetic rubber plant which Firestone plans to build in Communist Rumania parallels the steel which the United States sold to Japan prior to World War II. Americans got that steel back—at Pearl Harbor. . . . Firestone's plan to build a synthetic rubber plant in Communist Rumania can only strengthen the Communists and throw away American jobs.

As in all their publicity, in this flyer the Philadelphia YAF also urged people sympathetic with its protest to write to the company in Akron, Ohio.

The next week, the YAF marched in picket lines in front of two Firestone offices in Philadelphia, and the county chapter announced that the demonstrations were "the start of a series of statewide and nationwide protest actions against Firestone." The pickets carried signs that parodied a Firestone slogan: "When Red wheels are rolling the name is known as Firestone." [5] A press release issued by the chapter on April 5 said in part:

> It is up to YAF members coast to coast to organize these protests and voice our dissent. Please join with us. Arrange for your chapter to picket local Firestone stores. Distribute handbills urging the public to write the Firestone Tire & Rubber Co. and local newspapers expressing their disapproval of this action. The actuation and continuation of these demonstrations by you is vital in this nationwide effort.

The YAF did conduct demonstrations elsewhere—in Los Angeles, in Cleveland, and in a few cities on the East Coast.

The press reported that Firestone's franchised dealers were alarmed at what was happening. They were losing business to Goodyear, and they wanted the head office to do something quickly to quiet the conservatives. The company officers sent their Eastern region public-relations representative to visit YAF leaders in various cities, but he accomplished little. YAF officers found him "a sincere individual who believed Firestone was acting in the national interests," but, as the executive director later said, "a $10 million check . . . couldn't get us to call [the demonstrations] off." [6]

Firestone perhaps took some comfort as word spread that some Rumanian trucks and tractors had been photographed in Red China with Goodyear tires on them. Good-

[5] The original Firestone slogan was, "Whenever wheels are rolling, no matter what the load, the name that's known is Firestone."

[6] Bernard Gwertzman, "United States Embarrassed: Facing Boycott, Drops Rumania Deal," Washington *Evening Star,* May 8, 1965, as reprinted in *Congressional Record,* 111 (July 26, 1965), 18228.

year's request to the Commerce Department for a license to sell synthetic rubber to Rumania was also widely discussed. Goodyear promptly answered these charges: if any of its tires were in China, they had not been knowingly sold to anyone there by the company. They might have been purchased through intermediaries, of course. Furthermore, while the company had considered selling some rubber to Rumania, only samples were involved, and the company had decided not to sell even these.

Firestone executives appealed to various congressmen and government officials to defend their sale to Rumania but received little aid. On March 13, 1964, Secretary of State Rusk told the Senate Committee on Foreign Relations that "the use of trade with Communist countries for national purposes is a matter for national decisions. The volunteer efforts of individuals or organizations to impose their private notions on our overall trade policy can only frustrate the effective use of this essential national instrument."[7] Yet, a year later a State Department spokesman treated the Rumanian-Firestone deal as solely a private matter. When questioned during a press and radio briefing about the negotiations, he suggested that either the Rumanian government or the Firestone company be addressed, for "it's a matter between the two."

Firestone soon decided not to go through with its proposed sale. The adverse publicity and boycott were already hurting the company's competitive position, and the climax of the YAF's demonstrations was still to come. For this, the YAF planned to have a light plane fly over the Indianapolis Speedway on Memorial Day, during the famous annual 500-mile race, carrying streamer signs denouncing Firestone. The company based much of its tire advertising on the race, and to have all of it tainted by adverse YAF publicity would represent too serious a loss to bear.

IV

Firestone executives conferred with officials of the Department of State on April 16 to advise them that the company intended to end the negotiations with the Rumanians. The President's press secretary told reporters later that Firestone found the "pressure was so strong and the economic losses would be so severe that implementation . . . would be unsound." Four days later the decision was announced publicly. Firestone's public-relations representative sent a note to Dave Jones, executive director of the YAF in Washington, telling him that the sale of the synthetic rubber plant would not be made and asking him to bring public attention to the termination of the deal.

Six weeks after Firestone announced the cessation of negotiations with the Rumanians, Goodyear sent reproductions of several articles from *Human Events,* a conservative magazine, and *New Guard,* a YAF publication, reporting its own experience and Firestone's troubles to its sales representatives in the field. The purpose of doing this, according to a statement in *Wingfoot Clan* was "to enable [salesmen] to answer queries from customers, Goodyear dealers and competitive dealers." Accompanying the articles was a letter from the marketing manager of the tire division suggesting that "surely every Goodyear salesman will proudly show [one of the articles] to commercial accounts, competitive dealers—especially Firestone and Goodyear dealers."

Senator Fulbright spoke to the Senate on July 26 about "Public and Private Responsibilities in the Conduct of Foreign Relations," condemning both the YAF and Goodyear for having pressured Firestone to refuse to sell the plant to Rumania. He found the actions

> very disturbing indeed and very mischievous —when private groups or businesses or in-

[7] Statement by J. William Fulbright, Chairman, Committee on Foreign Relations, United States Senate, *Public and Private Responsibility in the Conduct of Foreign Relations,* July 26, 1965, p. 1.

dividuals take it on themselves, by act or omission, to alter or dictate or defeat official policies of the United States Government. This amateur policy making—or policy breaking—can be accomplished by almost any group or organization endowed with the conviction that it knows more about some aspect of foreign policy than anybody else and with the will to intimidate officials or other organizations that are not very hard to intimidate. It has been done by business interests seeking a competitive advantage, by organized labor, and by those sterling patriots whose self-designated task it is to keep the rest of us in line, loyal and true to the red, white and blue. . . .

The effect of the rupture in the Rumanian-Firestone negotiations almost certainly will not be the denial to Rumania of the synthetic rubber plants that it seeks. Synthetic rubber technology and equipment are available to Rumania quite readily from western European sources, or, for that matter, from the Soviet Union, and the probable outcome of the whole affair will be that Rumania will get her synthetic rubber plants but not from the United States. Instead of a healthy profit of Firestone, a solid gain for our balance of payments, and a positive step forward in the building of bridges to the East, the United States will have earned a harvest of ill will and a reputation for being quite incapable of executing policies decided upon by the President and the Department of State.[8]

The next day the *Wall Street Journal* reported that Universal Oil Products Corporation of Des Plaines, Illinois, had concluded an agreement with the Rumanian government to become the prime contractor to build a $22.5 million petroleum refinery in the Ploesti oil field. The Continental Illinois Bank & Trust Company in Chicago said it was lending Rumania $16,242,000 over seven years at 6 per cent interest to help pay for the plant. The Export-Import Bank was ready to guarantee 72.25 per cent of the contract price plus loan interest, totaling about $20 million. The refinery was to be adjoining the new synthetic rubber plant and would supply raw materials for it.

M. D. Gilchrist, vice chairman of Universal Oil, the *Journal* reported, said that his company "isn't trying to set foreign policy but is adhering to the policy of the federal government, which in June called for increased trade between the U.S. and Rumania." [9]

[8] *Ibid.*, pp. 1 and 5–6.
[9] July 27, 1965.

QUESTIONS

The Private Right to Frustrate Public Policy

1. Compare the Seafarers' reasons for its picketing of the *Cleopatra* with Goodyear's reasons for its refusal to deal with Rumania. In what ways are they similar and different?

2. Senator Fulbright condemned both the Seafarers and Goodyear for interfering with the day-to-day conduct of foreign policy, maintaining that this is the sole responsibility of the President. Critically evaluate his argument, explaining what kinds of activities of unions and corporations that affect foreign policy you would allow.

3. If the Seafarers were forbidden to use the boycott in such situations as those related in the case, what alternative means would be available for them to use to protect their interests?

4. Did Goodyear act responsibly in showing the articles from the right-wing magazines to tire dealers? To whom does Goodyear owe any responsibility?

5. After analyzing the campaign against Firestone, what advice would you give to a company in a similar situation? Do you think Firestone might have answered

its critics more effectively than it did? What would you have recommended that it do?

6. How do you explain the lack of any trouble encountered by the Universal Oil Products Corporation when it agreed to build a petroleum refinery for Rumania?

7. Did the State Department meet its responsibilities toward American seamen and Firestone in these two cases? If your answer is no, what else should it have done? If your answer is yes, do you judge the Seafarers and Goodyear irresponsible? Why?

chapter **5**

WHEN IS GOVERNMENT CONCERN INTERFERENCE WITH BUSINESS?

Business and government leaders are ambivalent in their attitude toward the free competitive market and the role of government in regulating or modifying market forces. In the fall of 1962, after his encounter with the managers of the steel industry over steel prices, President Kennedy declared his faith in the free market:

> The free market is a decentralized regulator of our economic system. The free market is not only a more efficient decision maker than even the wisest central planning body, but, even more important, the free market keeps economic power widely dispersed.[1]

Yet the President not only had "helped" the market roll back the price increases made by the steel companies but had offered, in January, 1962, wage and price guideposts as supplementary regulators of the economic system.

In an article entitled "What Business Wants from Lyndon Johnson," the February, 1965, issue of *Fortune* catalogued the various benefits business leaders hoped the President would grant. The "host of items designed to benefit particular industries" included such requests as tighter curbs on crude-petroleum imports, encouragement of wheat and flour sales to Russia and China through loan guarantees, a sympathetic attitude toward railroad mergers, more liberal depreciation guidelines, and better communications between government and business. But when businessmen looked at such government programs, designed to help other groups, as "hot lunches in our schools, Medicare, aid-to-education, urban renewal, and the anti-poverty program," they tended to perceive "fundamental questions." After listing the above programs in a speech, George Champion, chairman of the board of the Chase Manhattan Bank, posed three such questions and gave his answer to them in the case of guidelines:

> Do the government's new activities interfere with the operation of the free market system? Do they invalidate price as an index of the demand for products and services and of the costs incurred in their production? Do they weaken the regulatory force of competition?
>
> These are the questions we as a nation have always asked in trying to determine

[1] Harold W. Chase and Allen H. Lerman, *Kennedy and the Press* (New York: Thomas Y. Crowell, 1965), p. 326.

> whether government activities went too far, whether they tended to create a planned economy, to regiment industry, and to imperil economic freedom. When we raise such questions today with respect to some of our guidelines—and more particularly with the guideline approach—the answers come back resoundingly in the affirmative. [They are] interference with the free-market system.[2]

Business in the United States has not always, if ever, expected or wanted the government to maintain a "hands-off" policy. After sounding the sentiment of the commercial and financial leaders of his day, Alexander Hamilton wrote in his 1791 *Report on Manufacturers* that "the expediency of encouraging manufacturers in the United States, which was not long since deemed very questionable, appears at this time to be pretty generally admitted." He recommended that the government help business by imposing duties on imports, providing subsidies, establishing quality standards, sponsoring a stable banking system, and building roads and canals. Until after the Civil War businessmen unabashedly accepted Hamiltonian promotionalism by the government as part of their political creed. They saw government as a welcome partner in the success of business.

As business firms grew larger after the Civil War, absorbing small local companies and extending their influence over whole industries, agitation began for government regulation of their activities. Business leaders responded by changing the rhetoric of their speeches, emphasizing individualism and laissez faire economics rather than manifest destiny and the national good; but it is doubtful that they also changed their practices. They still looked to the government, not just to grant them favors but to help them tame the wild competitive forces of the free market. The more perceptive among them recognized that even regulation could often be turned to advantage. Richard Olney, a director on the boards of several railroads and prospective Attorney General under President Cleveland, reassured a railroad president worried about the newly created Interstate Commerce Commission:

> The Commission, as its functions have now been limited by the courts, is, or can be made, of great use to the railroads. It satisfies the popular clamor for a government supervision of railroads, at the same time that supervision is almost entirely nominal. Further, the older such a Commissoin gets to be, the more inclined it will be found to take the business and railroad view of things. It thus becomes a sort of barrier between the railroad corporations and the people and a sort of protection against hasty and crude legislation hostile to railroad interests. . . . The part of wisdom is not to destroy the Commission but to utilize it.[3]

Professor John P. Roche characterizes—perhaps too harshly—the businessmen of the late nineteenth and early twentieth centuries as composing "an opportunistic elite living at the public trough, nourished by state protection, and devoting most of its time and energies to evading Adam Smith's individualistic injunction."[4] To a remarkable degree business was successful for many years in promoting a government strong enough to restrain labor unions severely but too weak to be able to impose minimum wages. The public accepted without much question the busi-

[2] "Government by Guidelines: A New Threat to Economic Freedom," *Tax Foundation's Tax Review,* 26 (June, 1965), 23.

[3] Matthew Josephson, *The Politicos, 1865–1896* (New York: Harcourt, Brace & World, 1938), p. 526.

[4] "Entrepreneurial Liberty and the Fourteenth Amendment," *Labor History,* 4 (Winter, 1963), p. 3.

nessman's theory of a self-regulatory economy, paying little attention to the inconsistency between this theory and the business community's opportunistic practices.

The Great Depression of the thirties destroyed the theory and made necessary a close examination and reformulation of the relationship of business and government. Clearly the public—including workers and consumers—as well as business needed protection from the ruthless insecurity of unstable free markets. The nation required a mixture of government and business enterprise to insure prosperity and economic growth. As the government took on added responsibilities for the economic welfare and security of its citizens, public officials became increasingly concerned with prices, wages, investment policies, methods of cost accounting, and the level of profits. More and more businessmen were called to account for their actions not by the market but by government officials. Businessmen had intended that the government should do no more than help their businesses and safeguard their interests. They found, however, that it holds them responsible for their decisions.

As government and business try to meet their responsibilities and maintain a viable system that balances the claims of economic freedom and economic control, they encounter problems and come into conflict. Their relationship is one of tension and fluctuation as men in positions of leadership seek to define and pursue their respective interests, public and private. Some of the problems they encounter and a few of the contradictions between "ideology" and practice that occur are revealed in the following cases.

Interference or Sales Promotion?

KENNEDY AND STEEL PRICING

In April, 1962, the managing officers of the United States Steel Corporation and the President of the United States clashed dramatically over the issue of a price increase in steel. Most, but not all, of the managers of other major steel companies supported U.S. Steel's stand; backing the President were his chief advisors and aides in the Administration, the chairmen of various interested regulatory agencies, and a number of senators and representatives of both parties. The clash was not unique but simply the most recent of a number of encounters between public officials and the leaders of one of the nation's largest and most basic industries.

I

The first encounter between the steel industry and the government occurred before World War I, when the Taft Administration brought suit against U.S. Steel; the courts were asked to dissolve the giant concern, which was charged with antitrust violations under the Sherman Act. (At the time of its formation U.S. Steel had controlled approximately 65 per cent of the country's steel capacity.) Although the Supreme Court refused in 1920 to dissolve the company, in its opinion it conceded that U.S. Steel was guilty of an attempt—albeit unsuccessful—to monopolize the industry. The Court was much impressed with the attitude of U.S. Steel toward its competitors, summed up in Elbert Gary's term "friendly competition." Though U.S. Steel's share of industry sales declined in the succeeding years, the corporation remained big enough to keep its competitors "in line."

The depression of the 1930's was a disaster for the steel industry. From 1929–33 production declined by nearly 60 per cent, and employment fell by nearly 52 per cent. Of the 213,000 men working in 1933, 80 per cent were employed only part-time. In 1932, plants were operating at not quite 20 per cent of capacity. Under such conditions the stable structure of pricing began to break down as firms tried to sell enough steel to make some return on overhead and to increase plant utilization. Uncontrolled pricing seemed imminent when the National Industrial Recovery Act of 1934 was enacted. The Act permitted industry leaders to establish codes of fair competition with the approval of the President. For the first time in history the steel leaders could fix prices and be safe from antitrust regulations. Initially, they were enthusiastic over the government-sanctioned price fixing arrangement; for example, Charles M. Schwab, former president of the Bethlehem Steel Corporation, said that never before in his 50 years of experience had he seen a year "when the business could be conducted on a commonsense basis." After the Supreme Court declared the NIRA unconstitutional, the steel industry fell back upon its basing point system and price leadership tradition,[1] now bolstered by the government's encouragement to regulate the steel market.

During World War II, the prices of steel were a matter for government concern and were carefully regulated by the Office of Price Administration (OPA). Along with the price regulation was an intricate supply and allocation system. Rationing was abandoned by the government in 1946, but it was continued informally because the demand for steel was much greater than the industry's capacity could possibly meet. Industry leaders, the public, and the government insisted that prices be kept down. The large steel producers had decided to use their judgment in the allocation of steel rather than that of the market, necessitating the establishment of a kind of "private" OPA to ration steel among its many consumers. The government granted the industry temporary exemption from the antitrust laws in order to permit the various producers to cooperate in the new nonmarket allocation system. By 1948 a "gray" market in steel had clearly developed and was estimated to involve sales running to half a billion dollars annually;[2] the cause was the low price of steel. In 1950, after the beginning of the Korean war, many of the old price and allocation controls were again imposed on the industry.

The government had participated in the price and wage decisions of the steel industry during World War II and was willingly or reluctantly involved in the negotiations of almost every major labor agreement with the steel workers during the post-war period. In 1945–46, a strike was averted only when President Truman suggested that the companies grant a wage increase of 18.5¢ an hour coupled with a price increase of $5 a ton. The companies had previously offered 12.5¢ an hour with an understanding that the government might allow something more than $4 a ton increase in price. In 1949 the union called for a reopening of the agreement to negotiate wage changes and pension benefits. The companies rejected the union's requests, and negotiations became deadlocked. With the threat of a strike looming, President Truman appointed a fact-finding board to report on the issues and make a recommendation for settlement. The companies protested the appointment, strongly urging use of the Taft-Hartley pro-

[1] A *basing point system* of pricing allows firms, wherever located, to sell their product at a price equal to the price of the product sold at the "basing point" city plus transportation charges from the basing point to the customer. Thus, when Pittsburgh was the steel industry's basing point, a plant at Cleveland would sell steel to a Cleveland customer at the same price charged that customer by a Pittsburgh plant. *Price leadership* is the situation where all or most firms in an industry follow the lead of a single firm in setting prices.

[2] "That Daffy Gray Market," *Fortune,* 37 (May, 1948), 95.

cedures. As spokesman for the industry, Clarence B. Randall, president of the Inland Steel Company, declared:

> [The President] has proclaimed that wages shall be fixed by the government. This step is always the first one taken by those who set out to establish a socialist or corporate state. The fixing of profits comes next, and then when incentive is killed and production fails, the final step of nationalization follows. . . . I repeat—this [fact-finding board] is the repeal of collective bargaining—this is government wage-fixing, the inevitable consequence of labor monopoly.[3]

The Presidential board did not recommend a wage increase but did suggest the institution of a pension and insurance plan. The negotiators still could not agree and the strike, which began October 1, continued for a month. The final settlement was not dissimilar to that recommended by the board.

In 1952, with the steel industry under the wage and price controls of the Korean war, the most serious wage dispute up to that date arose. The Wage Stabilization Board considered the requests of the union and the counter-demands of the companies; it recommended a package of a 12.5¢ hourly wage increase plus added fringe benefits of 5.1¢ an hour. When the companies refused to accept the recommendations and a strike was imminent, President Truman seized the steel mills of the nation on April 8. Army officers occupied the offices at the mills and temporarily became directing operators of the properties. On April 23 the Office of Price Stabilization authorized a $3 price increase for steel, but no wage settlement ensued. On June 2 the Supreme Court ruled that the President did not have the power to seize the industry, and the long-delayed strike began immediately. Around the first of July, John Steelman, a special assistant to the President and acting Director of Defense Mobilization, offered a price increase of $4.50 a ton; on July 24, he increased the offer to $5.20. Once the latter price increase had been approved, a settlement came quickly, and the 55-day strike was ended. The union gained a 16¢-an-hour wage increase and a number of other benefits whose exact cost is difficult to measure.

In 1954 the steel union and management agreed to a wage package of 10¢–12¢ an hour, and the companies raised prices from $3–$4 a ton. The following year the two parties agreed to a 15¢-an-hour wage increase, and the companies raised prices by $7.50 a ton, with U.S. Steel setting the pattern followed by the other firms. In 1956 negotiations came to a stalemate and a 27-day strike followed. The strike was embarrassing in an election year and Administration leaders, particularly Secretary of Labor James Mitchell and Secretary of the Treasury George M. Humphrey, pressured the companies to get the idle mills open. The final settlement was a handsome one, the union gaining 45.6¢ over a three-year period. On August 6 U.S. Steel published a new schedule of prices that showed an average increase of $8.50 per ton, and the other companies promptly followed suit.

In 1959 the United Steel Workers and the steel industry became involved in a steel strike of record length, a 116-day walkout that ended only because of a government injunction. The dispute itself was finally settled only because of government intervention. The companies had offered a wage increase of about 10¢ an hour, a figure that was widely believed to be one the union could and would accept. Unemployment was high in steel towns, and the workers showed little inclination to strike. Management, however, turned its attention from wages to work rules and, on this issue, the workers and the union were united and determined not to yield. Secretary of Labor Mitchell issued a detailed statistical report on the economics of prices, wages, and productivity in the steel industry. He pointed out that between 1940 and the fiscal year 1959, basic steel prices increased 178 per

[3] Benjamin M. Selekman, Sylvia K. Selekman, and Stephen H. Fuller, *Problems in Labor Relations,* 2nd ed. (New York: McGraw-Hill, 1958), pp. 474–75.

cent while employment cost per ton (including wages and fringe benefits) for wage employees rose 131 per cent, and employment costs for all employees rose 153 per cent. He concluded, "The increase in average prices of steel products since 1940 has exceeded the rise in employment cost per ton of steel produced. This is true whether employment cost for wage employees alone is considered, or whether employment cost of all employees is taken into account." He and Vice President Nixon finally succeeded in getting the industry leaders and union negotiators to agree to a settlement. It was almost exactly what had been offered earlier in June by the companies, except that the work rules issues were partly deferred and partly assigned to negotiations by local groups at the various mills. When, after a night-long session, the agreement was reached Secretary Mitchell said: "It is my belief the steel companies will not need to increase prices immediately." And in fact steel prices were not increased until April, 1962.

In 1962 the government, labor, and the steel companies were again involved in working out a new agreement. In the fall of 1961 the President had publicly and privately asked the 12 largest steel companies to hold the line on prices when wages went up as called for by the existing contract. Coupled with the request was an implicit promise that, if prices held, the Administration would help hold the line against excessive wage demands in the spring. On February 6, Secretary of Labor Arthur J. Goldberg, acting on behalf of President Kennedy, urged the steel companies and the United Steel Workers to start negotiations as soon as possible in order to have a new contract by July 1. He emphasized the importance of a non-inflationary steel contract to vigorous economic recovery; continued recovery also required that there be no disruption of the industry by a strike. A little more than a week later management and USW officials began bargaining, the first time in the USW's nearly 26-year history that talks had begun at such an early date. Before the end of the month the talks collapsed. President Kennedy let it be known he wanted negotiations to begin again before May 1, a date suggested by the union.

In the middle of March the parties resumed their talks and by the end of the month had reached an agreement. The steel workers were to receive an average increase of 10¢ an hour later in the year but no immediate wage increase was included. An industry statement said that the new benefits would increase employment costs by about 2.5 per cent during the first year compared with an average annual increase of from 3.5 per cent to 3.75 per cent under the 1960 contract, and with 8 per cent a year in the period between 1940 and 1960. Conrad Cooper, chief industry negotiator, said that the settlement cost did not fall wholly "within the limits of anticipated gains of productive efficiency." He added that the accord represented real progress in the development of voluntary collective bargaining in the steel industry. According to the *Wall Street Journal,* some steel leaders believed that the settlement was non-inflationary. David McDonald, president of the USW, termed the settlement non-inflationary but would not put a price tag on it. "I am interested in benefits, not costs," he said. President Kennedy praised the settlement, saying that "it demonstrates that the national interest can be protected and the interests of the industry and of the employees forwarded through free and responsible collective bargaining." [4]

The formal contract between U.S. Steel and the USW was signed on April 6, nearly three months before the expiration of the old agreement. Such an early settlement was unprecedented in steel and rarely seen in any labor negotiations in the United States. A new development in industrial relations appeared to be emerging—the peaceful settlement of labor arrangements without the

[4] March 30, 1962.

threat and anxiety and pressure of a strike. At the government's insistence, a major industry and union seemed to have arrived at the same conclusion as Professor Clark Kerr, who had observed:

> [Collective] bargaining has a constantly deeper impact on society at large. It is no longer a side show, but is, instead, inextricably bound up with the effectiveness of the total economy. . . . Traditionally, collective bargaining has been concerned with the setting of wages, hours and conditions of work, usually on an annual basis. Increasingly, it is concerned with the progress of the industry and thus the economy in general.[5]

II

The cordial atmosphere that prevailed at the time of the new wage settlement was soon to be dissipated. On April 10, 1962, the executive committee of U.S. Steel decided to raise the price of steel by about $6 a ton from the current average price of $170. As soon as the decision was made, Roger M. Blough, chairman of the board, took a plane to Washington to notify the President, "as a matter of courtesy." Mr. Blough evidently felt the President would be interested since he had been calling for non-inflationary wage and price policies from all industry and labor. The President had argued that any development that set off a new wage-price spiral would stunt economic growth, keep unemployment high, cut into export sales, weaken the dollar, and further aggravate the outflow of gold.

In the meantime Leslie B. Worthington, president of U.S. Steel, announced the price increase in the following public statement:

> Since our last over-all adjustment in the summer of 1958, the level of steel prices has not been increased but, if anything, has declined somewhat. This situation, in the face of steadily mounting production costs which have included four increases in steelworker wages and benefits prior to the end of last year, has been due to the competitive pressures from domestic producers and from imports of foreign-made steel as well as from other materials which are used as substitutes for steel.
>
> The severity of these competitive pressures has not diminished; and to their influence may be attributed the fact that the partial catch-up adjustment announced today is substantially less than the cost increases which have already occurred since 1958, without taking into consideration the additional costs which will result from the new labor agreements which become effective next July 1.
>
> Nevertheless, taking into account all the competitive factors affecting the market for steel, we have reluctantly concluded that a modest price adjustment can no longer be avoided in the light of the production cost increases that have made it necessary.
>
> If the products of United States Steel are to compete successfully in the marketplace, then the plants and facilities which make those products must be as modern and efficient as the low-cost mills which abound abroad and as the plants which turn out competing products here at home. Only by generating the funds necessary to keep these facilities fully competitive can our company continue to provide its customers with a dependable source of steel, and to provide its employees with dependable jobs. But the profits of the company—squeezed as they have been between rising costs and declining prices—are inadequate today to perform this vital function.
>
> Our annual report, published last month, shows clearly the effect of this squeeze.
>
> In the three years since the end of 1958, United States Steel has spent $1,185,000,000 for modernization and replacement of facilities and for the development of new sources of raw materials. Internally, there were only two sources from which this money could come: depreciation and reinvested profit. Depreciation in these years amounted to $610,000,000; and reinvested profit, $187,000,000—or, together, only about two-thirds of the total sum required. So after using all the income available from operations, we had to make up the difference of $388,000,000 out of borrowings from the public. In fact, during the period 1958–61, we have actually borrowed a total of $800,000,000 to provide

[5] *New York Times,* April 18, 1962.

for present and future needs. And this must be repaid out of profits that have not yet been earned, and will not be earned for some years to come.

During these three years, moreover, United States Steel's profits have dropped to the lowest levels since 1952; while reinvested profit—which is all the profit there is to be plowed back in the business after payment of dividends—has declined from $115,000,000 in 1958 to less than $3,000,000 last year. Yet the dividend rate has not been increased in more than five years, although there have been seven general increases in employment costs during this interval.

This squeeze, which has thus dried up a major source of the funds necessary to improve the competitive efficiency of our plants and facilities, has resulted inevitably from the continual rise in costs over a period of almost four years, with no offsetting improvement in prices.

Since the last general price adjustment in 1958, there have been a number of increases in the cost of products and services purchased by the corporation, in state and local taxes, and in other expenses, including interest on the money we have had to borrow—an item which has jumped from $11,500,000 to nearly $30,000,000 in 1961.

And from 1958 through 1961, there have been industry-wide increases in steelworker wages and benefits on four occasions amounting to about 40 cents an hour, and also increases in employment costs for other employees. These persistent increases have added several hundred million dollars to the employment costs of United States Steel, without regard to future costs resulting from the new labor agreement just negotiated.

In all, we have experienced a net increase of about 6 per cent in our costs over this period despite cost reductions which have been effected through the use of new, more efficient facilities, improved techniques and better raw materials. Compared with this net increase of 6 per cent, the price increase of 3.5 per cent announced today clearly falls considerably short of the amount needed to restore even the cost-price relationship in the low production of 1958.

In reaching this conclusion, we have given full consideration, of course, to the fact that any price increase which comes, as this does, at a time when foreign-made steels are already underselling ours in a number of product lines, will add—temporarily, at least—to the competitive difficulties which we are now experiencing. But the present price level cannot be maintained any longer when our problems are viewed in a long-range perspective. For the long pull a strong, profitable company is the only insurance that formidable competition can be met and that the necessary lower costs to meet that competition will be assured.

Only with profits can a company improve its competitive potential through better equipment and through expanded research. In this latter phase we are constantly developing lighter, stronger steels which—ton for ton—will do more work and go much farther than the steels that were previously available on the market. They thus give the customer considerably more value per dollar of cost. As more and more of these new steels come from our laboratories, therefore, our ability to compete should steadily improve. But the development of new steels can only be supported by profits or the hope of profits.

The financial resources supporting continuous research and resultant new products, as well as those supporting new equipment, are therefore vital in this competitive situation—vital not alone to the company and its employees, but to our international balance of payments, the value of our dollar, and to the strength and security of the nation as well.[6]

The same day, April 10, Edmund F. Martin, president of the Bethlehem Steel Corporation, told a stockholders' annual meeting that "competition in the industry probably would prevent any general increase in steel prices because of the new labor contract. We should be trying to hold the line on prices. . . . We should be trying to reduce the price of steel, if at all possible, because we have more competition, particularly from foreign sources." He declined to say outright whether the cost of steel would go up after July 1, when the new two-year agreement with the USW

[6] *New York Times,* April 11, 1962.

was to go into effect. The next day, however, Bethlehem Steel announced a price increase that matched U.S. Steel's. Republic, Jones & Laughlin, Youngstown, and Wheeling also followed. Kaiser Steel, Inland Steel, and Colorado Fuel and Iron reported only that they were studying the situation.

III

President Kennedy made clear his feelings about the price increase in his opening statement at a press conference the afternoon of April 11:

> The simultaneous and identical actions of United States Steel and other leading steel corporations increasing steel prices by some $6 a ton constitute a wholly unjustifiable and irresponsible defiance of the public interest.
>
> In this serious hour in our nation's history when we are confronted with grave crises in Berlin and Southeast Asia, when we are devoting our energies to economic recovery and stability, when we are asking Reservists to leave their homes and families months on end and servicemen to risk their lives—and four were killed in the last two days in Vietnam—and asking union members to hold down their wage requests, at a time when restraint and sacrifice are being asked of every citizen, the American people will find it hard, as I do, to accept a situation in which a tiny handful of steel executives whose pursuit of private power and profit exceeds their sense of public responsibility can show such utter contempt for the interests of 185 million Americans.
>
> If this rise in the cost of steel is imitated by the rest of the industry, instead of rescinded, it would increase the cost of items for every American family. It would increase the cost of homes, autos, appliances and most other items for every American family. It would increase the cost of machinery and tools to every American businessman and farmer. It would seriously handicap our efforts to prevent an inflationary spiral from eating up the pensions of our older citizens and our new gains in purchasing power. It would add, Secretary McNamara informed me this morning, an estimated $1 billion to the cost of our defenses at a time when every dollar is needed for national security and other purposes. It will make it more difficult for American goods to compete in foreign markets, more difficult to withstand competition from foreign imports and thus more difficult to improve our balance-of-payments position and stem the flow of gold. And it is necessary to stem it for our national security, if we're going to pay for our security commitments abroad.
>
> And it would surely handicap our efforts to induce other industries and unions to adopt responsible price and wage policies.
>
> The facts of the matter are that there is no justification for an increase in steel prices. The recent settlement between the industry and the union, which does not even take place until July 1, was widely acknowledged to be non-inflationary, and the whole purpose and effect of this Administration's role, which both parties understood, was to achieve an agreement which would make unnecessary any increases in prices. Steel output per man is rising so fast that labor costs per ton of steel can actually be expected to decline in the next 12 months. And, in fact, the Acting Commissioner of the Bureau of Labor Statistics informed me this morning that, and I quote: "Employment costs per unit of steel output in 1961 were essentially the same as they were in 1958."
>
> The cost of major raw materials—steel scrap and coal—has also been declining. And for an industry which has been generally operating at less than two-thirds of capacity, its profit rate has been normal and can be expected to rise sharply this year in view of the reduction in idle capacity. Their lot has been easier than that of 100,000 steelworkers thrown out of work in the last three years. The industry's cash dividends have exceeded $600 million in each of the last five years, and earnings in the first quarter of this year were estimated in the February 28 *Wall Street Journal* to be among the highest in history.
>
> In short, at a time when they could be exploring how more efficiency and better prices could be obtained, reducing prices in this industry in recognition of lower costs, their unusually good labor contract, their foreign competition and their increase in production and profits which are coming this year, a few gigantic corporations have

decided to increase prices in ruthless disregard of their public responsibilities.

The Steelworkers Union can be proud that it abided by its responsibilities in this agreement. And this Government also has responsibilities which we intend to meet. The Department of Justice and the Federal Trade Commission are examining the significance of this action in a free, competitive economy. The Department of Defense and other agencies are reviewing its impact on their policies of procurement. And I am informed that steps are under way by those members of the Congress who plan appropriate inquiries into how these price decisions are so quickly made and reached and what legislative safeguards may be needed to protect the public interest.

Price and wage decisions in this country, except for very limited restrictions in the case of monopolies and national emergency strikes, are and ought to be freely and privately made. But the American people have a right to expect, in return for that freedom, a higher sense of business responsibility for the welfare of their country than has been shown in the last two days.

Some time ago I asked each American to consider what he would do for his country and I asked the steel companies. In the last 24 hours we had their answer.

The *Wall Street Journal* reported that "the timing [of the price increase] puzzles a good many steel users. Not only did the increase come precisely when it was likely to produce the maximum political anger, but it came when steelworkers and production had begun to drop as users started to work off inventories they had built as a strike hedge. Previously, steel men had said their price decisions would depend on 'market conditions.' " The across-the-board increase surprised some steel sales executives, for it raised the price of such products as pipe and wire for which demand had been weak. One steel company sales vice president told a *Journal* reporter, however, that his concern would rather sell a smaller volume at a "reasonable profit" than a larger volume "at a loss or near-loss." [7]

[7] April 12, 1962.

The *Journal* report continued:

Dr. Roy L. Reierson, economist and senior vice president of New York's Bankers Trust Co. calls the move "unfortunate" because of its likely effect on the nation's balance-of-payments problem. . . . [He] fear[s] the increase will cut into exports of steel and steel-containing items, encourage low-priced imports of these items and so increase the margin by which total U.S. payments to foreigners exceed income received from foreign sources. . . .

Though steel prices had been held steady for years before the current boost, they had earlier been going up much more rapidly than other industrial prices. Before the current increase, steel prices had climbed about 50 per cent since 1950, while the average of all wholesale industrial prices had risen about 22 per cent. During the same period the average weekly wage of a steel production worker has soared from about $68 to about $130 now—a rise of about 90 per cent—while average wages of all U.S. production workers rose 65 per cent to about $95 now from around $58 in 1950. The swift rise in steel prices in the mid-50's prompted many steel users to turn to foreign steel. Users uniformly indicate this [switch to] substitute materials and later to low priced process is likely to accelerate sharply with the current increase.

In Washington, Representative Emanuel Celler of New York scheduled a broad investigation of the steel industry by his House Antitrust Subcommittee, and Tennessee's Senator Estes Kefauver called for a Senate investigation. Administration officials in the departments of Commerce and Labor and the Treasury talked with managers of the Inland Steel Company and other businessmen throughout the country, explaining the adverse effects the price increase was going to have on our balance of payments. Officials also met with the managers of the Armco and Kaiser steel corporations. The chairman of the Federal Trade Commission announced that his agency had begun informal investigations of the steel companies to see if they had violated a certain consent decree of June, 1951; other government agencies and offices also announced investigations of various and somewhat vague kinds. Administration officials also met with officers of U.S. Steel and strongly expressed their view that the price increase should be rescinded. Representative William W. Scranton of Pennsylvania, a Republican candidate for governor of his state, wired U.S. Steel's Roger Blough that "The increase at this time is wrong—wrong for Pennsylvania, wrong for America, wrong for the free world. The increase will set off another round of inflation. It will hurt people most who can least afford to be hurt."

On April 13, Inland Steel announced that it would not raise its prices, and the Secretary of Defense ordered defense contractors to shift their steel purchases to companies that had not raised prices. A contract for more than $5 million of special armor plate for missile-launching submarines went to Lukens Steel Company, rather than being divided with one of the companies that had raised prices. Bethlehem Steel then announced that it was rescinding its price increase, and U.S. Steel rolled back its prices shortly thereafter.

IV

Senator Barry Goldwater of Arizona accused the Kennedy Administration of attempting to "socialize the business of this country. . . . When we have a President who takes it upon himself to set prices in this country, then I suggest that every man, woman and child knows what we are up against. We need no longer hold back and be careful about what we say about our opposition." In two separate editorials the *Wall Street Journal* discussed the rollback of steel prices:

> What was really at issue here, and still is, is whether the price of steel is to be determined by the constant bargaining in the market place between the makers and buyers of steel; you may be sure that if the makers guessed wrong the market would promptly change their decision. Or whether the price of steel is to be decided and then enforced by the Government. In short, the issue is whether we have a free market system or whether we do not. That, and nothing more.[8]

> Let us first of all be clear about just what the Government did. It said that a private company could not change the price of its product, a property right which is obviously basic to a free economy. In other words, the Government set the price. And it did this by the pressure of fear—by naked power, by vituperation, by threats, by agents of the State security policy. . . . Whatever the majority of contemporary Americans may feel, the fact is that their forefathers understood the connection between economic freedom and political liberty. Property rights, in their view, were basic, as basic as life itself. There is nothing abstract or academic about that proposition; it means purely and simply that free acquisition and disposal of property is the mark of a free man. All history shows that economic freedom is essential to the maintenance of free political institutions.[9]

[8] April 16, 1962.
[9] April 18, 1962.

THE FAIR-TRADE CONTROVERSY

Fair-trade laws are meant to prevent retailers from competing in the prices charged for brand-name goods and usually allow a company that makes or distributes a brand-name product to set a minimum price below which the retailer may not sell. Manufacturers espouse fair-trade arrangements partly because they keep price competition within bounds, helping to maintain a product's profitability by forbidding price cutting. Manufacturers also argue that the laws help maintain sales outlets and thus sales volume. Should profit margins on products be cut or eliminated through competitive pricing, retailers might drop the product or the whole product line and shift to another.

The advocates of fair-trade laws have been remarkably successful at the state level in getting legislative approval for fair-trade practices, but on the federal level they have suffered defeat after defeat. In 1952 Congress did pass the McGuire Act permitting the use of interstate contracts to fix resale prices within states that allow intrastate price-fixing contracts. The Act extended the reach of the Miller-Tydings Resale Price Maintenance Act of 1937, which affirmed the right of the states to enact state fair-trade laws. With the exception of the McGuire Act, however, fair-trade proponents made little headway in Washington until 1961. In that year a new wave of enthusiasm developed for a federal fair-trade law.

I

Prior to 1930 both federal and state courts consistently condemned schemes to maintain retail prices as a violation of both the Sherman Antitrust Act and the Federal Trade Commission Act. However, two methods of preventing price cutting were judged legal. First, manufacturers could refuse to sell to price cutters; under Section II of the Clayton Act a firm could select its customers if it did not do so in restraint of trade. Second, producers were permitted to fix the prices at which their *agents* sold the products.

The National Association of Retail Druggists has lobbied long and aggressively for state fair-trade laws. In 1931 it was successful in persuading California to enact the first of these laws. In practice the law proved to be ineffective, since retailers who did not sign contracts to abide by the manufacturer's or the distributor's price could continue to fix or to cut prices as they saw fit. The legislature amended the law in 1933, making illegal "willfully and knowingly advertising, offering for sale, or selling any commodity at less than the price stipulated in any contract entered in pursuant to . . . the Act, whether the person so advertising, offering for sale or selling is or is not a party to such a contract, is unfair competition and is actionable at the suit of any person damaged thereby."[1] Other states soon followed California's lead, and the Supreme Court upheld the state acts in 1936. By 1941 only the states of Missouri, Texas, and Vermont, and the District of Columbia were not covered by their own fair-trade laws.

In 1961 fair-trade advocates made a determined effort to secure federal approval of their arrangements. The timing of the new campaign reflected the spectacular growth of discount houses and the expansion of chainstore operations across the nation. Between 1950 and 1960, the number of discount houses rose from 2,000 to 14,000; it was estimated that by 1970 discount houses might account for 80 per cent of the retail business.[2] Their competition contributed to the disappearance of many independent retailers and drugstores and brought a heightened sense of insecurity to others that managed to stay in business. Victor LeBow, a New York City marketing consultant, reported that according to a survey based on the years 1947–54 a new retail business had only a 74 per cent chance of surviving the first six months, and a 50 per cent chance of staying open the first 2.5 years.[3] Dun and Bradstreet reports indicated that retail business failures had been rising for more than a decade. In 1960 they totaled 15,455; the rate of failure for that year came to 57 per 10,000, com-

[1] Clair Wilcox, *Public Policies Toward Business* (Homewood, Ill.: Richard D. Irwin, 1960), p. 379.

[2] *Wall Street Journal,* July 24, 1961.

[3] Quoted by Senator Proxmire in *Hearings* on S. 1722, Committee on Commerce, U.S. Senate, 87th Cong., 1st Sess. (Washington: Government Printing Office, 1961), p. 10.

pared to 42 per 10,000 in 1955 and 34 per 10,000 in 1950.[4]

Alert to these new developments, Senators Hubert Humphrey and William Proxmire introduced a "quality stabilization" bill in the Senate, and Representative Oren Harris introduced the bill in the House. Under the proposals, a retailer who sold a nationally branded item at a price lower than that set by the manufacturer would commit a federal offense; the intent of the bill was to protect small retailers from much price competition. Hearings on the new bill were soon begun before the Senate Commerce Committee.

II

The proponents of fair-trade laws had long argued that a federal act would strengthen the American system of free competition and serve the public interest. In 1951 Senator Humphrey (the son of a drugstore operator) had maintained that fair-trade legislation helps to protect and insure fair competition:

> I want to see the businessmen competing in the market place on the basis of skills, efficiency, ingenuity, hard work and service—but not on dollar power alone. And I might say that fair trade is not the only law on our statute books that limits unbridled unfair competition. Take a look at the antitrust laws, the Robinson-Patman Act, the Federal Trade Commission Act and many others. They definitely, like fair-trade laws, curb certain types of unfair competition in order to promote fair competition, and thus prevent the growth of monopoly power. . . .
>
> Fair trade is to the small businessman what minimum wages and fair labor standards are to labor, and what price parity is to the farmer. Fair trade is a process which is designed to provide minimum compensation to the distributor for the handling of the products of labor and the farmer who by law are assured minimum wages and costs of production. It is a process which seeks to afford equal opportunities for one to engage in the field of distribution without being subjected to the onslaught of sly and deceptive practices of a few giant resale price manipulators in the field. . . .
>
> Our free enterprise system cannot long endure if economic power is concentrated in relatively few hands. We must have large numbers of businesses, and we must make it possible for men to have a fair chance of success in business enterprise, if we are to avoid the statism about which there is much fear. Accordingly, the restoration of effective fair trade, as a bulwark for the preservation of our competitive small business economy, should have the support of every American citizen who believes in free enterprise.[5]

Speaking on the same subject before the Senate Commerce Committee in 1961, Senator Proxmire emphasized the need for fair-trade legislation in the public interest. It would, he claimed, reduce the cutthroat competition of discount houses, which causes a decline in the number of neighborhood stores and specialist stores and an increase in the size of retailing units as large producers integrate and squeeze out small manufacturers who try to compete directly at the retail level. The result, according to the Senator, was a serious loss to consumers, the disappearance of convenient neighborhood stores. He was of the opinion that average prices would decline slightly should fair trade be instituted. In support of his argument, he referred to the research of H. F. Ostland and C. R. Vickland,[6] who compared the retail prices of 50 well-known brand products sold in drugstores in 48 states for the period March–September, 1939, when retail prices were effectively maintained, with prices immediately before price maintenance had been instituted. They found an average drop of 0.9 per cent in the retail prices of those brands after fair

[4] Dun & Bradstreet, *The Failure Record Through 1960* (New York: Dun & Bradstreet, 1961), p. 3.

[5] *Congressional Record,* 98 (June 12, 1952), A3668.

[6] H. F. Ostland and C. R. Vickland, *Fair Trade and the Retail Drugstore* (Chicago: Druggists Research Bureau, 1940).

TABLE 1 Increase in Wholesale Prices (Percentages) January 1, 1959, over January 1, 1947

	FAIR TRADE	NON-FAIR TRADE	TOTAL
Pharmaceuticals	—	40.2	40.2
Proprietaries	21.3	27.4	25.6
Toiletries	19.8	42.3	31.0
Sundries	38.6	62.6	56.6
Total	24.8	41.2	36.5

SOURCE: Quoted in *Hearings,* p. 36.

trade became effective. Chainstores tended to raise their prices, but other stores reduced theirs.

Maurice Mermey, director of the Bureau of Education on Fair Trade in New York, supported Senator Proxmire's arguments. He presented data to prove the price benefit enjoyed by consumers in fair-trade states. Among his sources were the 1953 and 1960 McKesson studies.[7] The first examined prices from 1947 to 1952, and the second from 1952 to 1959. Both covered the same 201 drugstore products representative of the four categories that make up 80 per cent of the items most frequently sold in drugstores.

Mr. Mermey replied to some of the charges made by opponents of fair-trade laws:

> It has been said that fair trade breeds monopoly. It's quite a trick to develop a monopoly consisting of nearly 2 million business units—all small retailers.
>
> It has been said that fair trade prevents the efficient retailer from passing savings on to his customers. In fact, any retailer can share the benefits of his efficiency with his customers to his heart's content. First of all, he never has been under any obligation to deal in fair-traded goods. Second, even if he does he can sell them at any price he pleases provided he removes the trademarks or brand names which identify them. Further, fair-traded goods never accounted for more than 10 per cent of the retailer's stock. He has been, therefore, perfectly free to price cut the other 90 per cent as much as he pleased.
>
> It has been said that fair trade stifles competition. This is an extraordinary assertion in view of the unparalleled increase in the scope and intensity of competition during the very period of fair trade's existence.[8]

Many manufacturers favored the fair-trade bill. A spokesman for the Corning Glass Works of New York testified:

> The current situation is not caused by a new kind of efficient competition, because low overhead and cut-price retailing is not new. What is new is that so-called discounters have asserted a right to appropriate a well-known brand name regardless of the wishes of the manufacturer who created it, and to pick two or three of the best known and fastest selling items, which they advertise that they can sell, because of their efficiency, at 25 to 50 per cent below the prices charged by the old, poor, inefficient neighborhood store. They accept no responsibility for the service in terms of assortment, and will cheerfully abandon the line when it has served their publicity purposes.[9]

Michael Daroff of Botany Industries, president of one of the largest manufacturers of men's suits, bitterly told a Senate Com-

[7] McKesson and Robbins, Inc., *Study of Price Changes on 201 Fair-Traded and Non-Fair-Traded Drug Store Products* (New York: Bureau of Education on Fair Trade, 1953 and 1960).

[8] *Hearings,* p. 48.

[9] *Ibid.,* p. 138.

mittee of a Philadelphia discount house that had advertised "Botany 500" suits at $1.00 over the wholesale price. Botany had not sold this store any suits and so sent a man to check up. "People came in," Daroff reported, "and wanted to buy one of our suits. In fact, they had a big crowd in the store to try to buy the suits, but they couldn't fit them because they had either small sizes or some big sizes. The salesman said to him, 'You don't want to buy that brand. That brand is no good anyhow.' He said, 'Our own brand is better than that.' Not only are they killing us," Daroff concluded, "they are even knocking us." [10]

III

Those who fought against the proposed new federal fair-trade law based their opposition on the same principles recited by the law's advocates: the free competitive system and the public interest. The Consumers' Federation of St. Louis declared that fair-trade legislation was completely antithetical to any concept of price freedom and a free market, being wholly at variance with the basic philosophy of all antitrust laws and any idea of a free economy.[11] The Cooperative League of the U.S.A. passed a resolution opposing fair-trade legislation and condemning it as a threat to the economic system that made America strong.[12] Professor Joseph Klamon, a marketing expert, testified that in his opinion the attempt to pass fair-trade laws

> is an effort to repeal the law of supply and demand. It is idle to suggest that the proponents of this type of legislation want anything but higher prices. It is economically unworkable; it is an effort to take a change of venue from the economic arena, the free market place, to the political arena; to me it is bad law, bad economics, and very poor public policy.
>
> The interests of sellers and buyers are not always the same. The trade groups sponsoring the legislation do not confuse their interest with the public interest, rather, they identify their interest as the public interest.[13]

Professor Klamon found the most distasteful part of fair trade to be its effect upon prices. He believed that there is no doubt that consumers have to pay more for nationally branded products and cited the 1959 report on consumer prices by the Antitrust Division of the Justice Department. This report was based on a survey of prices of 132 items picked at random in cities not covered by fair-trade laws. Of the 119 items available in all of the cities, 77 sold below the price fixed for them in fair-trade cities. Robert Bicks, then head of the Antitrust Division, said that consumers purchasing these 77 items in the non-fair-trade cities surveyed could effect savings of as much as 27 per cent below their fair-trade value. On the basis of such findings, estimates were made that consumers would pay from $1 billion to $10 billion more annually for goods should Congress enact a federal fair-trade law.[14]

The opponents of fair-trade laws asked again and again at the Commerce Committee hearings why the public should not be allowed to benefit from the lower prices that discount houses and chainstores can afford as a result of lower operating costs. They also claimed that fair-trade laws do not necessarily work to the advantage of the small retailer. I. W. Abel, vice president of the Industrial Union Department, AFL–CIO, stated:

> Introduction of fair trade would promote the use of private brands. Discount houses and department stores would soon be forced to feature such brands at bargain prices.
>
> The small retailer would be stuck with the inventories of name brands which he could not discount or put on sale. He could not compete for the private brands with the bigger discounter or the big department store. Consumers would increasingly shun the small store with fixed prices.

[10] Martin Mayer, "Fair Trade or Foul: The Battle Rages Again," *Saturday Evening Post,* April 11, 1964, p. 67.
[11] *Hearings,* p. 61.
[12] *Ibid.,* p. 152.
[13] *Ibid.,* p. 63.
[14] *Ibid.,* p. 136.

> The big manufacturer could then have it both ways. He could set his retail prices to insure maximum profits, raising prices to the dealer in the process. He would also make the private brands for those seeking to avoid the impact of fair trade. He would be the major beneficiary all the way around.[15]

Opponents of fair trade also argued that fair-trade regulations were not only bad for the public and small retailers but unworkable as well. Such regulations had broken down in various states where they were allowed and had proved to be unenforceable. Many manufacturers had already voluntarily abandoned fair trade after finding maintenance and policing of their fixed fair-trade prices difficult. Professor Klamon suggested that the difficulty of enforcing fair-trade prices was inherent. Since consumers, for the most part, are influenced by rational buying motives, they compare quality, durability, value, and price of products. "Any effort by law to eliminate or restrict the opportunity of the consumers and the public to shop around for values and bargains," he said, "is legislating economic nonsense, and is doomed to failure." [16] He predicted that any federal fair-trade act would not be effective. Like the NRA, the Miller-Tydings Amendment, the McGuire Act, and the 45 state fair-trade laws—none of which worked very well—it would finally collapse. Representative Murray Dingell of Michigan agreed that "like prohibition, it will not be accepted by the general public, and its attempted enforcement will of necessity be uneven."

[15] *Ibid.*
[16] *Ibid.*, p. 66.

IV

In June, 1964, the Senate Commerce Committee tabled the quality stabilization bill, but its proponents have not given up their fight and hope to secure enactment at a later time. Ed Wimmer, vice president of the National Federation of Independent Business, maintained that the principle and intent of quality stabilization had been badly misrepresented as a price fixing scheme. In a letter to the *Wall Street Journal* he wrote:

> There was no distinction drawn in most editorials attacking the Quality Stabilization Act between a group of manufacturers who may get together and establish a fixed price on a certain kind of material or service or piece of equipment as against a manufacturer who merely fixes the price on a toaster, a watch, a lawnmower, or some other item below which no seller can go.
>
> Neither was there ever any real explanation that no manufacturer could even fair-trade or price-maintain a product that wasn't in competition with similar merchandise, which made it absolutely impossible for any maker of a name brand product to establish a price that would be unreasonably high without risking the loss of his market.
>
> I might also call your attention to the fact that such statements as those which indicate that price maintenance laws protect competitors from legal competition is an utter disregard of the facts. Once the fair-trade law or the Quality Stabilization Act is on the books, it is up to the manufacturer (and not the Government) to protect himself and his product under that law. It is an act enabling those who believe in fair competition to exercise their beliefs.[17]

[17] August 3, 1964.

QUESTIONS

Kennedy and the Steel Pricing Controversy & The Fair-Trade Controversy

1. How might one reconcile the argument that fair-trade laws strengthen the system of free competition while actions such as President Kennedy's weaken the free market?
2. "Fair-trade laws are passed with full hearings and legislative approval; Ken-

nedy acted hastily, rashly, and on his own. The former do not adversely affect the public interest and the market as does the latter." Explain your agreement or disagreement with this conclusion written by a student after reading the two cases.

3. "President Kennedy did nothing more than mobilize and use market forces to get the steel prices rolled back. Advocates of fair-trade laws, however, restrain normal market forces and thus do more injury to the public interest." Explain why you would agree or disagree with this statement made by a student after reading the two cases.

4. What losses and gains may be expected for a community if discount houses and large retailers drive small store owners out of business, as fair-trade advocates fear?

5. "President Kennedy acted as he did in 1962 because he knew very well the history of government run-ins with the steel industry." What lessons might Kennedy have drawn from the encounters of President Truman with leaders of the steel industry?

6. The *Wall Street Journal* said that the free acquisition and disposal of property is the mark of free men. Support or disprove the argument that economic liberty in the use of property and political liberty are linked together. In your answer, explain the relationship of the "use of the property" and "free men" and whether all restrictions on the use of property are also restrictions on "free men."

7. A cynical observer commented that advocates of fair-trade laws are only trying to get what the steel industry has had ever since 1901 when United States Steel was formed. Explain why you agree or disagree.

8. Write a memo to the president and directors of U.S. Steel, evaluating their policies in 1961–62 regarding wages and prices; give your suggestions for improving or changing any of those policies that injured the interests of the company.

Beneficial Adjustments or Dangerous Tampering?

PRICING IN ALUMINUM

On October 29, 1965, the Olin Mathieson Chemical Company announced a half-cent per pound increase in the price of both primary (ingot) aluminum and fabricated metal. The ingot price was raised about 2 per cent, from 24.5¢ to 25¢. Though Olin Mathieson, the fourth largest primary producer in the United States, accounted for only about 6 per cent of total production, it was immediately joined in its price increase by Reynolds Metal and Kaiser Aluminum, the second- and third-largest companies. Many observers confidently expected the giant of the aluminum industry, the Aluminum Company of America (Alcoa), quickly to fall into line.

I

The managers of all the firms in the aluminum industry had good reason to favor a price rise that autumn. While sales had increased between 1955 and 1964 by 42 per cent (from $1,531 million to $2,173 million for the Big Three alone, who account for about 85 per cent of the industry's primary production), profits had fallen. Alcoa and Kaiser had enjoyed their highest profits in 1956, and Reynolds had its best year in 1959. The combined return of the three companies in 1955 had been 17.7 per cent on net worth; this figure decreased by two-thirds by 1960, and in 1964 it was still only

7.3 per cent. Compared with the 12.1 per cent average return earned by the 500 largest American industrial companies in 1964, aluminum was not doing well.

The source of the industry's difficulties was that although production had increased rapidly by 1964 (up 63 per cent over 1955) capacity had risen still faster and was up 75 per cent. The excess capacity of the industry—together with aggressive competition—pushed prices down. The average industry ingot price, which had reached 26¢ a pound in 1960, fell steadily to a low of 22.6¢ in 1963.

From the low point in 1963, the ingot price had been raised four times, for a total increase of about 8 per cent, to 24.5¢.[1] By mid-1965, sales had picked up so well that the industry's production rate was very close to capacity, and in such a market many businessmen in the industry believed that another price increase would stick. *Modern Metals,* a trade magazine, suggested that firms could benefit by raising prices on unprofitable fabricated products, by stopping price shaving on ingots, and by reducing extended credit.

If aluminum prices were going to be raised again, it would have to be done carefully and with regard for the market, for although the Big Three controlled all but 15 per cent of primary production and accounted for about two-thirds of fabricated aluminum goods, competition in the industry was by no means absent. A half-dozen foreign companies sold thousands of tons of primary metal in the United States; the Aluminum Company of Canada was one of the largest firms, with sales in 1964 equal to 70 per cent of those of Alcoa and larger than either Reynolds or Kaiser. Also, more than 200 fabricating companies—casting firms, foundries, extruders, utensil makers, and producers of domestic aluminum building materials—sold in competition with the Big Three. These independent fabricators had vigorously pushed into the markets for some kinds of aluminum goods. Through low, promotional pricing, they had tried to develop a volume of sales sufficient to reduce their unit costs below the selling price. By 1965 these companies accounted for 61 per cent of extrusion sales, nearly double their share 15 years before. They had increased their sales of sheet and plate metal more slowly, up to about 26 per cent.

Price cutting by the independents affects the larger companies, but the Big Three usually do not change their price lists until the price cutting gets "out of hand" and threatens market stability. They then publish "firming" cuts that match the *de facto* market prices, and as soon as the market allows they follow with "firming" increases. The big integrated companies supply most of the metal to the independents and could hurt them badly by raising ingot prices and keeping fabricated prices down. They are mindful of antitrust prosecution, however, and have been careful not to squeeze too much. They have usually initiated or gone along with price changes in primary metal only when fabricated prices were changed, too, allowing a margin for the non-integrated, independent companies.

In recent years the Big Three have made other moves to improve the market other than simply raising prices; for example, they began to quote uniform delivery prices to reduce the temptation to shave prices by making allowances on freight charges. Alcoa also drastically reduced the number of price classifications for its fabricated products, and the other major producers followed suit.

II

When Olin Mathieson raised its prices on Friday, October 29, Kaiser and Reynolds quickly joined, and the industry waited to see what giant Alcoa would do. Alcoa's net income as a per cent of revenue in the first three quarters of 1965 had been only 6.4, no more than in 1959 and one-fourth less

[1] Data on production, prices, and profits from Gilbert Burck, "Aluminum: The Classic Rollback," *Fortune,* 73 (February, 1966), 108.

than in 1957. (Income as a per cent of capital was 5.5, considerably better than the 3.4 per cent of 1960 but far below the 7.3 per cent of 1957.)

One factor in Alcoa's decision was certain to be that federal government officials were very interested in the price increase, especially with its effect upon President Johnson's price-guidepost policy and the large purchases of aluminum by the Defense Department. From the President's home in Texas—where he was visiting at the time—came reports on Sunday, October 31, that the Secretaries of Defense, Treasury, and Commerce would meet the next day to discuss use of and sales from the huge stockpile of aluminum the government had accumulated. Joseph Califano, Special Assistant to the President, assured reporters that the meeting had nothing to do with prices but was called to consider ways in which the stockpile might be used to help meet defense needs and the country's balance-of-payments problem.

The *New York Times* published on November 1 a story (based on what its editors considered a reliable source) that President Johnson was "sputtering mad" over the price increases. A rumor spread, as well, that the President was ready to dump 500,000 tons from the stockpile onto the market. Alarmed industry leaders sought to find out exactly how the President felt about the price rise. John Harper, the president of Alcoa, called President Johnson in Texas, the *Wall Street Journal* reported, but an aide said that Johnson was not too concerned about the price rise. Furthermore, all government officials insisted there was no connection between the meeting of the Cabinet officers and the industry's price increase.[2]

On the basis of such assurances, Alcoa executives decided to raise their ingot price by the same amount as Olin Mathieson's. Moreover, they felt they could also increase the prices of fabricated products—representing 80 per cent of their sales—by an average of one cent a pound. On Friday, November 5, these increases were announced, and the other major companies immediately raised their prices for fabricated products to match Alcoa's. Alcoa spokesmen explained that the increase in fabricated product prices over the ingot price rise was necessary to achieve a level of earnings sufficient to finance expansion, modernization, and new product research and development; they also thought the increase was vital to insure growth, opportunities for employment, and an adequate return on investment, as well as to offset substantially increased labor costs.

III

For eight months representatives of the aluminum industry and the federal government had been meeting at irregular intervals to arrange for an orderly disposal of surplus aluminum in the government's stockpile. On November 3, only two days before Alcoa's price announcement, representatives of all the major aluminum companies met with government officials to continue these negotiations. The discussions began amicably; speaking for the government were Lawson B. Knott, Jr., administrator of the General Services Administration, who had hurried back from Paris to participate, and Paul R. Ignatius, Assistant Secretary of Defense for installations and logistics. Ignatius presented the aluminum problem as seen by the Department of Defense; military requirements were estimated to take up to 200,000 tons more in 1966 than the year before for a total of about 400,000 tons. To curb imports the government wanted to take at least half of that amount from the stockpile. According to Leon Hickman, Executive Vice President of Alcoa, the four largest companies had reached a

> firm agreement . . . to buy 200,000 tons in 1966 as part of a larger program which envisioned buying the entire stockpile at the

[2] November 12, 1965.

rate of 100,000 tons a year thereafter. . . . The Government recessed the meeting Friday night to call their supervisors and they did . . . while we waited. We were really hopeful that we had an agreement Friday evening, and the word came back in thirty or forty minutes that the Government would like to think it over overnight.[3]

The next morning Mr. Ignatius read a statement to the company negotiators—it was a press release that would be made public by Secretary of Defense McNamara in the afternoon:

Government representatives have reported to representatives of the aluminum industry that increased defense requirements for aluminum, as a result of our operations in Vietnam, make necessary the release of metal from the aluminum stockpile. Surplus aluminum in the hands of the government now exceeds the stockpile requirement by 1.4 million tons.

Disposal of this surplus has become increasingly necessary in the light of two serious problems:

1. Defense production will require the consumption in 1966 of between 300,000 and 400,000 tons of aluminum, approximately 150,000 to 200,000 tons more than in 1965.

2. Aluminum imports which adversely affect our balance of payments continue to rise. It is estimated that in 1966 foreign imports will total 600,000 tons—50 per cent greater than last year.

. . .

If government officials are to serve the national welfare and to protect the consuming public, the United States government has no alternative other than to take 200,000 tons of aluminum surplus and dispose of it at market prices in the national interest.

The press release then set forth five formulas under which the government was prepared to dispose of the surplus metal. The arrangement on which the companies had agreed that afternoon was not included. After finishing the statement, Mr. Ignatius explained that agreement could be reached if the industry were to buy 200,000 tons of stockpile ingots in 1966; on the other hand, there would be no further negotiations until the industry signed up for the 200,000 tons. The company officials found the terms of the government's statement harsh, as Mr. Hickman explained:

It spoke of the five proposals that the Government had made, all of them rejected by industry. It did not mention the proposal that we were negotiating on. . . . We pointed out that it would take weeks to reduce [the new terms of an] agreement to writing. Nevertheless, we had to give our answer right there. Three or four other companies in the industry weren't even there. It apparently made no difference. We said, "Well, we are concerned as we have been from the beginning of the stockpile program to get it behind us and get it out of the way. We're interested in the long range program. Can we have an understanding with you, if we buy your 200,000 unequivocally in 1966, of the framework of that larger deal: that is the 100,000 tons a year plus the flexibility to protect labor?" They said, "We can agree to nothing until you have agreed to take 200,000 tons. When you have done that, at some later mutually agreeable time, we will talk to you about whether there can be a longer range program."

We were, in effect and in actuality, given an ultimatum—very pleasantly, but it was a take it or leave it. Well, we obviously—we obviously—with respect to our solvency and our labor and our stockholders could not take that.

We asked if the negotiations could be continued on Sunday or Monday, if we could see other officials of the Government. The answer was "no" to every one of them. We said we could not take the offer that was before us without any assurance on the longer range program, at which point the meeting was adjourned without another date set to start.[4]

Both the chairman of the President's Council of Economic Advisers, Gardner Ackley, and the Secretary of the Treasury,

[3] From the transcript of Mr. Hickman's press conference, Mayflower Hotel, Washington, D.C., November 8, 1965.

[4] *Ibid.*

Henry Fowler, issued statements from the White House.

Statement by Gardner Ackley

The Council of Economic Advisers has reviewed the recent increases of aluminum prices in the light of the wage-price guideposts. It has concluded that these increases have no justification under the wage price guideposts and therefore are inflationary.

The increase in aluminum ingot prices is the fifth such increase in 25 months, for a total increase of more than 11 per cent. Primary aluminum is an industry with a productivity trend substantially above the average for economy; under the guideposts, such industries should not be raising prices.

In the first three quarters of this year, profits after taxes for the big three primary producers are as follows, compared with the first three quarters last year:

Alcoa—up 26 per cent
Kaiser—up 29 per cent
Reynolds—up 52 per cent
The big three producers combined—up 33 per cent

Profits for the three companies this year will be 80 per cent above the level of 1960. And prospects are excellent for further growth of production and profits at the prices prevailing before the latest increase.

. . .

Aluminum is one of the basic materials of our economy. Higher aluminum prices raise the costs of many products, both civilian and military. Production of primary aluminum in this country is highly concentrated, with 80 per cent of capacity in the hands of just three companies. This situation imposes a particular responsibility on these companies to consider the public interest in their pricing decisions.

Statement of Secretary Fowler

Release of surplus aluminum from the stockpile is an essential step to defend our balance of payments.

Imports of aluminum this year are expected to be 500,000 tons. This is far more than this country has ever imported. Until 1961, imports averaged about 200,000 tons a year. Imports have more than doubled in just four years. The cost of this deterioration to our balance of payments already exceeds $100 million.

Next year, in the absence of stockpile surplus releases, imports will again rise sharply. The primary aluminum industry is operating at 100 per cent of rated capacity. With rising demands from private users and an increase of approximately 200,000 tons in military needs, domestic production cannot keep pace. If the imbalance is partly met from foreign sources, as it would be, the rise in imports next year can be expected to constitute a substantial additional cost to our international trade balance.

. . . The use of the stockpile surpluses to help meet the needs of our military effort in Vietnam and to avoid further losses in our trade balance—without disruption of domestic markets—will be an important factor in protecting the position of the dollar in the world.

Secretary of Defense McNamara and Mr. Ackley declined to acknowledge any direct connection between the price increase and the release of aluminum from the stockpile. They admitted, however, that the extra supplies on the market were "bound to relieve some of the pressure on prices." The Secretary added, "It simply does not make sense for the Government to spend the taxpayer's money to buy increasingly large amounts of aluminum [for defense goods] when it holds 1.4 million tons which are surplus to any conceivable defense requirement." [5] He indicated that the government would bypass the basic producers, providing the stockpile ingots to defense contractors and paying them enough for the finished product to compensate them for processing the ingots. About 75,000 tons would be used for powdered aluminum (for bombs) and perhaps another 40,000 tons would be converted into matting for temporary military airport runways. The remainder would be sold at the "market price." With apparent reference to the higher aluminum prices just announced,

[5] *Wall Street Journal,* November 8, 1965.

McNamara suggested that many transactions "take place at other than the published price."

The 200,000 tons to be sold from stockpile in 1966 was equal to about 7 per cent of 1965's primary production of 2.8 million tons. Remelted scrap contributed about 765,000 tons, and imports furnished another 490,000 tons.

IV

Officials of Alcoa and Reynolds announced that they expected to maintain the new price increases, but Leon Hickman hedged Alcoa's affirmation by noting that all price changes "must be tested in the market place." Businessmen from around the nation supported the companies' firm stand. An executive of a chemical company in New York commented, "It's a rather sad state of affairs when we're told government will decide what wages we can pay or what prices we'll be allowed to charge. It suggests that government knows what's best about everything. Things like this can only be decided in the market place." And Merle Hostetler, an economist and a vice president of the Union Commerce Bank of Cleveland, complained that the government was "trying to regulate prices by word of mouth instead of letting competitive market conditions determine them." [6] David Rockefeller, president of New York's Chase Manhattan Bank, criticized government pressure on the aluminum companies in a speech before the American Petroleum Institute on November 9:

> We must beware of . . . the attempt to maintain price stability through the artificial and arbitrary control of wages and prices, rather than by the control of effective demand through the use of fiscal and monetary policy. The government's strong reaction to price increases in the aluminum industry is a profoundly disturbing case in point. We should keep clearly in mind the immeasurable contribution that free markets and free competition make to our economy and the essential role of wage and price flexibility.
>
> They must be able to move up and down in accordance with changing patterns of technology, product development, competition and consumer tastes. Given a level and a distribution of national income, it is the open marketplace which determines the best allocation of our human and material resources.
>
> Frankly, I am concerned about the tendency on the part of government to tinker with the price mechanism. Official guidelines for wages and prices, whether by decree or by a strong call for voluntary compliance, necessarily disrupt the vital role of flexibility in response to normal economic forces. And our economy has become so intricately interdependent that you simply cannot impose restraints in one area and blandly assume they will have no repercussions in other areas. I fear that we are in danger of backing inadvertently into a managed economy, and I am convinced that this is not the high road to the good life. The forces of the marketplace, which call forth the initiative and incentive necessary for a dynamic and progressive economy, can be blunted by overregulation. The fact is that free market forces work in the general public interest when there is least interference in the areas of decision-making. To spread government controls further is to risk severe damage to the efficiency of the market system.[7]

Administration officials did not appear to be impressed by the criticism from the business community, for they made known their plans to sell immediately 100,000 tons of surplus aluminum in a bid to test the market price. This was in addition to the 200,000 tons to be released the next year, in 1966. The sale must have been arranged quickly, for the responsible officials in the General Services Administration could not offer any details except that it would be through competitive bidding.

A spokesman for Kaiser Aluminum then called for a resumption of negotiations between producers and the government, warn-

[6] *New York Times,* November 9, 1965.

[7] From the transcript of Mr. Rockefeller's speech, "The Sound Ingredients of a Great Society."

ing that "continuing public expressions of disagreement . . . can only result in an unfortunate hardening of attitudes." Harlow J. Reed, executive vice president of Olin Mathieson, also asked for a new effort to solve the problem of the aluminum surplus in a manner compatible with "the health of the nation's economy." [8] The release of 200,000 tons from the stockpile would cost the industry about $100 million and would be bad enough, but another 100,000 tons would scramble markets all over the world. Selling to the highest bidder would enable secondary producers and fabricators to undersell the market, jarring the whole price structure maintained by the major producers.

In the meantime, Alcoa's John Harper had been meeting with Secretary McNamara. On November 10, just before the company released the news, the Secretary announced that Alcoa, in "a patriotic act of industrial statesmanship" was rescinding its recent price increase. In a news conference he maintained that the government could do little more than "establish guideposts and policies . . . it can persuade, but the ultimate responsibility for prices in our free-enterprise market system rests upon management as it's influenced by labor and consumer." [9] He also indicated that "it would be possible to limit the quantity of metal to be disposed of from the stockpile in 1966 to less than 200,000 tons." With the price decrease there was now less danger that the extra needs for aluminum would be met by imports.

Alcoa's decision to rescind the price increase was followed within hours by Reynolds, and officials of Kaiser and Olin Mathieson indicated they, too, would drop their recent price increase. The moves were not made happily. One company official expressed himself as "heartsick, bitter, and dejected. We might as well admit that future increases will need advance permission from the White House. This is no longer a free and competitive economy." [10]

An editorial of the New York *Herald Tribune* condemned the government's interference: "We have a far better mechanism than Presidential judgment for determining 'justified' price levels: the forces of a free market. An industry (such as aluminum) dominated by a few producers is often presumed to be non-competitive, when actually these often are the most fiercely competitive of all." [11]

Business generally argued that the market should have been allowed to justify the price, if it could. Merle Hostetler of the Union Commerce Bank of Cleveland, for example, argued: "These people wouldn't be raising prices if they didn't think demand would justify it. If they were wrong then it would have been adjusted in the

[8] *Wall Street Journal,* November 10, 1965.

[9] Burck, *op. cit.,* p. 229.

[10] The devotion of the aluminum company officials to a free and competitive economy has not always been singleminded. In 1964, the justice department charged six firms, Alcoa, Anaconda Wire and Cable (a subsidiary of Anaconda Copper), General Cable Corporation, Kaiser Aluminum, Olin Mathieson, and Reynolds with fixing prices and rigging bids on aluminum electrical cable from June 1958 to at least March 1961. Annual sales of the cable amounted to $70 million. Each company pleaded "no contest" to the charges, accepting punishment without conceding guilt. Each was fined $50,000. Companies charged with violating the antitrust laws often plead "no contest" and accept the judgment of the court to avoid a long trial and disclosure of evidence that customers could use to sue for triple damages. Without publicly available evidence, injured customers find proof of injury from the price rigging almost impossible to establish. In this case, though, many customers believed that they had a chance to prove that the aluminum companies were "submitting noncompetitive and collusive price quotations and bids to purchasers of aluminum conductor cable and the establishment, maintenance and protection of conspiratorial price structures so that competition would be restrained or eliminated and monopolistic conditions would prevail." By October 1965 over 100 utility firms had filed suit against the six defendants. See the *Wall Street Journal,* October 6, 1965.

[11] November 9, 1965.

market place." Senator Everett Dirksen of Illinois said, "If the aluminum people have been at it all their lives and don't know how to run the businesses, then who does? It's a simple question of arithmetic. If a company producing aluminum takes a look at its books and it is in the interest of stockholders and labor to increase prices, the arithmetic has to speak for itself."

V

On November 16, a week after the price rollback, the government and the aluminum companies announced agreement on a plan to dispose of the 1.4 million tons of surplus aluminum in the national stockpile. Though earlier discussions had dragged on for months the two parties reached accord after only two days of negotiations. In its announcement the Defense Department reported the terms of the agreement:

> The industry representatives and the Government representatives agreed in principle that the industry will purchase the surplus aluminum at an average rate of not less than 100,000 tons per year or the defense requirement, which ever is greater, but not to exceed 200,000 tons per year, except that in 1966 the minimum quantity to be purchased will be not less than 150,000 tons.[12]

Aluminum company officials were pleased to secure an agreement for orderly disposal of the stockpile metal. They had long considered it a sword of Damocles hanging over the industry. In 1952 when the government undertook to stockpile 2 million tons of aluminum in anticipation of a five-year war, Leon Hickman warned his industrial colleagues that the government one day is "going to clobber us with it."

While not unaware of the potential threat a stockpile posed for the industry, company officials saw in it a number of advantages. First, in the 1950's it offered a way for aluminum producers to expand production facilities with little risk of oversupplying the market. Under the Defense Production Act of 1950 Congress permitted the stockpiling of products needed by the armed services and in short supply during the Korean conflict; it encouraged the aluminum industry to double its capacity, promising each firm the right to sell to the stockpile any aluminum from the new plants not required for defense uses.

The second advantage of the stockpile sales became apparent as time went on. Though most of the new plants began producing only after the end of fighting in Korea, the companies were able to continue to sell metal into the stockpile under the original contracts. Administrators appointed by President Eisenhower allowed the companies to vary sales in such a way as to stabilize and even to raise prices in the market. During the period 1952–58, when the bulk of the stockpile was accumulated, the price of aluminum rose steadily. In 1950 aluminum ingots sold for 17.5¢ a pound and in 1957 for 28.1¢ a pound. When the price dropped 2¢ a pound in March, 1958, ingot prices were stabilized and even recovered 0.7¢ a pound as the companies sold 323,128 tons to the stockpile.[13] These sales amounted to about 15 per cent of the industry's total production at a time when it was lagging behind capacity by one-third to one-fifth. In effect, stockpile sales had become an industry subsidy.

The stockpiles were already overfull during most of the period of accumulation and had been since 1954. In that year the Defense Department changed its planning assumption about the probable length of a big conventional war from five to three years. Smaller stockpiles, sufficient for only three years, were then required. The Eisenhower administration, however, moved slowly to bring stockpile buying in line with the decisions of the Defense Department,

[12] *New York Times,* November 17, 1965.

[13] Robert F. Lanzillotti, "The Aluminum Industry," in Walter Adams, ed., *The Structure of American Industry,* 3rd ed. (New York: Macmillan, 1961), pp. 202, 210, 218–19.

declaring only in 1958 that materials accumulated in excess of the three-year war needs were surplus. Even more slowly did the government then or later dispose of the excess metal in the stockpile. By October, 1965, so little aluminum had been sold from it that there was 3.2 times as much held as was needed to meet requirements.

Despite the huge size of the stockpile, most aluminum company officials seemed to believe that the government was not likely to use it in a way detrimental to their interests. After all, they had secured passage of a provision in the Defense Production Act forbidding sales that would disrupt the market; further protection of their interests seemed assured by another requirement that most of the stockpile could be sold only with prior Congressional authorization.

PRICING IN COPPER

In November, 1965, the American copper industry rescinded a price increase under circumstances similar to those encountered by the aluminum industry a week earlier. In both cases the President used his power to make sales from government stockpiles to undermine a price change that threatened his "anti-inflationary" programs. The rollback of copper prices, however, elicited no such chorus of criticism from the business community as had the aluminum rollback.

I

In a number of ways the American copper companies faced problems not unlike those that confronted the aluminum firms. In 1965, copper was in short supply and demand for it was strong. Strikes in the United States and in Chile—which accounts for about 15.5 per cent of world copper production—had reduced supplies, and the Rhodesian crisis threatened to cut off the output of Zambia;[1] at the same time, defense demands for copper products, particularly for brass ammunition cases, had increased rapidly. The price of U.S. copper had risen five times since early 1964, from 31¢ a pound to 36¢ a pound, yet major companies had not made outstanding profits.

On October 20, 1965, the government of Chile ordered the Kennecott and Anaconda companies to raise the price of exported Chilean copper by 2¢, to 38¢ a pound. Producers throughout the world quickly complied with the rise, leaving only the price in the United States at 36¢ a pound. After waiting 13 days, the Copper Range Company announced that it was raising its price to 38¢ a pound; all the other producers followed suit except Kennecott, which is the largest American producer of refined copper and with Anaconda and Phelps-Dodge comprises most of the domestic industry.

For some time industry leaders had debated the wisdom of raising prices. Domestic producers had resisted suggested increases because they feared loss of copper markets. The higher copper prices go, experts argued, the faster industrial consumers will switch to competing materials; they pointed out that copper had already lost sales in the electrical field and that many pipe and tube products are no longer made of copper. In the United States companies that formerly used copper for drainage, waste, and vent plumbing are increasingly

[1] In 1965 the United States produced 1,361,049 tons of new, primary copper; Zambia produced 759,258 tons and Chile 644,786 tons. The unilateral declaration of independence on November 11, 1965, by the government of Ian Smith, prime minister of Rhodesia, threatened to disrupt rail service from Zambia to Mozambique. Zambian producers had no alternative transportation route to the rail line that crossed Rhodesia.

using plastic. Aluminum has gained a strong foothold among manufacturers of underground and overhead electrical cable, and it is being used in commercial and residential wiring as well. Furthermore, research into the use of low cost sodium as a conductor for high voltage transmission lines and into the sandwiching of other metals with copper promises more substitution for and reduced sales of copper.

A few industry officials felt that the price of copper in 1965 was still modest and probably should go higher, given the short supply and heavy demand. The president of the Copper Range Company suggested that a higher price to meet increased demands would stimulate an increase in supply by making it worthwhile to produce more metal. The 38¢ price would enable his company to process lower-grade ores that were uneconomical when sold at 36¢. Other producers who favored the increase advanced the same argument, maintaining that holding down the price perpetuated the copper shortage by keeping marginal mines out of production. They argued further that attempts by copper users to substitute other metals or materials had often proved difficult, if not impractical. Switching to a substitute metal often involves retooling, redesigning the product to accommodate differently shaped parts, reestimating costs, and making myriad other adjustments, all expensive and time-consuming for copper users. Such a change involves a risk; the user must gamble that the spread between the prices of copper and its substitute will continue long enough for him to recover his investment in the changeover.

Copper prices had been in turmoil for some time when the Copper Range Company acted in November 1965. Chile had initiated a price increase in May, and by June copper futures on the London Metal Exchange had risen to over 52¢ a pound. By the middle of November, copper for delivery in the first quarter of 1966 was selling in London at 66.5¢ a pound and the U.S. price for secondary copper, or copper refined largely from scrap, had jumped to as much as 70¢ a pound. Nearly one-third of American copper comes from imports and scrap, since the country produces only about 1.3 million tons from domestic sources but consumes some 2 million tons annually.

The low price of primary copper forced the producing companies to ration their sales, limiting the amount of metal shipped to each customer. Even with the rationing not all users were able to secure copper from the producers. Many independent fabricators, for example, had to turn to the expensive secondary market for their supply, and even some of the producing companies were forced to buy premium-priced copper to fulfill contracts with some of their regular customers.

II

On the evening of November 17, just one week after he had reported Alcoa's backdown on its price increase, Secretary of Defense Robert S. McNamara hurriedly called a press conference in Washington to announce the government's intention to sell 200,000 tons of copper from the defense stockpile. The press had earlier reported rumors that the administration was anxious to roll back the increase in the copper price, but the smallness of the surplus in the copper stockpile—4 per cent above defense requirements—seemed to give the President little leverage compared to what he had enjoyed in dealing with the aluminum companies. Earlier in the year the government had transferred 110,000 tons of copper from the stockpile to the mint for use in new coins. Left in the stockpile were 810,000 tons, of which 775,000 tons were defense reserves, required for a three-year non-nuclear war. A release of 200,000 tons would dispose of the surplus and cut deeply into the required reserves. However, under a provision of the 1946 Strategic and Critical Materials Act, the President was authorized to release reserves if in his judgment the action would contribute to the common defense.

Secretary McNamara presented a four-point program to reduce what he called inflationary pressures on copper prices that might "seriously impair our defense effort in Vietnam." He reported that there had been discussions during the preceding seven to ten days between government officials and leaders of the copper industry; they had reached an understanding that stockpiled metal was to be disposed of in an orderly way at from 38¢ to 36¢ a pound, depending on the quality of the metal and other factors. Release of copper from the stockpile would, he thought, "go far to satisfy the increasing demands of the domestic market."

To conserve the domestic supply the government proposed to control exports of copper and scrap for an indefinite period. The Defense Department would also recommend that Congress suspend the import duties on copper to encourage a greater flow of the metal into the country. The Secretary refused to discuss directly the 2¢ a pound increase, and when reporters pressed him for a statement on prices he repeated the statement made the week before: "I don't believe price increases are warranted in any major commodities today." [2] He suggested that each company would have to make its own price decisions.

While the copper producing companies issued no formal statements about the release of the stockpiled copper, a number of officials indicated their approval. A spokesman for the Phelps-Dodge Corporation said, "This additional metal is badly needed by U.S. industry to meet defense requirements growing out of the war in Vietnam. This additional supply should tend to bring down the very high prices which have been charged by nonproducers." [3] An official of Revere Copper and Brass, a major fabricator, expressed his satisfaction with the government's action; output had been curtailed, he said, because of the copper shortage.

Various government officials informally suggested to reporters that they would be happy to see the price of secondary copper knocked down by the stockpile release. Most industry spokesmen told news reporters that they believed the President's action was primarily aimed at relieving the short supply and thus preventing bottlenecks from developing in the industries dependent upon copper products. They thought it unlikely that the release of the metal would force a rollback of the producer price; the wide spread between producer and secondary prices and the extremely tight supply would maintain an upward pressure. They hoped the main effect of the government's move would be to stabilize the price of secondary copper and to bring it closer to the producer price. On November 18, the day after McNamara's announcement, copper futures for secondary metal did drop 2¢ a pound, and they were expected to continue down.

III

On November 19, just two days after the government released the stockpiled copper, C. J. Parkinson, president of Anaconda, announced that his company was rescinding its recent 2¢ a pound increase, explaining that the move was "forced by circumstances beyond our control." He told reporters that he had not seen the President except on television and had seen no other officials than White House aides; the price move, he said, was taken "by this company after a great deal of thought and was not based on any other considerations."

Phelps-Dodge quickly followed Anaconda's lead, and the smaller companies also dropped their prices back to 36¢ a pound. Some companies, such as the Copper Range Company, initiator of the increase, moved reluctantly. James Boyd, its president, complained that "I haven't seen

[2] *Wall Street Journal,* November 18, 1965.
[3] *Ibid.,* November 19, 1965.

yet that this release from the stockpile will affect the market," but he admitted that he would study the situation.

There were no editorials in business or financial publications condemning the government's release of stockpiled copper nor were there accusations by businessmen that the government was using the stockpile to force down the price of copper. H. S. Houthakker, an economics professor at Harvard, commented upon the incident, however, in a letter to the *New York Times:*

> The effort to roll back the producer price of copper . . . appears to be misdirected. The trouble with the copper market is not that the producer price is too high, but that it is too low. . . . The leading producers sell their output at a fixed price to some favored large customers for fear they might otherwise switch to aluminum. The more vulnerable users who cannot find substitutes have to buy in the dealer market, where the price is about 50 per cent higher. Whether this two-price system is legal is something that the antitrust lawyers might well look into. But it is clear that it aggravates and perpetuates the imbalance in the copper market. The favored users who buy at the lower price are precisely those who could most easily use substitutes, whereas the dealer price is inflated by the low elasticity of demand of the others. . . . To bring order into the copper market it is necessary to restore a single price.[4]

Later, in 1966, Representative Thomas B. Curtis of Missouri criticized the Administration's intervention in copper. "I think we have gone beyond that [using the stockpile for military purposes, not just to help along the industry] in copper, for example, where we are in real short supply. . . . Frankly . . . they were trying to . . . take care of a price problem. I would say . . . that this is being done at the neglect of future military needs."

Senator Paul Douglas of Illinois answered Representative Curtis. ". . . we largely purchased these raw materials to keep prices from falling. I do not see why we cannot use the same stockpile to keep prices from rising. This is not merely a bailout, this is also a stabilizing factor. . . . As a practical measure a lot of this stuff was bought to keep prices up. We all know the raw materials lobbies that operate through both Houses of Congress." [5]

[4] November 28, 1965.

[5] The statements of Representative Curtis and Senator Douglas are found in Hearings before the Subcommittee on Federal Procurement and Regulation of the Joint Economic Committee, *Economic Impact of Federal Procurement,* 89th Cong., 2nd Sess., January 24 and March 23 and 24, 1966, pp. 127–28.

QUESTIONS

Beneficial Adjustments or Dangerous Tampering?

1. How do you explain the "business" criticism of the Administration's rollback of aluminum prices but the absence of "business" criticism of the rollback of copper prices?

2. If a large private purchaser of aluminum were faced with a rise in the price of the metal and had the means to bargain for a lower price, should the purchaser seek the lower or accept the higher price? If the purchaser is the government, explain how its actions should differ.

3. How did the Administration "attempt to maintain price stability through the artificial and arbitrary control of . . . prices" in these two cases, as David Rockefeller implied?

4. How "free and competitive" were the markets in aluminum and copper before the Administration rolled back prices?

5. Compare the way in which the stockpiles of aluminum and copper were handled by the government in the fifties and in 1964. What arguments would you make that the government acted irresponsibly (or responsibly)?

6. Assume you were a spokesman for a major aluminum company and were asked to answer the November 6, 1965, statement of the Council of Economic Advisers or of the Secretary of the Treasury. Prepare a brief, concise report suitable for public distribution.

7. After reading these cases a foreigner commented: "Firms in both the aluminum and copper industries, as well as the government, are involved in economic planning and control while camouflaging their actions in the rhetoric of the free market." What evidence in these cases can you find to support or deny this opinion?

section **3**

THE SOCIAL FUNCTION OF THE MARKET

In asking how scrupulously a corporation or union must look out for the welfare of the public at large we raise an issue that has long troubled political theorists: How can a community reconcile its public needs with the private purposes of its citizens? Individuals, organizations subordinate to the state, and government must respect each other's interests if they are to maintain for long a peaceful, viable community. The alternatives to mutual respect are clear enough. On the one hand, if government disregards the interests of the governed and their institutions, the result is tyranny, a not uncommon though hardly commendable form of national rule. On the other hand, if citizens serve only their private interests and show no concern for the requirements of community life, an ordered, civilized society is hardly possible.

More than 2,300 years ago Plato noted that men are not self-sufficient in meeting their many wants; they are, he said, mutually dependent upon one another. Society is thus based on a system of services whereby each person both gives and receives, benefiting others and the whole society as well as himself. Plato argued that men who properly understand their own natures and who live within a state that provides them the opportunity to develop their capabilities fully will naturally serve the social interest. Later students of politics had less faith in this potential reasonableness, perceiving in men a flaw of selfishness that impairs the co-ordering of private and social interests.

In the sixteenth century, Niccolò Machiavelli made much of this selfishness, which he assumed was an important constituent of human nature. He sought neither to eradicate it nor to change it but argued, instead, that governors should use it to further their larger purposes. What was required was some means of controlling the private pursuits of men or, better, of harnessing them to serve the otherwise unmet needs and requirements of society. Machiavelli proposed, as his means, force and law. A little more than a century later, the English philosopher Thomas Hobbes took up Machiavelli's suggestion and presented a systematic argument that government must bend men's selfish egotism by law or by force to meet the needs and demands of the state; in turn, this would limit the antisocial inclinations of men and permit them to enjoy the protection and benefits of organized society. His state, the Leviathan, endowed as it was with absolute power to order and coerce its members, did not appeal to men who valued constitutional checks upon the government as well as the citizenry; nor did it fit well with the increasingly popular social theory of individualism.

John Locke was one among many philosophers who rejected Hobbes's absolute state, although he did not refute the supposed ground of its necessity, since he accepted the presumption that self-interest is a fundamental and compelling trait of men. Locke simply assumed that the behavior of men was different from that postulated by Hobbes. He rejected the idea that without a powerful, unlimited government men would lapse into "a war of all against all," and asserted a final harmony of nature that "somehow good will be the final goal of ill." Without exploring the means by which the two endeavors would converge, he insisted that the pursuit of selfish, private interests and the protection of the common good came to the same thing. It remained for the classical economists—drawing their doctrines from the exposition of Adam Smith, the analyses of David Ricardo, and the utilitarian theories of Jeremy Bentham—to discover in the free, competitive market the mechanism that made fully comprehensible the type of convergence assumed by Locke.

According to the new economics, the market resolved the problem of any conflict between private interests and public good so long as monopolies or other obstacles did not block its operations. Each person sought his self-interest through the market; in selling his labor or producing goods for sale, competition guided him, as if by an "invisible hand," into the service of the community. Whereas Plato believed man had to be taught to respect the social good, and Hobbes believed the state must force men to serve it, the political economists of the late eighteenth and early nineteenth centuries insisted man need only pursue self-gain; the competitive market would take care of the common good. Alexander Hamilton expressed a widely held point of view when he wrote that "everyman ought to be supposed a knave; and to have no other end, in all his actions, but private interests. By this interest we must govern him; and by means of it, make him cooperate to public good, notwithstanding his insatiable avarice and ambition." [1]

In guiding men along the paths of civic virtue, the competitive market relieved individuals of social responsibility. If, as sellers, they offered what buyers wanted, they made profits, which served simultaneously as private reward and as public proof that they served the community! Apologists for the market claimed it accomplished even more than this harmonizing of public and private interests, however; it was also a moral system that justly enriched or impoverished men according to their contribution to the market and so to society. The market thus determined the just wage and the just price, in this way impersonally and autonomously answering a question with which philosophers, prophets, and priests had long wrestled. The market relieved businessmen not only of responsibility for the public interest but also of any further ethical concern for those with whom they dealt in the market. Subsistence wages for meat packers, dangerous conditions in coal mines, and dawn-to-dusk hours for garment workers were simply the requirements of the market, not the judgments of employers. However bad the conditions allowed by the market, they were the best possible

[1] Saul K. Padover, "The 'Singular' Mr. Hamilton," *Social Research,* 24 (1957), 174.

given the circumstances. Attempts to improve them by interfering in the market would produce far worse consequences.

The classical economists declared that the market performed two functions that are actually quite different and sometimes incompatible, if not contradictory. Insofar as the market encourages producers to provide efficiently the quantity, quality, and kinds of goods that best will resolve the various conflicting consumer demands and satisfy the multitudinous wants of those who buy, it may well tend to produce social harmony. In its other function of distributing wealth and income, however, it may promote dissension and exacerbate rivalries. The market is a rationing system as well as a stimulator of production, and while people may be pleased at the amount and variety of the national product, they may be most dissatisfied if they do not get what they consider their fair share of it.

The market does not and apparently need not provide equality in its rationing function but only a reasonable and equitable distribution—one in line with people's experience and expectation. In the United States the top 5 per cent of income units receive just under 20 per cent of all personal income; the lowest fifth of all units receive not quite 5 per cent. This pattern of income distribution is a bit more even or equal than the pattern of 30 years ago when, in the midst of the Great Depression, the top 5 per cent accounted for over 25 per cent of all income, and the lowest fifth received only 4.1 per cent. It is perhaps worthy of note that in few other nations is income distributed as equally as in the United States; throughout most of the world the distribution is skewed toward far greater extremes.

Today, few economists and fewer politicans hold the market in as high esteem as was common two or three generations ago. Interference with the competitive market through governmental regulation, prohibitions, and subsidies, while often promoted in the nineteenth and early twentieth centuries, were nevertheless not as easily accepted and regularly practiced then as they are now. However, neither the economists and politicians nor the public are ready or willing to abolish the market. Though we recognize it as a device of our own creation rather than the divine instrument of natural order that its ardent nineteenth-century devotees thought it, we also know that the competitive market is an extremely useful instrument. The functions it performs are valued so highly that private persons or groups are not usually allowed to interfere with them except through or with the permission of the government. Private interference with the market infringes upon the prerogatives of government and threatens the social results promised by the market system. Even if a privately initiated restrictive action is undertaken with good intent and for apparently defensible reasons, its result is a denial of due process through either government or market procedures that is almost sure to raise questions of justice more insistent and problems of social harmony more contentious than those produced by the operation of the market itself.

chapter **6**

PRIVATE REGULATION OF THE MARKET

Ordinarily we do not emphasize the market's rationing functions. It is more pleasant to dwell on the wondrous responsiveness of the market to the complex variety of demands made by consumers. Basic economic texts rightly draw attention to the amazing array of transactions and the vast system of interdependent organizations required to produce each morning a "typical" American breakfast of eggs, bacon, milk, sugar, coffee, and orange juice. But that same market produces quite a different breakfast for the many people unable to pay the prices of these foods that are taken so much for granted. If a citizen does not have sufficient income to pay for certain goods in the market, he cannot enjoy a share of them.

The rationing function of the market serves a useful—and, indeed, necessary—purpose. Since the supply of goods and services is too limited for everyone to have all he desires, they must be rationed in some fashion. When color television sets were first mass-produced, for example, the industry simply could not produce enough to provide one for every person who would have liked one. Because the price of the first models was high—over $500—many consumers could not or would not buy one, and demand and supply were brought into rough correspondence. The rationing of the superfluities of daily living such as television sets hardly excites our concern. The rationing of such essentials as food, clothing, health services, and shelter is a more sensitive issue, however. One result of the play of market forces in the United States is that some people are unable to get sufficient quantities of good food and habitually suffer malnutrition. The market channels resources into gaudy gambling casinos in Las Vegas at the same time that it denies building materials to slum dwellers.

Such distributions can be explained and defended if they are the results of a free, competitive market. Presumably they reflect the sum of all the demands of the nation's consumers—a composite social judgment. On the other hand, some people's demands carry exceptional weight because they have great wealth; and for each person who can command more than the average quantity of goods there is at least one who commands less. Thus the market can be harsh and divisive as it appears to favor one person, group, or class over another.

In wartime the nation becomes acutely aware of the market's rationing function. The normal inequities of its results are seen in a new light because of the government's request for equal sacrifice, the need for common effort, and the demand for military service. In recent major wars the government has suspended the free market and instituted its own pricing and rationing systems. Some goods were rationed because they were in short supply and critically needed by the military—for example, rubber in World War II—but others appear to have been made subject to price controls and rationing largely to avoid the inequities of the free market's distribution. A case in point is meat; the manner in which it was distributed during World War II illustrates American attitudes toward the market as a rationing device. Civilian per capita consumption of meat during that war was higher than at any time during the 1930's, and in 1944—when it reached almost 153 pounds—it was at its highest level since 1909. There was no shortage of meat then; at least, meat had been in much shorter supply many times before. Nevertheless, the government did not allow the market to distribute and ration it according to the dollars consumers might wish to bid for it. Instead, each person was issued a quota of "stamps" that entitled him to buy a certain quantity of meat. The reasons for adopting this non-market rationing were made clear by government officials; ". . . if uneven or unfair distribution of necessities causes bitterness, then our home morale will suffer drastically,"[1] said one official. According to another, a "maldistribution of food would react unfavorably on the war effort."[2]

In peacetime we do not worry as much about uneveness or unfairness in the market. Few Americans, for example, accused the market of maldistribution of meat in the 1950's. Yet between 1950 and 1958 per capita civilian consumption of meat dropped 9 per cent, falling below the level of consumption for the war year 1944. An important cause of the drop was the combination of a 19 per cent rise in the price of meat and a 66 per cent increase of unemployment from 2,822,000 to 4,681,000 workers. Millions of people had to forego eating as much meat as they liked. Given an unequal share of the market's rationing "stamps" (dollars), they received an unequal ration of meat. This is a result that we accept; on the whole, Americans go along with the market's distributions, believing that its impersonal workings are probably no worse and perhaps considerably better than those of any other system readily available.

The social tensions that accompany rationing are often overlooked by those who attempt to control the market. When unions or other groups attempt to interfere with the market's decisions, they may encounter a reaction on the part of those adversely affected that is surprisingly vigorous because of the strains already present. Private interference with the market may distort production or waste resources—and it is often condemned on these grounds—but it is most abrasive in its effects on the market's rationing. If private persons or groups add to or take from the well-being of others without the sanction and

[1] From a radio speech by Connecticut State Rationing Administrator, Chester Bowles, March 9, 1942. Quoted in William J. Wilson, "The Price Control Acts of 1942," *The Beginnings of OPA*, Part 1, Office of Temporary Controls (Washington: Government Printing Office, 1947), p. 39.

[2] From a statement by Joseph A. Kershaw, first chief of the Ration Banking Branch, Office of Price Administration. Quoted in Joseph A. Kershaw, *A History of Ration Banking*, Office of Temporary Controls (Washington: Government Printing Office, 1947), p. 1.

mediation of the competitive market or the government, they may wield social power in an essentially irresponsible way.

The cases that follow illustrate the problems created when private organizations or groups interfere with market processes. The reader should decide whether or not the interference in these instances, though privately undertaken, was socially responsible and whether its results were desirable.

Benefits and Mischiefs of Private Action

STEEL AND THE GRAY MARKET

From the end of World War II until 1949 and from the start of the Korean war until 1952, a large number of American steel companies passed up profits that they might easily have earned; at the same time, industry spokesmen condemned those who made profits by selling steel at prices consumers were ready and willing to pay. Earlier, steel company officials had indeed played an important part in the successful business campaign to have government price controls lifted at the end of the war, but that did not indicate that they were opposed to price control and market allocation as such. Rather, they established their own price system and attempted to enforce its rules themselves; this situation existed until early in 1949.

Soon after the Korean war began, the National Production Authority established a schedule of priorities for access to supplies of steel. Firms not engaged in war production were allowed to buy a certain percentage of their normal material supplies wherever and whenever they could; this meant that these nonpriority firms were given a hunting license rather than direct allocations. Faced by the explosive demand conditions that naturally followed from such an artificial system, large suppliers nevertheless kept their prices down and allocated their scarce products as before.

While large producers seemed reluctant to make maximum profits, many small operators showed no such inhibitions. Brokers, finders, expediters, and warehouse operators appeared everywhere, ready to provide or to hunt steel. Often they dabbled in other commodities in short supply—caustic soda and nails, for example—as well as steel; their capital equipment was little more than a telephone, and their assets were largely the contacts they had in the industry. Many were accused of being nothing but fronts for well-established firms that did not want to get openly involved in such unseemly transactions. The collective operations of these traders came to be known as the "gray market" in steel.

One cannot precisely define the gray market, but some of its characteristics may be described. First, many businessmen condemned those who bought and sold on the gray market as little better than wartime black-marketeers; on the other hand, after 1946 government price controls no longer existed, and high as the gray market price might go, it was completely legal. Second, the gray market existed side by side with the "regular" market. The same steel was bought and sold at two different prices; favored customers of steel producers and suppliers—usually large companies—paid a low price on the regular market; smaller or less favored new firms had to scrounge the market for steel and pay two to five times more on the gray market.

After the war many American consumers became familiar with a two-price system when they tried to buy such scarce goods as automobiles and refrigerators; farmers contended with it when purchasing farm machinery. Steel was the most important product to have a second price on a gray market, however. It was a basic material, and its sales were large. One authority estimated that in 1947–48 as much as 5 per cent of all steel was sold on the gray market. In some sections of the country the gray market was much bigger; in 1947–48 it accounted for 15 per cent of steel sales on the West Coast,[1] while in the Los Angeles area, in particular, about one-third of the sheet and strip steel sold early in 1948 went through the gray market, a decline from an even higher figure in 1947.[2]

I

The immediate cause of the flourishing gray market in steel during the period 1946–49 was the high demand created as every manufacturer rushed production to meet the vast backlog of consumer demand that had built up during the war years of rationing and defense production. Later, the government's need for additional steel during the Korean conflict generated the same kind of extra demand and encouraged the gray market to reappear. In both cases the supply-demand forces of an open, competitive market would have adjusted to the excess demand by raising prices to a level high enough to cut out many marginal purchasers. Appropriate as such a result may seem for a competitive market, it would nevertheless have undoubtedly produced cries of monopoly, profiteering, and gouging from those faced with the high prices. Steel company executives were not anxious to disappoint excitable customers and lay themselves open to public charges of being ruthless, exploiting monopolists.

Even though they kept their prices down, the large steel producers did not escape criticism. Many economists and congressmen accused the steel industry of failing to expand its capacity after World War II. Although it had increased blast furnace capacity during the war by 21 per cent, the industry increased it in the next five years by only 6 per cent. The reluctance of industry leaders to expand capacity further stemmed from the bitter experience of the Great Depression of the 1930's. By 1932 production of steel ingots and castings had fallen to one-fourth of 1929's output, and during the best year in the thirties, production was only 85 per cent of that in 1929. Much more than half of the industry's capacity simply lay idle for over a decade. During the war, at the insistence of government officials, the industry increased ingot capacity from 81.6 million tons to 91.9 million tons in 1946. In 1947, about 87 million tons of this capacity could be used, and this meant that some 60 million tons of finished steel could be produced (quite a lot of steel is lost in the lengthy process of converting raw steel into saleable goods). Final production of finished steel goods was far short of the estimated domestic demand of 67 million tons.[3]

In 1947 Congress authorized the establishment of a system of "voluntary" allocation of steel; this system continued until early in 1949 to meet the demands of various government programs essential to defense and foreign policy. These programs required about 17 million tons of finished steel yearly for "freight cars, shipbuilding, plumbing and heating equipment for houses, line pipe and other facilities for the oil and gas industries, exports to the 16 Marshall Plan countries, other priority exports, military requirements, Atomic Energy Commission projects, and barges for inland waterways." [4]

Many businessmen, government officials, and members of Congress felt that the demand for steel so greatly exceeded capacity that the industry's planned 3-million ton addition to capacity in 1947 was far too skimpy. The Senate Small Business Sub-

[1] "That Daffy Gray Market," *Fortune,* 37 (May, 1948), 95.
[2] *Business Week,* September 28, 1948, p. 73.
[3] *U.S. News & World Report,* August 8, 1948, p. 39.
[4] *Ibid.,* p. 40.

committee presented a report that summarized the research findings of three governmental departments in support of its view that more steel producing facilities were needed:

> The Department of Labor estimates the 1950 demand for ingot steel, under conditions of full employment, at between 98 and 120 million tons. The Department of Commerce calls for a minimum of 99.5 million tons. The Department of Agriculture . . . predicts a demand for 110 million tons.[5]

Steel spokesmen dissented from these views, stating that the current shortage was temporary, the result of an unusual situation brought about by pent-up domestic demand and the wartime destruction of steel capacity abroad. They pointed to the small demand during the Depression in describing steel as a feast-and-famine industry. To increase capacity rapidly would lead to a repetition of the 1939 situation when steel production had been only 62 per cent of capacity. Research reports prepared for the industry indicated an average yearly steel consumption of no more than 59 million to 75 million tons for the post-war period. In 1946 steel spokesmen had confidently argued that the industry had sufficient capacity to fill orders "to 1975 at least"; further, they expected no order backlog until after 1947 at least.[6] (The average annual production of steel, 1950–64, was 103 million tons, ranging from a low of 85 million to a high of 127 million tons.)

Senator James E. Murray of Montana reminded several company witnesses testifying before the Small Business Subcommittee that in 1941 steel company officials had opposed increases in capacity on much the same grounds as they were doing in 1947, even though steel capacity had had to be increased by 15 million tons before the end of the war. He proposed that the government underwrite the cost of constructing new capacity immediately. Financing of private construction could be handled through Reconstruction Finance Corporation loans, or the government could undertake construction directly as it had done during the war.

The Small Business Subcommittee hearings reflected the fact that steel capacity was now a political issue, with the government and many steel consumers on one side and steel company executives and many businessmen on the other. During 1947 and 1948, after the companies granted wage increases, they raised the price of steel. These price hikes added fuel to the fires of political controversy. After the first such increase in 1947, and with a second rise likely before the end of the year even though steel profits were at a high level, Senator Estes Kefauver of Tennessee announced that he was appalled by the industry's pricing behavior and its refusal to expand capacity. He announced:

> We have now an opportunity to see whether those who in debate on the [Taft-Hartley] labor bill were so opposed to monopoly are actually against monopoly, or are only critical of monopoly when it appears in the field of labor itself.[7]

Senator Edward Martin of Pennsylvania was also aroused by what he thought was the industry's restriction of capacity as well as by the questionable practices involved in steel distribution. At the conclusion of the hearings by the Small Business Subcommittee in September, 1947, he lectured the industry leaders:

> As the heads of steel companies you cannot be expected to bear the entire blame [for gray market practices]. However, you certainly cannot escape all the responsibility for the abuses revealed by this investigation. You have the power to control it by the exercise of your leadership and your authority. . . . I tell you this frankly. . . . If evils like the steel gray market and other abuses which have developed, and similar racketeering in other lines of business do not end,

[5] *Ibid.*, October 3, 1947, p. 33.
[6] *Ibid.*, August 8, 1948, p. 41.

[7] *New Republic*, September 8, 1947, pp. 10–12.

> don't be surprised when Uncle Sam moves in as a traffic cop.
>
> I realize that steel is a tough business. But in the steel business, as in any other business, management has no more right to adopt a "public be damned" attitude than has labor or government.[8]

Benjamin Fairless, president of United States Steel, defended his company and the industry generally. He retorted:

> The policy followed by the United States Steel Corporation has been just the reverse of a "public be damned" attitude. . . . We have tried to distribute our steel production equitably among many thousands of steel users in a way designed to serve the best interests of the country as a whole.[9]

In a speech delivered before the Baltimore Chamber of Commerce, Fairless blasted governmental intervention in the steel industry:

> I do not fear Fascism because it killed the three great nations which adopted it. . . . I do not fear socialism because, in Europe today, socialism is living on the dole, and America is the only country on the earth that is able to foot the bill. . . . But when somebody in Washington starts telling me how much he loves the free enterprise system and how he proposes to save it from itself, I shake in my very shoes. I wonder why it is that these self-appointed saviors of our national welfare always seem to miss the point . . . that our American system is the only one left in the world that is not controlled by power-hungry politicians, who would literally hack it to death on the pretext of saving its immortal soul. . . . I have been through so many congressional inquisitions that no self-respecting skeleton would hide in my closet on a bet.[10]

II

The steel industry was able to maintain its private allocation system and keep what in effect was a price ceiling on steel products because a few firms controlled most of the production, because these firms had long worked together under an arrangement of "price leadership," and because the cost of entry was high enough to discourage any serious new competition. The conditions that supported the maintenance of private allocation and price controls did not necessarily insure efficient management of the system, however. Steel companies supposedly gave allocation priorities to old and large customers. One steel executive explained that allocations were not "hard and fast," but that they did "reflect a past relationship." [11] When it was advantageous to do so, however, company salesmen took on promising new customers—thousands in total—before the demands of old customers were satisfied. Practices varied. Some old customers got all their steel requirements filled, while others did not; in some cases expanding needs were taken into account and in other cases they were not. An orderly market became impossible; whether a company badly needed steel or not and whether the price it was ready to pay was high or low did not seem to affect the availability of steel. If steel did become available, there was no assurance where it would turn up. Several large producers—among them Norge Appliances, which had to operate at 60 per cent of capacity in 1947—and a host of smaller producers had to cut back production severely because of steel shortages. In many cases, small firms went out of business because they could not get the steel necessary to produce goods that they were virtually assured of selling.

Many a user learned the hard way just how uncertain steel allocations were. Partly because of their efforts to maintain the industry's basing-point pricing [12] despite freight rate increases, steel companies began to close out old accounts in distant territories, leaving customers there with no regular steel supply at all. The behavior of

[8] *Newsweek,* September 22, 1947, pp. 67–68.
[9] *Ibid.,* p. 67.
[10] *Ibid.,* May 1, 1950, p. 58.

[11] *Fortune,* 37 (May, 1948), 170.
[12] See p. 108 in Chapter 5.

a division of the National Supply Company, a major pipe manufacturer, was the subject of a report in *Fortune* magazine. When its officers decided that the company no longer could or would absorb the $4–$6 per ton freight charge from its Pittsburgh mill to Chicago (the nearest basing point to its midwestern customers), the National division closed off its accounts in five midwestern states. When these customers offered to pay National or any rival supplier the freight charges, the steel companies replied that such practices were "uneconomical" or would violate policy. Suddenly cut off from their normal supply of steel, the users turned to the gray market for relief.

The steel shortage gave the large steel companies an opportunity to increase their share of manufacturing finished steel goods. Naturally, they filled their own steel needs first before supplying unfinished steel to non-integrated firms. They also reaped a competitive advantage by raising prices for unfinished steel and lowering prices on finished steel goods. Through such tactics the large steel producers were able to eliminate many small firms. For example, by the late 1940's the basic steel producers accounted for nearly 85 per cent of domestic steel-drum output, compared with roughly 7 per cent during the 1930's. And between 1945 and 1949, U.S. Steel's sales of iron ore to outsiders declined from 9.2 million tons to 4 million tons.[13]

Executives of small firms reacted to this kind of pressure by protesting the "unfair competition" of the "monopolistic" companies and charged corruption, bribery, and payoffs. In looking into the matter, the Senate Small Business Subcommittee turned up few cases of actual malpractice. On March 8, 1948, *Newsweek* announced one of these rare finds in the following terms: "The Senate Small Business Subcommittee investigating the gray market in steel had spent months hunting for an elephant. Last week it bagged its first game: a mouse."[14]

The mouse was M. J. Courtis, an account clerk with Carnegie-Illinois Steel in Chicago. Courtis lined up a customer, the Steel City Welders Corporation of Gary, Indiana, that was willing to pay $200 a ton for steel. Then Courtis got in touch with Copco Steel and Engineering Corporation of Detroit, a Carnegie-Illinois customer. Courtis informed Copco that if it would ship the necessary sheets to Steel City Welders, he would see that Copco's orders from Carnegie-Illinois were expedited. Courtis and a friend collected the difference between the $96 a ton Copco charged and the $200 a ton which Steel City Welders paid. The two expediters collected over $32,000 in "fees" before they were caught.

Large firms such as Allis-Chalmers, Fruehauf Trailers, International Harvester, and White Motors were not much affected by petty shakedowns of this sort. Enjoying well-established supplier relations, they could usually satisfy their needs through regular trade channels. Not infrequently, however, they found that they had to purchase large quantities of metals for which there was little demand—stainless and brass—in order to secure the steel they wanted.

When the large companies were pressed too hard by the steel shortage, they had the financial reserves to engage in "conversion" or to buy steel mills outright. Conversion began as the practice of trading scrap steel for a much smaller amount of finished steel. Since the scrap dealers were able to sell finished steel on the gray market for handsome prices, they gained most of the advantage in this kind of conversion, so the steel companies put an end to it. Later, user companies financially strong enough to carry large steel inventories practiced conversion by buying ingots and semifinished steel from firms short of finishing facilities and contracting with other steel firms that had surplus finishing capacity for

[13] Walter Adams, "The Steel Industry," in Walter Adams, ed., *The Structure of American Industry,* 3rd ed. (New York: Macmillan, 1961), pp. 154–55.

[14] p. 65.

final processing. A user needed the cooperation of the steel firms involved, of course.

The risks of conversion convinced a number of steel users that outright ownership of a steel mill made better business sense. Borg-Warner bought Superior Sheet Steel of Canton, Ohio; General Electric bought Mahoning Valley Steel; Apollo Steel was acquired by a syndicate of 25 steel users; and Studebaker bought Empire Steel.[15] Not all arrangements of this type worked out as planned, unfortunately. Kaiser-Frazer, for example, bought into Portsmouth Steel, a company controlled by the Cleveland financier Cyrus Eaton, in order to supply its new automobile assembly lines in the old Ford bomber plant at Willow Run, Michigan. Despite its holdings in the company, one year later Kaiser lost Portsmouth's monthly steel allocation of 23,000 tons. Kaiser was then forced to purchase pig iron from a War Administration plant in Cleveland and to finish up to 15,000 tons of steel a month at a mill leased in Findlay, Ohio. Any steel over this amount had to be processed at the Kaiser-owned blast furnace at Provo, Utah.[16]

Even if a user secured a small hand mill's production after buying into it, the cost was higher than for the steel produced by the large integrated companies. Borg-Warner's newly acquired Superior Sheet Steel was probably one of the most efficient hand mills, yet its costs were 50 per cent higher ($130–$140 a ton for hot-rolled sheets) than those of large continuous mills.

III

For those not fortunate enough to have allocations in the regular steel market, good connections, or sufficient resources to buy a small steel mill, the only way to get steel was to shop in the gray market. Steel for the gray market came from a variety of sources. The main source was the resale of steel by customers who received priority allocations but found that they could make more money selling their allotment than by using it themselves. A manufacturer might also receive delivery of only one kind of steel—sheet—when he needed deliveries of wire as well to keep his assembly lines going. He would thus find himself with a temporarily unusable surplus of sheet. The sensible response to this situation was to find another buyer and turn his surplus inventory into cash.

Imports of steel from countries eager to take advantage of the attractive high prices in the United States to secure scarce dollars added to the gray market supply. Ironically, many of the nations involved were those to whom the United States was allocating $55-a-ton steel under terms of Marshall Plan agreements. While Congress debated the European Recovery Program, British tin plate was being readily sold in the United States at 17¢ a pound, against the U.S. list price of 7¢; and Belgian hot-rolled sheets were being offered to Americans and bought by them at prices ranging from $265 to $335 a ton in Antwerp.[17]

A third and minor source of steel in the gray market was the kind of leakage from the regular market exemplified in the case of M. J. Courtis, the Small Business Subcommittee's "mouse."

How the gray market operated in detail to distribute the steel obtained from these sources and the kind of men who ran it were revealed in the investigations conducted in 1952 by the Senate's Select Committee on Small Business under the chairmanship of Blair Moody of Michigan. The gray market promoters were men of ingenuity; in other circumstances they might have been hailed as able entrepreneurs.

One of the gray market operators whose activities the committee thoroughly examined was Seymour Waldman of Chicago, owner of the Emergency Steel Service Corporation of Skokie, Illinois. In 1946, the

[15] *Fortune,* 37 (August, 1948), 175.
[16] *Business Week,* November 27, 1948, p. 20.
[17] *Fortune,* 37 (May, 1948), 173.

resources of this company consisted of only $5,000 in capital, a small office in Chicago's Loop rented for $25 a month, Waldman's own nimble mind, and a willingness to hunt for hard-to-get steel for needy processors. At first, Waldman advertised his services by mail, stamping and addressing the envelopes himself. By 1951 the firm employed 25 people, including five salesmen who ran up phone bills of $4,000 a month; annual sales were around $7 million, with profits at $280,000.[18] Waldman admitted that over 50 per cent of the firm's business consisted of buying and selling steel at prices considerably above those at which preferred buyers bought steel from the mills. Where Waldman's company fit in the overall pattern of gray market steel transactions appears in the following passage from the Select Committee's report:

> Harry Phillips of the Ohio Valley Tool & Die Co., Steubenville, Ohio, was the first link in the chain. He purchased the steel from the Weirton Steel Co. and the Fort Pitt Steel Co. at prices ranging between $5.20 and $5.80 a hundredweight. He sold the steel to his brother, Matthew Phillips of the M. & E. Co., New Cumberland, W. Va., at $7.50 a hundredweight. Matthew sold it to a Pittsburgh broker, Isadore Forman, at $10. Forman sold it to the Martin Co. of Cleveland at $10.40. The person who bought it for the Martin Co. then turned around and sold a portion of the shipment in the name of Metal Associates at $10.50 to Emergency Steel Service of Skokie, Ill. Emergency finally sold the steel to an end user, the Daisy Manufacturing Co. of Plymouth, Mich., at $10.95 a hundredweight plus 40 cents in phantom freight charges and "Federal tax." Metal Associates sold the balance of the shipment to K. & G. Steel of Chicago at $11.10 a hundredweight. K. & G. in turn sold it to Aldan Steel at $11.95. Aldan sold it to Chevrolet-Indianapolis at $15.45. Thus, in one series of deals, the steel was bought and sold by six different brokers, and in the other series of deals seven brokers managed to take a hand in extending the "daisy chain." Throughout the transactions the steel never left Steubenville, Ohio, until it was sold to the end users, the Daisy Manufacturing Co. and Chevrolet-Indianapolis.[19]

Some of the agents who had traded Waldman's steel before it got to him were, if anything, even more nimble than Waldman himself. Jay Freidman, the "person" mentioned by the committee as buying steel for the Martin Company, was shown to be doing the selling for Metal Associates as well.[20] Isadore Forman, the Pittsburgh broker, told the committee that he did not have a warehouse for steel or use steel in any way. His sole source of steel was the M. & E. Company, with whose management he had close ties of friendship. He also admitted that he did not allow government regulations to interfere with his business. Regulation No. 98 issued by the Office of Price Stabilization in 1951 required all steel producers and sellers to list the highest price they had charged during 1951 and prohibited any higher price; this regulation remained in effect until the end of the Korean war. When government officials questioned Forman about his steel business he pointed out that he was a contractor; when they appeared at another time to investigate contracting, he argued that he was a steel broker.

The final purchasers of the steel in the "daisy-chain" described by the committee were apparently not always aware of the complex transactions that preceded the sales to them. Lester Carlin, the purchasing agent for Chevrolet-Indianapolis, a job shop producing parts for Chevrolet trucks, said that he was only following company policy in buying steel from established firms that had steel warehouses. When he was informed that he might have purchased the $345 a ton steel at $200 through another broker, he was quoted as saying, "It has been an

[18] *Newsweek,* December 31, 1950, pp. 72–73.

[19] U.S. Senate, *Report of the Select Committee on Small Business, The Gray Market in Steel* (Washington: Government Printing Office, 1952), p. 7.

[20] *Ibid.,* pp. 12–13.

education here today. I can assure you of that." [21]

The other end user was the Daisy Manufacturing Company, a producer of air rifles, BB shot, and toys. Cass Hough, executive vice president, testified that Daisy employed about 500 people and that approximately 40 per cent of the population of Plymouth, Michigan, was dependent upon the company. He pointed out that Daisy was limited by the National Production Agency's restrictive order to produce only 58 per cent as many goods as it had manufactured in 1949. Daisy was not allocated the steel needed to reach that level of production, however, nor was it given a priority rating; it could not get steel from primary producers, for it had only a hunting license. Thus, for Daisy the alternatives were laying off its work force or buying steel on the gray market.[22]

The Select Committee's Detroit hearings produced other startling findings. Two members of the Intelligence Unit of the Bureau of Internal Revenue in Detroit, for example, were reported to have engaged in gray market transactions on behalf of brokers. The operations of the Oakman Manufacturing Company provided another case study that revealed the peculiarities and opportunities of the gray market. Nathan and Harry Freedland, the two owners of Oakman, had been arrested before the war on charges of running handbooks. The company's main business ostensibly was making metal stampings for a large number of customers, including the Chrysler Corporation and the Hudson Motor Car. Testimony brought out that another 40 per cent of their business involved selling steel. Oakman bought steel at $60 a ton from large steel producers and sold it to end producers at prices ranging up to $375 a ton. The Freedland brothers readily admitted that they carried on their gray market operations through two dummy corporations, L. & M. Steel and Clements Steel. According to a committee report:

> The L. & M. Steel Company was named for Louis and Mary Labovitz who were shown to be related through marriage to the Freedland brothers. Louis Labovitz testified that he received $35,000 a year for receiving checks and other mail at his home. He carried the materials to the offices of Oakman Manufacturing Company where Max Derin, the purchasing agent for Oakman, kept all records for L. & M. . . .
>
> Mrs. Yetta Dubin, nominal head of the Clements Steel Company . . . identified the Clements Steel Company as "a selling agency for the Oakman," and stated that she was a sister-in-law to Nathan Freedland. She said that she was paid $100 a month for signing checks in the name of the Clements Steel Company. She also received mail addressed to the company at her home and delivered this mail unopened to the company purchasing agent, Max Derin, at Oakman.
>
> Testimony of other witnesses disclosed that the steel passing through the L. & M. Steel Company and the Clements Steel Company went principally to the Ambassador Steel Company and the V. & R. Steel Company.
>
> Hyman Freedland, head of Ambassador Steel, stated that he was a brother of Nathan and Harry Freedland and that he did a monthly business of $35,000 in buying and selling steel. Hyman could not identify any of the nominal officers of the L. & M. Steel Company or the Clements Steel Company. He said that his brothers at the Oakman Manufacturing Company handled all the details on steel coming to him through L. & M. and Clements.
>
> Victor Rothberg, owner of the V. & R. Steel Company, testified that he conducted his business from his home. He was uncertain as to the amounts of steel he had handled in the past year. Committee records indicated that Rothberg had sold 3,000 tons since March 1951. When asked if this was a

[21] U.S. Senate, *Hearings before a Subcommittee of the Select Committee on Small Business, Steel Gray Market* (Washington: Government Printing Office, 1952), p. 129.

[22] *Report*, p. 9.

fair statement, Rothberg replied that it was not, that he "handled more than that." [23]

IV

In its report, *The Gray Market in Steel*,[24] the Select Committee strongly condemned gray market practices and steel middlemen.

> Your committee is hopeful that the new OPS regulation, CPR 98 . . . will provide the teeth necessary to put the gray market operators out of business. These parasites of the steel industry perform absolutely no useful economic purpose. They are in the market for all the traffic will bear. Most of them have little or no experience in the steel business. They were drawn to it like bees to honey when they saw the opportunity to make a "fast buck." They will remain in it as long as the shortages continue. Then, as in World War II, they will move into greener fields, perhaps to war surplus or other scarce commodities. Whatever they do and wherever they may be, one may be certain that they will be trading on another's hardship. Small businessmen in other fields, hard pressed for other scarce materials and commodities, will be encountering the same names and faces.
>
> The gray market in steel has been a vicious and reprehensible thing. The small businessman has not been the only victim. Big business has felt its effects too. The entire economy has suffered. The net effect of gray markets in steel and elsewhere, has been to inflate prices and to increase the cost of the defense program. In these days when economy is essential to the well-being of the nation, America can ill afford gray markets. They must be stamped out wherever and whenever they arise.[25]

Seymour Waldman of Emergency Steel disagreed strongly with the committee's conclusions. He pointed out that the gray market and its practices were neither surprising nor bad, since GNP had grown three-fold and the number of manufacturing firms had increased from 235,000 in 1941 to 307,000 in 1951. He maintained that industry had outgrown the pattern for steel movements that had served in an earlier period and claimed that the gray market distributors who handled 18 per cent of the nation's steel output performed a valuable and necessary service:

> There was a need and there still remains a need for a redistribution service (now termed a daisy chain) in order to place steel where it is required in this vast, greatly expanded industrial structure which exists in this country today. How can any single distributing firm keep abreast of the metal requirements of 307,100 companies? If a distributor is doing a good job in his area he will have many opportunities to be of real service by locating material for manufacturers that is material that they require for production and which is not currently in stock. If distributor A needs steel for an account and distributor B has that item available is not the national security furthered if that scarce item is moved into production?
>
> Let us go one step further. . . . D may have had the offering from B or perhaps B offered to E, another distributor who offered to D. Of course, the price will increase each time the steel changes hands but without the profit incentive this scarce material would not move. We have used an extreme example involving many middlemen, but we maintain that even such a movement as described is not only beneficial to all parties involved but is also for the national good.
>
> A descriptive analogy might be the purchase of corporate stock without a stock exchange. What a difficult time one would have in purchasing a given stock if he had to locate another individual somewhere in this country who owned the desired stock and wanted to sell it! [26]

Mr. Waldman also argued that the accusations and charges leveled against steel distributors contradicted some of the established underpinnings of our society:

[23] *Ibid.*, pp. 19–20.
[24] *Report.*
[25] *Ibid.*, p. 25.
[26] *Hearings*, pp. 140–41.

It is exceedingly unfortunate that proceedings of this should be referred to by the somewhat nebulous term "gray market query." . . . In a capitalistic system where price controls are not present, prices of goods or commodities supposedly are controlled by supply and demand. On the one hand we are told that profit incentive is the backbone of our American democracy and on the other we are maligned by some quarters for attempting to make profits. In the minds of the average laymen the term "gray market" connotes something evil, something akin to the illegal black market. . . . [Those who accuse us] realizing the futility of criticizing the profit incentive free-enterprise system while at the same time conducting an ideological war against communism, change the charge to "profiteering." [27]

[27] *Ibid.*, pp. 139–40.

CIVIL RIGHTS AND SELECTIVE PATRONAGE

Encouraged by the Supreme Court's 1954 decision that "separate but equal" schools were unconstitutional, American Negroes began a revolution to achieve their full social and political rights as citizens. Their first major success came in December, 1956, when a boycott of Montgomery, Alabama, buses succeeded in forcing an end to segregated seating on public transportation. In cities and towns across the nation, in north and south, Negroes and sympathetic whites began to use "sit-ins" to obtain restaurant and lunch counter service for Negroes, "freedom rides" to eliminate segregated bus and rail transportation, "stand-ins" to gain open admission to theaters, parks, and swim clubs, and "kneel-ins" to open churches. A notable characteristic of this social movement was that Negro ministers usually played a leading role in organizing and directing the efforts to do away with segregation.

I

In Philadelphia, Pennsylvania, a group of Negro ministers had become increasingly concerned with the high and rising rate of unemployment in their community. The unemployment rate for Negroes had risen from 4.5 per cent in 1954 to 10.7 per cent in 1959 and was almost twice that of whites. The ministers believed that discrimination was a major cause of the higher unemployment, for Negroes were often the last to be hired and the first to be laid off; furthermore, they were seldom hired for the more secure white-collar positions. The ministers were especially concerned with arbitrary discrimination against Negroes in the higher paying prestige jobs. Having learned that a Negro had few opportunities to be promoted to good jobs, however well trained or qualified he might be, many Negro youths lost hope. Understandably, they saw no use in preparing themselves for jobs that were denied them. Discrimination thus tended to keep Negroes at the bottom of the job heap and to encourage them to drift into the ranks of the unemployable. Either without jobs at all or subject to frequent job losses, they received low incomes and could accumulate few resources; this economic weakness made them vulnerable to further economic retaliation when they attempted to exercise the rights normally available to and enjoyed by American citizens.

Federal fair-employment regulations and the fair-employment statutes of a number of states had made only modest contributions to opening jobs for Negroes. The Philadelphia ministers were convinced that for many years white employers had joined with their workers and the unions in a massive, tacit, and effective "shut-out" of Negroes. This shut-out was not a legally imposed program, however; most job discrimination was the result of habit, custom, inertia, and unthinking decisions by those who made employment policy in private companies. Successful attacks upon discriminatory hiring, the ministers decided, would thus have to be primarily through private, non-legal programs. Further, the Negroes would have to use their own strength.

Philadelphia's population was just over two million people, of whom 535,000 were classified as non-white; these persons were mostly Negroes. The Negro community commanded a total income of between $600 million and $800 million with which to purchase goods and services. The group of ministers discovered that though Negroes made up nearly 27 per cent of Philadelphia's population, they held less than 1 per cent of the prestige jobs in the city's companies and firms. "Prestige jobs" were defined as those filled by junior executives, supervisors, clerical workers, skilled tradesmen, driver-salesmen, and other employees who came into close personal asociation with other personnel and customers. Although Negroes comprised one-quarter of the population of the city, the ministers thought it reasonable that Negroes should fill jobs at every level in the job structure roughly in proportion to their number in the nation's population as a whole, about 10 per cent; as a goal for the beginning of their program they set an even lower figure than this, however.

Their aims were to get business firms immediately to hire some Negroes for prestige positions and to stop arbitrary discrimination against all Negroes in hiring. To achieve these goals the ministers worked out a technique that would permit them to make their demands with full knowledge of each firm's situation and to back these demands, once they were made, with increasing pressure until they were met. They called this technique the Selective Patronage Program (SPP), and described it as "moral persuasion by withdrawing economic support." [1]

Many of the characteristics of SPP reflected careful preliminary legal investigation. Uses of private economic power, such as withholding credit, denying supply, or refusing patronage, were unrestricted by law if exercised individually and voluntarily. Concerted use of economic power might also be legal if the participants joined freely and voluntarily. The more organized the use of economic power, the more likely it was to become subject to the prohibitions of conspiracies in restraint of trade. Since SPP skirted a gray, uncertain area of the law, the ministers tried to avoid legal entanglements by not using the word "boycott" and by not establishing any organization or electing any officers or directorate. They ran the program on an *ad hoc* basis with *ad hoc* leadership and spokesmen for each encounter with a new company.

II

In late spring, 1960, the Rev. Leon Sullivan, Philadelphia Zion Baptist Church, and a group of other ministers met with the president and the personnel manager of the Tasty Baking Company. They had already successfully requested another company to hire more Negroes. After discussing Tasty's hiring practices and the distribution of Negroes in its work force, the ministers asked the company to hire two Negro driver-salesmen, two Negro clerical workers, and three or four Negro girls in the icing department. No Negroes were currently working in the jobs they asked be filled, for traditionally these categories had been "white." Mr. Pass, the personnel manager, argued that Tasty did not discriminate; its record of hiring Negroes was excellent, and there had been hundreds of Negroes in the company's employ. The

[1] The story of the SPP is based largely on materials in Hannah Lees, "The Not-Buying Power of Philadelphia's Negroes," the *Reporter,* 24 (May 11, 1961), 33–35; the *Wall Street Journal,* January 8, 1963; "How Negro Pressure Gets Jobs," *U.S. News & World Report,* 55 (August 12, 1963), 30–32; and other news reports in the *New York Times* and the *Wall Street Journal.*

ministers were not impressed. They wanted Tasty to hire Negroes for some positions of dignity and responsibility, and they would settle for nothing less than their demand.

Mr. Kaiser, Tasty's president, countered that he had no need just then for any more clerical workers or driver-salesmen; further, he did not appreciate being pushed. However, he agreed to hire more Negroes as the need arose. The ministers said they would give Tasty two weeks to hire the required number of Negroes. If the positions they had named were not filled by then, the SPP would go into effect.

Tasty did not meet the ministers' demands within the two week period. The next Sunday Negro ministers in 450 churches throughout greater Philadelphia explained the situation to their congregations, "exercising their democratic right to advise their friends what to buy and where," as one put it. They told their congregations that as individuals they were not going to buy any Tasty products until the stated quota of Negroes was hired, but they added that it was up to each individual to decide whether to do something to help the drive for Negro freedom. Approximately 125,000 Negroes decided to support SPP. Two weeks later Tasty had not yet capitulated, so the ministers urged their congregations to intensify the SPP. Signs advertising Tasty's slowness in hiring Negroes began to appear in bars, barber shops, and beauty parlors. As the program continued, it gained supporters from among Negro fraternal organizations, social clubs, and newspapers. The NAACP also endorsed it. When after eight weeks Tasty announced it had hired two Negro driver-salesmen, two Negro clerical workers, and some half-dozen Negro icers, almost all of Philadelphia's Negroes had joined in the SPP.

The white community of Philadelphia was almost completely ignorant of what had happened. The three newspapers with big circulation in Philadelphia ignored the selective patronage campaign. The editors explained that they did not want to aggravate racial tensions. Noting that newspaper publicity for boycotts would almost certainly increase their chances of success, one editor said, "We did not want to be put in the position of helping with publicity something we don't know whether we can agree with, either morally or legally."

Late in September, 1960, a group of ministers called on officials of the Pepsi-Cola company and asked that Negroes be hired for certain positions. When the request was rejected, the ministers announced that an SPP against Pepsi would begin on the following Sunday, October 2. Sales of Pepsi-Cola fell sharply on Monday and Tuesday. On October 4, Pepsi sent a telegram to the ministers announcing its willingness to follow their hiring suggestions. The SPP continued for two full weeks, however, for the ministers' policy was not to call an end to a program until the new employees were actually at work.

Two other soft drink companies found the ministers' requests reasonable; they complied quickly and suffered no withdrawal of patronage. Two baking companies, Bond Bread and Freihofen Bread, learned from Tasty's experience and also avoided any trouble. The ministers approached a number of oil companies—Esso, Cities Service, Mobile, and Atlantic—and found the officials quite sympathetic to their demands. Atlantic already had about 25 Negroes in such clerical and executive jobs as chemist, psychologist, and sales promotion staff worker, and reported itself well pleased with the quality of work done by its Negro employees and with general office morale.

Two other oil companies did not respond as quickly to the ministers' demands. Since both the Gulf Oil and the Sun Oil companies faced difficult problems with seasonal hiring and in dealing with their unionized workers, company officials did not see how they could immediately change their hiring practices. Gulf Oil was approached at the height of the winter heating season when its highest complement of employees had already been hired. Its officials did not even respond to the request of Rev. Joshua Licorish of the Zion Methodist Church for an appointment. After waiting three weeks he and the other ministers brought Gulf's lack of cooperation to the notice of their congregations. The following Monday, Gulf's switchboard was jammed with customers cancelling fuel-oil contracts. With sales showing a sharp drop, the company moved fast; within a week it had arranged for the ministers to talk over the hiring problems with its officials and the union leaders involved.

The ministers had stipulated that new Negro employees must not be the first laid off. The union men said they were sympathetic with the Negro aims but not when these aims ran counter to hard-won union gains. Layoffs strictly followed seniority under their agreement with Gulf. If the newest drivers were not laid off, all drivers hired for the season's peak would have to be kept on with no work. The ministers chose not to be a party to featherbedding, and they wanted to avoid an open conflict with the union over displacing unionized white workers. An agreement was accordingly reached that the company would hire three Negro truck drivers; the union agreed they could become union members but insisted they would be laid off first if they were lowest in seniority. Twelve days after SPP began, Gulf had hired the required Negroes.

Sun Oil Company also found the ministers tough in their bargaining but willing to be flexible in meeting difficult problems. The Rev. Alfred G. Dunston, Wesley African Methodist Episcopal Church, was the spokesman for the ministers. He and a number of his colleagues met with company officials on February 3, 1961. Though the company pointed out that it had hired two Negro clerks at the Marcus Hook refinery the year before, in addition to employing many Negroes who had long tenure there, the ministers were more impressed with the facts that of the 1500 office staff workers only two were Negroes and that there were no Negro truck drivers.

Two weeks after this meeting Rev. Dunston asked Sun to hire 24 additional Negroes, 19 for the office (the same number as employed by Atlantic, whose administrative installation was about the same size), 3 permanent truck drivers, and a products salesman. All were to be hired within a month. Sun officials objected that they could not be expected to hire truck drivers just as the heating season was ending; moreover, they did not think they could find so many qualified Negroes in only four weeks.

By March 19, the ministers' deadline, the company had interviewed 19 Negro applicants for clerical work but had hired only one; the others failed to qualify by the standards used. Sun had also hired a Negro salesman and upgraded a Negro mechanic to driver. Since their demands had not been met, the ministers urged their church members to support an SPP against Sun. The withdrawal of patronage continued for a month and a half; the ministers estimated that it cost Sun some $7,000 a week. Before the SPP ended Sun had hired all of the required office workers, and the ministers had settled for the company's promise to upgrade other Negroes to truck drivers as job openings became available.

Officials of other companies, unable to believe that they could be accused of discrimination against Negroes, underestimated the resolve and strength the ministers possessed. Early in March, 1961, a delegation of ministers told Mr. William Dickinson, managing editor of the Philadelphia *Bulletin,* that it expected him to hire 28 additional Negroes for specific jobs such as reporter, copy boy, and librarian as well as for positions in various clerical and press-operations positions. Dickinson replied that this "came as a great surprise to us. We thought we were well integrated. We had about 50 Negroes in editorial, supervisory, and other white-collar jobs, in addition to about 650 Negro newsboys." He promised to hire Negroes but was unable to meet the deadline. Withdrawal of patronage was in effect from April 15 to June 10, when the paper finally hired the last of the Negroes that the ministers had specified.

One of the *Bulletin*'s competitors, the Philadelphia *Inquirer,* hired an additional 39 Negroes, met its deadline, and thus avoided any SPP against it. A number of other employers also met the deadlines, but some complained that they had had difficulty in finding enough Negro girls to qualify for office work. Many reported that they had lowered their requirements in order to secure the number of workers required, though none explained what the requirements were or how they had been set. One businessman said that his company had had to retrain its new Negro employees before they could fill the more demanding posts. The ministers sent numerous applicants to the companies, telling the hiring officials that if they couldn't find qualified people, that "is your problem."

The personnel manager of the Great Atlantic and Pacific Tea Company was so sure no charge of discrimination could be made against his company that he gave a ministers' committee the company's personnel records to study. In the fall of 1962 the committee members carefully analyzed the 2,000 jobs in A&P's 150 stores in the area and in its general offices. They found that about 11 per cent of the employees were Negroes, but no Negroes were employed in the 250-man general office staff, few held jobs as cashiers and checkers, and not enough were in the meat and dairy product departments. Further, Negro workers complained that they faced job restrictions in warehouse jobs. The ministers asked that these restrictions be eliminated, that 60 Negroes be hired in the stores, and that at least 6 be added to the office staff.

A&P officials were astonished by these demands, but since 20 other companies had already complied with the ministers' requests and 6 had suffered under SPP they agreed to add Negroes as fast as job openings appeared. The ministers replied that the company had a month to hire the 60 Negroes. When the manager complained that the deadline was unrealistic, the ministers gave him another month. By December 9, 1962, the company had still not put Negroes in two of the positions specified, and the ministers announced an SPP against A&P. On February 4, 1963, the ministers announced that the company had more than met the minimum requirements, having hired, upgraded, or retrained at least 80 Negroes for higher-paying positions.

III

Mr. Ruby Hurley, NAACP director for the Southeastern region said, "The cash register has a way of talking to the . . . businessman that beats anything I know of." Other leaders pointed out that the boycott is less likely to lead to violence and police curbs than are sit-ins and other public demonstrations. Rev. Ralph D. Abernathy, an Atlanta Negro leader who had been jailed seven times for integrationist activities said, "Nobody wants to go to jail, but everybody can safely switch to another brand of bread or stop buying someone's soda pop." [2]

Several of the Philadelphia companies approached by the ministers reported that they were not unhappy with the results. More qualified Negro job seekers began to show up once Negroes learned that they might have a good chance of being accepted and that they certainly would be considered for jobs. An oil company official revealed that his parent organization had begun to hire more Negroes in other cities as a result of the Philadelphia experience: "The result is we're now getting some crackerjack Negro salesmen." He also said that

[2] *Wall Street Journal,* January 8, 1963.

sales had increased since the boycott. Other firms, including banks and insurance companies, heeded the lesson of the SPP campaigns and for the first time began to employ Negroes in "sensitive" jobs that put them in direct contact with the public. The influence of the patronage program was thus more far-reaching than its direct effects. After moving against only 24 firms by late 1963, the ministers estimated that at least 4,000 new jobs for Negroes had opened up in these companies and others in Philadelphia.

Some Philadelphians wondered if other groups might be encouraged to try to get jobs for themselves through force; potentially, competing boycotts would create a nasty situation. A few people wondered aloud if the ministers might not be charged one day for violating city and state fair-employment practice laws on the ground that they were pressuring employers to hire on the basis of race. A report from Chicago in September, 1963, suggested that such concerns were not unfounded. The Department of Justice and the Cook County state attorney's office had begun an investigation of the Negro Labor Relations League. Employers had complained that the League had tried to extort money from them under the guise of seeking more employment opportunities for Negroes. League officials were alleged to have demanded contributions from businessmen and to have picketed with "Unfair to Negroes" signs those who refused.

Churchmen were especially concerned about the use of economic pressure by Negroes, since the churches, through their ministers, were organizing and leading the forceful programs of action. The National Council of Churches issued a statement that explored the ethical problems involved in such a program:

> Whereas in the past, economic suppression of practically every known form has been practiced in seeking to maintain the secondary status of Negroes and other non-whites, today the tables are being turned and a new spirit of economic aggressiveness is emerging on the part of those previously suppressed. . . . [The organized withdrawal of patronage] has become increasingly effective today because downtown merchants, especially, are growing vulnerable to competition from suburban stores and many depend for a substantial percentage of their business on the mid-city non-white residents. This type of economic pressure has been one of the most productive methods used to secure justice in the field of business. The technique of selective buying, as practiced in the North and East, has in addition produced little or no violence.
>
> It is significant to note also that in recent years responsible business managements, in determining the location of new plants, are increasingly influenced by the record of racial relations in the various communities under consideration. At this point both economic realism and a growing business consciousness of larger responsibility to owners, workers, suppliers, and customers are working against discrimination. Such developments are helping more and more community leaders to discover that discrimination is bad business, as well as bad social ethics.[3]

In the preface to the resolution on boycotts and economic pressure the General Board of the National Council of Churches declared:

> In view of the increasing significance of, and frequently mounting bitterness and tension in, the use of economic pressures in racial situations, the National Council of Churches recognizes that economic pressure is not simply good or evil in itself but must be judged in terms of the ethical ends it serves and the restraint and discipline with which it is used.[4]

[3] *Background Paper of Information: Use of Economic Pressures in Racial Tension,* General Board, National Council of Churches, 1963.

[4] *Resolution on Use of Economic Pressures in Racial Tensions,* Approved, General Board, National Council of Churches, June 8, 1963.

QUESTIONS

Benefits and Mischiefs of Private Action

1. "We cannot safely allow private groups to define the public interest for they will almost always twist their definition in such a way that it becomes merely a cover for their own interest." Do the actions of the steel companies and of the Negro ministers in the two cases support or repudiate this statement? Carefully note both the private and public interests involved.

2. "The Negro ministers appealed to the consumers to support their campaign, and thus consumer sovereignty was preserved. The steel managers, however, disregarded the market, substituting their judgment for that of the consumers. Clearly the steel companies are more to be condemned." Explain why you would agree or disagree with this statement.

3. If you would allow Negroes to operate a Selective Patronage Program (SPP), upon what principle would you base your decision to permit or forbid a White Citizens' Council to organize a boycott of firms employing Negroes?

4. List the short-term and long-term consequences for the steel companies should they choose in a time of short supply and high demand (a) to keep prices below "market demand" and to allocate production among consumers, or (b) to let the market fix prices and allocate steel. Which of these alternative actions would you recommend for a steel company to follow?

5. How would you distinguish the SPP from the racket wherein an organization sells "protection" under threat of injury to a business?

6. The Senate Select Committee condemned the gray-marketeers of steel as "parasites" who "perform absolutely no useful economic purpose"; Mr. Waldman contended that they were profit-seeking practitioners of free enterprise. With whom do you agree and why?

7. "Using the argument of the National Council of Churches one can justify not only the SPP and the steel companies' pricing policy in the mid-1940's and early 1950's but also anyone who rigs prices and shares markets. Such businessmen always can argue that they serve the ethical end of stabilizing markets, eliminating destructive cut-throat competition, and dampening wildly gyrating prices. As long as they act with discipline and restraint, they should not be condemned." Explain why you agree or disagree.

8. Mr. Fairless maintained that U.S. Steel tried to distribute steel "in a way designed to serve the best interests of the country as a whole." What evidence is there to support or disprove his statement?

chapter **7**

ESCAPE FROM COMPETITION

In 1889 Andrew Carnegie wrote in praise of competition:

> It is here, we cannot evade it, no substitutes for it have been found; and while the law may be hard for the individual, it is best for the race, because it insures the survival of the fittest in every department. We accept and welcome, therefore, as conditions to which we must accommodate ourselves, great inequality of environment, the concentration of business, industrial and commercial, in the hands of the few, and the law of competition between these, as being not only beneficial, but essential for the future progress of the race.[1]

He deftly included within his definition of competition the business forms that were then being denounced as monopolizing trusts.

The penchant for praising competition while supporting non-competitive practices is common among Americans. An ambivalent attitude toward competition bedevils economists, politicians, and jurists quite as much as businessmen and unionists. However much competition may be praised, it is usually found, first, to be more appealing in theory than in practice; second, to be more "practical" for the other fellow than for oneself; and third, to be best appreciated, in any case, if it is conducted in a "fair" and reasonable way.

Americans accepted the competitive system and became its advocates at a time when it was able to function only imperfectly, when its scope and impact were limited by the narrow effective range of the American market. Until the early 1830's each community needed to be largely self-sufficient. Local businessmen—the shoemaker, the miller, the blacksmith—with the help of local labor produced most of the goods and services sold. Uncertain and costly transportation kept non-local goods out of the market, and such competition as existed was mediated by face-to-face dealings between customer and producer. Since shops were small, workers and their employers dealt with each other personally. Competition in these circumstances, while sometimes sharp, was not often apt to be carried too far. It was a democratic way of conducting business; it permitted quite free and open entry, since capital requirements were seldom large, and it encouraged a middle class of small tradesmen, merchants, and more or less skilled workers.

[1] Andrew Carnegie, "Wealth," *North American Review,* 148 (June, 1889), 65.

As turnpikes and canals began to open the whole country to commerce after the 1820's, markets grew in value and expanded in area. Boston-made shoes were sold in Ohio and South Carolina; flour milled in western New York State could be easily shipped and sold along the whole East Coast. Ironware from New Jersey and Pennsylvania began to be sold in quantity throughout the Old Northwest. The spread of the railroads after 1850 shattered whatever protection distance was still providing for local producers and merchants. Competition became national in scope and impersonal in operation; for the first time buyers and sellers began to feel the full force of the competitive market.

In exchange for the benefit of an increased flow of goods at cheaper prices, the expanded market began to exact a cost. To meet the threats as well as the opportunities of the market, producers increased the sizes of their plants and invested in new and expensive machinery. The heavy overhead charges that resulted from these investments, combined with the ruthless—even brutal—competition that followed the Civil War, brought uncertainty and instability in the marketplace and too often reduced profits or brought mounting losses. Businessmen discovered that wider competition involved the risk of faster and more widespread ruin than they had believed possible.

American laborers had become disenchanted with free competition even before businessmen; they saw clearly how competition between employers could force down wage rates and erode working conditions. Skilled workers such as carpenters and shoemakers began to amalgamate local unions into city and national federations to increase their bargaining power and their ability to resist competitive wage cuts.

Businessmen had no single answer, comparable to the union, to the rigors of competition; from the 1870's until World War I they experimented with one arrangement after another in hope of finding a way to bring about greater stability, to restrain cutthroat competition, and to avoid price wars and bankrupting below-cost sales. Except in rare situations, these attempts to limit competition were seldom successful. Companies merged with their competitors to form larger units, but often the only result was that rival companies were able to enter into even stronger competition than before. Businessmen set up pools to fix prices and to assign market shares, and they formed trade associations to police the agreements reached and to establish fair trade practices; but as soon as a pool member thought he might win some advantage by selling below the agreed price, he would undercut his associates, and the pool soon would be a shambles. James J. Hill, builder of the Great Northern Railway, explained that "a starving man will usually get bread if it is to be had and a starving railway will not maintain rates." [2]

To secure tighter control of the individual competing firms within an industry, businessmen turned to a new form of business organization, the trust. John D. Rockefeller set the pattern for trusts when he created the Standard Oil Company in 1879. Rockefeller was appalled at the waste and inefficiencies of uncontrolled competition in the oil industry and set about ending damaging competition by organizing practically the entire industry into a single unit. Owners of the various member firms that entered into Rockefeller's combination retained title to their

[2] Thomas C. Cochran and William Miller, *The Age of Enterprise*, rev. ed. (New York: Harper & Row, 1961), p. 141.

property, but a single trust management made all production and pricing decisions for 90 per cent of the refining carried on in the United States. The benefits of this arrangement were so obvious that in industry after industry—salt, sugar, leather, lead, and cottonseed oil, among others—businessmen quickly formed trusts in imitation. Legal problems soon arose, however; the courts ruled that for a corporation to join a trust was *ultra vires,* that is, beyond its lawful powers. Trusts thus became unenforceable, if not illegal. As a result, the trust form dropped from favor, but the term "trust" lived on and was applied invidiously to any large corporation or business combination. In 1890 the term appeared in the title of the Sherman Antitrust Act, one of the first major pieces of federal legislation designed to regulate and to keep in check monopolies bent on restraining free trade.

Many of the nation's leading businessmen were convinced that some means had to be found to regulate unrestrained competition. Rockefeller believed that the merger, consolidation, and cooperation of firms was absolutely necessary. He maintained that "the day of the combination is here to stay. Individualism has gone, never to return." [3] Andrew Carnegie also made clear his preference for the rational order of monopoly—under his control in his particular industry, of course. A few economists joined with these princes of industry in questioning the value of unrestrained competition, whose passing was taken to be inevitable —if not always a blessing—as companies joined together, particularly after 1888, into larger and larger units under holding-company charters.[4] One economist argued in 1893 that antitrust "legislation will be in vain. The age of competition as we have known it is gone forever. As well try to waken the dead." [5] Other observers insisted that the increasing sizes of firms did not necessarily mean increasing monopoly. Justice Holmes warned in his dissent in the Northern Securities case of 1903 that business combinations as such should not be declared illegal. To do so would, in his opinion, "disintegrate society so far as it could into individual atoms. If that were [the Antitrust Act's] intent I should regard calling such a law a regulation of commerce as a mere pretense. It would be an attempt to reconstruct society."

A reconstruction of society appeared to be what some anti-monopolists wanted. Vice President Thomas R. Marshall declared in 1913, "The people were told in the last campaign that trusts were a natural evolution, and that the only way to deal with them was to regulate them. The people are tired of being told such things. What they want is the kind of opportunity that formerly existed in this country." [6] Walter Lippmann ridiculed such an outlook as one held only by those who could think the United States might again become "a nation of villagers." [7]

[3] Allan Nevins, *John D. Rockefeller,* I (New York: Charles Scribner's Sons, 1940), 662.

[4] In 1888 New Jersey amended its corporation laws to read: "Any corporation may purchase . . . the capital stock [of] any other corporation or corporations of this or any other state. . . ." Prior to this time most states had generally forbidden corporations to own the stock of other corporations, though they sometimes made special exceptions.

[5] Richard Hofstadter, "What Happened to the Antitrust Movement?" in *The Business Establishment,* Earl F. Cheit, ed. (New York: John Wiley, 1964), p. 121.

[6] Richard Hofstadter, *The Age of Reform* (New York: Random House, 1960), pp. 248–49.

[7] Hofstadter in Cheit, *op. cit.,* p. 123.

Ridiculous this view may be, for modern technology allows and even requires us to maintain vast business organizations. Even if antitrust laws were vigorously enforced, the distribution of business corporations within our major industries would not differ greatly. The government broke the pre-1945 monopoly of the Aluminum Corporation of America, but in 1958, 96 per cent of all shipments of primary aluminum were made by only four companies. While competition may have been increased, entry into the industry is not easy.

Large corporations are technologically desirable. Perhaps the ideal corporation in a given industry need not be as large as most of the existing giant firms, but it must be far larger than any neighborhood or village business if we are to continue to enjoy the abundant products we consume in our urban society. Yet there lingers on in our antitrust policies as expressed by the courts a suspicion of bigness; it may be well founded. "It is possible," wrote Judge Learned Hand in his decision in the Aluminum case, "because of its indirect social or moral effect, to prefer a system of small producers, each dependent for his success upon his own skill and character, to one in which the great mass of those engaged must accept the direction of the few." [8]

The following materials explore some of the problems of competition and monopoly. In the first pair of cases, a union and a company in the same industry attempt to escape some of the insistent—and, each maintains, the destructive—effects of competition. In the second pair, a union and a company introduce innovations in their respective industries to increase efficiency and to improve operations, among other purposes. Each case reveals some of the gains as well as some of the losses of monopoly.

[8] U.S. v. Aluminum Co. of America, 148 *Federal Reporter,* 2nd Series, 416, 427 (1945).

Escape from Competition

LOCAL UNION NO. 3, IBEW

The Great Depression that began in 1929 racked the American business system. The competitive market seemed to produce misery and woe for businessmen and workers alike, and it hardly appeared to be protecting the public interest. Profits disappeared for most firms, while the earnings of workers lucky enough to keep their jobs in the manufacturing industries shrank to an average of $17 a week in 1933 as the unemployment rate rose to 24.9 per cent. The general price index had dropped by 28 per cent since the peak year of 1929, and companies cut back production again and again as unsold goods continued to pile up. Competition appeared to have gone rampant; it was forcing people to work long hours for pitifully low wages, and it was destroying any profits by driving down prices even as it left markets glutted. Many businessmen despaired of the market correcting itself. To remedy the dismal situation they began to advocate a program that would limit and tame the forces of competition. Gerard Swope, for example, president of General Electric, advocated in 1931 the "Stabilization of Industry." He proposed a new constitution for industry designed to stabilize production and consumption as well as to provide workers with security and employment. Companies were to organize themselves into trade associations that would outline trade practices, business ethics, methods of standard accounting, and cost practices. The associations were also to collect and distribute information on the volume of business, inventories, production standards, and prices. Franklin Roosevelt's new Administration adopted a form of this program, incorporating it in the National Industrial Recovery Act of 1933. The NIRA encouraged firms to draw up industry codes of "fair" competition to regulate prices, product quality, and wages. To satisfy labor, the act also provided for minimum wages, maximum working hours, and the right of collective bargaining.

I

Responding to the encouragement of the NIRA, Local No. 3 of the International Brotherhood of Electrical Workers of America (IBEW)—led by its able and energetic business agent, Harry Van Arsdale, Jr.—undertook a campaign in 1934 to organize workers engaged in the manufacture and installation of electrical equipment in New York City. The manufacturers of switchboards and control panel boards, whose workers were the primary target, claimed that any wage increases would prohibit them from competing with large national manufacturers such as General Electric. They proposed that the union protect them and the workers' wages by keeping non-New York City-manufacturers' products out of the city market; in return they would encourage the union's organizing drive. Together they could agree upon, set up, and enforce their own private code. The proposal appears to have been accepted, for by the end of 1934 the workers employed by New York City's principal switchboard and panel board manufacturers had joined Local No. 3. Since the new members were denied full membership rights, however, and had no vote or voice in union affairs, one may suspect that the manufacturers' encouragement as much as union inducement persuaded them to join.

The voluntary code accepted by Local No. 3 and the electrical manufacturers in New York City provided for an exchange of information concerning bids to be made for contracts and the establishment of "standards" for bidding. When submitting a bid, each contractor was to calculate his estimated labor cost and then add to it as overhead 35 per cent of his labor cost and 10 per cent of his cost of material. Every bid also was to contain provisions reserving to the contractor the right to furnish all the materials used as well as labor supervision; builders could not purchase electrical supplies themselves for use or installation by the contractors. The agreed-upon fair-practice rules were to be interpreted by a Voluntary Code Authority—consisting of various representatives of the contractors, electrical equipment manufacturers, and the unions—which could impose fines for violation of the code.

Local No. 3 took it upon itself to enforce the code by making sure that no contractor with whom it negotiated used or installed any electrical equipment that was not union made. Like other building trades unions, Local No. 3 acted as an employment agency for construction employers, furnishing competent union members to fill job positions upon request. These unions thus helped to order and to stabilize what otherwise would be a chaotic labor market, since construction companies usually have no permanent place of work and no permanent labor force.

Not only did Local No. 3 enforce the code, but it added some embellishments. It forbade the use of preassembled equipment not manufactured by "fair" shops, that is, union shops in New York City. Firms not on the "fair list" found the New York market almost completely closed to them as a result, and any employer who tried to evade the restrictions quickly felt the weight of union disapproval. Local No. 3 did not hesitate to strike or boycott any defector, and it could shut down any construction operation because all building trades unions in the city respected each other's picket lines. If one struck, all the others stopped work.

Both union members and employers benefited from the union-policed codes. The members received higher wages, shorter hours, and protected jobs; the New York electrical manufacturers enjoyed an exclusive market within the city, and the electrical contractors were able to charge a 10 per cent commission on the cost of all materials purchased. According to Justice Black of the United States Supreme Court:

> The combination among the three groups, unions, contractors, and manufacturers, became highly successful from the standpoint of all of them. The business of New York manufacturers had a phenomenal growth, thereby multiplying the jobs available for the Local's members. Wages went up, hours were shortened, and the New York electrical equipment prices soared, to the decided financial profit of local contractors and manufacturers. The success is illustrated by the fact that some of the New York manufacturers sold their goods in the protected city market at one price and sold identical goods outside of New York at a far lower price.[1]

II

Out-of-town manufacturers saw the sales of their products in New York City dwindle. In December, 1935, the Allen Bradley Company of Milwaukee, Wisconsin, and nine other electrical equipment firms located outside New York City brought suit against Local No. 3 in the southern New York district court, charging that the union had entered into a conspiracy in restraint of trade in violation of the antitrust laws.[2] They also accused Local No. 3 of engaging in an unlawful boycott by refusing to handle or to work on goods manufactured by companies outside New York and of threatening builders and contractors who purchased goods from them.

Local No. 3 denied the charges. Its officers contended that the union activities were directed toward the improvement of the workers' conditions and as such were immune from prosecutions under the antitrust laws. The union also argued that Allen Bradley and the other complaining employers had refused to enter into collective agreements with the union, thus creating a labor dispute and justifying the union's actions.

Because the facts of the cases were complicated and involved, the Court referred the case in 1938 to a special master who was to hear testimony and make findings. These hearings lasted two and a half years. Four hundred witnesses testified, 1,700 exhibits were offered, and 2,400 pages of testimony were presented. Finally, in November, 1942, the special master presented to the court 374 findings of fact and 26 conclusions of law. After considering them, on June 10, 1943, Judge Francis Caffey found Local No. 3 guilty on several counts. His opinion stated that:

> 1. Local 3 had a right to enter into closed-shop agreements and to decide with whom it would enter into such agreements, and the union had a right to determine whom it should accept or reject as members if its decision was reasonable and not arbitrary.
>
> 2. Local 3's strikes against city projects for the purpose of getting employment for its construction members were unreasonable and unlawful.
>
> 3. The plaintiff companies were entitled to an injunction restraining the defendants from doing the acts charged in the com-

[1] Allen Bradley v. Local Union No. 3, IBEW, 325 U.S. 797 (1945), p. 800.

[2] The Sherman Act itself contains no specific mention of labor unions, although unions were frequently prosecuted under it. The Clayton Act of 1914 amended the Sherman Act with the intention of exempting labor unions from prosecution as monopolies. Section 6 of the Clayton Act states: "The labor of human beings is not a commodity or an article of commerce. Nothing contained in the antitrust laws shall be construed to forbid the existence and operation of labor, agricultural, or horticultural organizations, instituted for the purpose of mutual help . . . nor shall such organizations, or the members thereof, be held or construed to be illegal combinations in a restraint of trade, under the antitrust laws."

plaint as recommended by the special master.

4. The plaintiff companies were entitled to a judgment declaring that the acts of the union violated the Sherman Act.[3]

Local No. 3 brought an appeal. On October 12, 1944, Judge Charles E. Clark of the Federal Court of Appeals for the Second Circuit reversed the lower court's decision, charging that "the very verbosity and superfluity of the findings have not aided the decision as much as doubtless expected." He found the lower court's order to stop all the practices mentioned in the special master's 374 findings ambiguous. He noted, too, that unions did not necessarily forfeit the protection afforded by the Clayton and later acts when they combined with non-union groups, particularly when the union's activities were directed, as in this case, toward the self-interest and the protection of the workers.

III

Allen Bradley and the other electrical manufacturers in turn appealed the case to the Supreme Court. On June 18, 1945, Justice Black delivered the majority opinion. He presented a succinct summary of Local No. 3's activities as seen by the court.

> Using conventional labor methods, such as strikes and boycotts, it [Local No. 3] gradually obtained more and more closed-shop agreements in the New York City area. Under these agreements, contractors were obligated to purchase equipment from none but local manufacturers who also had closed-shop agreements with Local 3; manufacturers obligated themselves to confine their New York City sales to contractors employing the Local's members. In the course of time, this type of individual employer–employee agreement expanded into industry-wide understandings, looking not merely to the terms and conditions of employment but also to price and market control. Agencies were set up composed of representatives of all three groups to boycott recalcitrant local contractors and manufacturers and to bar from the area equipment manufactured outside its boundaries.[4]

The problem in this case, according to Black, was a narrow one: "Do labor unions violate the Sherman Act when, in order to further their own interests as wage earners, they aid and abet businessmen to do the precise things which that act prohibits?"[5]

In delivering the majority opinion, Justice Black supported the district court in declaring the union wrong. He recognized that there long had been two opposing views of the limits to union activities under the Sherman Antitrust and Clayton Acts. According to one view, Congress approved the antitrust legislation only to eliminate high consumer prices imposed by industrial combinations or business monopolies. The second view was that the antitrust acts covered all classes of individuals and organizations and therefore that *all* combinations, business or otherwise, that interrupt the free flow of trade are unlawful. The latter view, according to Black, was prevalent until the passage of the Clayton Act in 1914, after which the former point of view was more closely followed.

Justice Black declared that in the Wagner Act of 1935 Congress had more recently decided to protect the right of labor to organize and to encourage collective bargaining. The policy of protection and encouragement of unions conflicted with the earlier policy of assuring competition among businesses in the marketplace. The problem for the court was to decide how far Congress intended union rights to restrict active competition.

> It must be remembered that the exemptions granted the unions were special exceptions to a general legislative plan. The primary objective of all the Antitrust legislation has

[3] Allen Bradley Co. v. Local Union No. 3, IBEW, 145 *Federal Reporter,* 2nd Series, 215 (1943).

[4] Allen Bradley v. Local Union No. 3, IBEW, 325 U.S. 797 (1945), pp. 799–800.

[5] *Ibid.,* p. 801.

been to preserve business competition and to proscribe business monopoly. It would be a surprising thing if Congress, in order to prevent a misapplication of that legislation to labor unions, had bestowed upon such unions complete and unreviewable authority to aid business groups to frustrate its primary objective. For if business groups, by combining with labor unions, can fix prices and divide up markets, it was little more than a futile gesture for Congress to prohibit price fixing by business groups themselves. Seldom, if ever, has it been claimed before, that by permitting labor unions to carry on their own activities, Congress intended completely to abdicate its constitutional power to regulate interstate commerce and to empower interested business groups to shift our society from a competitive to a monopolistic economy.[6]

Justice Roberts agreed with the majority in reversing the circuit court's decision; however, he felt that the manufacturing firms were as guilty as the union.

In two branches of industry, the manufacturers and the employers, one by one, succumbed to union pressure and entered into agreements. Was not such action in each instance conspiracy? Are more than two parties required to conspire, and did not each of those conspiracies, to some extent, hinder and restrain interstate commerce and affect the market and the competitive price situation? As each agreement was consummated, the market was, to that extent, closed and the boycott against out-of-city manufacturers tightened.[7]

Justice Murphy disagreed with the majority because he felt the union had not in any true sense aided or abetted a primary violation of the Act by supporting and enforcing employers' agreements. He further argued that the mere fact that the union pursued its own self-interest with the aid of others rather than solely through its own activities would not be decisive of statutory liability. "What is legal if done alone should not become illegal if done with the assistance of others and with the same purpose in mind. Otherwise a premium of unlawfulness is placed on collective bargaining." [8]

[6] *Ibid.*, pp. 809–10.

[7] *Ibid.*, p. 818.

[8] *Ibid.*, p. 820.

THE ALLEN BRADLEY COMPANY

The great price conspiracy of the electrical equipment industry that became public in 1960 might have remained hidden if some of the firms involved had not accused the Tennessee Valley Authority, then under the management of General Herbert D. Vogel, of being unpatriotic and socialistic because it turned back their bids submitted in a competition involving major purchases of machinery. Having received from American firms bids that were within a few cents of being identical, General Vogel believed it would be wise to ask for bids from British, Swiss, and Belgian firms. Piqued at losing a major customer, General Electric denounced the TVA decision. Company spokesmen warned that buying such major electrical equipment as generators and turbines from foreign countries would leave the United States vulnerable in time of war when spare parts and services from abroad would be difficult to get. Moreover, company officials implied that such purchases were hardly patriotic, since foreign goods were made by workers who received low, almost slave-labor wages.

I

Annoyed at General Electric's attack on TVA, General Vogel ordered the domestic bids published. He pointed out at the same time that even if General Electric's prices were to be reduced to reflect a labor cost of zero, they would still be higher than those of the British. TVA could hardly believe that the lower foreign prices were simply the result of lower labor costs; inefficient and costly methods of production in American firms and perhaps rigged pricing offered a better explanation.

Senator Estes Kefauver of Tennessee, Chairman of the Subcommittee on Antitrust and Monopoly, began to investigate the charges made by TVA. Spurred on by the subcommittee's hearings in Knoxville and by the evidence TVA had collected, the Justice Department intensified its own investigation of pricing in the electrical equipment industry. The department made little progress until, by a lucky chance, it came into possession of a cache of papers that revealed the elaborate clandestine techniques used by the industry to rig their prices and share markets.

Early in 1960 the Justice Department secured indictments against 29 electrical equipment companies and 53 company executives, charging conspiracy to restrain trade. Robert Bicks, chief of the Justice Department's Antitrust Division, described the conspiracies as involving "a pattern of violations which can fairly be said to range among the most serious, the most flagrant, the most pervasive in the history of the Sherman Antitrust Act." Much to everyone's surprise the presiding judge sentenced several of those who pleaded guilty to jail terms of from three months to a year. The Sherman Act provides for such penalties, but they have seldom been applied.

Among the business executives sentenced to jail was Mr. Fred Loock, president of the Allen Bradley Company. He had pleaded guilty, explaining to the *Wall Street Journal* his participation in the conspiracy: "No one attending the gatherings [in the electrical controls industry] was so stupid he didn't know [the meetings] . . . were in violation of the law. But it is the only way a business can be run. It is free enterprise." He argued that "we also need protection against buyers," and the meetings gave the companies involved such protection. Loock gave as an example of the perfidy of buyers the behavior of a major Detroit manufacturer who told one electrical equipment firm that a competing firm had offered a lower price on some items sold by both. "By discussing the matter, which was not true, among ourselves, we were able to iron out the problem." He concluded, "I believe that in an industry where money is necessary to continue research and development of products we should have some protection against the crookedness of some buyers." [1]

Loock spoke from long experience in the electrical equipment industry and specifically with the Allen Bradley Company, which is a relatively small firm with annual sales ranging between $75 million and $100 million in radio components and control devices for electric motors. Loock had joined the company in 1910 immediately after leaving high school. He became president in 1949, and his salary when he was sentenced was $130,000 a year. He received no stock options or bonuses, and he had never owned a share of the company's stock.

II

The segment of the electrical equipment industry in which the Allen Bradley Company operates, the industrial control or motor control sector, is a highly concentrated one; nine firms are responsible for three-quarters of its annual sales, which totaled about $350 million in 1960. As in the rest of the electrical equipment industry, capital investments are large. The high overhead costs that result tempt companies to cut prices when business is slow, and in the past price instability had caused serious problems throughout the industry. Accordingly, Justice Department sources maintained that for many years—no one is quite sure how many—representatives of the control equipment manufacturers conspired to rig prices. The conspiracy certainly went

[1] *Monopoly Power and Economic Performance,* Edwin Mansfield, ed. (New York: W. W. Norton, 1964), pp. 81–82.

back to the period immediately following World War II, and there are indications that it probably originated in the early thirties under the NIRA. Though particular arrangements changed over the years, the purpose and general operating method of the conspiracy did not.

The specific pattern of conspiracy in the control equipment sector, revealed at the trial in 1960, apparently dated from the end of the Korean war. During that war the industry was urged by government officials to increase capacity to meet the expanding needs of the country. By the time the heavy investments had been made, however, the war was over. In 1954–55 a buyer's market developed, leading to a collapse of pricing arrangements and what industry officials called the great "white sale." Prices on some equipment dropped by as much as 50 per cent. To avoid these costly competitive wars in which everyone was hurt, Loock and other executives set up a price conspiracy on a firmer basis.

The industrial control equipment companies divided their joint efforts into three tasks: to maintain market price levels on the various existing products, to fix prices for new products, and to allocate business among the companies. Their intent and accomplishment was to control the prices, terms, and conditions for the sale of their equipment. Customers were classified so that all sellers would grant the same discounts to any particular buyer. Representatives often decided what new products should be placed on the market and what the price for an acceptable new product should be. Officials of the several firms met often to ensure that none deviated from the price and marketing arrangements agreed upon. In short, price competition was virtually eliminated for 75 per cent of the sales in the electrical control industry.

Naturally, the illegality of the activities required an elaborate system of devices and camouflage. The conspirators could regularly meet while attending association gatherings whose purposes were open and legal. For example, the industrial control equipment manufacturers were able to get together at the Homestead Hotel in Hot Springs, Virginia, for the annual meetings of the National Electrical Manufacturers Association (NEMA), Industrial Control Section. They also discussed their business before or after the annual meetings of the Industrial Control Advisory Committee at Camp Keystone, North Bay, Ontario, or at the NEMA annual convention in Atlantic City, New Jersey. As the need arose, the conspirators called meetings to discuss particular problems. The current chairman of the Industrial Control Advisory Committee of NEMA usually arranged the illegal meetings to coincide with scheduled NEMA meetings. Notices of meetings were given out carefully by telephone calls at home or by written notices sent in plain envelopes without return addresses.

In the years prior to 1955 for which the government had documentary proof of a conspiracy, General Electric had exercised price leadership in the electrical control industry. After this date, General Electric representatives attended meetings only sporadically. Nevertheless, GE was informed of all impending developments and it, in turn, notified the representatives of the other companies of GE's approval or disapproval of an action taken or proposed.

The Justice Department obtained substantial evidence of meetings and even records of the subjects discussed. Mr. Baddra Rashid of the Department of Justice made the results of these meetings public knowledge during the Philadelphia trials. Some of the topics covered were reported as follows: [2]

[2] The topics cited were reported in the press at the time of the trial and may also be found in *Hearings before the Subcommittee on Antitrust and Monopoly of the Committee on the Judiciary,* U.S. Senate, 87th Cong., 1st Sess., *Administered Prices,* "Price Fixing and Bid Rigging in the Electrical Manufacturing Industry," Parts 27 and 28.

1. In August, 1955, a meeting was held in Maine. All defendants except General Electric were present. It was agreed that prices should be increased by 10 per cent and that Cutler-Hammer should initiate the price increase in November.

2. A meeting was held in November, 1955, in Atlantic City to determine the effect that the 10 per cent price increase was having on the market.

3. In April, 1956, at a meeting held in Cleveland, the conspirators decided to follow some of GE's recent price increases and not to follow others. Shortly after this, GE rescinded the price increases that the other firms had not followed.

4. In 1957 the problem of how to price a new product became a vexing issue. At a meeting in Hot Springs, Virginia, in May, it was the consensus that the new Cutler-Hammer Double O starter should sell for about two-thirds of the price commanded by the present form of starter and should be placed on the market about January 1, 1960. At a meeting in Atlantic City in November, 1957, the representatives tried to persuade Cutler-Hammer officials not to introduce a lower priced, lower quality starter. Cutler-Hammer argued that a market for such a starter existed and was not well served by the needlessly high quality starters available. Afraid of stimulating competition, the other conspirators insisted that Cutler-Hammer introduce a higher quality starter and keep up the price. Cutler-Hammer finally agreed in January, 1958, not to bring out its proposed cheaper model.

III

In testimony given at a hearing of the Kefauver Subcommittee after the trial, Loock claimed that he was not guilty of fixing prices even though he had pleaded guilty to charges of doing so. He maintained that Judge Ganey told the defendants that since a conviction was essential to the Justice Department, he would throw the book at them if the Department were forced to present all its evidence in connection with the charges already brought and if they were found guilty. Loock said:

> There was no question in Philadelphia but that a plea of guilty on the part of all indicted people was essential to the Government, and that is what they were after. . . . [That] is the impression that the government has wanted to create with the country, that the entire electrical industry was just a low-life industry. The control industry was dragged into this case on a technicality pure and simple.[3]

Loock maintained that he and his company had not made sealed bids except in special cases involving projects in which there was some assembly work or construction that was not part of normal production:

> I do not remember that Allen Bradley Company has ever bid on a sealed bid, and if so, I would say it was in connection with the purchase or repair parts or something. . . . The sealed bid serves only one purpose and that is to give the chiseler an excellent chance. So far as the Allen Bradley Company is concerned, we build quality apparatus. We just simply cannot compete with the tin-knocker,[4] and he has a field day on these sealed bids.[5]

Furthermore, according to Loock, Allen Bradley did not do business with the government. He stated that the government required sealed bids, which was against Allen Bradley policy, and also that the government wasted company time and money with such red tape as requirements for blueprints of standard parts.

The secret meetings for the purpose of fixing prices with which the government was so concerned did not actually take

[3] *Hearings,* Pt. 28, pp. 17464–65.
[4] According to Loock, a tin-knocker is a fellow who "has a little shack somewhere and has a hammer and a tinsnips, and with the aid of those efficient tools builds the cabinet which encloses the control apparatus which we build."
[5] *Hearings,* pp. 14471–72.

place, according to Loock. It was true that there had been meetings of representatives of firms in the motor-control industry; he recalled that these meetings occurred as early as 1919. It was also true that occasionally general price levels were discussed, but these discussions took place after price changes had gone into effect. Moreover, price level discussions were held only when the cost of labor and material required a price increase:

> What I want to also point out, in fairness to our control industry, is that these illegal meetings, as you term them . . . always followed a cost increase. We never had these meetings when there wasn't a cost increase, and, furthermore, the records show that we never did anything other than to offset the cost increase. . . . We did not fix prices. . . . I am telling you that all we did was recover costs.[6]

Discussions among the firms were necessary if they were to protect themselves against chiselers:

> I want to point out that we have good competitors and we have competitors not so good. The thing that the Government did not bring out, the fact that the Government was acquainted with, was that our price increases always followed an increase in the cost of labor. . . . When costs go up there is only one alternative, and that is to increase prices. . . . The reason for these several meetings at which an increase in prices was discussed was because, among our competition, we had some who couldn't—[7] who would agree to the price increase, who would agree to the fact that the price increase was necessary—as a matter of fact, one of the competitors pled the last time for a price increase which I did not want to go along with, and we had to get the increase into a range of a week to ten days, or two weeks, because if that were not done, then the competitors that I am talking about could easily go out with the old prices and solicit business from customers on the plea that they were giving the customer the benefit of a lower price, and thus take business away from the so-called decent competition. Subsequently, that cost also having gone up, when they had to increase prices, they would go back to the same customers and on a plea that they had done something for the buyer, that he should continue to buy from them.[8]

However, Loock stated that all these manufacturers had many other problems in common. Most of the meetings were held for the purpose of discussing these problems. The only reason that prices were discussed was to get a general price increase in a relatively short time. This was to protect the good competitor who was forced to raise prices because of rising costs.

According to Loock, it ought to be remembered that the first firm to raise its prices suffered the most from loss of business. He stated that if prices were raised in a short period of time, this shortened the period in which the "good" competitor might lose business to the unscrupulous competitor.

[6] *Ibid.*, pp. 17490–91.

[7] Loock broke the sentence off here, leaving the implication that these were competitors who could not be "persuaded" to go along with the others.

[8] *Hearings*, p. 17464.

QUESTIONS

Escape from Competition

1. Analyze the reasons given for the "monopolizing" actions of Local No. 3, IBEW, and the Allen Bradley Company and indicate how forbidding such actions would serve the public interest.

2. If unions acting alone are to be permitted to restrain trade to protect the "labor of human beings," why should companies not be allowed to restrain trade

in like fashion to protect the labor, efforts, and human interests of managers and stockholders?

3. Unions argue that they protect workers against unfair competition and unscrupulous employers. Evaluate Loock's argument that businesses selling in the market need protection against unfair buyers and unscrupulous competition.

4. Assuming that Loock was right when he maintained that the electrical equipment companies only recovered costs when they met to adjust prices, explain how you would justify their actions.

Efficiency v. Monopoly

STANDARD OIL COMPANY OF CALIFORNIA

The Antitrust Division of the Department of Justice brought suit in 1947 against the Standard Oil Company of California for entering into supply or requirement contracts with independent dealers to secure the exclusive right to supply them with petroleum products and automobile accessories.[1]

I

At the time the suit was brought Standard was the largest seller of gasoline in the West; its fuel was sold through its own service stations, to the operators of independent service stations, and to industrial users. In 1946 its sales through company-owned service stations [2] amounted to 6.8 per cent of the total taxable gallons sold in the seven-state Western area; sales under exclusive supply contracts with independent service stations added another 6.7 per cent; and sales to industrial users accounted for 9.5 per cent. Standard's combined sales through these outlets thus amounted to 23 per cent of the total taxable gallons sold in the area. Retail service-station sales by Standard's six leading competitors made up 42.5 per cent of the area's total taxable gallons; the remaining retail sales were divided among more than 70 small companies. All of Standard's major competitors relied upon exclusive supply contracts. In 1948 only 1.6 per cent of all retail outlets were what are known as "split-pump" stations, that is, stations that sell the gasoline of more than one supplier.

Before 1934 Standard Oil usually sold its petroleum products through independent service stations whose owners entered into agency agreements with it. In that year Standard adopted the first of its several exclusive supply contract forms, and by 1938 such contracts had wholly superseded the agency method of distribution. Company officials favored the new, exclusive relationship with dealers because it gave them better control of distribution and lowered costs significantly. Since the exclusive supply contracts proved economical, the company argued that both the industry and the public benefited from their use. Certainly the contracts did not seem to have given the company a competitive advantage, for between 1936 and 1946 Standard's sales of gasoline through independent dealers remained at a practically constant proportion of the area's total sales; its share in the sales of lubricating oil declined slightly during the period, from 6.2 per cent to 5 per cent of the area total. Standard's sales of tires and batteries for 1946 were proportionately higher than they were in 1936, but they were somewhat lower than for some intervening years, and even in the best year during the period they

[1] Standard Oil Company of California *et al.* v. United States, 337 U.S. 293 (1949).

[2] These stations were managed by a wholly-owned Standard subsidiary, Standard Stations, Inc.

never exceeded 2 per cent of the total sales in the Western area.

As of March 2, 1947, exclusive supply contracts with Standard had been entered into by the operators of 5,937 independent stations, or 16 per cent of the retail gasoline outlets in the Western area. These stations purchased from Standard $57.6 million worth of gasoline and $8.2 million worth of other products in 1947. Some outlets were covered by more than one contract, so that about 8,000 exclusive contracts were in force. These contracts were of several types, but a feature common to each was the dealer's obligation to purchase from Standard all his requirements of one or more products. Two types, covering 2,777 outlets, obliged the dealer to purchase from Standard all his requirements of gasoline and other petroleum products as well as tires, tubes, and batteries. Of the remaining written agreements, 4,368 bound the dealer to purchase only Standard's petroleum products. Several hundred other independent dealers had made oral contracts to sell only Standard's gasoline. In some instances dealers who contracted to purchase from Standard all their requirements of tires, tubes, and batteries, had also agreed orally to purchase from Standard their requirements of other automobile accessories. Of the written agreements, 2,712 were for specific terms of various lengths; the rest continued in effect from year to year but were terminable "at the end of the first six months of any contract year, or at the end of any such year, by [one party's] giving to the other at least 30 days prior thereto written notice. . . ."

The government based its case on the argument that the exclusive contracts were in clear violation of Paragraph 3 of the Clayton Act,[3] and the district court upheld this view. In its decision enjoining Standard from enforcing or entering into exclusive supply contracts with independent dealers, the court held that the procedural requirement of showing an actual or potential lessening of competition or a tendency to establish monopoly was adequately met by proof that the contracts covered "a substantial number of outlets and a substantial amount of products, whether considered comparatively or not." The facts proved that large numbers and amounts were affected; thus, the court reasoned, an illegal lessening of competition was an automatic result. The very existence of the contracts deprived dealers of the opportunity to deal in the products of competing suppliers and denied suppliers access to the outlets controlled by those dealers.

The court excluded as immaterial testimony bearing on "the economic merits or demerits of the exclusive contract system as contrasted with the system which prevailed prior to its establishment." The court showed no interest in data that would have shed light on the comparative status of Standard and its competitors before and after the adoption of the new system. The court also considered it unnecessary to make findings, on the basis of the evidence that was admitted, as to whether the number of Standard's competitors had increased or decreased since 1936 when the exclusive control system began or whether the number of their dealers had increased or decreased.

II

The company appealed the decision to the Supreme Court, which upheld the lower

[3] The paragraph states that "It shall be unlawful for any person engaged in commerce, in the course of such commerce, to lease or make a sale or contract for sales of goods, wares, merchandise, machinery, supplies or other commodities, whether patented or unpatented for use, consumption, or resale within the United States . . . on the condition, agreement, or understanding that the lessee or purchaser thereof shall not use or deal in the goods . . . of a competitor or competitors of the . . . seller, where the effect of such condition, agreement, or understanding may be to substantially lessen competition or tend to create a monopoly in any line of commerce."

court. Writing for the majority, Justice Frankfurter said:

> The issue before us . . . is whether the requirement of showing that the effect of the agreements "may be to substantially lessen competition" may be met simply by proof that a substantial portion of commerce is affected or whether it must also be demonstrated that competitive activity has actually diminished or probably will diminish. . . .
>
> Standard's share of the retail market for gasoline, even including sales through company-owned stations, is hardly large enough to conclude as a matter of law that it occupies a dominant position, nor did the trial court so find. . . . Requirements contracts . . . may well be of economic advantage to buyers as well as to sellers, and thus indirectly of advantage to the consuming public. In the case of the buyer, they may assure supply, afford protection against rises in price, enable long-term planning on the basis of known costs,[4] and obviate the expense and risk of storage in the quantity necessary for a commodity having a fluctuating demand. From the seller's point of view, requirements contracts may make possible the substantial reduction of selling expenses, given protection against price fluctuation, and—of particular advantage to a newcomer to the field of whom it is important to know what capital expenditures are justified—offer the possibility of a predictable market. . . .
>
> Yet serious difficulties [attend the attempt to rest our decision upon the test of economic consequences of the agreements]. We may assume, as did the court below, that no improvement of Standard's competitive position has coincided with the period during which the requirements-contract system of distribution has been in effect. We may assume further that the duration of the contracts is not excessive and that Standard does not by itself dominate the market. But Standard was a major competitor when the present system was adopted, and it is possible that its position would have deteriorated but for the adoption of that system. When it is remembered that all the other major suppliers have also been using requirements contracts, and when it is noted that the relative share of the business which fell to each has remained about the same during the period of their use,[5] it would not be far-fetched to infer that their effect has been to enable the established suppliers individually to maintain their own standing and at the same time collectively, even though not collusively, to prevent a late arrival from wresting away more than an insignificant portion of the market. If, indeed, this were a result of the system, it would seem unimportant that a short-run by-product of stability may have been greater efficiency and lower costs, for it is the theory of the antitrust laws that the long-run advantage of the community depends upon the removal of restraints upon competition.
>
> Moreover, to demand that bare inference be supported by evidence as to what would have happened but for the adoption of the practice that was in fact adopted or to require firm prediction of an increase of competition as a probable result of ordering the abandonment of the practice, would be a standard of proof, if not virtually impossible to meet, at least most ill-suited for ascertainment by courts. Before the system of requirements contracts was instituted, Standard sold gasoline through independent service-station operators as its agents, and it might revert to this system if the judgment below were sustained. Or it might, as opportunity presented itself, add service stations now operated independently to the number managed by its subsidiary, Standard Stations, Inc. From the point of view of maintaining or extending competitive advantage, either of these alternatives would be just as effective as the use of requirements contracts, although of course insofar as they resulted in

[4] This advantage is not conferred by Standard's contracts, each of which provides that the price to be paid by the dealer is to be that "company's posted price to its dealers generally at time and place of delivery."

[5] Upon the request of Standard, its six largest competitors filled out questionnaires showing the number of retail dealers who distributed their products during the years 1937–46. Though their position relative to each other fluctuated, the figures showed that as a group they maintained or improved their control of the market. Together with Standard, these six companies distributed, as of 1946, through 26,439 of approximately 35,000 independent service stations in the Western area.

a tendency to monopoly they might encounter the anti-monopoly provisions of the Sherman Act. As [the company] points out, dealers might order petroleum products in quantities sufficient to meet their estimated needs for the period during which requirements contracts are now effective, and even that would foreclose competition to some degree. So long as these diverse ways of restricting competition remain open, therefore, there can be no conclusive proof that the use of requirements contracts has actually reduced competition below the level which it would otherwise have reached or maintained.

We are dealing here with a particular form of agreement . . . and not with different arrangements, by way of integration or otherwise, that may tend to lessen competition. To interpret that section as requiring proof that competition has actually diminished would make its very explicitness a means of conferring immunity upon the practices which it singles out. Congress has authoritatively determined that those practices are detrimental where their effect may be to lessen competition. It has not left at large for determination in each case the ultimate demands of the "public interest," as the English lawmakers, considering and finding inapplicable to their own situation our experiences with the specific prohibition of trade practices legislatively determined to be undesirable, have recently chosen to do. Though it may be that such an alternative to the present system as buying out independent dealers and making them independent employees of Standard Stations, Inc., would be a greater detriment to the public interest than perpetuation of the system, this is an issue, like the choice between greater efficiency and freer competition, that has not been submitted to our decision. We are faced, not with a broadly phrased expression of general policy, but merely a broadly phrased qualification of an otherwise narrowly directed statutory provision. . . .

If in fact it is economically desirable for service stations to confine themselves to the sale of the petroleum products of a single supplier, they will continue to do so though not bound by contract, and if in fact it is important to retail dealers to assure the supply of their requirements by obtaining the commitment of a single supplier to fulfill them, competition for their patronage should enable them to insist upon such an arrangement without binding them to refrain from looking elsewhere.

We conclude, therefore, that . . . observance by a dealer of his requirements contract with Standard does effectively foreclose whatever opportunity there might be for competing suppliers to attract his patronage, and it is clear that the affected proportion of retail sales of petroleum products is substantial. In view of the widespread adoption of such contracts by Standard's competitors and the availability of alternative ways of obtaining an assured market, evidence that competitive activity has not actually declined is inconclusive. Standard's use of the contracts creates just such a potential clog on competition as it was the purpose of Paragraph 3 to remove wherever, were it to become actual, it would impede a substantial amount of competitive activity.

III

Justice Douglas dissented from the majority opinion and in strong, blunt words expressed his fears about the Court's attitude toward antitrust:

The economic theories which the Court has read into the Antitrust Laws have favored rather than discouraged monopoly. As a result of the big business philosophy underlying [decisions of the court], big business has become bigger and bigger. Monopoly has flourished. Cartels have increased their hold on the nation. The trusts wax strong. There is less and less place for the independent.

The full force of the Antitrust Laws has not been felt on our economy. It has been deflected. Niggardly interpretations have robbed those laws of much of their efficacy. There are exceptions. Price fixing is illegal *per se*. The use of patents to obtain monopolies on unpatented articles is condemned. Monopoly that has been built as a result of unlawful tactics, e.g., through practices that are restraints of trade, is broken up.[6] But

[6] See United States v. Griffith, 334 U.S. 100; Schine Theatres v. United States, 334 U.S. 110; United States v. Paramount Pictures, 334 U.S. 131, 172.

Those cases have largely expended the force

when it comes to monopolies built in gentlemanly ways—by mergers, purchases of assets or control and the like—the teeth have largely been drawn from the Act.

We announced that the existence of monopoly power, coupled with the purpose or intent to monopolize, was unlawful. But to date that principle has not shown bright promise in application. Under the guise of increased efficiency big business has received approval for easy growth. In [a recent] case United States Steel—the giant of the industry—was allowed to fasten its tentacles tighter on the economy by acquiring the assets of a steel company in the Far West where competition was beginning to develop.

The increased concentration of industrial power in the hands of a few has changed habits of thought. A new age has been introduced. It is more and more an age of "monopoly competition." Monopoly competition is a regime of friendly alliances, of quick and easy accommodation of prices even without the benefit of trade associations, of what Brandeis said was euphemistically called "cooperation." While this is not true in all fields, it has become alarmingly apparent in many.

The lessons Brandeis taught on the curse of bigness have largely been forgotten in high places. Size is allowed to become a menace to existing and putative competitors. Price control is allowed to escape the influences of the competitive market and to gravitate into the hands of the few. But beyond all that there is the effect on the community when independents are swallowed up by the trusts and entrepreneurs become employees of absentee owners. Then there is a serious loss in citizenship. Local leadership is diluted. He who was a leader in the village becomes dependent on outsiders for his action and policy. Clerks responsible to a superior in a distant place take the place of resident proprietors beholden to no one. These are the prices which the nation pays for the almost ceaseless growth in bigness on the part of industry.

These problems may not appear on the surface to have relationship to the case before us. But they go to the very heart of the problem.

It is common knowledge that a host of filling stations in the country are locally owned and operated. Others are owned and operated by the big oil companies. This case involves directly only the former. It pertains to requirements contracts that the oil companies make with these independents. It is plain that a filling-station owner who is tied to an oil company for his supply of products is not an available customer for the products of other suppliers. The same is true of a filling-station owner who purchases his inventory a year in advance. His demand is withdrawn from the market for the duration of the contract in the one case and for a year in the other. The result in each case is to lessen competition if the standard is day-to-day purchases. Whether it is a substantial lessening of competition within the meaning of the Antitrust Laws is a question of degree and may vary from industry to industry.

The Court answers the question for the oil industry by a formula which under our decisions promises to wipe out large segments of independent filling-station operators. The method of doing business under requirements contracts at least keeps the independents alive. They survive as small business units. The situation is not ideal from either their point of view or that of the nation. But the alternative which the Court offers is far worse from the point of view of both.

The elimination of these requirements contracts sets the stage for Standard and the other oil companies to build service-station empires of their own. The opinion of the Court does more than set the stage for that development. It is an advisory opinion as well, stating to the oil companies how they can with impunity build their empires. The formula suggested by the Court is either the use of the "agency" device, which in practi-

of Hartford-Empire Co. v. United States, 323 U.S. 386—an indefensible decision whereby the Court allowed those who had built one of the tightest monopolies in American history largely to retain their ill-gotten gains and continue their hold on the economy. The philosophy of that decision can be summed up in the words Brandeis used to describe the decree effecting a so-called dissolution of the American Tobacco Co. He said that its defenders "appear to have discovered in the Constitution a new implied prohibition: *'What man has illegally joined together, let no court put asunder.'* " *The Curse of Bigness* (1935), p. 103.

cal effect means control of filling stations by the oil companies or the outright acquisition of them by subsidiary corporations or otherwise. Under the approved judicial doctrine either of those devices means increasing the monopoly of the oil companies over the retail field.

When the choice is thus given, I dissent from the outlawry of the requirements contract on the present facts. The effect which it has on competition in this field is minor as compared to the damage which will flow from the judicially approved formula for the growth of bigness tendered by the Court as an alternative. Our choice must be made on the basis not of abstractions but of the realities of modern industrial life.

Today there is vigorous competition between the oil companies for the market. That competition has left some room for the survival of the independents. But when this inducement for their survival is taken away, we can expect that the oil companies will move in to supplant them with their own stations. There will still be competition between the oil companies. But there will be a tragic loss to the nation. The small, independent businessman will be supplanted by clerks. Competition between suppliers of accessories (which is involved in this case) will diminish or cease altogether. The oil companies will command an increasingly larger share of both the wholesale and the retail markets.

That is the likely result of today's decision. The requirements contract which is displaced is relatively innocuous as compared with the virulent growth of monopoly power which the Court encourages. The Court does not act unwittingly. It consciously pushes the oil industry in that direction. The Court approves what the Antitrust Laws were designed to prevent. It helps remake America in the image of the cartels.

UNITED MINE WORKERS OF AMERICA

In 1958 Raymond Phillips, his brother Burse, and Jim Pennington found themselves in trouble with the giant United Mine Workers Welfare Fund. The three men had gone into partnership in 1952 as the Phillips Brothers Coal Company; now the Welfare Fund's trustees had brought suit against the partners to collect back royalties of about $56,000. This suit was not the first instance of "union trouble" that the partnership had faced, but it was the most serious. The company could not possibly raise the sum claimed, which was greater than the total profits and almost three times the net profits earned since the company began. The alternatives open to the partners seemed to be to have the suit dismissed in court or to go out of business.

I

Phillips Brothers was a small mining operation in which each of the partners had invested $9,000; another $100,000 had been borrowed to purchase several expensive pieces of equipment. The partners were workers as well as managers. Raymond Phillips performed all the bookkeeping chores, but his chief job was maintaining the equipment in good repair, for he was the company's only mechanic. Pennington worked at the tipple—weighing, loading, and crushing coal. Burse Phillips worked in the strip pits, operating the mining and loading machines.

Phillips Brothers began operations in mid-1952. The next year a United Mine Workers organizer, Ed Daniels, made several trips to the Phillips' mine to urge the partners to sign the union's standard labor contract, the National Bituminous Coal Wage Agreement. Pennington later described Daniels' persuasive approach as follows: "The UMW man came by and told us to sign up or he'd bankrupt us." [1] The partners objected that signing would also

[1] Nat Caldwell and Gene S. Graham, "The Strange Romance Between John L. Lewis and Cyrus Eaton," *Harper's*, 223 (December, 1961), 25.

bankrupt them; while they were just starting out, they could not afford to meet the union wage scale or to pay the 40¢ a ton royalty to the Welfare Fund required by the Agreement. Daniels' reply to this, according to the partners, was that they could work out their own arrangements with their three workers, none of whom then belonged to the UMW; as for the Welfare Fund, they would be expected to pay only what they could. Though the partners doubted that the union would be as easy with them as Daniels suggested, they had no alternative but to agree to its terms. In October, 1953, the Phillips Brothers Coal Company signed the National Bituminous Coal Wage Agreement.

Eighteen months later—in April, 1955—an armed band of men stopped at the Phillips mine. Similar bands traveled in caravans through the hills between isolated communities and had become frequent visitors to non-union mines throughout West Virginia, Kentucky, and Tennessee. In some cases, there had been newspaper reports of buildings burned and machinery wrecked before the visitors continued on their way. A spokesman for the mob that appeared at the Phillips property told Raymond Phillips to shut his mine and keep it shut until notified he could open it again. Phillips was also advised to get his men signed up with the UMW. The partners subsequently sought out Daniels and reminded him of what he had said earlier, but he told them they could not expect to run a union mine with non-union men. The UMW secretary for District 19 also told them that all of the men would have to join and added that their company would have to pay its back royalties to the Welfare Fund. Faced with the full force of the union, the partners gave in. All those working at the mine except Raymond Phillips, who was designated "boss," signed with the UMW.

The Phillips Brothers Coal Company made profits of $28,542 in 1955 and paid royalties on about 5,600 tons of coal; at that time the company's annual production averaged about 36,000 tons. After unionization, however, the firm's financial position began to worsen; profits dropped by 25 per cent in 1956, and in 1957 the company recorded a loss of $20,385.[2] As profits decreased the partners decided to stop paying the royalty. They may have gained some added courage in this step from the knowledge that they were not alone; many other small mines had been hit just as hard and had also stopped paying royalties.

In 1958 the Welfare Fund trustees moved to recover the money due—or, as many of the independent mine operators thought, to put them out of business for good—by bringing suit against more than 40 small companies. Though the defendant companies had signed the National Bituminous Coal Wage Agreement and apparently obligated themselves thereby to make the royalty payments in question, they contended that the UMW had forced them to accept the agreements through a program of terrorism. More significantly, and much to the surprise of the trustees, the Phillips Brothers partners and their lawyer, John A. Rowntree, charged both the UMW and the Welfare Fund trustees with conspiring with the major coal companies to monopolize the coal industry in violation of the Sherman Antitrust Act.

II

It was probably little more than rumor that first suggested to the partners their defense of charging a UMW conspiracy. One such rumor involved the 1955 strike by UMW miners in the Sequatchie Valley; when this strike was broken by shipments from the Nashville Coal Company and the West Kentucky Coal Company, newspaper reports suggested that the UMW had earlier bought into these very companies. Local union officials and miners shrugged off the

[2] Reply Brief of Respondents in the Supreme Court of the United States, United Mine Workers of America v. James M. Pennington *et al.*, October Term, 1964, No. 48, pp. 102, 123.

implication that the UMW was helping to defeat its own members who worked in the valley's small, thin-seamed mines; such reports were just the propaganda of union haters, they said.

Although rumors of this sort might not have made effective court evidence in 1958, the UMW was not in a position to counter them with a convincingly flat denial. Early in 1960, well before the Phillips litigation reached final settlement in the Supreme Court, the UMW filed its first public financial report as required by the new Landrum-Griffin Act (Labor-Management Reporting and Disclosure Act of 1959), and the rumors received a shocking confirmation. The report showed that the union was a substantial investor in the strikebreaking concerns, which were two of the country's largest coal mining companies.

The UMW had acquired for over $2 million about 10 per cent of the common stock of West Kentucky Coal and for $2.5 million all of the 50,000 shares of the preferred stock. The preferred shares acquired voting rights when dividends were in arrears, as they had been since April, 1958. The UMW also held substantial blocks of the stock of West Kentucky Coal and its subsidiary company, Nashville Coal, as collateral on loans.[3] The terms of the loans relieved the borrower of personal liability upon surrender of the collateral. The loan notes were renewed annually. If the creditor did not pay the interest, usually because dividends were not paid on the collateral stock, it was added to the principal of the renewal note. If the stock declined in value, there was no demand for additional collateral. One of the loans, amounting to over $2.5 million and secured by 90,600 shares of common stock, was to Cyrus S. Eaton, chairman of the board of West Kentucky Coal and Nashville Coal as well as chairman of the board of the Chesapeake and Ohio Railway Company and an investor in, or manager of, many other companies. The union's direct and indirect interest in the two coal companies totaled over $25 million, giving it control through outright ownership or collateral holdings of more than one-half of West Kentucky's stock and an influential if not controlling voice in Nashville Coal.

[3] Pennington v. United Mine Workers of America, 325 *Federal Reporter,* 2nd Series, 813 (1963).

III

Suspecting that the UMW might be involved in major financial dealings with some of the big coal operators and working hand-in-glove with them, the Phillips partners and their lawyer reviewed the history of labor-management relations in coal since World War II to find evidence that would support their theory of conspiracy. They believed that they had found what they were looking for in the sharp change they noted in UMW policy after 1950. This change, they charged, showed that the UMW had ceased to be primarily a representative of the coal miners throughout the country and had become instead an economic empire favoring the large coal companies that could use machines and so further the efficiency of coal production.

Prior to 1950, the coal mining industry had long been plagued by overproduction, strikes, and strife. Except in wartime, miners typically worked less than 200 days a year. All too frequently coal piled up "on the grass" and, if the union did not call a strike, unemployment spread throughout the coal districts. John L. Lewis, president of the UMW since 1925, deplored the instability of the industry and sought to remedy it through union action. In 1949 the union's *Journal* declared, "Since the coal industry, of its own accord, cannot get together and exhibit the business acumen necessary to protect its employees and the business and population of the mining communities, the duty of performing this public service devolves upon the only stabilizing force the industry has ever known—the UMWA [United Mine Workers of America]."

The union already had experimented with work stoppages described by Lewis as "brief stabilizing periods of inaction during which cessation of all mining will occur." It had also proposed a three-day work week as a solution to the problem of over-production. Industry leaders opposed the union's program for a shorter work week and higher wages; it made no economic sense, as Lewis later admitted himself. The controversy resulted in numerous big strikes. From 1945 through 1950 an average of 10.4 million man-days were lost through work stoppages each year. (From 1950 through 1960 the days lost through work stoppages averaged only one-thirteenth as many.)

Lewis had never held a naïvely idealistic view of trade unionism. In 1925 he had said that it "is a phenomenon of capitalism quite similar to the corporation. One is essentially a pooling of labor for purposes of common action in production and sales. The other is a pooling of capital for exactly the same purposes. The economic aims of both are identical—gain." [4] Neither did he see anything romantic about miners in dark, dirty, and dangerous mines. He had for years maintained that the sooner men could get out of the mines and be replaced by machines the happier he would be and the better off the men would be. In 1947 Lewis told a Congressional committee:

> The UMWA . . . [had taken] the position that the only way in which the standard of living could be increased . . . would be by increasing the productivity and lowering the unit costs and utilizing the genius of science and the automatic machine . . . and the usage of power to do the work of human hands, and the UMW educated its membership through the years to an acceptance of that policy. . . .
>
> As the result of that policy, the UMW . . . declared that the miners had a right to participate, through increased wages and shorter hours and improved safety and better conditions, in the increased productive efficiency of the industry, holding that there were three parties to the profit by increased proficiency and greater production: (a) the investor who was given a larger return and a more secure investment; (b) the mine worker who would get higher wages and shorter hours, improved safety conditions; and (c) the consumer of the product who could buy this product at a lower unit cost.[5]

The UMW's policy of accepting mechanization as long as the miners' shared in the benefits was one of long standing, going back to the early 1900's. Since 1933 Lewis had also made clear the union's interest in discouraging inefficient, marginal operators, believing that they could not serve the best interests of the working miners. For his approval of mechanization and his aid in furthering it in coal mining, Lewis received much public acclaim as a farsighted industrial statesman.

The rapid introduction of machines into coal mining resulted in an impressive gain in productivity. Between 1949 and 1960 the output per man-hour almost doubled, far outstripping the productivity gains of manufacturing. Though employee compensation per man-hour increased by 71 per cent during the same period, employment costs per ton actually dropped by almost 11 per cent. The public benefited primarily through low or lower electric power rates. The price of coal sold to electric utilities dropped by about 3 per cent during the fifties, whereas the price of oil rose nearly 10 per cent and the price of gas doubled.

The 160,000 miners who continued to work in the coal pits in 1960 enjoyed higher wages and better conditions than

[4] John Hutchinson, "Captain of a Mighty Host: A Note on the Retirement of John L. Lewis," *Yale Review,* 50 (September, 1960), 42–52.

[5] Morton S. Baratz, *The Union and the Coal Industry* (New Haven: Yale University Press, 1955), pp. 71–72.

they ever had before, but there were 234,000 fewer jobs than there had been 11 years before—a 60 per cent decline! For over a decade an average of 400 jobs disappeared weekly. Small mines had closed, and many of the operators and their employees found themselves part of the permanently unemployed. The rapid displacement of workers and the readjustment of coal markets left in the southern Appalachians a pocket of festering misery that was to become a national problem. Those hardest hit blamed the union and the big operators for ruining them.

In their suit against the UMW the Phillips partners accused the union and the few big companies in the area of attempting to solve the problems of the coal industry by an illegitimate concerted effort to squeeze out the small operators and to destroy the jobs of the bulk of the miners. To achieve their goal of a stable, prosperous industry paying high wages, both the union and the big companies took steps to exclude the production, marketing, and sale of non-union coal. As evidence of this alleged conspiracy, the partners presented both the 1952 National Bituminous Coal Wages Agreement, which forbade signatory companies from leasing coal lands to non-union operators, and the 1958 Agreement, which contained the additional provision that the companies were not to buy or sell coal mined by companies that did not pay the wage rates specified elsewhere in the Agreement. The results of these provisions soon made themselves felt. Since the major companies held extensive reserves and were rapidly adding to them, small non-union operators were denied access to hundreds of thousands of acres and billions of tons of coal. After 1958, the small operators who had nonetheless managed to hold a coal claim but who were unable to pay the union wage scale or Welfare Fund royalties were forced to market their coal in direct competition with the big companies; they could no longer sell their output to these companies and thus avoid the difficulties and expenses of marketing their coal directly to industrial users.

IV

Additional evidence available to the partners and relevant to their charge involved the Tennessee Valley Authority. In the mid-1950's TVA began to build and operate large coal-fed steam plants for the generation of electricity. The resulting expansion of TVA's demand for coal opened a vast new market and created excellent opportunities for the development of small mines in Tennessee and Kentucky, including the mine of the Phillips partners. TVA's purchases of coal increased from 500,000 tons in 1950 to approximately 20,000,000 tons in 1956. The coal was bought through bids in both a term and a spot market. The spot market involved small orders to be delivered within a short time and offered definite advantages to small, financially weak companies that could not afford the risks and heavy investments involved in long-term commitments.

Non-union firms began to flourish because of sales to TVA. Lewis and the UMW felt that such growth threatened the union's position and its wage standards and so moved to squeeze small firms out of this new market. In 1955 the UMW and two large coal producing companies, the Consolidated Coal Company and the Pocahontas Fuel Company, prevailed upon Secretary of Labor James P. Mitchell to make use of the powers available to him under the Walsh-Healy Act [6] and to determine a minimum wage in the coal industry for work done under government contract. The union contended that TVA was buying coal "at starvation prices, at intolerable and unjustified prices." The Secretary agreed, and he set a minimum wage for the bituminous

[6] The Public Contracts Act, passed in 1936, permits the Secretary of Labor to fix the minimum wages that must be paid in the manufacture or supply of all goods purchased by the federal government.

coal industry twice as high as the minimum for any other industry under the Walsh-Healy Act.

At the 1956 convention of the UMW, Secretary Mitchell explained his action:

> I have had occasion, as Mr. Lewis has indicated, to work with your organization in the Department of Labor on many fronts. . . . As you know, about a year ago the Secretary of Labor, for the first time in history, found a minimum wage in the coal industry which controlled the wages that were to be paid to workers who worked on government contracts. We purposely sought that determination in order to exclude from government bidding those non-union mines which are a detriment to the industry. And I think by and large we have succeeded, except for certain areas of government purchasing which still have to be, shall I say, investigated. Twenty-five per cent, at the moment, of the TVA purchases are made under contracts less than $10,000, which excepts such purchases from the determination of the Walsh-Healy Act. I have set in motion a study of the TVA purchasing policy to see if there is any evasion of the Walsh-Healy determination on the part of the TVA. I don't know whether there is or not, but if there is, you can be sure that we will correct it. . . . I propose to continue this enforcement policy, because I believe it is in the interest not only of the worker but is in the interest of the fair employer to prevent the chiseling, non-union employer from competing in the market place with fair labor employers who hire union labor.[7]

The Phillips Brothers Coal Company and other small companies were able to escape the Walsh-Healy restrictions by limiting their annual spot-market TVA sales to less than $10,000. The union and the large companies began to try to close this loophole. They met with the TVA directors in 1956 to urge them to reduce the Authority's spot-market purchases from 25 per cent to 10 per cent of the total. They also suggested that spot contracts for coal not shipped at the time specified be automatically canceled. When TVA did not immediately act on their suggestions, they seem to have acted on their own. According to the allegation of the Phillips Brothers, the large companies—particularly the two in which the UMW had an interest—then began to dump coal on the spot market in a further attempt to drive the small operators out of business.

Toward the end of 1956 the price of coal on the spot market began to decline; it continued downward through 1957 and 1958, finally reaching a very low figure in 1958. During 1956, 1957, and 1958, Pittsburgh-Midway Coal, Peabody Coal, West Kentucky Coal, and Nashville Coal, four of the big coal-producing companies, made offerings of large tonnages on the TVA spot market at generally declining prices, and a number of these bids were successful. Evidence indicated that one of these companies, West Kentucky, had usually sold coal extensively in the middlewestern utility market, especially up and down the Mississippi Valley. Despite the fact that demand in this market had held up well, West Kentucky began to throw distress coal into the TVA market. The behavior of Nashville Coal was similar. After 1956 West Kentucky showed a great decline in its profits and in 1958 and 1959 reported losses. Officials of West Kentucky Coal, Nashville Coal, and Peabody Coal reported that they had not made separate analyses of the profits on the coal sold to TVA. The president of Peabody Coal stated that he was "afraid to look at some of them [the figures]."

V

The heavy offerings of coal on TVA's spot market at distress prices adversely affected Phillips Brothers and the other small operators; they were being bankrupted and eliminated as competitors. The jury that initially heard the case concluded that more than coincidence was involved when the

[7] Pennington v. United Mine Workers, *op. cit.*, pp. 814–15.

companies in which the UMW had an interest dumped big tonnages on the spot market at low and declining prices at the same time that the union was attempting to eliminate or drastically reduce that very market. Though the union contended that as a labor organization it had always acted in the interests of its members and that it was motivated by legitimate labor goals—securing union standards of wages and better conditions of employment—the jury found it guilty of violating the antitrust law. Damages were fixed at $90,000, a sum that was to be trebled in accordance with the law.

The case was appealed to higher courts and finally in June, 1965, the Supreme Court of the United States declared that unions are not exempt from the antitrust laws if they and employers make agreements to secure uniform labor standards throughout an industry. Writing for the majority, Justice White said:

> It is true that wages lie at the very heart of those subjects about which employers and unions must bargain and the law contemplates agreements on wages not only between individual employers and a union but agreements between the union and employers in a multi-employer bargaining unit. The union benefit from the wage scale agreed upon is direct and concrete and the effect on the product market, though clearly present, results from the elimination of competition based on wages among the employers in the bargaining unit, which is not the kind of restraint Congress intended the Sherman Act to proscribe. We think it beyond question that a union may conclude a wage agreement for the multi-employer bargaining unit without violating the antitrust laws and that it may as a matter of its own policy, and not by agreement with all or part of the employers of that unit, seek the same wages from other employers.
>
> This is not to say that an agreement resulting from union-employer negotiations is automatically exempt from Sherman Act scrutiny simply because negotiations involve a compulsory subject of bargaining, regardless of the subject or the form and content of the agreement. . . . But we think a union forfeits its exemption from the antitrust laws when it is clearly shown that it has agreed with one set of employers to impose a certain wage scale on other bargaining units. One group of employers may not conspire to eliminate competitors from the industry and the union is liable with the employers if it becomes a party to the conspiracy. This is true even though the union's part in the scheme is an undertaking to secure the same wages, hours or other conditions of employment from the remaining employers in the industry. . . . There is nothing in the labor policy indicating that the union and the employers in one bargaining unit are free to bargain about the wages, hours and working conditions of other bargaining units or to attempt to settle these matters for the entire industry. On the contrary, the duty to bargain unit by unit leads to a quite different conclusion. The union's obligation to its members would seem best served if the union retained the ability to respond to each bargaining situation as the individual circumstances might warrant, without being straight-jacketed by some prior agreement with the favored employers. . . .
>
> [T]he policy of the antitrust laws is clearly set against employer-union agreements seeking to prescribe labor standards outside the bargaining unit. One could hardly contend, for example, that one group of employers could lawfully demand that the union impose on other employers wages that were significantly higher than those paid by the requesting employers, or a system of computing wages that, because of differences in methods of production, would be more costly to one set of employers than to another. The anticompetitive potential of such a combination is obvious, but is little more severe than what is alleged to have been the purpose and effect of the conspiracy in this case to establish wages at a level that marginal producers could not pay so that they would be driven from the industry. And if the conspiracy presently under attack were declared exempt it would hardly be possible to deny exemption to such avowedly discriminatory schemes.
>
> From the viewpoint of antitrust policy, moreover, all such agreements between a

group of employers and a union that the union will seek specified labor standards outside the bargaining unit suffer from a more basic defect, without regard to predatory intention or effect in the particular case. For the salient characteristic of such agreements is that the union surrenders its freedom of action with respect to its bargaining policy. Prior to the agreement the union might seek uniform standards in its own self-interest but would be required to assess in each case the probable costs and gains of a strike or other collective action to that end and thus might conclude that the objective of uniform standards should temporarily give way. After the agreement the union's interest would be bound in each case to that of the favored employer group. It is just such restraints upon the freedom of economic units to act according to their own choice and discretion that run counter to antitrust policy.

Thus the relevant labor and antitrust policies compel us to conclude that the alleged agreement between UMW and the large operators to secure uniform labor standards throughout the industry, if proved, was not exempt from the antitrust laws.[8]

Justices Douglas, Black, and Clark concurred in the decision, adding the following comment:

> Congress can design an oligopoly for our society, if it chooses. But business alone cannot do so as long as the antitrust laws are enforced. Nor should business and labor working hand-in-hand be allowed to make that basic change in the design of our so-called free enterprise system. If the allegations in this case are to be believed, organized labor joined hands with organized business to drive marginal operators out of existence. . . . The only architect of our economic system is Congress. We are right in adhering to its philosophy of the free enterprise system as expressed in the antitrust laws . . . until the Congress delegates to big business and big labor the power to remold our economy in the manner charged here.

VI

Justice Goldberg dissented and was joined by Justices Harlan and Stewart. In part he argued:

> Despite allegations of conspiracy, which connotes clandestine activities, it is no secret that the United Mine Workers, acting to further what it considers to be the best interests of its members, espouses a philosophy of achieving uniform high wages, fringe benefits, and good working conditions. As the *quid pro quo* for this, the Union is willing to accept the burdens and consequences of automation. Further, it acts upon the view that the existence of marginal operators who cannot afford these high wages, fringe benefits, and good working conditions does not serve the best interests of the working miner but, on the contrary, depresses wage standards and perpetuates undesirable conditions. . . . Consistent with this view, the Union welcomes automation, insisting only that the workers participate in its benefits. . . . It would seem [in the majority's opinion, however] that unions are damned if their collective bargaining philosophy involves acceptance of automation. . . .
>
> [Further] there were allegations that a part of the conspiracy of the large coal operators consisted of collusive bidding on the TVA spot market of West Kentucky Coal Company, Nashville Coal Company, and two other coal operators, for which the Union allegedly shared responsibility. It was asserted that the effect of this alleged collusive bidding was to drive down the prices on the spot market and thereby injure the small coal operators. Although the [lower court] apparently accepted this position, it did not deal directly with the question of whether the evidence was sufficient to show the Union's participation in the alleged scheme. Rather [it] relied upon the fact that the

[8] United Mine Workers of America v. Pennington *et al.,* 381 U.S. 657 (1964). The majority opinion ruled that the joint efforts of the union and the large companies to influence the Secretary of Labor and the TVA directors could not be used as evidence of violation of the antitrust laws. It said, "Such conduct is not illegal, either standing alone or as part of a broader scheme itself violative of the Sherman Act." The Court therefore remanded the case for further proceedings, consistent with its decision.

Union was a major stockholder in West Kentucky and had substantial interests in Nashville. . . . The ownership of a controlling or substantial interest in a company which conspires with others in violation of the antitrust laws does not in itself impose antitrust liability on the owner. Rather the owner must be shown to have participated knowingly and actively in the alleged illegal activity.

QUESTIONS

Efficiency v. Monopoly

1. In the Standard Oil of California case the court dismissed the "economic merits or demerits" of the exclusive contract system as immaterial to the decision. In the United Mine Workers case Justice Goldberg charges that the opinion of the majority condemns a union's collective bargaining philosophy if it involves acceptance or automation. Defend the argument that the court's conception of public interest is too narrow. Defend the argument that the court's conception of public interest is broader than that encompassed by mere economics.

2. What are the gains and losses to the community when large companies and big unions "squeeze out" small, independent businessmen or operators as Standard Oil of California was free to do and as the Mine Workers did? Take into account the benefits and costs of the innovative changes sponsored by Standard Oil and the Mine Workers.

3. Why do you agree or disagree with Justice Douglas' opinions in the two cases?

4. Justice Frankfurter suggested that Standard Oil of California might be trying to stabilize the oil market both for its benefit and for that of its customers; John L. Lewis maintained that the union had to act as a stabilizing force in the industry for the benefit of investors, workers, and consumers. Do you believe the stability provided in each case was in the public interest and, if so, why?

5. Justice Douglas argues that the court's decision in the Standard Oil case allows—if it does not encourage—the company to buy out the independent dealers and control oil distribution. The government thus promotes monopoly. In the United Mine Workers case, Phillips accused the UMW and the large coal companies of using the government to help monopolize the coal industry. Do you find in these cases that the government contributed to monopoly practices? Might the government promote monopoly in order to serve the public interest?

6. The outcomes of the Standard Oil of California and UMW cases suggest that as a matter of public policy we may have to choose between efficiency and competition. Under what conditions or circumstances does such a choice have to be made?

chapter **8**

BUSINESSMEN: ENTREPRENEURS OR BUREAUCRATS?

Businessmen and union leaders not infrequently argue that the power they are believed to possess is merely putative. The chief executive officer of a large national manufacturing firm once complained that he and his managers were in an almost hopeless situation; they were buffeted so severely by circumstances, opponents, and competitors that he foresaw only a dark future for his firm and the industry. First, they had suffered a long and costly strike and had then had to settle without gaining their demands to be able to operate their plants more efficiently. Second, the government was threatening to impose price guidelines upon them, and the antitrust division of the Justice Department was continually lurking about, looking for an excuse to prosecute. Third, foreign competition had made large inroads into the firm's markets abroad, and at home substitute products were eating away at sales. In sum, he saw no relief, no room for maneuver, and no chance for initiative. He and his associates were hemmed in and restricted—powerless pawns of a society that no longer encouraged efficient, profit-seeking business.

The particular complaints of this businessman may have been born of temporary setbacks to the company and his own ineptitude, but their general tone is not untypical. Most business and union leaders probably also feel that they act as conditions and situations dictate rather than as men who impress their will upon events and give them direction. So convinced are businessmen and union leaders—like almost all managers within large bureaucracies—of their limited power that they seldom identify those who act or make decisions within the organization. Things happen, decisions are made, and transactions are accomplished, but these proceed apparently without the help of personalities. The people involved become puppets of circumstances or of tendencies and forces within the industry. Although muckraking journalists and biographers once pictured swashbuckling captains of industry who shaped their industrial as well as their political and social environment, businessmen today are inclined to portray themselves as competent professionals who adapt themselves to forces set in motion by others.

There are, of course, constraints on the businessman's freedom of action and on his power; many considerations must enter into his judgments and decisions, among them the power and demands of politicians, organized consumer groups, and employees. Such realities, and not simply the self-pity of businessmen, were reflected in the popularity of an article published in the *Harvard Business Review* that described how even routine business decisions could only be made in consultation, almost hourly, with government representatives.[1] And James R. Hoffa of the Teamsters Union could undoubtedly tear a similar page from his own calendar to reveal the magnitude of limitations on union leaders in conducting what he not unrealistically terms "the union business." Indeed, the prolonged legal battle he carried on with the Department of Justice might well have intimidated and frustrated a person of less initiative and imagination.

In addition to the objective constraints they actually face, however, managers also operate in an environment of values and beliefs that reinforces their self-image of essentially passive response. The thought that businessmen, along with angry Presidents, aggressive trustbusters, and hard-bargaining unionists, might be accountable for even some of the major developments in our society is not readily entertained by most citizens. The idea that the business community responds to the initiative of others is perpetuated by the news media as they regularly report "Wall Street reactions" to Presidential press conferences, the statements of labor leaders, and other significant events. The pictures occasionally drawn of businessmen as "robber barons," "malefactors of great wealth," or "economic royalists" have never replaced the less colorful one of the businessman as a manager who minds his own business, adjusting its detailed operations to meet contingencies triggered by others. Indeed, if we omit the Progressive era and the Great Depression, we can generalize that businessmen have usually been regarded as rational economic agents who simply make decisions "at the margins" guided by the best information available to them, straightforward criteria of profitability, and their individual consciences.

The crucial factor influencing business judgment is now commonly thought to be the degree of "confidence" in the state of the economy. Americans are influenced in this belief more by the reasoning of academic economists than by the judgment of social critics. Arthur F. Burns, chairman of the Council of Economic Advisors during the Eisenhower Administration, president of the National Bureau of Economic Research, and a Columbia University economist, has emphasized the importance of business confidence and lent his support to the view that the individual businessman is an "intervening variable" who is almost totally dependent on and vulnerable to the acts, demands, and even attitudes of others. In a sweeping appraisal of the performance of the American economy in the postwar era, Burns related changes in the economy to variations in the level of business confidence, which in turn he linked in detail to specific public policies, union demands, and Presidential attitudes toward the business community.[2] We need not examine here the kinds of congressional policies,

[1] Gilbert H. Clee, "The Appointment Book of J. Edward Ellis," *Harvard Business Review,* 40 (November–December, 1962), 79–92. Some readers were given pause by the editorial blurb at the beginning of this article that identified the author as the director of a leading consulting firm who had not permitted the annoyance of having to keep appointments with bureaucrats to prevent him from the successful "reorganization of foreign and domestic states."

[2] Arthur F. Burns, *The Management of Prosperity,* "The 1965 Fairless Lectures" (New York: Columbia University Press and Carnegie Press, 1966).

Presidential attitudes, or union postures that Professor Burns believes heighten business confidence and that are conducive to socially beneficial investment and managerial decisions. The important point is that the views of Burns and other economists reinforce the image of the businessman as a technician who has little freedom in shaping the character of American life.[3]

Professor Burns' view of the businessman is completely consistent with—indeed, it is a corollary of—the priority assigned the market mechanism in economic theory. According to the theory, competitive pressures operate *in the long run,* so as substantially to limit the discretionary range and effect of business decisions. However, as John Maynard Keynes pointed out, in the long run we are all dead. In the short run, businessmen sometimes enjoy considerable discretion and find ample room for initiative. We do an injustice to the boldness, the genius, and the imagination of businessmen to describe their work as merely the outcome of grinding market forces. Consider the following description by a Supreme Court Justice of the massive merger of 37 steel companies into the United States Steel Corporation in 1901; it was, he said,

> an evolution, a natural consummation of the tendencies of the industry on account of changing conditions, practically a compulsion from "the metallurgical method of making steel and the physical method of handling it," this method, and the conditions consequent upon it, tending to combinations of capital and energies rather than diffusion in independent action. And the concentration of powers . . . was only such as was deemed necessary, and immediately manifested itself in improved methods and products and in an increase of domestic and foreign trade. Indeed an important purpose of the organization of the corporation was the building up of the export trade in steel and iron. . . .[4]

To describe the creation of U.S. Steel as the result of "natural tendencies" and "technological compulsions" is to overlook the carefully plotted strategies and inspired maneuvers of such men as Charles M. Schwab who worked hard to bring about the merger. We need not be surprised, however, that the men involved accepted its description as an impersonal, natural event. To introduce people into the drama would raise awkward questions about the power amassed by the men who controlled the $1.4 billion corporation that produced half the pig iron, 60 per cent of the structural steel, and 90 per cent of the bridge steel in the nation. From certain points of view, such questions might be better left unexplored or even unasked.

There are several important qualifications to acceptance of the theories of general business helplessness in the face of events and government action. The interaction between government and business has often been clearly very profitable for business. Much of the entrepreneurial skill displayed by business in the prosperous period dating from the end of World War II has been dedicated to making imaginative and inventive use of the opportunities afforded by government subsidies, tax reductions, contracts, and investments in such things as air-

[3] This image is perpetuated in literature, film, and in TV "Easterns," in which the businessman is typically portrayed as an "organization man," a "Babbitt," a "tired businessman," or a "man in a grey-flannel suit" rather than as a swashbuckling entrepreneur.

[4] "Opinion of the Court," Justice McKenna, United States v. U.S. Steel Corporation, 251 U.S. 419, 437–38.

ports, roads, schools, and research.[5] Indeed, one can hardly begin to account for the enormous gains in the American economy since 1945 without recognizing the business initiative that imaginatively combined these and other welfare benefits with private funds and managerial expertise. The business leaders that *Fortune* admiringly calls the "New Breed" have learned to capitalize upon the opportunities offered them in the form of governmental programs. Gilbert Clee concludes his tale in the *Harvard Business Review* about the depressing web of government bureaucracy and red tape with the somewhat ironic observation that managers must learn to negotiate more effectively the labyrinthian corridors of political power. And the investment firm of Merrill Lynch, Pierce, Fenner & Smith, in a pamphlet on the investment prospects arising from America's growing efforts to solve pressing domestic problems, extolls "the economic virtues of a free society" and reminds its clients of "the lucrative markets created by forthcoming social problems." [6]

Another reason for discounting the modesty of top industrial leaders about their impact on the economy is the estimate of their importance implicit in the salaries they pay themselves. In one year, the 66 highest executives of the General Motors Corporation received more income from salaries, bonuses, and other financial benefits than the combined total salaries of the President and the Vice President of the United States, the members of the Cabinet, the Supreme Court, the Senate, the House of Representatives, and 48 state governors.

Antitrust cases, pricing conspiracies, and the other scandals that are reported with oppressive monotony in the daily pages of the *Wall Street Journal* constitute a further argument against believing that consumers, political figures, and labor leaders determine economic processes, while business leaders are merely passive instruments. The degree to which it is possible, for example, to build stout, though perhaps illegal, shelters against the chill winds of the marketplace suggests that businessmen have a good deal more power than is acknowledged in their rhetoric.

Consider the situation that came to light when the price conspiracy in the electrical equipment industry was revealed. In 1959 the Tennessee Valley Authority asked for bids to deliver a 500,000 kilowatt turbo-generator and awarded the contract to C. A. Parsons & Co., Ltd., of England. General Electric, whose bids had been eliminated as too high, complained that the English firm's bid was unfair because its labor costs were 40 per cent lower than comparable American wages. This wage differential, GE maintained, accounted for the more than $6 million difference between the American bids and the lower bid by Parsons. In answering these charges of unfairness, TVA's chairman, General Herbert Vogel, calculated that the British firm's bid would have been $4 million to $5 million lower even if General Electric had paid its labor—including engineers, draftsmen, and other salaried personnel, as well as hourly rated factory workers—nothing!

It is by no means clear that the two American companies that bid in the TVA competition were subject to the discipline of the marketplace as they set their

[5] Business has also profited from government pollution control and stockpiling programs. With respect to antipoverty projects, see Ivar Berg and Marcia Freedman, "Job Corps: Business Bonanza," *Christianity and Crisis,* 25 (May 31, 1965), 115–19.

[6] "The New American Horizon," Securities Research Division, Merrill Lynch, Pierce, Fenner & Smith, Inc., New York, May, 1966.

prices for turbo-generators. At the very least, the market had failed to promote efficient production. The companies could not come within striking distance of Parsons' bid even though the British firm had to overcome the handicaps of a tariff of $1.5 million (about the size of its wage bill) and a "Buy American" requirement that foreign bids had to be at least 20 per cent lower than any domestic bid for a government agency to accept them.

The normal pricing policies in several American industries suggest as strongly as the sporadic instances of outright price conspiracies elsewhere that businessmen have considerable power to shape their destinies. Deftly analyzing the incomplete data on automobile pricing disclosed in congressional hearings and other sources, Daniel Bell concluded that the management of General Motors sets automobile prices so that they will return a profit even when production may be no more than 35 per cent or 40 per cent of capacity. When sales are high, economies of scale become operative and unit costs dip below those used in the low sales years as a basis for determining prices, thus insuring the automaker substantial profits.[7] Similarly, in the steel industry, the break-even figure in the 1960's has been reliably reported at 48 per cent of capacity. Presumably prices could be lowered to reflect the economies that set in when high levels of production are achieved; instead, profits soar as prices remain stable or even rise.

Stories of old-fashioned initiative, business acumen, and entrepreneurial derring-do on the American economic scene still appear often enough to constitute a final reason for rejecting the theory that businessmen are helpless. By no means are all managers tired bureaucrats, as the case of one company that had been losing money will illustrate. Anxious to avoid a financial failure, the managers of this company wondered what to do with a large and useless inventory of wallpaper cleaner that would not sell. With intelligence—and no little sense of humor—they relabeled it "Play-dough" and in the first two years alone sold several million dollars' worth of it across toy counters.

If the role of business leaders in making vital economic decisions needs to be reexamined in an atmosphere cleared of foggy ideologies, at least as much attention should be focused on the role of union leaders. Union officials claim that they are hamstrung by the combined workings of union democracy, government surveillance of their financial operations, rapid technological change that stalks after the jobs they seek to control, and unemployment rates that exert downward pressure on wages. Like some business managers, however, some labor leaders have capably turned events and challenges into opportunities and advantages, so no general theory of the natural weakness of union leadership can be taken at face value.

Thus, when employers and congressmen sympathetic with them insisted, in the Taft-Hartley Law of 1947, that labor–management agreements be construed as legal contracts, the union cause seemed at first to have suffered a setback. Employers anxious to avoid pressures from the organized segments of the labor market and wishing to obtain government aid in achieving greater stability in their complex business operations had wanted "no strike" clauses in labor agreements, coupled with provisions for the arbitration of disputes, to be made enforceable in the courts; with the Taft-Hartley Act they were successful. Union leaders were not slow to see the advantages of property ownership that the con-

[7] *New York Review of Books,* 3 (September 10, 1964), 12.

strual of agreements as contracts implied, however; they have since managed successfully to husband their members' investments in their jobs by contesting unilateral managerial decisions to modify work procedures and to relocate production facilities. What at first seemed government persecution of unions was recognized as an opportunity and was turned to good use by alert labor leaders.

Union leaders are also a good deal less the victims of changing technology than they portray themselves to be in disputes with their counterparts in corporations over such issues as work loads, crew sizes, and working rules. For example, Harry Bridges, president of the West Coast longshoremen's union,[8] negotiated with an employer group a ground-breaking "modernization and mechanization" agreement that opened the way for far-reaching technological changes in the manner of loading and unloading seagoing cargo. The stevedoring companies were enabled by the agreement to cut crew sizes, use larger sling loads, and employ forklift trucks and other mechanical devices. As a result of these reforms, turn-around time for West Coast-based ships has been substantially reduced, and longshoremen share—in accordance with the terms of the original agreement—a portion of the benefits that accrue to the companies. Only the slowness of some of the employers to take advantage of the permissive clauses in the contract has kept the union from enjoying even greater returns on its forward-looking policies.

Another leader who has refused to be daunted by changing technology is Edward Swayduck, president of the Amalgamated Lithographers Union of New York. Swayduck is an even more individualistic entrepreneur than Bridges and has led his union on an independent course in pursuit of the opportunities for growth in the areas of his members' interests. His union regularly finances research on new methods and applications of lithography. The union's contributions to the art of packaging alone have been notable; it has also added a great deal to the advertising industry's array of techniques for catching the eye and the interest of the consumer.

Not all union leaders grasp opportunities to exploit their business environment, of course, any more than business executives typically exploit all the opportunities afforded them by the presence of unions. Some formerly aggressive union leaders have now virtually given up in the face of the difficulties and pressures that confront the labor movement in America. Unions have not achieved much influence as representatives of the swollen ranks of white-collar workers, and they have been less than completely successful in preventing rank-and-file members brought into the fold in earlier periods from embarrassing defections, secessions, and even occasional subversions of their bargaining efforts. Whether unions have even succeeded in raising wage levels in America is a matter of considerable dispute among economists. As for their social impact, the vulnerability of many unions to criticism from congressional investigating committees and militant civil rights leaders is by now a matter of public record.

In sum, we may well be skeptical of the bland innocence and agonized helplessness that have become central themes in the rhetoric of businessmen and union leaders. The captains of industry are not merely "dependent variables" in reality, whatever place economists may assign them in the world of their elegant but oversimplified equations. Business managers are neither as powerless nor as

[8] The International Longshoremen's & Warehousemen's Union.

rational as they and others often claim. Nor are union leaders as subversive of capitalist institutions and values nor as omnipotent as their critics would have us believe. Their own complaints against the effects of laws are less than compelling; their exploitation of the market and its price systems are sometimes impressive; their capacity for consolidating or expanding their organizational gains are perhaps less than their abilities to manage their organizations with bureaucratic expertise.

At the same time that we make room for a better differentiated view of business and union leaders than that offered by conventional stereotypes, it is well to note that a new breed of politically astute entrepreneurs, outside both unions and corporations, has appeared, almost unnoticed on the American scene. Little attention has yet been given to the heads of private foundations, the university scholars, and the government leaders who have quietly moved to become initiators in recent years. The Ford Foundation has played a major role in the economic development of the new countries of Africa; the Carnegie Foundation has regularly broken new ground in education, which, in turn, figures very significantly in the growth of the U.S. economy; the Atomic Energy Commission, the National Aeronautics and Space Administration, and the Department of Agriculture have contributed enormously to the peaceful application of nuclear energy, the development of computer technology and "miniaturization," and an unbelievable output of foodstuffs, respectively. Clark Kerr, formerly president of the University of California at Berkeley, and George Taylor of the University of Pennsylvania have broken numerous impasses between corporations and unions while teaching the nation much about effective leadership of large organizations.

A host of quasi-public agencies gives testimony to the fact that old-fashioned entrepreneurship is appearing in some new guises. A noted economist reminds us that the Tennessee Valley Authority, the many turnpike authorities, port authorities, and regional "conferences," and a number of housing and urban renewal agencies represent new forms of "enterprise structures." "These structures have become so large and extensive," he writes, "that when Robert Moses, a New York civil servant, was at the height of his activity in the middle 1950's, he had the best claim to the title of the nation's outstanding entrepreneur." [9] A review of Mr. Moses' activities and relationships is indeed suggestive of the variety of entrepreneurial opportunities still present in America. One of the newest enterprise structures is the Communications Satellite Corporation; it was invented by public servants and politicians, working in collaboration with private citizens, to capitalize on space-age opportunities.

Initiative and creativity are of significance to our economic system wherever they are found, and economic doctrines that overlook the importance of entrepreneurial "bureaucrats" in governmental and quasi-public agencies ought to be modified to fit current reality.

The four cases that follow focus on four American leaders. The careers and actions of Roger Blough and Robert Moses help one to move beyond received doctrines and to identify the conditions under which entrepreneurial or bureaucratic responses are likely to appear. John Paul Getty and David Dubinsky have

[9] Eli Ginzberg, "The Passing of an Economy That Never Was," *Columbia Journal of World Business,* 1 (Summer, 1966), 133–38.

been obliged to confront some circumstances that might have evoked a number of different managerial strategies. A review of the choices that they have made and the conclusions that they have reached suggests some additional dimensions of the entrepreneurial role in America. These cases represent the kind of evidence that must be considered in determining who are the initiators and who are the passive responders in America today; they also warn us that a useful definition of entrepreneurship is not easy to formulate.

Expressions of the Entrepreneurial Spirit Today

ROGER BLOUGH

The chairman and chief executive officer of the country's largest steel producer, United States Steel Corporation, is, by his position alone, an important and leading businessman. Nevertheless, Roger M. Blough, who had been elected chairman of the board of U.S. Steel in 1955, was almost unknown to the public when in 1962, much to his surprise, he found himself the highly publicized antagonist of President John F. Kennedy in a struggle over a price increase the steel industry had just announced. Blough's picture appeared on the covers of newsmagazines, his news conferences were televised, and his comments made headlines across the country. He appeared to be a man of deep convictions about his company's pricing policy, calmly convinced that it was right, and stubbornly, though quietly, insistent that the President had no right to try to change it. Faced with Kennedy's hastily but skillfully organized opposition to the price rise, however, he prudently accepted its rescission.

I

Until Roger Blough became vice chairman in May, 1952, and heir-apparent to Benjamin Fairless, then president and chairman of U.S. Steel, few people outside the company had ever heard of him. He had served as an associate counsel in 1939–40, helping U.S. Steel prepare testimony for the investigation of the Temporary National Economic Committee. Fairless later reported why Blough had impressed him:

> No one could have asked anyone more questions than he asked me the first time I met him. We were weeks preparing answers to questions which might arise during the investigation. I noticed that young Blough had thoroughness, tenacity, the ability to get below the surface in order to develop facts. He made a deep impression on me. When an opening came up in the legal end of U.S. Steel in 1942, I suggested him for the job.[1]

In 1942 Blough was appointed general solicitor in charge of all legal matters for the United States Steel Corporation of Delaware, the holding company that guided the activities of the many subsidiaries making up the steel giant. He reorganized the legal department, centralizing work that had been carried on in each of the scattered subsidiary companies. In the following years he also participated in labor negotiations, helped work out financing programs, and showed himself an increasingly able and adept administrator. He took major responsibility for reorganizing the sprawling, semiautonomous subsidiaries, finally transforming them into divisions of one central corporation that determined both general policy and specific production programs. He also pushed hard for a standard cost system

[1] Eleanor Harris, "Mr. Big of Big Steel," *American Weekly,* August 17, 1958.

throughout the company so that better management control might be maintained.

Within 10 years Blough had won the confidence of the board of directors, and he was designated chief executive officer when Fairless retired at age 65 in 1955. Fairless explained why he and the board wanted Blough:

> He handles people so cleverly that the decision is reached without any fanfare. He has many assets, but if I had to narrow them down to one, I would say that Roger's greatest ambition is to have a job well done—and he's perfectly willing to give others the credit. He's an organization man, not an individualist. And he has real modesty; he's not an actor at all.[2]

Blough himself had suggested that businessmen play only a modest role in the activities of running and developing the modern corporation; in the main they adjust to the pressures of the market and respond to the demands made upon them. Businessmen, he suggested, can accomplish only what the public allows them to do. For example, corporations have grown large not because businessmen and managers created them, but rather because the American people wanted them to become large organizations. Consumers, investors, and workers regulate or destroy business, and they—not businessmen—"have led business to develop from the entrepreneurship to the partnership to the modern corporation 'where hundreds of thousands of persons provide the necessary capital and share the risks involved.' "[3]

In delivering the 1959 McKinsey lectures at Columbia University, Blough explained the benefits and opportunities of being an "organization man":

> The heart of the matter is that, through these freely formed and constantly evolving [corporations], generative forces of great originality rise far above the individual imagination of any of its members, enhancing the role of *every* man and giving breadth and scope even to him who may be called the uncommon man. . . . To sum up, our group member grows as a person through adjustment, through training, through doing important things with the group and for the group and hence for himself. . . . In fact our corporate associate has, in the Aristotelian view, provided himself with great opportunities for real happiness because his activities are virtuous.[4]

That the board of directors of United States Steel should select an organization man for the corporation's chief executive is hardly surprising, for they have themselves divided management duties and responsibilities among a number of officers. Three of these officers—the chairman, the chairman of the executive committee, and the chairman of the finance committee—are the ruling triumvirate. They exercise their control through the Operating Policy Committee, in which they are joined as members by the general counsel and the six executive vice presidents for functional areas. Aiding the members of the OPC in running the big, complex organization are 17 administrative vice presidents and 28 ordinary vice presidents. U.S. Steel is thus not run by any single man, but by the balanced judgment of men expert in their particular fields. Leslie B. Worthington, president and chairman of the executive committee, has explained that "with our different backgrounds we don't always see eye to eye, but until we agree, we never quit."[5]

Once the Operating Policy Committee reaches an agreement, Blough speaks for it and the corporation. Because of U.S. Steel's size and prestige in the business community, Blough has also often been a spokesman for the entire steel industry in congressional hearings and in public speeches. He has

[2] *Ibid.*

[3] "Are Corporations Big Enough?" *Business Week,* March 23, 1954, p. 196.

[4] "The Corporate Key to a Greater Society," McKinsey Foundation Lectures, 1959 (text of lectures), pp. 21 and 30.

[5] *Forbes,* August 1, 1964, p. 19.

been well rewarded for his services to his corporation; his salary is more than $265,000 a year, and generous stock options enabled him to own over $2 million worth of shares by 1962.

II

In his first reports to the stockholders and in speeches to the public, Roger Blough discussed the principal problem that he thought would face U.S. Steel in the decades between 1955 and 1980. The corporation needed to invest at least $360 million a year in modernizing existing plants and equipment and in new facilities that would increase its steelmaking capacity by more than 50 per cent; though the investment was large, it would do no more than maintain the corporation's share of the expanding steel business. Securing the funds for the required investment had been and would continue to be extremely difficult, Blough maintained, because of inflation:

> It has not only wiped out the benefits of all of the technological progress which has occurred in our plants and our mills, but it has cut our profit margins far below the levels which prevailed in the earlier years of our corporate life. But that, of course, is only part of the story; for while inflation has been shrinking our profit margin on the one hand, it has been generating the need for a substantial increase in profits on the other . . . [because] the cost of our equipment we buy for our steel mills has been rising at the rate of almost 8 per cent each year during the past ten years. . . .[6]

As Blough saw the problem, he and his fellow executives had available four possible ways of generating sufficient revenue within the corporation for the required investment. They could raise prices, cut wage costs of production workers, seek higher depreciation allowances from the government, or lower per-unit costs through further reorganization and the introduction of radical changes in steelmaking technology. To some extent they meant to seek funds in each of the four ways; but Blough made clear in his speeches that he and the other managers favored the first three over the fourth, for they seemed to entail less risk and would most surely and easily supply the needed funds.

Steel prices had moved upward persistently throughout the fifties, but the most rapid and largest increases occurred after Blough became chairman of U.S. Steel. Between 1955 and the end of 1958 the price of finished steel increased by about 28 per cent; over the same period, the prices of all manufactured goods went up by about 10 per cent. Senator Estes Kefauver asked Blough to explain the policy followed by U.S. Steel in establishing prices; specifically, he wondered why all the steel companies listed the same prices and why no price ever seemed to come down. Blough replied:

> My concept is that a price that matches another price is a competitive price. If you don't choose to accept that concept, then of course, you don't accept it. In the steel industry we know it is so. . . . For anyone to assume that prices are not competitive because some producers raise the price the same as other producers, I think is, as I said before, simply an erroneous assumption.[7]

Competition had brought steel prices to their high level, Blough asserted. This explanation did not satisfy congressmen, newspaper editors, and scholars; they accused the steel companies of raising prices after every round of wage negotiations more than enough to make up the additional costs of the new agreement with the union. Not competition, they said, but steel managers taking advantage of an oligopolistic market situation determined steel prices. After 1958, President Eisenhower took a strong stand against further rises in the price of steel;

[6] "Inflation as a Way of Life," an address delivered before the National Editorial Association, Chicago, November 9, 1956.

[7] U.S. Senate, Committee on the Judiciary, Subcommittee on Antitrust and Monopoly, 86th Cong., 1st Sess., *Hearings On Administered Prices,* Pt. II (1957), pp. 312 and 314.

his Secretary of Labor pointed out that while the steel companies justified their price increases by citing rising total labor costs, the relevant figures were not total but unit costs. Steel prices had far outdistanced these costs—employment costs per ton—all through the 1950's.

Besides growing political and popular criticism of the steel industry's pricing policy, the threat of foreign imports made further increases hazardous. By the late 1950's prices for many American steel products ranged as much as 10 per cent above world steel prices. In December, 1958, the United States became a net importer of steel for the first time in its modern history. Blough pointed out that despite the rising productivity in U.S. Steel's mills and in those of the rest of the industry,

> the fact remains that we are rapidly losing the technological margin that we had over other nations, and that has thus far supported American wages at levels high above those prevailing elsewhere in the world.[8]

Since neither he nor other leaders of the steel industry were in favor of tariffs or import restrictions at that time,[9] the only important way to meet the foreign competition, according to Blough, was to keep wage costs down:

> Despite all that we and the Government may do to promote our competitive position, the final decision rests with the American working man, and with his delegated leaders. For the fact remains that in the last analysis the only one who can fully protect the American workman is the American workman himself. If he can keep wage costs from mounting while rising productivity brings our total costs into competitive balance with foreign costs, then truly I believe that he can expect to see the greatest era of prosperity our nation has ever known.[10]

III

In 1959 Roger Blough threw himself into a crusade to protect American steelworkers against loss of their jobs to foreign workers by persuading them to restrain their wage demands. First, of course, union power had to be confronted and contained. Again and again Blough denounced the overwhelming power exercised by unions, forcing companies to agree against their wills to high, non-competitive wages. He warned of the "glacier-like forces of a powerful labor movement" and the power of labor unions that add up to "a force which no one company or even any one industry could begin to equal—a force which will surpass the strength of any group of private organizations this country has ever known."[11] He argued that since World War II there had been "no restraining force upon their wage demands, and [the unions] have demonstrated their power to shut down a whole industry until their demands are met to their satisfaction."[12] That had been the situation in the past. In 1959, however, when a new labor agreement was to be negotiated, Blough was ready to apply restraints: U.S. Steel would agree to no more than a modest wage increase of about 10 cents an hour (or 3 per cent), and it would also demand an end to all work rules that in management's view were restrictive and contributed to inefficiencies.

Under U.S. Steel's existing labor agreement with the United Steelworkers of

[8] "A Talk of Two Towns," address before the Annual Meeting of the Cleveland Chamber of Commerce, April 17, 1958, pp. 10–11.

[9] Leslie B. Worthington, president of U.S. Steel, called for a temporary additional tariff on steel and pig-iron imports on February 8, 1967. Prior to this, he and other leaders had sought to limit imports by charging foreign companies with illegally "dumping" steel products in the U.S. and then selling them at prices below those charged in their home markets.

[10] *Ibid.*, p. 17.

[11] *Free Man and the Corporation* (New York: McGraw-Hill, 1959), pp. 62–63 and 65.

[12] *Statement,* before the Subcommittee on Antitrust and Monopoly of the Senate Committee on the Judiciary, April 24, 1959. Public Relations Department, United States Steel, New York, p. 7.

America, management had the right to change any and all work rules made obsolete by technological change; furthermore, union officials had offered to work jointly with management to get rid of any inefficient or unreasonable practices. In 1959 management asked for much more; it wanted freedom to eliminate any and all rules that set the amount, quality, and manner of work to be done—the standards by which one told how fast was fast and how fair was fair. In effect, the managers of U.S. Steel were asking the steelworkers to finance their own technological displacement. By changing the rules, managers could get more work at the same price, thus lowering costs per unit. Lower costs and the same or higher prices would provide more funds for reinvestment in new machines and equipment, and these in turn would make possible the same or greater output using fewer workers.

Despite these obvious effects of technological change, the steelworkers did not oppose it as such and had never restricted its introduction; all they questioned in 1959 was the desirability of asking the workers to finance it themselves. Productivity in the steel industry had increased about 10 per cent between 1955 and 1959; technological advances already implemented permitted the steel industry to produce 6 million more tons of steel, using 16,000 fewer production workers, in the first half of 1959 than in the same six months of 1955. However, with jobs already disappearing because of technological change, the steelworkers union had little sympathy for the argument that its members ought to work harder to provide investment funds for U.S. Steel. In 1959 the corporation held nearly half a billion dollars of readily marketable securities and possessed an additional working capital of $615.5 million in cash and securities. Many critics argued that with funds as large as these available, the corporation's executives needed only to be bold, imaginative investors if they wanted to hurry the pace of change; they hardly needed to play the role of penny-pinching, whip-cracking employers short of investment funds.

Blough and his fellow executives were perhaps reluctant to reduce the liquidity of U.S. Steel's financial position in 1959; at any rate, they maintained their bargaining demands, and in consequence the corporation suffered the longest steel strike in American history—116 days. It was stopped only when President Eisenhower declared it a national emergency and secured an injunction. In the settlement subsequently worked out with the help of Vice President Nixon, the workers agreed to accept a wage increase they had rejected before, and management agreed not to make further changes in work rules. While Blough did not gain for U.S. Steel the savings in labor costs he had wanted, the wage increase was the industry's smallest of the post-World War II period. He declared that "from the standpoint of the steel industry of the United States remaining competitive in world markets and from the standpoint of the steel industry being able to provide jobs, the trend [of wage costs] is somewhat better than it was in the 1950's." [13]

IV

U.S. Steel (and the steel industry) still needed additional help if it was going to hold its markets. Blough had done as much as he could to hold down wage costs; now he suggested that the company would have to increase its efforts to improve steel technology. Since the gains of such improvement would be recorded only in the long run, however, he began to urge certain reforms that would provide more immediate benefits. In late 1960 he declared:

> Much of the difficulty we now face in acquiring improved tools more rapidly would be alleviated if the Government's tax laws recognized that the existing depreciation al-

[13] "Business Has a Mandate, Too," address before the 67th Annual Dinner Meeting, Illinois Manufacturers Association, Chicago, December 15, 1960, p. 13.

lowance . . . is woefully inadequate because of inflation. . . . The time has come, I think, to recognize that every industrial foreign country against which American goods must compete has more liberal depreciation laws—in most cases *much* more liberal—than has the United States. And something should be done about it! [14]

During its first year the new Kennedy Administration did not increase depreciation allowances, and the thoughts of steel executives apparently turned once again to the short-run remedy of a general rise in the price of steel. Early in 1962, President Kennedy proposed that average national productivity be used as a guidepost in raising wages and in increasing and cutting prices; however, the executives of U.S. Steel decided to raise steel prices in April, 1962, with no reference to the suggested guideposts. Blough personally announced to the President the action already taken. As we noted in detail in Chapter 5, President Kennedy reacted strongly; within a few days U.S. Steel rescinded its price increases, and at a press conference Roger Blough ruefully commented, "Well, I think you gentlemen can readily see that I do not know anything about politics."

V

Because they were only partially successful in their drive to keep wage costs down and were completely defeated in the attempt to raise prices, Blough and the other U.S. Steel executives decided in 1962 that they must increase revenues by completing the reorganization of the corporation and by improving its technology to make it truly competitive. They were determined to give the lie to a saying common in the industry that "you didn't have to be good to make money in steel—you merely had to produce it a little cheaper than U.S.S., which didn't make steel very inexpensively at all." [15]

The record of U.S. Steel between 1955 and 1962 was sluggish and in need of a change; sales and profits were down about one-third. Edwin H. Gott, executive vice president for production, explained that everyone had become complacent. For too long the company had been used to a seller's market; now it was content to hope that the market would return by itself. Robert C. Tyson, chairman of the finance committee, explained that in the past the company's "primary job was to get out production and our concern was in that and other directions [rather than making drastic organizational changes]." Leslie B. Worthington, the corporation's president, admitted that finally, "we started looking for better ways of doing things; we wondered what we did wrong." [16] Chairman Blough himself conceded that in the late fifties and early sixties U.S. Steel suffered from a corporate organization that was out of step with the changing times. He had not followed through and completed the reorganization, begun under Fairless in the early fifties, from holding company to a true operating steel company. A writer for *Forbes* reported after talking with Blough that company executives had, for some time, looked for excuses to put off ending the careers of men they knew and liked. They delayed the painful task of pulling mills out of communities, breaking with tradition, and making tough decisions.

A shakeup was clearly in order, and Blough and other executives began making a drastic change in U.S. Steel, doing things, as one executive vice president put it, that "you didn't think possible before." First, they planned consolidations of overlapping positions and duplicated work that eventually would eliminate a fifth of the company's 26,000 managerial positions, ranging from foremen to vice presidents. The number of sales officers, for example, was cut from 53 to 29, and all salesmen were now required to sell all products in a given market rather

[14] *Ibid.*, p. 14.

[15] "U.S. Steel Strips for a Fight," *Business Week,* September 28, 1963, p. 114.

[16] "United States Steel: Ready to Go," *Forbes,* August 1, 1964, pp. 18–23.

than to continue specializing in a single product. Several thousand white-collar clerical workers were let go as well.

As a second reform, the executives of U.S. Steel finally decided to invest in some of the radical technological processes that had already been adopted abroad and by most of the other major American steel companies. Their decision was eased by the fact that in 1962 Congress enacted a 7 per cent tax credit for business expenditures on major equipment, and the Treasury revised its depreciation rules to allow easier accumulation of investment funds. The effect was to increase corporations' net cash flow and to raise the after-tax rate of return on new investments. These changes, along with a recovery in sales, helped persuade the U.S. Steel executives that the time was indeed ripe for investing in the new processes already available. In 1963 U.S. Steel put into operation a basic oxygen furnace with a 1,500-ton capacity and in 1965 added others with a capacity of 6,000 tons. It planned to spend from $500 to $600 million a year on new plants and equipment, at least through 1968.

VI

Some critics have suggested that the conversion from the open hearth to the basic oxygen process at U.S. Steel clearly reflected the particular quality of Roger Blough's entrepreneurship during his first years as corporation chairman. Foreign steel firms had been using basic oxygen furnaces for commercial production since 1952. As early as 1955 studies indicated that the basic oxygen process could cut construction costs by half or more and reduce operating costs about 40 per cent below those of the open-hearth process. Blough and the rest of U.S. Steel's executives had not been anxious to invest in the new process, however; during the years of reduced sales in the fifties they preferred to rebuild, improve, and increase their open-hearth capacity. Finance committee chairman Robert Tyson explained, "Nobody who has efficient open-hearth furnaces is going to throw them out to buy oxygen furnaces. We waited until we needed to replace old capacity." [17]

Though U.S. Steel and the other steel companies did begin to build substantial basic oxygen plants in the mid-sixties, the steel industry as a whole showed little interest in advancing the technology with any speed. In 1964 its expenditures on research and development amounted to only $116 million—less than 1 per cent of the value it added to its products. In comparison the rubber industry spent $159 million, 40 per cent of the value added to its products, and steel's research and development spending was less than one-tenth that of the chemical industry.[18]

John McDonald, writing in *Fortune,* was highly critical of U.S. Steel and the other big steel producers; he concluded, "The fact is that much of this new capacity [of the fifties and early sixties] was in effect obsolete when it was built. The new plants certainly didn't do much for the industry's productivity." [19] Herbert G. Lawson, a reporter for the *Wall Street Journal,* noted in October, 1966, that U.S. Steel had been embarrassingly slow to adopt the basic oxygen process. Lawson, like McDonald before him, noted that for years U.S. Steel had been a cash-rich company, "in a beautiful position" to invest quickly and heavily in the new, highly productive processes. Since 1955, U.S. Steel had held in cash or in highly liquid securities anywhere from about one-fourth to over one-third of its total assets. It conservatively set money

[17] *Ibid.,* p. 20.

[18] U.S. Department of Commerce, Bureau of the Census, *Statistical Abstract of the United States, 1966* (Washington: Government Printing Office, 1966), Table 1143, p. 771; *Reviews of Data on Science Resources* (Washington: National Science Foundation, December, 1966), p. 5.

[19] "Steel is Rebuilding for a New Era," *Fortune,* 73 (October, 1966), 135.

aside for a project before the project was started. During the period 1955–65, the company kept an average of $437 million in earmarked low-paying securities; these dollars could have been earning much higher returns if they had been invested more boldly.

Though these business publications suggest that U.S. Steel has been something less than enterprising during Blough's term as chief executive, Professor William Haller, Jr., observes that the corporation's managers

> may have given a practical demonstration of the saying traditionally ascribed to Andrew Carnegie that "pioneering don't pay." At any rate, the strategy of waiting until one's competitors have developed a process to the point where big bug-free, low cost plants can be built may be sound business. The plants actually designed for the large firms seem to fit this description. . . . It is natural enough not to monkey with a winning team; the open hearth was a familiar and an easily improvable technique; and an opportunity to lower costs may not, under these circumstances, have seemed sufficiently attractive to justify a change in the established ways of doing things.[20]

[20] William Haller, Jr., "Technological Change in Primary Steelmaking in the United States, 1947–65," *The Employment Impact of Technological Change,* Appendix, Volume II (Washington: Government Printing Office, 1966), pp. 184–85.

ROBERT MOSES

For over 40 years Robert Moses built bridges, parks, highways, terminals, dams, power houses, and monumental public structures on a scale that amazed and pleased some New Yorkers and outraged others. In the unlikely office of New York City Parks Commissioner, he made himself a power to be reckoned with by mayors from LaGuardia to Lindsay and governors from Al Smith to Nelson Rockefeller. He disputed with cabinet officials and bested even Presidents of the United States who dared try to thwart his projects. He was a tough, able administrator who possessed a robust ego, the nerve and boldness of a conquistador, and extraordinary intuition.

One of his biographers declared that the closest parallel to Moses' career in government was to be found in industry, where the "American genius for integration and unification" has perhaps been most apparent.[1] Al Smith also saw in him the kind of drive and initiative that possessed the great business innovators; Moses, he said, "promotes public business like a rugged individualist."

[1] Cleveland Rodgers, *Robert Moses, Builder for Democracy* (New York: Holt, Rinehart and Winston, 1952), p. xx. Foreword by H. V. Kaltenborn.

I

Moses asserted his individuality early in his career. While still an undergraduate at Yale in 1909 he proposed that the college use a portion of the gate receipts from football to support other sports, including the swimming team of which he was a member. He presented his proposal as a challenge to Walter Camp, Yale's famous football coach, who was amazed at the audacity of the student in presenting so absurd a demand. Moses won his point, however, by taking his case to the college newspaper and publicizing the logic and common sense of his proposal. Not only did Yale adopt the practice of using football to finance its entire sports program, but so did other colleges.

Later, while studying at Oxford, Moses became interested in government service. He wrote a dissertation on the development of the British civil service and presented it for his doctoral degree from Columbia University in 1914. Still pursuing his interest in government, he then joined the Bureau of Municipal Research in New York as a student-worker and was soon appointed to a staff position. His studies in and reports on civil service standards, budgetary programs, and public administration brought him recognition from those concerned with improving the quality of government operations. In 1919 Governor Al Smith made Moses chief of staff of the State Reorganization Committee, a newly appointed group that had been assigned the task of recommending ways to make the state government more responsible and efficient.

New York had adopted its state constitution in 1894; it was verbose, badly organized, and confusing. Over the years, amendments had created a hodgepodge of 187 overlapping agencies, boards, and offices. Moses prepared the Committee's report, recommending the use of a state budget and the reorganization of the government into 18 centralized departments responsible to the governor. His detailed analysis, cogent arguments, and carefully drafted bills helped Smith secure legislative approval for most of the recommendations.

At about this point in his career Moses became interested in parks and parkways; what attracted him to them is unknown. At the time, New York's park programs were unimportant and seemed to offer no promise to an ambitious man. Some 24 different agencies loosely administered the state's few, scattered parks, and none had any active plan for developing them or building an extended system of parks to serve the rapidly growing urban population in the state's major cities.

In 1922 Moses drew up a brochure entitled *A State Park Plan for New York*. It was primarily a proposal for a $15 million bond issue to begin the development and extension of existing parks and the acquisition and development of additional parks and parkways. Moses drafted a bill embodying his plan and authorizing the bond issue, and by intensive lobbying and persuasive arguments secured its approval. He then managed to arrange his appointment to the unsalaried post of chairman of the advisory state council, which would oversee the expenditure of the funds available; he also picked up another unsalaried administrative post as president of the Long Island State Park Commission. He held these two posts for some 39 years, until 1963. In 1927–28, Moses served as New York's Secretary of State and remained in Albany to run the state government while Al Smith campaigned for the Presidency. During these Albany years Moses developed the capacity to handle several jobs at the same time, and he served an intensive apprenticeship in the craft of applied politics. He later remarked that he had learned his practical education in the facts of public life at the feet of Governor Al Smith.

From 1924 on Moses devoted a part of his energies to the creation of Jones Beach, a 17-mile-long stretch of sand on a barrier island off the south shore of Long Island. His five-year fight against parochial village officials who refused rights of way and wealthy landowners who did not welcome the prospect of city hordes invading their preserves was as colorful and loud as only Moses knew how to make it. He campaigned through towns and villages on Long Island, promising a miracle playground for the public, displaying blueprints, and arousing either intense enthusiasm or bitter opposition.

The state legislators who had to appropriate the funds for the park Moses was promoting were skeptical that very many people from New York City would travel 40 miles to get to a new beach when Coney Island Beach was right at the end of an existing subway line. Further, there wasn't even any road to Jones Beach since it lay out beyond a marsh. Worst of all, the barren sandstrip rarely rose more than two feet above sea level and thus seemed subject to flooding and destruction at any time. Using park money already available, Moses set out to meet the objections of his critics.

He dredged sand from the marsh and dumped it on the beach until it was 14 feet above sea level. The dredging opened a boat channel for fishermen. Finally the legislature appropriated $150,000 for a beach pavilion.

The sum that had been authorized was only enough to construct the foundation of the bathhouse in Moses' original plans. Undaunted, Moses used the money to put in the foundation and went back to Albany for more. He disposed of a subsequent appropriation for a water tower in the same way, using the little money he got to build the bottom half of the campanile-like structure he wanted. He then invited the legislators to come down to the beach for a "dedication" and to persuade them to provide the rest of the money necessary to finish the work.

Though he got his money eventually, peevish legislators frequently cut off the funds. Several times Moses could not pay his bills. His engineers began to buy supplies in towns 20 or more miles away when local credit ran low. Once, when the contractor building the causeway across the marsh to the beach ran out of funds just as he was about to complete the job and the banks refused to provide additional credit, Moses asked his mother to lend the necessary $20,000. He berated the state government as a sink of unimaginative men who wallowed in routine and waste. "Trouble was," he later declared, "those boys just could not see anything better than a hat-rack. Our problem was to provide a playground with lots of space for a city of seven million people, and we wanted a place of high standards." [2]

After the development of Jones Beach and while he was building parkways to link the city with the far reaches of Long Island, Moses undertook a new project, the creation of Bethpage State Park. Once again he had to demonstrate his knack for overcoming obstacles. He had secured an option on 1,400 acres of land 37 miles from New York City. The state legislature refused to appropriate the million dollars required to buy the property, but Moses adeptly sidestepped this block to his plans. The Long Island Park Commission, of which he was president, established a self-liquidating corporation, the Bethpage Park Authority. In 1934 it sold a million-dollar bond issue, which was to be retired out of the fees charged golfers who used the park. The park was soon in operation, and by late 1936 Moses had constructed highways that tied the park to the Long Island parkway system. Rather than pay off the bonds, he refinanced them after 1938, with legislative approval, and used the resulting funds for other park developments.

Moses was convinced that parks and parkways did not just happen; he made them happen because he had an interest in them. Whatever the difficulty and however frustrating democratic procedures were, he argued that almost anything could be done if the public could be mobilized to support it and if "there are leaders available, ready and eager to take advantage of the logic of events." [3] Men had to take responsibility and they had to act; nothing else really counted if accomplishment was the goal.

> [My] experience taught me to be wary of salvation by new organization charts and efficiency installations. . . . Men, not charts and measures, make good government. The ideal thing, of course, is to have first-class men operating first-class machines, but first-class men can operate any machine and third-rate people cannot make the best and most modern gadgets work. Budget, efficiency and planning surveys usually avoid the big immediate problems in favor of small economies, or propose long-run revolutionary plans not realizable in our lifetime.[4]

[2] Edmond S. Fish, "New Swimmin' Hole," *Saturday Evening Post,* July 5, 1941, p. 51.

[3] Rodgers, *op. cit.,* p. 110.

[4] Robert Moses, *Working for the People: Promise and Performance in Public Service* (New York: Harper & Row, 1956), p. 39.

II

Although Moses had proved himself an aggressive, bold public servant of initiative and imagination in appointive offices, he failed in his attempts to win elective offices. In 1933 the new Fusion Party considered Moses and came close to choosing him, but finally selected Fiorello H. LaGuardia as the candidate it would run against the current minion of Tammany Hall for Mayor of New York City. When LaGuardia won election, he offered Moses any post he wanted in the city government; Moses chose to become Commissioner of City Parks, presiding over a reorganized department that gave him jurisdiction over parkways as well as parks. The following year he ran as the Republican candidate for governor against the popular incumbent Herbert H. Lehman and lost badly.

Moses' political campaigns in no way slowed down his other work. Governor Lehman had appointed him to head a State Emergency Public Works Commission early in 1933, and in a matter of weeks he had produced an extensive, state-wide program of revenue-producing projects. The new Administration of Franklin D. Roosevelt, still debating relief measures, borrowed a number of ideas from the Moses program, and many state and county governments adopted the policies and procedures he had established.

As Parks Commissioner-designate, Moses drew up plans for his forthcoming work before LaGuardia's inauguration and before legislation was passed fixing his status and consolidating the agencies he was to command. He already knew what powers he would need to administer and expand the city's network of parks and highways, for he had drafted most of the laws creating and defining the many other offices he had held. He also recognized that the widespread unemployment and massive government relief spending could be turned to his advantage. With four consulting engineers he began a survey in mid-November of every park and parkway in greater New York. When he took office on January 19, 1934, he was ready with plans for 1,700 relief projects to employ 80,000 men; along with the plans he furnished estimates of costs, the equipment required, and the kinds of labor needed, as well as maps and photographs of each area where work was to be done.

His energetic administration showed a new face of government in New York City. Ten months after Moses had taken over the Parks Department, Oswald G. Villand wrote in the *Nation:*

> No sooner had Mr. Moses taken hold of the New York City park situation than an immediate improvement was manifest. He overruled political pulls, threw influential yacht clubs off city property, drove out squatters, requisitioned idle reservoirs for new parks, demanded land abandoned for prison use, and invigorated and stimulated the whole Parks Department.[5]

The speed with which old parks were cleaned up and new ones appeared amazed New Yorkers. When Moses fired off a letter to the commissioner of sanitation, objecting to the piling of garbage cans along the sides of certain parks, the commissioner jokingly asked how his men were to know when they left garbage cans on a street one day that a new park would appear there the next!

In 1936, LaGuardia asked Moses to take over, in addition to his other offices, the chairmanship of the Triborough Bridge Authority. This agency had been set up to plan and build a complex of roads and bridges to ensure a smooth flow of traffic between the Bronx, the borough of Queens on Long Island, and the upper east side of the island of Manhattan, but incompetent personnel had made only a start in construction of this key link in the city's transportation system. Its engineering and financ-

[5] October 17, 1934, p. 427.

ing were both inadequate. Moses had already demonstrated that he could get bridges built as well as parkways and parks. In 1934 he had been appointed sole member of the Henry Hudson Parkway Authority, and he immediately arranged to sell $3.1 million worth of bonds to build a toll bridge connecting the northern tip of Manhattan with the Bronx and a parkway down the west side of the island. He had pushed the construction energetically, and LaGuardia wanted the same drive applied to the proposed Triborough Bridge. Moses happily accepted the new unsalaried assignment, seeing in it an opportunity to exercise power on a scale that matched his vision.

> From the beginning it has been our conception that the function of the Authority is not merely to build and maintain certain water crossings within the city, but to help solve metropolitan arterial and recreational problems. . . . [I]t has long been a cherished ambition of mine to weave together the loose strands and frayed edges of New York's metropolitan arterial tapestry. . . . The Triborough Bridge has provided the warp on the metropolitan loom, the heavier threads across which the lighter ones are woven.[6]

Moses hired new engineers, arranged for tolls that would make the bridge a self-liquidating project, sought federal loans and grants, and in two years and eight months completed the massive work. It is more than a bridge; it is, in fact, made up of 16 bridges—four over water and twelve over land—14 miles of ramps and connecting highways, and many small parks and recreational areas tucked into corners and loops of the structure.

Shortly after he took over the Triborough Bridge project, a group of prominent citizens asked Moses to serve as the executive officer of a commission to plan a world's fair in New York in 1939. Always happy to put himself in a position to advance his own plans by getting other things done, he later wrote, "I welcomed them with open arms. The fair was obvious bait for the reclamation of the [Flushing] meadow."[7] Flushing meadow was a wasteland of muddy flats in Queens across which ran a 90-foot mountain of refuse and ashes; Moses had for some time wanted to clean up this eyesore and transform it into a park. He therefore agreed to cooperate in building a world's fair, but only on condition that Flushing meadow be selected as the site and that the site be converted to a park and given to the city when the fair was over. His terms were accepted, and, having planned his activity beforehand, he secured possession of the whole meadow before land speculators could move in. Within six months, bulldozers working day and night had leveled the mountain of waste, dredged two lakes, and covered the area with topsoil to make it ready for landscaping and the construction of buildings.

Throughout the thirties, the forties, the fifties, and into the sixties Moses continued to undertake new projects. In 1954 Governor Thomas E. Dewey made him chairman of the Power Authority of the State of New York with the responsibility of financing and constructing two major power projects, one at Niagara Falls and the other on the St. Lawrence River. The total cost came to almost $1.4 billion. He admitted, "I do not know anything about kilowatts, but I know how to get things done." Not only did Moses complete the power projects two years ahead of schedule, but he managed to carry out the development of a series of parks and recreational areas in the Niagara region, which he had planned a quarter of a century before. He relished the fight that had been put up by five utility companies to stop his power program, declaring, "[They are] supported by powerful allies, but [they operate] without much of a grasp of public relations and public opinion as

[6] From a talk given by Moses, July 11, 1941; Rodgers, *op. cit.*, p. 97.

[7] Robert Moses, "From Dump to Glory," *Saturday Evening Post*, January 15, 1938, p. 72.

they are today. I think we can lick them to the ground. If not, they will be in the courts for a long, long time with no hope of ultimate victory." [8]

By 1966, Moses could count among his accomplishments the construction of 7 bridges, 2 tunnels, the New York Coliseum, the East Side Airline Terminal in Manhattan, the Battery Park Garage, and miles of city, state, and federally aided expressways, parkways, and highways—all of which returned revenues of almost $56 million in 1965. On Long Island he had established 16 state parks and 140 miles of parkways; in New York City he had added 611 playgrounds, 15 swimming pools, 4 golf courses, and 223 tennis courts. During his tenure as Commissioner of Parks, 1934–60, he increased the city's total park area from 14,000 acres to 34,245 acres.

III

Not all of Robert Moses' projects worked out well; he was not always right in his planning or successful in accomplishing all that his plans promised. Mayor LaGuardia once told him that "when you are wrong I know nobody who can be more wrong." The housing programs that he directed in the 1950's bogged down in red tape, and critics of his handling of slum clearance accused him of ruthlessness in displacing tenants from condemned buildings; some of these housing programs also came close to being tainted with outright corruption. New York's second World's Fair, 1964–65, over which he noisily presided, turned out to be a colossal money loser; its creditors received payment on only a small portion of their claims, and the surpluses with which Moses had hoped to build more parks remained nothing but a dream.

Moses has seldom simply ignored criticism. He attacks his critics with colorful invective and arrogance. "Critics don't build things—New York has long been known as the easiest place to get headlines and the hardest place to get results," he has said. He categorizes most of his critics as "long-haired men and short-haired women . . . the professional vomiters and mudslingers . . . with their excited, maggoty brains, and the rattlesnake element in the press." [9]

He is equally harsh on government officials with whom he disagrees. He once wrote, in a letter to a fellow commissioner:

> [Your] letter ranks high among the most asinine communications from a public official I have had the privilege of seeing in many years, and I boldly claim to have been the waste-basket for a lot of this stuff.[10]

That architects condemn the commonplace and prison-like appearances of his buildings, that city planners rebuke him for a lack of imagination in failing to re-create the city in a fundamentally new form, and that conservationists believe his roadways and parks despoil as much scenery as they preserve do not bother Moses. He sees his work as nothing exalted or grand; it is prosaic, often grimy, and always necessary. He explained to an audience at Princeton University:

> When Kubla Khan decrees a stately pleasure dome, Frank Lloyd Wright or Le Corbusier is sent for. I get into the picture when there is a remote, disputed barrier beach, an abandoned salt meadow, or a run-down, ragged, misused shore front to be reclaimed, a narrow parkway right-of-way to be torn foot by foot from reluctant, embattled and avaricious real estate owners and subdividers, or a forlorn gas house and slum to be carved out with an ax or scalpel.[11]

IV

Moses believes that the work of public officials is not well understood; it need not be any more dull, routine, or filled with drudgery than private employment. Moses insists that Americans have built up

[8] Moses, *Working for the People,* p. 167.

[9] *Newsweek,* January 13, 1964, p. 45.

[10] Rodgers, *op. cit.,* p. 305.

[11] *Ibid.,* p. 239.

a mystique of private management. There is today almost as much bureaucracy in big business as in government. In the largest corporation the full-time working heads control policy as little as the top management staff in government. . . . The recent electrical equipment monopoly conspiracy suits show . . . that there are men who make good colonels in business under proper supervision, but should never be generals. Another moral is that corporations get so gigantic that monopoly controls them. . . . We put trusting faith in written rules of business management. . . . The sad, bitter, unromantic, and unpalatable truth seems to be that those qualities of leadership which build and inspire institutions yield to no formulas, rules, and panaceas. . . .[12]

Moses also insists that there are no fixed and unchangeable areas in which public and private officials function independently. Both are needed everywhere, for they complement each other. The vast automobile industry, for example, depends upon the government officials who plan, build, and maintain the highways, bridges, and tunnels that make the automobile a useful vehicle. He points out that without the streets, parks, pure water supply, and waste disposal provided by government, house builders would have a sorry market for their products. There are opportunities in public service for virtually every sort of talent, according to Moses:

> All that a person needs is strong nerves, backbone, ability to argue a case by written and spoken word, the instinct for combat, the hide of a rhinoceros, and a willingness to work like a dog for an occasional rain-washed bone.[13]

[12] Speech at the School of Business, Fordham University, December 1, 1962.

[13] Moses, *Working for the People,* pp. 12–13.

QUESTIONS

Expressions of the Entrepreneurial Spirit Today

1. Roger Blough suggested that businessmen can accomplish only what the public allows them to do; Robert Moses insisted that almost anything can be done if the public can be mobilized and leaders take advantage of events. Which view best expresses the realities of the world as you understand it? What are these realities?
2. Under what conditions will Blough's conclusion be valid that the "generative forces of great originality rise far above the individual imagination of any members [of an organization], enhancing the role of *every* man"? Were these conditions present in U.S. Steel during his employment in it? In the city government of New York during Moses' tenure as its Parks Commissioner?
3. Do Americans have a picture of government work as dull, routine, and filled with drudgery as Moses asserts? Why? Is the picture of work in business corporations significantly different? Has the rise of the large corporation changed the picture?
4. Critically examine the opinion of Professor Ginzberg (p. 189), that in government and public service entrepreneurial talents may have great scope to develop and operate.
5. Analyze Blough's strategy for meeting the problems confronting U.S. Steel in the fifties and sixties, noting its strengths and weaknesses. Why did it commend itself to the managers of the corporation?
6. In what ways did Moses show himself to be an entrepreneur?
7. What would you say is the most essential difference between the leadership

of Blough and Moses as it affected the public? What differences are there in the ways the organizations they headed served the public (i.e. people outside the organization)? Is one more "public" or "private" than the other? Explain.

8. Moses suggested an effective leader of a large organization need not be a technical expert but only a man who "knows how to get things done." Is this the quality you would expect to find in a successful businessman? Why?

New and Old Style Employers in Industry

DAVID DUBINSKY AND "FOUR"

Many unions have hundreds of thousands of members scattered throughout the United States. In 1960 three unions reported over 1,000,000 members, four claimed a membership between 500,000 and 1,000,000, and 36 smaller unions had more than 100,000 members. Organizations of such size cannot be run efficiently and successfully by a few part-time officers. They require professional administrators and staffs to handle the complicated detail of the organization, coordinate the grievance and arbitration work and collective bargaining in the hundreds of locals, and manage the variety of other activities in which unions are now involved—investing, publishing, education and training, organizing, court proceedings, political lobbying, and community affairs.

The staff personnel of the largest unions have sometimes felt it necessary to organize to bargain with their employer, the union. By bargaining collectively, they have come to believe, they can better protect their interests and working conditions. The clerical employees of many unions, among them the International Ladies' Garment Workers Union, are represented by the Office Employees International Union. Organizers for the AFL–CIO formed their own union in 1957, the Field Representatives Federation. By 1962 this organization had helped advance the cause of union organizers in at least six major unions. In May, 1961, the staff organizers of the International Union of Electrical Workers secured recognition for a staff organization, the Council of Industrial Organizers, as their bargaining agent. Not all unions, however, have been as ready as the Electrical Workers to recognize the unionization of their own employees who hold positions as sensitive as that of organizer. One of the more reluctant organizations has been the International Ladies' Garment Workers Union (ILGWU), famous for the labels it manages to have attached to the clothes made by its members.

I

Although the ILGWU gave its general consent to the unionization of its clerical staff, it strongly resisted the repeated attempts of a group of its union organizers and business agents to gain recognition for the Federation of Union Representatives (FOUR) as a bargaining agent. The ILGWU is a large union with a good-sized staff. In 1963 it had 446,554 members in 461 locals. Though over 41 per cent of its membership is concentrated in the New York metropolitan area, the rest is scattered over 39 states, Puerto Rico, and Canada. To service an organization of such geographic dispersion and to handle the problems of its huge membership, the union employed a staff of 1,795 persons.

Early in 1960 FOUR leaders began their campaign to organize the 200–300 business agents, organizers, educational directors, and other personnel who do union-label and political work in the ILGWU. A major complaint among these workers was low wages; organizers, for example, began at $65 a week and averaged only $100. The campaign began quietly and informally; FOUR was not defined as a formal organization until December 11, 1960. When a Boston newspaper reported the activities of the group a week later, the leaders sent a telegram to ILGWU President David Dubinsky notifying him that they believed a majority of the union's organizers wished to be represented by FOUR. Part of the telegram stated:

> In the interest of the welfare of the ILGWU and of a harmonious and constructive relationship, we offer to submit to an impartial card check to prove our majority status. We must advise you that if we do not receive a favorable reply during the week of December 18, 1960, our membership has instructed us to petition the NLRB for a representation election.[1]

President Dubinsky replied that the request for a union of organizers inside the union posed an important policy decision which he did not feel he was authorized to make alone; he would have to refer the matter to the next meeting of the General Executive Board, which was to convene six weeks later in Atlantic City, on January 30, 1961. Dubinsky informed the FOUR leaders that he did not understand how there could be any need for a bargaining organization, since the usual opportunity to take care of complaints was always available:

> As to your allegations concerning grievances, you are certainly aware and were recently advised that the door to my office has always been open to any individual or group. That policy still stands. However, it should be made clear that the record shows that not one of the persons involved in your group has come to me with any complaints or any problems.
>
> Insofar as your complaints are concerned, I am, as I have always been, willing to see you, any other individual or any other group. All that is required is a call to my secretary for an appointment.[2]

On January 27, 1961, two members of the FOUR executive committee, Constantine Sedares and Marvin Rogoff, wired Dubinsky that they would appear at the General Executive Board Meeting. Dubinsky responded by inviting to the meeting any staff member who wanted to discuss his problems, but on condition that he not attempt to represent any organization unrecognized by the ILGWU. As a result, the FOUR members did not appear. After its meeting, the union's General Executive Board (GEB) issued a condemnation of FOUR, arguing that its activities, if successful, would split the ILGWU:

> For many years, the ILGWU has negotiated with unions representing its clerical, secretarial and like employees. But in the 60 years of its existence, its business agents and organizers have always been considered as the very spirit and soul of the union, as missionaries in labor's crusade and not simply as employees engaged to perform a job for pay by an employer called the union.
>
> Between them and the union they serve there has never been a barrier such as divides employers and employees, and as a result many of them have been able to rise to top posts in the ILGWU. It is our considered view that a "union-within-a-union" inevitably must evolve into a factional caucus directed at control and determination of union policy for its own special and private interests. . . .
>
> The duties of the business agents are directional in nature. Business agents are entrusted not only with contract enforcement but also with providing guidance to the discussion and determination of union policy. In many instances and communities they are spokesmen for the union. In their work they are the embodiment of the union. Anyone in this category bargaining collectively with the ILGWU would in effect be sitting on both sides of the bargaining table. The GEB has, therefore, instructed the ILGWU legal staff to oppose recognition of a bargaining unit in this category.[3]

In addition to the statement attacking FOUR, the Board set up a review committee to study and evaluate personnel matters, to consider grievances and suggestions of staff members, and to make policy

[1] *Justice,* February 15, 1961.
[2] *Ibid.*
[3] *Ibid.*

recommendations to the General Executive Board.

At the board meeting Dubinsky strongly expressed his view that a union is not a business but "a crusade, a movement, a banding together of working people to defend their interests and to promote the general welfare of the community and the world in which they live." He felt that it was an ironic quirk of fate that he and other ILGWU leaders should be characterized and treated as employers. One of FOUR's leaders had earlier accused the ILGWU of being "hypocritical, guilty of failing to practice the principles it preaches, and in effect, playing the traditional part of the niggardly employer." To these charges, which had appeared in the New York *Herald Tribune,* Dubinsky replied in a speech to the GEB meeting:

> I spent time in a Czarist jail because I was part of a struggle to free people, not because I was paid to agitate. The founders of the ILGWU starved themselves into sickness and death, faced beatings and crippling, gangsters and prisons because they felt that this was their responsibility to their consciences and to their fellow workers. Never did it occur to us that in facing these sacrifices, we were grasping for a "job."
>
> If it was a job we wanted—with the usual benefits of shorter hours and greater income —we all could have had such "jobs" because over the years the offers to leadership elements of our union to take well-paying management positions have been plentiful. We chose to stay with the labor movement not because it paid better, not because it offered more security, not because it offered greater leisure, but because it was our dedication, our struggle, our belief—our very lives. What a bitter joke that we are now characterized as "management" in relation to our comrades-in-arms.[4]

II

In spite of the ILGWU's protests, the National Labor Relations Board held hearings in January, 1961, to decide if it should conduct a representational election among the union's organizers. On April 14, 1961, the Board ordered that a certification election be held, ruling that organizers, business agents, and educational directors were employees and that the ILGWU was an "employer engaged in commerce" under the terms of the Labor-Management Act. The officers of the ILGWU were outraged; an editorial in their newspaper *Justice* denounced the NLRB's decision:

> The ILGWU cannot be reduced to the same status as the United States Steel Corporation or General Motors. There is all the difference in the world between the exploitation of human labor through which business transforms it into profits and the dedicated responsible service to a union which many have rendered with no thought of personal gain. . . . A union is not a business. It is not an employer exploiting employees for profit; it is not a boss engaged in commerce. A union is a crusade. . . .[5]

The election ordered by the NLRB was held on May 12, 1961, and the editor of *Justice* again denounced the procedure:

> If the ILGWU is a company, what goods or services is it producing at a price for profit? . . . Calling the ILGWU a "company" is a direct insult to every member of this union.[6]

After counting the ballots, the NLRB reported that FOUR had received 115 votes; 100 voters were against it; one ballot was declared void; and 33 ballots were challenged, 9 by the NLRB and the remaining 24 by the two parties to the dispute. Since neither side had a clear majority, the election was inconclusive. Later the regional director of the NLRB recommended that the ILGWU be sustained on 10 challenges, which kept the pro-FOUR vote at 115. Thirteen votes challenged by FOUR were nevertheless admitted, raising the anti-

[4] *Ibid.*

[5] May 1, 1961.

[6] May 15, 1961.

FOUR vote to 113. The 10 remaining ballots were to be unopened and held in abeyance until the NLRB could decide whether the individuals who had cast the ballots had been discharged illegally. Eight were not to be admitted: on October 3, 1961, the NLRB sustained FOUR's challenge against them on the grounds that the voters who had cast them were supervisors. The admissibility of the other two remained contingent upon the outcome of an appeal. Since FOUR received a majority of the total valid ballots cast, the regional director recommended that it be certified at once as the statutory representative in the bargaining unit.

Final certification of FOUR awaited the outcome of the ILGWU's appeal to the NLRB. In the meantime the union's officers had no intention of dealing with FOUR, and they conducted a strong campaign against it and its leaders. The ILGWU's *Justice* printed a selection of letters-to-the-editor denouncing FOUR for attempting to split the ILGWU, not utilizing officially recognized channels of protest, and being "pork choppers." (This degrading term in union slang refers to union members interested only in take-home pay.) Ray Bramucci of the Eastern Region Staff of the ILGWU wrote that personal feuds, not poor pay, lay behind the FOUR effort. While FOUR emphasized economic inequities as the sole basis for its organization, Bramucci recognized another reason:

> Far more important than money in the formation of FOUR is the overriding bitterness of a number of FOUR officers towards the ILGWU and its leadership. This was the "blood and thunder" of the organization of FOUR—the hatred of a manager or vice-president, bitterness over the differences of opinion concerning politics, dislike for union procedure—not Blue Cross and Blue Shield.[7]

FOUR retaliated to the harsh accusations from within the ILGWU by trying to embarrass the union whenever and wherever it could. A FOUR contingent crashed the 1961 New York City Labor Day parade and marched independently of the ILGWU. Its members passed out pamphlets along the parade route calling the ILGWU's anti-FOUR policy a "disgrace to the labor movement" that was undermining the "collective bargaining of professional workers, social workers, teachers, and other governmental employees." They charged Dubinsky with "Tammany tactics" and "union busting" and being unfit to serve on President Kennedy's Committee on Labor–Management Policy. Later in the same month, at the convention of the Massachusetts Federation of Labor, FOUR distributed a leaflet attacking the ILGWU; in November, at an outdoor rally for Mayor Wagner held in New York City's garment district just prior to the 1961 mayoralty election, FOUR tossed anti-ILGWU pamphlets from rooftops onto the speaker's platform. Throughout January, 1962, members of FOUR picketed ILGWU headquarters in New York City.

Colorful as FOUR's tactics were, they had slight effect upon the ILGWU, but the garment union's delaying fight decimated the smaller organization's ranks. FOUR began to degenerate into a nuisance, not a threat, as its resources dwindled and many of its original members resigned. A number of the members were suspended by the ILGWU, which accused them of collecting funds for the support of FOUR and of filing false work reports. Other members of FOUR had left it when they were promoted to higher posts in the garment union, in effect joining "management."

The ILGWU's General Executive Board reported on FOUR to the union's National Convention in May, 1962. It recommended that FOUR should be considered a faction, not a union, and that the official policy of suppressing it be continued. The convention delegates agreed, supporting the GEB report by a majority of about 9 to 1. In his summary remarks, just prior to that voting, Dubinsky expressed his views about FOUR:

[7] *Op. cit.*, June 1, 1961.

> Neither I, nor Stulberg [Secretary-Treasurer of the ILGWU] nor any vice-president, nor any manager, nor any assistant manager is an employee. We don't want anyone serving the cause of our union unless he becomes part of us. When they [the business agents] go to speak to workers, to adjust complaints, we don't want the workers to feel that they are dealing with hired help.[8]

After alluding to the factional strife that existed in the ILGWU during the 1920's, Dubinsky vowed that the union would never again be subjected to such disruption, particularly when the factionalism in question was inspired by outside influences. This, he explained, was the case with FOUR, the "union-within-the-union," and was his justification for rooting it out.

III

Not all people familiar with the labor scene saw in FOUR a threat as great as that seen by Dubinsky and his fellow officers in the ILGWU. Many labor experts felt that the employees who wanted to be represented by FOUR had as much right to organize as other professionals who already had unions—teachers, actors, musicians, airline pilots, and engineers, for example. Norman Thomas, who ran for President many times on the Socialist Party ticket, issued a strong condemnation of the ILGWU's position:

> Times and conditions have changed since the heroic days of struggle in the needle trades when very often there wasn't cash on hand to pay anybody's salary. Salary schedules for elected union officials are now generous and promptly paid. The union collectively now has very substantial assets. It is in a position to extend collective bargaining to its own employees. That right is by no means inconsistent with the health and prosperity of the industry in which it prevails. How can it be inconsistent with the well-being of a strong union to grant employees the privileges which it has won for its members in relation to the employees?
>
> The fact that both sides accept the principle of collective bargaining through unions of their own choice ought to make for fraternal settlement of rules on wages and working conditions. It will not further the [cause of] labor when a great union turns against the right of its own employees to organize.[9]

While FOUR was gaining public support of this kind, the dispute over the certification election continued to move slowly through the hearings and appeals procedures of the NLRB. At last, more than 13 months after the election was held, the NLRB—on June 22, 1962—ordered two of the remaining challenged ballots opened.

FOUR had received 115 votes; there were 113 ballots against it, and two challenged. When the Board opened the two challenged ballots, it found, as had been expected, that they were in favor of FOUR. The NLRB certified FOUR on August 6, 1962, and two days later the officials of FOUR sent a registered letter to David Dubinsky that submitted a list of bargaining demands and requested him to meet and bargain with them. The letter was returned marked "refused." On several occasions thereafter the ILGWU refused to bargain with FOUR and refused to furnish it with information concerning the wages, hours, and fringe benefits of FOUR's members. The ILGWU's defense for this apparent violation of the law was that the eight unopened votes set aside the previous October as having been cast by supervisors should not have been set aside. The ILGWU argued that it had not been given a hearing on these ballots and so had been denied due process of law; therefore, the certification of FOUR was invalid, and the ILGWU was under no obligation to bargain.

On April 29, 1963, the NLRB affirmed the finding of Trial Examiner Samuel S. Singer that the ILGWU had been afforded a full hearing and that the certification of FOUR was therefore valid. It further ruled that the ILGWU had violated the law by refusing to bargain with a certified union. An order was again issued requiring that the ILGWU bargain with FOUR.

[8] *Ibid.*

[9] New York *Herald Tribune,* May 11, 1961; reprinted in *Justice,* June 1, 1961.

Meanwhile, FOUR had undertaken separate NLRB proceedings, charging the ILGWU with unfair labor practices. FOUR accused the big union of violating the Taft-Hartley Act:

(1) by interrogations, warnings, directions, solicitations and threats;
(2) by the transfer and discharge of [two leaders of FOUR], and by the refusal to transfer [a member of FOUR];
(3) by the reduction and/or elimination of allowances for per diem, auto expenses, and telephone calls;
(4) by increasing job tasks and duties;
(5) by failing to grant wage increases in accordance with past practices; and
(6) by establishing committees to consider and resolve grievances and to make wage recommendations and by promising benefits to encourage employees to present their grievances to said committees.[10]

The NLRB trial examiner, and later the NLRB itself, found the ILGWU innocent of discriminatory practices with respect to charges 2, 3, and 4. On the one hand, it was decided that the leaders of FOUR were fired for just and sufficient reasons before their union activity became known; the reduction of certain allowances was not out of line; and no finding was made that job duties had been increased. On the other hand, the NLRB upheld FOUR on charges 1, 5, and 6, finding that the ILGWU had violated the law and ruling that it had to continue to grant the customary wage increases, to cease conducting the extraordinary group meetings, and to stop its private interrogations. In its findings the Board noted the irony of the case:

> The record here showed [several] situations where the acts and conduct of Respondent's officers and supervisors, departing from the protected area, plainly tended to interfere with, restrain and coerce its employees in the right themselves to enjoy what they had so long preached, *as Respondent's disciples,* to the employees of other employers—to bargain collectively with their own employers through representatives of their own choosing.[11]

The General Counsel of the NLRB accused the ILGWU of carrying out a ruthless antiunion campaign to stamp out a union of its own employees. The primary reason for this total, bitter, and intensive opposition to FOUR could be found, he believed, in president Dubinsky's identification of FOUR with an evil that required a religious fervor to counter it. The ILGWU considered its organizers as missionaries, not employees; if they began to consider themselves employees, they would begin to seem like heretics.

On August 2, 1963, the NLRB rejected the ILGWU's appeal to reconsider its decision to certify FOUR. A spokesman for the ILGWU stated that the union planned to appeal this certification through the appropriate legal channels, beginning with the United States Circuit Court of Appeals. The spokesman continued:

> The ILGWU maintains its original position that policymaking officers of a union are not a proper bargaining unit under the National Labor Relations Act. . . . The official union position holds that present labor laws were not intended to grant a political faction of union officers the immunity and privileges of a collective bargaining agent.[12]

[10] 142 NLRB 84.

[11] 142 NLRB 112–113.

[12] *New York Times,* May 1, 1963.

JEAN PAUL GETTY

By 1965 Jean Paul Getty had been widely recognized as the richest living American and one of the world's richest men. The Getty Oil Company, of which he is president and chief stockholder, is at the apex of a large and complex corporate structure. It includes about 40 companies, from the Tidewater and Skelly oil companies to firms that own hotels (including the luxurious Hotel Pierre in New York), make trailers, and sell life insurance. According to *Newsweek,* Getty's phenomenal success can be laid to a few basic factors: "his passion for grasping industrial and technological detail, especially in oil geology," his penchant for buying at depressed prices and holding for the long-term gain, and his father's wealth, a factor that is frequently overrated.[1]

I

George Getty, Paul's father, was a Minnesota lawyer who became a millionaire when oil was discovered on a 500-acre piece of land he owned in Oklahoma. He then moved his family to California and successfully bought and sold oil leases in the California fields. Paul Getty attended college in California, spending two years at the University of Southern California and the University of California at Berkeley before studying economics for a year in England at Oxford. In 1914 he arrived in Tulsa, Oklahoma, 21 years old and ready to begin buying and selling oil leases with his father's backing on a 30–70 profit split and with a $100 a month allowance. Nineteen months after his arrival, Paul was a millionaire.[2]

George Getty died in 1930 and left control of 95 per cent of his $10 million estate to his wife. Paul received only $500,000, presumably because the senior Getty did not approve of his son's private life. (By this time, Paul had been married and divorced three times within six years.) In 1932, in the depth of the Depression, Paul's mother finally gave him control of the family fortune. He immediately began to buy oil stock and real estate at cheap Depression prices. He also launched his monumental 19-year battle with Standard Oil of New Jersey for control of the Tidewater Oil Company. At the time, its assets were about $200 million; when Getty finally obtained control in 1951, they were three times as large.

During World War II, Getty requested a commission as a naval officer, but instead he was asked to take over the direction of the Spartan Aircraft Company in Tulsa. After the war, when the future of the aircraft industry appeared uncertain, Getty bought Spartan from Skelly Oil and turned it into a prosperous producer of mobile homes and auto trailers.

In 1948, Getty initiated his most formidable coup. He outbid several international oil companies for the Arabian oil rights in the 2,500-square-mile Neutral Zone between Kuwait and Saudi Arabia, offering King Saud $9.5 million in cash, $1 million a year whether he hit oil or not, to be applied against $.55 a barrel royalty, and 25 per cent of the company's net profits for the Neutral Zone."[3]

As usual, Getty's investment paid off handsomely and has continued to do so. In addition to the usual form of drilling, Getty decided to drill in the Neutral Zone's neglected Eocene rock formation, only 1,200 feet below the earth's surface. Costs were considerably lower for such drilling; an Eocene well would cost an average of $30,000 and one week's drilling, while a standard well cost $200,000 and took six weeks. Oilmen doubted that he had undertaken a commercially feasible project, but Getty's new strike doubled his share of Neutral Zone production, which rose from 5.8 million barrels in 1956 to 11.1 million barrels in 1957. To transport his oil, he bought and built a $200 million tanker fleet; to process it, he scrapped Tidewater's huge, outmoded refinery in Bayonne, New Jersey, and replaced it with the world's most modern refinery—built at a cost of over $200 million—15 miles south of Wilmington, Delaware.

II

In addition to being one of the world's richest men, Getty is also one of the world's

[1] March 7, 1960, p. 100.
[2] *Time,* February 24, 1958, p. 90.
[3] *Ibid.,* p. 92.

most outspoken and over the past several years has vigorously expressed his views of business. Getty observed several years ago that people frequently told him he was lucky because he started in business at a time when a man could still make millions. He felt, however, that he would rather begin his career today than when he did, for today there are "'more opportunities for a man to achieve wealth and success . . . than ever before." In his view, a great many men without imagination have been hiding behind excuses for the last 20 years in order to cover up their lack of initiative and their desire for security at almost any price. These excuses, according to Getty, include the threat of communism, anti-American feelings abroad, the high tax structure, and exorbitant labor costs. He does not believe that these excuses are valid; rather, the primary threat to America's leadership is, in his opinion, that timid businessmen won't show the rest of the peoples of the world that our system can best help them to raise their standards of living. This practical objective, not ideology and politics, is, after all, a people's major concern.

Although taxes are too high to suit him, many fortunes have been made since World War II, and he has little sympathy "with the fears and complaints expressed by the calamity howlers of our present day and age." [4] He has even less patience with those who claim they are worried by high labor costs: "Excessive labor cost is a handy excuse to cover inept management's inability to meet competition." [5] The glaring need of our age, says Getty, is not for a more advanced level of technology but for the better industrial and commercial leadership that can come only from alert, energetic younger men who see and understand the opportunities that exist and who are willing and able to accept and assume the responsibilities of such leadership.

Getty feels that the primary function of industrial and commercial management is to obtain results through people. Consequently, sound management psychology will motivate, direct, encourage, and inspire people so that their efforts will result in the achievement of their firm's objectives. Fortunately, the business community has recognized its past neglect of the human material that forms the most valuable asset of any business and has now done a great deal to develop a more enlightened viewpoint. However, Getty thinks that serious mistakes are still made. For example, he points out that far too many executives at all levels still fail to comprehend that sound management psychology, like charity, begins at home. While elaborate public relations schemes may accomplish much, a better start can be made with the nearest stenographer, machinist, or salesclerk:

> No psychological weapon is more potent than example. . . . If [an executive] makes a habit of spending three hours over lunch, he has no right to complain when his secretary dawdles an extra ten minutes over her coffee. . . . There are those who adopt a "what is permitted the gods is not permitted the cattle" attitude, blandly assuming their rank bestows privileges but also grants licenses. Typical of this genus is the man who issues menacing warnings about pilfering and the personal use of company property . . . yet . . . will blandly spend hours dictating personal letters to his secretary and will send subordinates out to run his personal errands on company time.[6]

Practices like this exert a strong adverse influence on subordinates. Workers hear about these things quickly through the grapevine, and when this occurs morale and output plummet in the "god's" department. Morale can also suffer through other deficiencies in executive integrity, such as bluffing, buck passing, and lack of fairness to and trust in employees.

III

Getty thinks that managers all too often have underestimated the mental abilities of

[4] *True,* June, 1958, p. 21.
[5] *Ibid.,* p. 26.

[6] *Playboy,* January, 1965, p. 135.

workers and union personnel and overestimated the importance of executives. He has not found workers and union officials to be ignoramuses. They resent management's attempts to mislead or misinform them and are quite likely to rebel against such treatment. Approaches that fail to show respect for workers and their representatives can often lead to labor problems. However, if given the truth, virtually all union leaders cooperate as much as they are able consistent with their responsibilities to union members.[7] From his experience Getty has concluded that union aims are seldom inconsistent with those of the employer, for the workers do not want to see their employer go out of business.

Getty believes that an important part of personnel policy is to let the worker know that he is important to the company. Cheap stunts and tinsely morale-building schemes won't work; the only answer is to believe in the importance of workers and mean it. Any executive who doesn't believe that rank-and-file employees are really important doesn't have a proper sense of proportion or know what makes his business tick.

> It's hardly difficult to imagine situations in which the hourly-wage employee is far more important than the salaried executive. Thomas Jones may have the exalted title of third assistant vice-president, and he may—and probably does—consider himself indispensable. But my guess is that he's far more expendable than, say, a crack punch press operator on the assembly line.
>
> Were Jones to vanish suddenly from the scene, his secretary—and he's sure to have at least one—can probably run things until he returns or until a replacement is found for him. In any case, the company will keep on going without Jones. But the absence of a punch press operator may well halt a production line—and, in the last analysis, it's the production line and the products which come off it that count most.[8]

Businessmen and the public put unions and management on an unequal footing, in Getty's opinion, by the way they react when rare cases of abuse or racketeering occur in labor organizations. Just because a few unions are bad and a few union leaders are crooked does not mean that we should do away with unions. Some businessmen are crooked too, but the lesson of that fact is certainly not that we should condemn the entire system of private ownership:

> Newspapers sometimes carry crazy stories about bank officials embezzling their depositors' funds. Despite these incidents, banks continue to flourish. No one in his right mind would dream of suggesting that the entire banking system should be abolished because of occasional larceny. Yet let even a single union—or even a local—turn sour, and a loud alarm is raised castigating all organized labor.[9]

To him the "all too familiar" organization man who habitually and consistently denounces organized labor is ridiculous. At the same time that most of the young executives and business students interviewed in a recent survey declared themselves to be against unions, 75 per cent of them cited security as the principal reason they worked for or hoped to work for a large corporation. Getty feels that it is illogical and inconsistent for admittedly security-seeking organization men to oppose labor's search for a similar degree of security.[10]

Labor's two basic aims, a fair share of the wealth it helps create and a recognition of its own importance, seem quite reasonable to him. He is willing to recognize the right of labor to organize and bargain with management because one of the basic human desires is to seek a better life, and most people seek it through more pay and shorter hours. There are, of course, limits to what management can give. It is management's responsibility to convince labor of this, define these limits clearly and reasonably, and furnish irrefutable facts to prove its case.

Getty points out that while the complex

[7] *Playboy,* March, 1964, p. 86.
[8] *Ibid.,* p. 142.
[9] *True,* June, 1958, pp. 24 and 26.
[10] *Playboy,* March, 1964, p. 86.

operational framework of modern business rests on mass production, mass production itself must rest on mass consumption and mass markets. Labor forms a sizeable segment of our mass markets, and labor's high earnings and consequent high buying power represent an important factor in our national prosperity.[11]

The myth that labor is out to wreck the free enterprise system, despite labor's contributions to it, has been strongly nurtured by some businessmen. Getty feels that the majority of U.S. labor leaders do not desire any of the alternatives to our present system. The facts that our economy is thriving and that it has burgeoned during the years that unions gained their greatest strength would seem to refute the argument that organized labor is wrecking or seeking to wreck our economy.[12]

Labor knows that it has a big stake in business. It also wants business, in turn, to realize that it has a big stake in labor. Although he doesn't carry a union card or pay dues, Getty says that he is a "union man," because he feels that labor unions are our greatest promoters of prosperity and our most formidable bulwarks against social or economic totalitarianism.[13]

[11] *Ibid.*

[12] *Ibid.*

[13] *True,* June, 1958, p. 24.

QUESTIONS

Old and New Style Employers in Industry

1. Explain the difference in Getty's attitude toward unions in general from that of Dubinsky toward FOUR. How might the nature of the oil industry influence Getty's appreciation of unions?

2. What conditions of our economy and changes in society have produced paternalism by employers such as Dubinsky and acceptance of unions by employers such as Getty?

3. Do you approve the protracted resistance to FOUR by Dubinsky and his union? Why? Some observers feel that Dubinsky defeated not only a particular group of workers who wanted to organize, but also a national labor policy that was meant to insure their right to organize and bargain collectively. Examine the rights of the larger organization as well as those of the workers.

4. Getty says that the complaints of managers about excessive costs serve as a handy excuse to cover up their own inability to meet competition. In what sense, if any, is this criticism applicable to Roger Blough's management of U.S. Steel?

5. Examine the pros and cons of Dubinsky's argument that non-profit, nonbusiness organizations should not be faced with the same requirements as profit making, private businesses.

6. Under what circumstances may Getty be right that a third assistant vice-president is more expendable than a punch press operator? Under what circumstances may he be wrong? Which set of circumstances is found more often in American business, in your opinion?

section **4**

THE INDIVIDUAL IN THE WORLD OF BUSINESS

Americans traditionally have expressed hostility toward organizations and bureaucracies, usually identifying them with the highly suspect "Big Government." Recently, however, many people have begun to realize that much more of American life than the government is now bureaucratized. Schools, businesses, unions, churches, fraternal clubs, interest groups—all are governed by bureaucrats and operate within a framework of bureaucratic rules in which "standard operating procedures" replace *ad hoc* decisions. Students have discovered that large universities are vast impersonal organizations in which they may lose their identities; they have demonstrated against being treated as so many IBM cards to be sorted, classified, and counted. Once students have become management trainees, they are sometimes dismayed to find themselves not Captains of Industry but corporals in the rear ranks of the white-collar armies that have conquered and now occupy the nation's major firms. Bureaucracy is a fact of life, however, and by the time today's students and trainees become 35-year veterans of business routine, having advanced year by year to higher positions, they probably will have learned to live with bureaucracy—and how to use it for their own purposes.

Certainly many Americans will work in large organizations, for employment is heavily concentrated in a few large industrial firms. Twenty-five of the largest industrial corporations employed 20 per cent of all persons working in manufacturing in 1965; the 500 largest employed 55 per cent—10 million workers. The change of the United States from a nation of self-employed to a country of employees has accompanied, and undoubtedly was caused by, industrialization. In 1910, more than half of all Americans lived in rural areas; most of them were self-employed and worked on their own farms. Since then the proportion of the work force that is self-employed has declined markedly. The self-employed made up about one-fourth of the labor force at the beginning of World War II; by 1960 they numbered only one in seven. In less than a generation, the self-employed segment of the work force was reduced by nearly 40 per cent. The heroes of Jeffersonian democracy, the men who could "hold their heads high before all the powers of the state and all the great landlords and financial barons in the world,"[1] would seem to be an ever diminishing influence in American society.

[1] Gaetano Mosca, *The Ruling Class,* 1st ed. (New York: McGraw-Hill, 1939), p. 285.

Despite the decline of self-employment, Americans have continued to hold in high esteem its values, traditions, and institutions. Political theorists, for example, have made much of the middle-class virtues of land-owning farmers, artisans in their small shops and independent businessmen. Upon these sturdy citizens they have built their theories of stable, democratic institutions, thus indicating their acceptance of a maxim pronounced by de Tocqueville over 130 years ago:

> If a state of society can ever be founded in which every man shall have something to keep and little to take from others, much will have been done for the peace of the world.[2]

The commitment of Americans to the protection of the self-employed has found popular expression in legislation and government programs as well as in scholarly treatises. The fair-trade laws were designed to protect small retailers from too much competition; the Small Business Administration aids little and middle-sized firms (up to the size of American Motors!) that find the market inhospitable; price support programs subsidize farmers,[3] many of whom are hardly the yeoman agriculturalists of colonial times; [4] and the Defense Department is charged with the responsibility of scattering a fair share of procurement subcontracts among little businesses. Such laws and programs are designed to encourage democratic individualism by keeping alive a truly competitive economy, which is believed to be conducive to a political system in which all citizens have an equal say.

If Americans want to continue to foster individualism and the values it promotes, they will have to protect it not only among small businessmen and farmers, but also within the ubiquitous industrial bureaucracies of the big corporations. In his famous book, *Human Problems of an Industrial Civilization,*[5] Professor Elton Mayo of the Harvard Business School suggested that individualism could be maintained by providing employees with a "home away from home" in the factory. Within the surrogate family of the corporate team, he suggested, managers could help promote creativity and loyal criticism among the workers by making their work less tedious and thus relieving them of their ennui, or weary dissatisfaction.

On the basis of studies conducted at Western Electric's Hawthorne plant in Chicago,[6] colleagues of Mayo concluded that modern employees respond to the normlessness and rootlessness—the "anomie"—of urban-industrial life by forming work groups. They join groups to escape the anomie of their lives, and they express their hostility toward the people and forces that impersonally direct them by engaging in such "irrational" activities as strikes, slowdowns, sabotage, and restriction of output. According to Mayo, if managers were competent in human relations they would see employees as whole men and not simply as wage slaves.

[2] Alexis de Tocqueville, *Democracy in America,* II (New York: Vintage Books, 1954), p. 266.

[3] Farm price supports were originally conceived as a balance to and an integral part of tariff policy, which was in turn an early measure to limit competition.

[4] The Census of Agriculture showed in 1960 that farms were larger than ever. Nine per cent of all farms, those over 500 acres, accounted for 61.5 per cent of all farm acreage.

[5] New York: Macmillan, 1933.

[6] F. J. Roethlisberger and W. J. Dickson, *Management and the Worker* (Cambridge: Harvard University Press, 1939).

They would satisfy the need of employees to belong, to be made to feel valuable as people rather than merely useful as just pairs of working hands. The ideal manager would come from a university-trained elite, and he would be alert to the psychological needs of all his subordinates. He would satisfy his employees by making them feel like members of a team, integrating them into factory society through a comprehensive program of communications that would encourage complaints to be sent upward and, at the same time, allow settlements of workers' problems to be sent down along with orders and directives.

Following Mayo's lead, sociologists, anthropologists, and psychologists in growing numbers turned their attention to elaborating methods and programs that might reduce or eliminate industrial conflict and might help achieve higher productivity. A human relations movement grew up about the implicit notion that the problem of employees could be substantially liquidated by managerial *noblesse oblige;* autocracy could be made benevolent and thereby palatable to all. The efforts of employees to organize unions, to get better wages, and to improve their conditions of work were regarded largely as the result of frustrations, poor communications, and a misguided class consciousness rather than as a democratic pursuit of democracy and enhancement of individual dignity at the place of work.

Not all scholars were confident that the new human-relations managers would be any more benign than autocrats of old. Erich Fromm examined the situation of the individual in modern industrial organizations in *The Escape from Freedom* [7] and found a problem not considered by Mayo. The growing dependence of Americans upon corporations for their livelihood offered an all-too-attractive opportunity to escape the burdens of responsibility. Corporate employees, Fromm believed, were allowing themselves to be made into pliant servants, thus contributing to the creation of a dangerous industrial power capable of destroying a free society. Under the authoritarianism of the organizations to which they belong, employees can deny that they exercise initiative and claim they simply act as they must to keep their jobs. (Since Fromm wrote, this age-old tendency to clothe behavior in organizational dress has been described with some new terms, among them "copping out," a pejorative term often used by Negroes to describe white rationalization for discriminatory behavior toward minorities, and "Eichmanism," which may be defined as the denial of personal responsibility for immoralities perpetrated under orders.) Such escape is psychologically attractive, Fromm maintained, because it relieves people of the responsibility that freedom implies.

Professor Daniel Bell analyzed the workings of the American industrial system and, like Fromm, was uneasy over what he saw. In a devastating critique of the meaning of work in America,[8] he argued that industrial engineers design jobs to serve machines, not to serve workers, and that managers unmindfully arrange work so that it both distresses and demeans employees. Bell likens the occupational experience of Americans to the fate of Ixion, who was tied, according to the Greek myth, to a perpetually revolving wheel in the depths of Hades. Professor Bell wonders why we do not consider rearranging the tasks in mass-production industries so that work could be parceled out for men to perform in their homes or in their communities after the fashion of the putting-out system in early nine-

[7] New York: Farrar and Rinehart, 1941.

[8] "Work and Its Discontents: The Cult of Efficiency in America," *The End of Ideology* (Glencoe, Ill.: The Free Press, 1960).

teenth-century England; workers might thus be spared time-consuming travel and the oppressive experience of working on long assembly lines and in big, impersonal factories. If we were to consider our production process in terms of its full human costs as well as its material benefits, he suggests, its efficiencies would seem less impressive than we commonly make out.[9]

Perhaps the most popular new critic of large organizations in the sixties has been Professor Chris Argyris.[10] He, too, focuses upon the psychological impairment of individuals who are dependent upon a hierarchy of superiors and caught in narrowly specialized jobs that demand but a fraction of a person's capabilities and deaden his spirit with repetitious bureaucratic routine. Argyris concurs with the criticisms by Fromm and Bell, but he considers the alienation of employees from managers a more crucial problem of industrial life. Where Mayo focused on the irrationality of workers, Argyris insists that the problem of the worker can be solved only if managers are attentive to the findings and suggestions of the behavioral sciences as they apply to themselves. "Human beings," Argyris writes, "are not simple and they deserve the consideration of not being manipulated by trick or specious methods." We may infer that manipulation by scientific methods is preferable and that psychologists and others can help managers to overcome their own and their employees' irrationalities.

Argyris maintains, as do other contemporary social scientists, that organizations need not oppress employees or stultify their abilities. Organizations that, in fact, do have these effects reflect the insecurity and distrust nursed by their managers, whose personalities and authoritarian styles get in the way of an objective arrangement of organizational priorities that would permit their employees to "actualize" themselves. Good management seeks to elicit the cooperation of employees and to direct their energy into beneficial forms of creativity and away from "strategies of independence" (to use Thorstein Veblen's charming euphemism for attempts to subvert authority). To achieve this end, Argyris counsels managers to know themselves and to develop through group discussions and such devices as "T Groups"[11] more sensitive responses to their subordinates' needs.

The psychological problems of employees and managers are real and deserve attention, but they need to be seen in the perspective of the other problems with which a democratic society must deal if it is to preserve, and enhance if possible, the values of individualism in an industrial world of large organizations. Mayo and Argyris have assumed that the *manner* in which managers exercise their authority rather than its *legitimacy* is the most pressing issue. This assumption overlooks the tentative, qualified basis of managerial authority in the American society.

[9] Bell also makes short shrift of sociological investigations showing that the greatest proportions of Americans are satisfied with their work in big organizations. Since most employees have little or no knowledge about working conditions that might be different from those confronting them in a given job, Bell finds their responses to survey researchers something less than revealing. For a discussion of this research see Robert Blauner, "Work Satisfaction and Industrial Trends in Modern Society," in W. Galenson and Seymour Martin Lipset, *Labor and Trade Unionism* (New York: John Wiley, 1960), pp. 339–60.

[10] *Personality and Organization: The Conflict Between System and the Individual* (New York: Harper & Row, 1957).

[11] Training Groups are organized along the same lines as psychiatric group therapy sessions; participants are encouraged to engage in candid discussions about each other and thus to facilitate the individual's understanding of his effect on others.

Consider briefly the arguments in defense of a manager's exercise of power over his employees. The first argument involves the claim of ownership; managers either own the means of production or act as agents for the owners, and this is regarded as a source of power. Authority based only upon ownership surely cannot be honored by even the staunchest defenders of property rights, however, for rights to the use of property extend no legal rights over people. An owner may use his property as he sees fit, but if he wishes another to help him use it or work it in some way, he must secure that man's voluntary agreement. Managers of large firms often have been able to get persons in need of jobs—almost any job—to agree to terms that narrowly restrict their freedom as workers in the plant; but those restrictions and the authority given managers came from the "voluntary" contracts made by the workers, not from the right of property. To argue that ownership gives some men power over other men is to be at odds with the underlying concept of democratic society. That ownership, in fact, does provide power over other men only indicates how far our practical world is from the theoretical one.

The second argument in defense of managerial authority is based on the recognition of practical need; someone, after all, must exercise leadership, provide direction, and coordinate various activities for the organization. The existence of the need, however, hardly justifies the particular processes by which American organizations select their leaders or the range of decisions and directives these leaders claim as their special prerogatives. Organizations need coordinators, but coordination may be carried on—and is carried on—in many different ways. In return for financial aid, for example, banks and other creditors not infrequently make demands that severely limit the range of initiative and choice open to the management of a particular organization; unions sometimes do the same, demanding a voice in determining not only wages, hours, and conditions of work but also investment and pricing.

Every time employees negotiate a work contract, either individually or collectively, management's authority is subject to question and open to possible limitation. The recent attempts by engineers to organize professional associations to bargain for them, the new-found militancy of teachers in demanding collective bargaining, and the appearance of bargaining organizations for such groups as insurance agents, gasoline retailers, and automobile salesmen and dealers suggest that managerial authority will increasingly and openly be challenged by white-collar employees.

However, managers do not cease to be managers when limitations are placed on their authority over employees, any more than they cease to be managers when a rise in the price of a raw material limits its further usefulness. An able manager tries to overcome such limitations by exercising his authority with more vigor in areas still open to him or in new areas he creates for himself. The problems of authority and subordination are, thus, constantly being debated. One cannot assume that they will be resolved in favor of the particular division of power commonly found at present in industrial organizations.

The emphasis of Mayo and Argyris in particular, but also of Fromm and Bell, on the psychological well being of individuals obscures the fact that organizational imperatives of predictability and effectiveness often require decisions that conflict with the interests and values of employees. Good will, sensitivity, and an appreciation for human relations simply do not eliminate or even deal effectively with the clashing needs and requirements of employees and their organizations. Reconciling organizational and individual rights presents us with frustrating dilemmas and harsh choices; there are no easy answers or sure theories to guide managers or employees as they contend with the multiple contingencies involved.

The cases that follow will illuminate some of the problems within and among the organizations that concern us most in a business society. They suggest that organizations may pose various threats to individuals, some of them very concrete, some of them more intangible and of a psychological kind studied by many contemporary social critics.

chapter **9**

CORPORATE INTERESTS AND INDIVIDUAL RIGHTS

When the courts of the United States called the corporation a person, they satisfied the American mythos of individualism, preserved the legal fiction of the classical liberal state, and continued the illusion that the country had a simple, Smithean, and competitive market system. But of course the real nature of the organization was not changed. Masking a corporation with the form of a person is comparable to stretching the hide of a flea over a boxcar and declaring the result to be in truth (or in law, at any rate) a flea! A boxcar-sized flea would be a monstrosity and might be expected to cause trouble. Similarly, any large organization, whether it is called a person or by some other name, is a creation with which the private individual cannot easily deal.

Individuals who clash with a corporate organization—a business firm, labor union, university, foundation, hospital, or church—will quickly find that it is no ordinary person. General Motors, for example, with its 745,000 employees, is a leviathan; so is the million-member United Automobile Workers union. Should an assemblyline worker find reason to bring suit against either organization, he would find it treated as a person on an equal footing with himself before the court. But in terms of resources available for hiring lawyers and experts, the individual and the organization would be most unequal, and the outcome of the case would be influenced by this fact.

The power that corporate organizations wield affects the livelihood, opportunities, positions, and occupations of individuals, often unfavorably. In confronting or competing with such organized groups, individuals must face the corporate strength and resources that the combination can mobilize. The individual may come off second best, not because his product is less serviceable, his idea is less creative, his interests less worthy of consideration, his services inferior, his arguments poorer, or his actions more reprehensible, but rather because he is not able to bear the costs, hire the lawyers and the experts, or maintain the image necessary to meet the organization as an equal.

In our society, organizations are ubiquitous. One scholar has pointed out that their "number is countless and the variety of these social groupings is abundant and complex. No aspect of the life of the individual is untouched by them.

Modern man is literally conducted from the cradle to the grave by [them]." [1] We have emphasized what happens when the interests of an individual and an organization clash, but individuals also benefit greatly from the activities of corporations. The job opportunities offered by corporations are vast, giving greater scope to the diverse abilities and interests of our people than has ever before been imaginable. Individuals do not have to follow the occupations or take the jobs of their fathers; neither do most of them have to bend their bodies and wills to agricultural work as has most of mankind through most of history. The range of skills and talents now required in our industrial, organizational society promises a freedom of job choice, if one is educated, that is almost overwhelming. We may also believe that from the efficient operation of business organizations we receive the goods and services to satisfy our consuming habits and that the effective operation of unions protects the community against sweat shop conditions, low wages, or the insecurity of unemployment. For such benefits we may gladly encourage organizations by providing them with special privileges.

While most people benefit from the activities of organizations, a number may suffer. The problem is to assure society the benefits of combinations while preserving a wide scope for individual pursuits and protecting individual rights and interests. Some writers suggest that the interests of both the community and individuals can be safeguarded only if corporate organizations are broken into smaller components, more nearly to approximate the perfectly competitive system of economic theory. The romanticists among them suggest on the one hand dissolving large corporations into a number of smaller firms and on the other hand limiting unions to single plants and prohibiting industry-wide collective bargaining. However, while smaller companies and unions than now exist might be economically feasible, modern technology will hardly allow a return to the job shops or individually owned and run business firms of the early nineteenth century, and one may ask if anything less would achieve the result desired. Even the smallest automobile company directly employs 30,000 people, and Kaiser Steel, a company that accounts for less than 2 per cent of American steel capacity, employs 11,000 workers. Both organizations seem large indeed, compared to any single individual whether within or without the firm; either is big enough to exert powerful pressure upon any individual who should clash with it.

Another solution to the problem of reconciling the interests of organizations and individual rights, which has long been advocated and practiced, is to form counterorganizations. Long ago Proudhon declared "multiply your associations and be free!" Industrial workers, among others, followed that advice; they organized unions to bargain collectively that they might check the sometimes harsh and capricious orders of managers and employers. Few would now deny that unionists enjoy at their places of work a freedom their unorganized predecessors did not know.

Unfortunately unions, too, are organizations, combinations of workers in which the individual may be lost and forgotten. The largest unions are now served by huge bureaucracies, and even the smaller unions must assemble a sizeable staff to manage effectively and efficiently their negotiations and administrative duties. Such bureaucracies generate needs of their own that do not necessarily square

[1] Earl Latham, *The Group Basis of Politics* (Ithaca, N.Y.: Cornell University Press, 1952), p. 1.

with the interests and concerns of individual members. Workers may join a union to ease the burdens of serving a business corporation that they regard as an impersonal master only to find that they have become subject to another master just as large, powerful, and removed from their direct control.

Union members of like interests who feel that their union has neglected them might form a new association with the hope of finding expression and protection for their individuality. Such a development, if successful and repeated, might lead to a continual line of organizations receding back to the individual himself or some small group. The strength of such smaller groups would, however, pale before the force of the larger overreaching organizations, buttressed as they are with ample treasuries, professional talent, and legal protections and immunities.

We face a dilemma: as organizations benefit and extend the freedom of individuals, they often do so by regimenting and disciplining their members, thus limiting their freedom. Professor A. V. Dicey clearly pointed out the issue over 60 years ago:

> The right of association has a paradoxical character: a right which from one point of view seems to be a necessary extension of individual freedom is, from another point of view, fatal to that individual freedom of which it seems to be a mere extension. . . . This paradox raises a problem which at this moment in all civilized countries perplexes moralists and thinkers no less than legislators and judges: How is the right of association to be reconciled with each man's individual freedom? Curtail the right of association and personal liberty loses half its value. Give to the right of association unlimited scope and you destroy, not the mere value, but the existence of personal freedom.[2]

In practice, of course, the degree to which corporate organizations can or do infringe upon the rights of individuals is limited. The inattention of managers to detail and the dependence of the staff upon procedural routine may leave many gaps in the enforcement of discipline through which an individual member may escape to enjoy at least some freedom. The ponderous style and cumbersome performance of large organizations often provides opportunities for individuals to compete with them successfully. The small firm profitably operating in the shadow of a larger company or a number of unorganized workers in the midst of a unionized shop is not unknown. Depending upon the inefficiencies and faults of organizations to guarantee the interests of individuals either within or outside of an organization, however, is precarious. A society that values individualism as highly as America does is not apt to be satisfied with it.

Deciding whether group interests—in particular the interests of business organizations and unions—should prevail over the interests of individuals is not easy. Yet the interests of the organization and the individual clash repeatedly, and both parties appeal to the public and to the government for support. Businessmen and union leaders usually defend the interests they represent with arguments of efficiency, responsibility to their stockholders—or members, as the case may be—and the public good; to accommodate the individual, they usually claim, would inflict much injury for little gain. They may be right, but it would be wise to consider these arguments with care and examine their assumptions skeptically. The arguments of the protesting individuals also should be subject to the same

[2] "The Combination Laws as Illustrating the Relation Between Law and Opinion in England During the Nineteenth Century," *Harvard Law Review,* 17 (1904), 514.

careful scrutiny. Individuals who charge corporations or unions with infringing their rights can be as self-righteous and self-serving as those who speak for organizational interests. They may have little or no appreciation of the interests of the wider group and no concern whatever for community interests.

In deciding who must pay the costs of individual freedoms, and in balancing the claims of corporate or organizational rights against those of individuals, more questions can be posed than answers confidently given; more problems are raised than solutions found. Yet in the practical world of daily affairs in industry and business, managers, union leaders, employees, union members, judges, and arbitrators have to find answers and provide solutions. The following cases illustrate attempts by such people to deal with the conflicting interests of organizations and individuals. Examine them critically.

The Organization and Religious Liberty

MARY ELLEN BENSON

Mrs. Mary Ellen Benson of Milwaukee, Wisconsin, missed three of five scheduled monthly meetings of Local 356, United Papermakers and Paperworkers Union, to which she belonged. In accordance with its by-laws the union assessed her a $5.00 fine. When she refused to pay the fine the local brought suit against her in County Court, its counsel arguing that union rules provided for, and past practice sustained, the application of a fine.[1]

"The union meetings come on Sunday morning," said Mrs. Benson, "exactly at my [Protestant] church time. I've told them [the officials of Local 356] over and over again that I will never go to their meetings as long as they are on Sunday—and I still won't. I should never have to pay the union or anybody else for my freedom on Sunday. I thought the Constitution gave us the right to freedom of worship. I just wish I could find someone who cares . . . who is willing to stand up and be counted." She said she could not quit the union "because then I would be out of a job." The local enjoyed a union shop under its agreement with the company; a worker had to join the union within 30 days after being hired or relinquish his job.

Local 356 argued that it would be unfair to other members to grant Mrs. Benson special dispensation from the attendance rule; the local's president pointed out that the membership had voted to meet on Sundays. During World War II the company had scheduled work seven days a week, and when production slackened enough to require only six days the members approved Sunday as a meeting day. There had been no moves made by the membership to change the time since then. A representative of the International confirmed the local's autonomy in scheduling meeting time and also observed that a number of unions, including the Typographers, had held meetings on Sunday. Attendance on Sunday is often better than on work days, and so the local's schedule contributed to more participation by members in union decisions and to a more informed, active membership.

The parties met in the chambers of county judge Robert J. Meich for a pretrial conference. Mrs. Benson admitted missing the meetings. Judge Meich praised her motives and expressed admiration for the unswerving convictions of a woman who places her

[1] Details of this case were obtained by the authors in interviews with union officials.

religion above her livelihood, but he advised that "past court decisions make it clear the union has the right to assess the fine." Mrs. Benson agreed on the advice of counsel to pay the $5.00 fine and court costs of $5.40.

EDWIN E. SHAW

Mr. Edwin E. Shaw had been employed at the Ottumwa, Iowa, meat packing plant of the John Morrell Company since 1947. On December 11, 1950, he was discharged for his persistent refusal to report for scheduled Saturday work of the pork cut gang. Some years before, he had begun to attend services at the Seventh Day Adventist Church, which observes the Sabbath on Saturday, and ultimately he and his wife were baptized into that faith. Since October, 1950, he had refused all Saturday work.

Shaw was suspended after successive absences on three Saturdays. He protested the company's action, and the union's grievance committee supported him. The company lifted the suspension and agreed to look into possibilities of assigning Shaw a job not requiring a Saturday work assignment. After an examination of all jobs that Shaw could fill, however, management concluded that no such spot existed.

Shaw was scheduled to work on Saturday, November 4, 1950, but he did not report; he was suspended and then reinstated without pay. Shaw was similarly scheduled for work and did not show up on the next Saturdays worked—November 18, November 25, and December 2. In each instance, Shaw was suspended and thereafter permitted to go back to his job, though without pay for the time lost during the processing of the grievance. When he failed to show up again on December 9, the company discharged him.

Shaw entered a new protest. The company and union officials were unable to settle the grievance this time and took the case to Harold M. Gilden, the arbitrator designated in their labor agreement, for final resolution. The union argued that Shaw's discharge was contrary to Paragraph 7 of the union's contract with the company in that it constituted discrimination against Shaw on religious grounds.[1] The company countered that Shaw's religion had nothing to do with the case; it had disciplined him for refusing to work and that "Shaw must be responsive, to the same degree as all other workers, to the work schedule" for his department. "The contract," the company representative said, "authorizes Saturday work and this scheduling practice has been followed for many years." When Shaw's pastor testified, he informed the arbitrator that performing work on Saturday was not only against Shaw's conscience but ultimately would lead to his expulsion from church membership.

In his decision, the arbitrator upheld Shaw's discharge. He wrote:

> In the touchy situation in which the world finds itself these days, the importance of upholding religious freedom cannot be overemphasized. While great credit is due Shaw for his faithful adherence to his convictions . . . [I] cannot permit these considerations to detract from or otherwise influence a sound, analytical appraisal of the points here involved. . . . The underlying principle, and this applies to all religious beliefs, is that the employees bear the responsibility and obligation to faithfully abide and adhere to the work schedules fixed for them. Where, as in some plants, a replacement system is invoked to facilitate religious observations and still provide for job performance, there

[1] "The company further agrees that it will not discriminate against any employee or applicant because of race, sex, color, creed, nationality, or because of membership in the Union."

is no quarrel. But where this pattern is not recognized or established, and a conflict arises, the employee must yield his religious scruples in favor of his job duties or resign. Many persons faced with this alternative have decided in favor of their religion, and often the choice has not proved an unhappy one. . . . To adopt a special rule excepting Shaw from working his work schedule would be unfair to other employees and discriminatory against them. Shaw himself must realize that if a new rule was made to accommodate each and every religious conviction, the plant's work schedules would soon be reduced to a haphazard and chaotic level.[2]

[2] *Labor Arbitration Reports,* 17 (Washington: Bureau of National Affairs, 1952), 282.

QUESTIONS

The Organization and Religious Liberty

1. Evaluate the argument used in both cases that to exempt certain workers from the attendance rules of their organizations would be unfair to other members.
2. How was the freedom to worship of Benson and Shaw affected by the decisions in these cases? Has each been especially penalized for wanting to worship as he or she pleased, or is each being asked to recognize that there are certain limits and restrictions on religious liberties in a pluralistic society?
3. How and why would your opinion of the decision in the Benson case differ if the United Papermakers and Paperworkers had ordered all locals to hold meetings on Sundays?
4. The arbitrator in the Shaw case declared that "if a new rule was made to accommodate each and every religious conviction, the plant's work schedules would soon be reduced to a haphazard and chaotic level." What conditions would be necessary for such a situation to result in fact? Are such conditions likely to exist in a city the size of Ottumwa (population in 1950 about 35,000)?
5. "The original purpose of unions was to protect workers from overbearing employers. Now we find that workers have only exchanged the old master for a new one in the guise of the union itself." What arguments both for and against this statement can you find in the Benson case?
6. In what ways are the two cases similar and in what ways are they different? Why should a union, as well as a profit-making company, have a concern for organizational efficiency?

The Organization and the Right of Livelihood

SENN v. TILE LAYERS PROTECTIVE UNION

In 1935 Paul Senn was engaged in the tile contracting business under the name of "Paul Senn & Company, Tile Contracting." Senn was a plasterer by trade but had turned to tile laying in 1931 as construction work in Milwaukee declined. Joining him in the business was William Neider, who resigned from the Tile Layers Protective Union. Arnold Holly, a suspended union tile layer, worked for the partners. The business was small; it was conducted in the main from Senn's own residence, although it had a showroom elsewhere. From time to time the company employed one or two extra journeymen tile layers and one or two helpers as required by the amount of work Senn contracted. Since Senn worked with his own hands, setting tile and performing other manual work on the job, he was able to underbid other contractors who abided by union rules and restrictions against such labor. During the course of the year he worked on about 40 jobs and earned a net income of $1,500. Of this amount, $750 was attributable to his own labor; the rest, his profit as a contractor, was not enough by itself to support him and his family. Small as these sums of money were, they were sufficient to attract the attention of the Tile Layers Protective Union and give rise to an important test case.[1]

I

Neither Senn nor any of his employees was a member of the Tile Layers Protective Union, Local No. 5, or the Tile Layers Helpers Protective Union, Local No. 47, nor had they any contractual relations with either union. Indeed, Senn could not become a member of the tile layers union since its constitution and by-laws required, among other things, that a journeyman tile setter should have acquired his practical experience through an apprenticeship of not less than three years. Senn had not served such an apprenticeship.

For some years prior to 1935 tile layers had suffered high unemployment in Milwaukee. Some, like Senn, had become independent contractors seeking small jobs at cheap prices simply to secure some work. Their willingness to cut wages and to ignore the standard requirements about working conditions allowed them to bid successfully for jobs union members might otherwise have filled. The unionized contractors argued that such competition undermined union standards and that they could not continue to maintain their agreed-upon wages, hours, and working conditions if independent, non-union contractors kept taking business away from them. Unless all contractors observed union standards, none of them could. The independent contractors not only endangered the hard won gains of the Tile Layers Protective Union but threatened the very existence of the union as well. They were taking work away from union members at a time when membership had already fallen drastically. The Tile Layers Protective Union Local No. 5 had 112 members in 1929, but by January, 1936, it had only 41 members. In an attempt to save itself and to secure more work for its members, the union had begun an organizing campaign.

Because so many contracting companies were small—an employer working with a few employees—the union members decided that they could protect their work standards and their jobs only by insisting upon the following provisions as a part of the labor agreement:

> Article III. It is definitely understood that no individual, member of a partnership or corporation engaged in the Tile Contracting Business shall work with the tools or act as Helper but that the installation of all materials claimed by the party of the second part as listed under the caption "Classification of Work" in this agreement shall be done by journeymen members of the Tile Layers Protective Union, Local No. 5.

The union organizers tried to persuade Senn to become a union contractor. They asked him to sign an agreement in form substantially identical with those entered into by about half of Milwaukee's tile laying contractors. Senn would agree to the union's terms for wages and hours only if Article III was eliminated. He maintained that he could not carry on his business unless he could continue to lay tile himself. The Tile Layers replied that an exception for Senn was impossible; the inclusion of the provision was essential to the union's interest in maintaining wage standards and spreading work among its members. The union made clear that it did not want a contractor, skilled or unskilled, to work with the tools of the trade with the men when there was not enough work to go around. The president of Local 5 expressed the hope that, if contractors did not work,

[1] 301 U.S. 468 (1937).

members of the union could find work and would be able to be taken off relief. Moreover, to eliminate Article III from the agreement with Senn would, they said, discriminate against contractors already unionized, all of whom had signed agreements containing Article III.

Senn refused either to sign the agreement or to unionize his shop, and the president of Local No. 5 warned him that the union would do everything "to harass and put things in his way." Carrying out their threat, Local No. 5 and Local No. 47 declared Senn "unfair" and sent the following letter to all local contractors and architects:

> Some time ago we presented to each individual tile contractor in the city a copy of our new agreement in which we specified what constitutes a bona fide contractor and who should install the work. Not having heard from some of these so-called tile contractors in a given time, we beg of you to contact the list of fair contractors listed below in awarding the tile work in your building operations. If in two weeks' time anyone outside this list is awarded tile work we will then picket such jobs, contractors' or architects' offices, or employ other lawful means to help us in our fight to better the conditions of our trade.

II

In December, 1935, about five months after the two union locals had circulated their letter about Senn, they began to picket his place of business. The pickets were peaceful; they patrolled in an orderly fashion, usually only during working hours, and took an hour off for lunch. Apparently they did not physically obstruct Senn's business or physically intimidate his customers. They simply carried banners, one with the inscription, "P. Senn Tile Company is unfair to the Tile Layers Protective Union," and another with the request, "Let the Union tile layers install your tile work."

On December 28, 1935, Senn brought suit in the Circuit Court of Milwaukee County against Locals No. 5 and No. 47 and their business agents. He sought an injunction restraining picketing and particularly "publishing, stating or proclaiming that the plaintiff was unfair to organized labor or to the defendant unions." The trial court refused injunctive relief, but the unions agreed to cease picketing at the place of work and to send no more letters to architects and contractors. The Wisconsin Anti-Injunction Act, passed only a short time previously, prohibited the issuance of an injunction in a "labor dispute" if the pickets or strikers conducted themselves lawfully. The court found that the controversy was a "labor dispute" and that the picketing was lawful in that it was conducted solely in furtherance of the dispute.

Senn then appealed to the Wisconsin Supreme Court, which affirmed the judgment of the trial court and denied a motion for rehearing. The majority held that though Senn was not eligible for membership and none of his employees was a union member the picketing constituted a "labor dispute" within the meaning of the state law because Senn's business injured the union's interests in threatening the organized workers' wage scales and work standards. The minority vigorously dissented, pointing out that the unions were trying to coerce Senn into barring himself from a lawful calling. They were thus depriving him of liberty and property without due process of law, in violation of the Fifth Amendment.

Encouraged by the strong dissent of the state supreme court, Senn appealed to the Supreme Court of the United States. There his counsel argued:

> The right of a citizen to work in a lawful business in a lawful manner, the right to follow any of the ordinary callings of life, is an inalienable right. A state legislature cannot deprive citizens of the United States of this right, and, *a fortiori,* it cannot be taken away by labor unions under color of a statute. It is the bounden duty of courts to protect this right. A man may not barter away his life or freedom, nor be forced by labor unions to relinquish them.

The union conceded that Senn had the right to work with his hands and tools as long as he conducted a nonunion shop:

> He may do so, as freely as he may work his employees longer hours and at lower wages than the union rules permit. He may bid for contracts at a low figure based upon low wages and long hours. But . . . since Senn's exercise of the right to do so is harmful to the interests of their members, they may seek by legal means to induce him to agree to unionize his shop and to refrain from exercising his right to work with his own hands.[2]

III

In a five-to-four decision the Court affirmed the judgment against Senn. Justice Brandeis delivered the majority opinion:

> There is no basis for a suggestion that the unions' request that Senn refrain from working with his own hands, or their employment of picketing and publicity, was malicious; or that there was a desire to injure Senn. The sole purpose of the picketing was to acquaint the public with the facts and, by gaining its support, to induce Senn to unionize his shop. There was no effort to induce Senn to do an unlawful thing. There was no violence, no force was applied, no molestation or interference, no coercion. There was only the persuasion incident to publicity. As the Supreme Court of Wisconsin said, "Each of the contestants is desirous of the advantage of doing business in the community where he or they operate. He is not obligated to yield to the persuasion exercised upon him by respondents. . . . The respondents do not question that it is appellants' right to own his own business and earn his living in any lawful manner which he chooses to adopt. What they are doing is asserting their rights under the acts of the Legislature for the purpose of enhancing their opportunity to acquire work for themselves and those whom they represent. . . . The respondents' act of peaceful picketing is a lawful form of appeal to the public to turn its patronage from appellant to the concerns in which the welfare of the members of the unions is bound up."
>
> The unions acted, and had the right to act as they did, to protect the interests of their members against the harmful effect upon them of Senn's action. . . . There is nothing in the Federal Constitution which forbids unions from competing with non-union concerns for customers by means of picketing as freely as one merchant competes with another by means of advertisements in the press, by circulars, or by his window display. Each member of the unions, as well as Senn, has the right to strive to earn his living. Senn seeks to do so through exercise of his individual skill and planning. The union members seek to do so through combination. Earning a living is dependent upon securing work; and securing work is dependent upon public favor. To win the patronage of the public each may strive by legal means. Exercising its police power, Wisconsin has declared that in a labor dispute peaceful picketing and truthful publicity are means legal for unions. It is true that disclosure of the facts of the labor dispute may be annoying to Senn even if the method and means employed in giving the publicity are inherently unobjectionable. But such annoyance, like that often suffered from publicity in other connections, is not an invasion of the liberty guaranteed by the Constitution. It is true, also, that disclosure of the facts may prevent Senn from securing jobs which he hoped to get. But a hoped-for job is not property guaranteed by the Constitution. And the diversion of it to a competitor is not an invasion of a constitutional right. . . . One has no constitutional right to a "remedy" against the lawful conduct of another.

IV

Mr. Justice Butler and three other Justices dissented, arguing in part as follows:

> The clauses of the Fourteenth Amendment invoked by plaintiff are: "No State shall . . . deprive any person of life, liberty, or property without due process of law; nor deny to any person within its jurisdiction the equal protection of the laws." Our decisions have made it everywhere known that these

[2] Senn v. Tile Layers Protective Union et al., 301 U.S. 469–70 and 478.

provisions forbid state action which would take from the individual the right to engage in common occupations of life, and that they assure equality of opportunity to all under like circumstances. Lest the importance or wisdom of these great declarations be forgotten or neglected, there should be frequent recurrence to decisions of this court that expound and apply them.

While this Court has not attempted to define with exactness the liberty thus guaranteed, the term has received much consideration and some of the included things have been definitely stated. Without doubt, it denotes not merely freedom from bodily restraint but also the right of the individual to contract, to engage in any of the common occupations of life, to acquire useful knowledge, to marry, establish a home and bring up children, to worship God according to the dictates of his own conscience, and generally to enjoy those privileges long recognized at common law as essential to the orderly pursuit of happiness by free men. *Meyer* v. *Nebraska.*

The right to follow any of the common occupations of life is an inalienable right. It was formulated as such under the phrase "pursuit of happiness" in the Declaration of Independence, which commenced with the fundamental proposition that "all men are created equal, that they are endowed by their Creator with certain inalienable rights; that among these are life, liberty and the pursuit of happiness." . . . I hold that the liberty of pursuit—the right to follow any of the ordinary callings of life—is one of the privileges of a citizen of the United States. Concurring opinion of Mr. Justice Bradley in *Butchers' Union Co.* v. *Crescent City Co.*, approvingly quoted in *Allgeyer* v. *Louisiana.*

Included in the right of personal liberty and the right of private property—partaking of the nature of each—is the right to make contracts for the acquisition of property. Chief among such contracts is that of personal employment by which labor and other services are exchanged for money or other forms of property. If this right be struck down or arbitrarily interfered with, there is a substantial impairment of liberty in the long-established constitutional sense. The right is as essential to the laborer as to the capitalist, to the poor as to the rich; for the vast majority of persons have no other honest way to begin to acquire property, save by working for money. *Coppage* v. *Kansas.*

It requires no argument to show that the right to work for a living in the common occupations of the community is of the very essence of the personal freedom and opportunity that it was the purpose of the amendments to secure. *Truax* v. *Raich.*

The object that defendants seek to attain is an unlawful one. . . . The principles governing competition between rival individuals seeking contracts or opportunity to work as journeymen cannot reasonably be applied in this case. Neither the union nor its members take tile laying contracts. Their interests are confined to employment of helpers and layers, their wages, hours of service, etc. The contest is not between unionized and other contractors or between one employer and another. The immediate issue is between the unions and plaintiff in respect of his right to work in the performance of his own jobs. If as to that they shall succeed, then will come the enforcement of their rules which make him ineligible to work as a journeyman. It cannot be said that, if he should be prevented from laboring as helper or layer, the work for union men to do would be increased. The unions exclude their members from jobs taken by non-union employers. About half the tile contractors are not unionized. . . . Between union members and plaintiff there is no immediate or direct competition. If under existing circumstances there ever can be any, it must come about through a chain of unpredictable events making its occurrence a mere matter of speculation. The interest of the unions in the manual labor done by plaintiff is so remote, indirect and minute that they have no standing as competitors. Under the circumstances here disclosed, the conduct of the unions was arbitrary and oppressive.

Moreover, the picketing was unlawful because the signs used constitute a misrepresentation of the facts. One of them declared plaintiff "unfair" to the tile layers union and, upon the basis of that statement, the other sign solicited tile work for union tile layers. There was given neither definition of the word nor any fact on which the accusation was based. By the charge made, there was implied something unjust or inequitable in his attitude toward labor unions. But there was no foundation of fact for any such accusation. There was no warrant for characterizing him as "unfair" or opposed to any legitimate purpose of the tile layers union or as unjust to union men. There is no escape from the conclusion that the unions intended by the picketing they carried on to misrepresent plaintiff in respect of his relation to, or dealing with, the tile layers union and by that means to deprive him of his occupation.

UNITED STATES v. GENERAL MOTORS

In November, 1962, the Justice Department accused the General Motors Corporation, three Chevrolet dealer associations in Southern California, and a number of General Motors and dealer association officials of illegally conspiring to bring pressure on Chevrolet dealers to stop them from selling new cars to "discount houses." [1] The Department charged the company and the associations with violating Section I of the Sherman Act, the relevant part of which reads: "Every contract, combination in the form of trust or otherwise, or conspiracy, in restraint of trade or commerce among the several States, or with foreign nations is declared to be illegal. . . ."

I

Chevrolets are ordinarily distributed by dealers operating under a franchise from General Motors. The dealers purchase the cars from the manufacturer and then retail them to the public. The relationship between manufacturer and dealer is incorporated in a comprehensive uniform Dealer Selling Agreement, which does not restrict or define those to whom the dealer may sell. Neither does it fix the selling price or limit the territory within which the dealer may sell. The franchise agreement does, however, contain a "location clause" which prohibits a dealer from moving to or establishing "a new or different location, branch sales office, branch service station, or place of business including any used-car lot or location without the prior written approval of Chevrolet."

[1] 384 U.S. 127 (1966).

In the late 1950's, "discount houses" in the Los Angeles area that sold consumer goods or provided "referral services" began offering new cars to the public at alleged bargain prices. Their sources of supply were the franchised dealers. By 1960 a number of individual Chevrolet dealers, without authorization from General Motors, had developed working relationships with these establishments. A customer could enter one of the discount houses and examine the literature and price lists for automobiles produced by several manufacturers. In some instances, floor models were available for inspection. Some of the establishments negotiated with the customer for a trade-in of his old car and provided financing for the purchase of his new car.

The relationship with the franchised dealer took various forms. One arrangement was for the discounter to refer the customer to the dealer. The car would then be offered to him by the dealer at a price previously agreed upon between the dealer and the discounter. In 1960, a typical referral agreement concerning Chevrolets provided that the price to the customer was not to exceed $250 over the dealer's invoiced cost. For his part in supplying the customer, the discounter received $50 per sale.[2]

Another common arrangement was for the discounter to negotiate the sale himself, the dealer's role being simply to furnish the car and to transfer title to the customer at the direction of the discounter. One

[2] United States v. General Motors Corporation, Supreme Court of the United States, No. 46, October Term, 1965, April 28, 1966, p. 3.

dealer furnished Chevrolets under such an arrangement, charging the discounter $85 over the invoiced cost, with the discounter getting the best price he could from his customers.

These were the two principal forms of trading involved in this case, although within each there were variations, and there were schemes that fit neither pattern. One dealer, for example, paid his referral service one-third of the gross profit on each sale, up to $75, there being no fixed price at which the sale was to take place. The same dealer earlier had paid a flat fee of $17.50 for every referral, whether or not the sale was consummated.

At least one discount house actually purchased its cars from cooperating dealers and then resold them to its customers. In this arrangement, referred to in the trade as "bootlegging," the customer did not receive a new-car warranty. General Motors, while disapproving of the practice, did not declare this a violation of the location clause of its franchise agreement. In those arrangements that General Motors and the dealer associations did claim violated the location clause, title to the new car passed directly from dealer to retail customer, who thus obtained a new-car warranty and service agreement.

There must also be distinguished the ubiquitous practice of using "bird dogs"—informal sources who steered occasional customers toward a particular dealer in return for relatively small fees, often a bottle of liquor. General Motors did not consider this practice a violation of the "location clause" and had even endorsed it as a useful technique for boosting sales.

By 1960 these methods for retailing new cars were in wide use. Of 100,000 new Chevrolets sold in the Los Angeles area in that year, some 2,000 represented discount house or referral sales. One Chevrolet dealer attributed as much as 25 per cent of his annual sales to participation in these arrangements, while another dealer reported making between 400 and 525 referral sales in a single year.

II

Approximately a dozen of the 85 franchised Chevrolet dealers in the Los Angeles area were furnishing cars to discounters in 1960. As the volume of these sales grew, the non-participating Chevrolet dealers located near one or more of the discount outlets began to feel the pinch. Seventy per cent of the local Chevrolet dealers were located within five miles of one or more of the 23 discount houses or referral outlets. Dealers lost sales because potential customers received, or thought they would receive, a more attractive deal from a discounter who obtained his Chevrolets from a distant dealer.

Franchised dealers are required to maintain adequate facilities for service operations as well as for sales and must also sell parts and accessories. All Chevrolet dealers have a contractual obligation to General Motors to perform warranty service on new Chevrolets regardless of where the cars were purchased. The proper performance of the service and parts obligations imposed by the Chevrolet Dealer Selling Agreement contributes importantly to customer good will and the overall profitability of a dealership. However, analyzed on a departmental basis, and allocating to the service and parts departments their share of the dealership administrative expenses, these departments of the Los Angeles metropolitan area dealers generally operated at a loss. An independent study using these methods by Price Waterhouse, showed that the typical Chevrolet dealer in the Los Angeles metropolitan area incurred an annual loss in the 1960 operation of the service and parts departments of approximately $14,000.

Discount sales did undercut the prices at which franchised dealers were able to, or chose to, compete. Two persons who had purchased Chevrolets, one on referral and the other in a discount house "sale," testified that they had compared the prices of other dealers but found the discount and referral prices lower. Dealers and their salesmen complained to General Motors about sales lost through inability to meet the discounters' price. Moreover, the discounters advertised and actually provided auto loans at interest rates substantially lower than those offered by GMAC, the General Motors financing subsidiary.

Other evidence suggested, however, that it was not just price alone that induced customers to purchase Chevrolets through the discounters. One customer testified that he preferred the discount house because he thereby avoided the haggling over price that seems an inevitable part of purchasing a car in the orthodox way. Others apparently assumed, without bothering to confirm by comparison shopping, that discount stores would offer lower prices. This assumption was encouraged by discount house advertising, which promised "the lowest price anywhere" and "savings of hundreds of dollars." A number of dealers thought that customers were taken in by the discounters. One said, "I believe a lot of people went into a discount store just because it had a sign up 'Discount House' and just willy-nilly bought a car without any knowledge as to what the car could be purchased for. Consequently our salesmen would lose the deal."

The discounters vigorously advertised Chevrolets with alluring statements of price savings as well as with assurances that all Chevrolet dealers were obligated to honor new-car warranties and their contemplated free services. General Motors does indeed require Chevrolet dealers to service Chevrolet cars, wherever purchased, pursuant to the new-car warranty and service agreement. Accordingly, dealers were increasingly called upon to service, without compensation, Chevrolets purchased through discounters. Perhaps what grated most was the requirement that they "precondition" cars so purchased—make the minor adjustments and do the body and paint work necessary to render a factory-fresh car both customer- and road-worthy.

III

On June 28, 1960, at a regular meeting of the Losor Chevrolet Dealers Association, member dealers discussed the problem of discount operations and resolved to bring it to the attention of Chevrolet's Los Angeles zone manager, Robert O'Connor. Shortly thereafter, a delegation from the association called upon O'Connor, presented evidence that some dealers were doing business with the discounters, and asked for his assistance. O'Connor promised he would speak to the offending dealers. When the dealers became convinced that no action was going to be taken, Owen Keown, a director of Losor, took matters into his own hands. First, he spoke to Warren Biggs and Wilbur Newman, Chevrolet dealers who were then doing a substantial business with discounters. According to Keown, Newman told him that he would continue the practice "until . . . told not to" by Chevrolet, and that "when the Chevrolet Motor Division told him not to do it, he knew that they wouldn't let some other dealer carry on with it." Other dealers selling to discounters responded in a similar way.[3]

When Keown reported the offending dealers' responses to the Association's annual meeting in Honolulu on November 10, 1960, the members agreed immediately to flood General Motors and its Chevrolet Division with letters and telegrams asking for help. Salesmen, too, would be asked to write. Keown described the decision as a means of getting "the assistance of the higher eschelon officials of Chevrolet and General Motors in bringing about an end to the discount house sale of Chevrolets."

[3] United States v. General Motors Corporation, Supreme Court of the United States, No. 46, October Term, 1965, April 28, 1966, pp. 5–6.

Hundreds of letters and wires descended upon Detroit, all of them protesting the "unfair" competition. Within a week Chevrolet's O'Connor was directed to furnish his superiors in Detroit with "a detailed report of the discount house operations . . . as well as what action we in the Zone are taking to curb such sales."

An inter-office memorandum, circulated among General Motors officials immediately prior to formulation of corporate policy vis-à-vis the discounters stated that "it would appear that one of the real hazards of condoning this type of operation is that discounted prices are freely quoted to a large portion of the public." Moreover, the memorandum noted that some discounters advertised that they would finance new-car purchases at an interest rate of 5.5 per cent, a rate substantially lower than that available at franchised Chevrolet dealers through GMAC. Since General Motors is intensely concerned that each of its dealers has an adequate "profit opportunity," it is interested in the price realized by dealers. By mid-December, General Motors had formulated a new policy. GM officials felt that if the discount houses were to continue,

> [they] would have a very serious and detrimental effect on the operation of General Motors Corporation, and that it eventually would seriously affect the sale of Chevrolet cars and possibly other General Motors products, in the event that the practice was taken up extensively among the other lines . . . and if it did we felt this would destroy the very carefully planned and constructive system of distribution that we had worked for so many years to establish, and in which we had such a very substantial investment of time, effort and money, to bring our operation to the degree of success that we enjoy today.[4]

The officials also disliked discount houses for not promoting Chevrolet sales but instead taking orders for any make of cars. Since they did not promote sales of Chevrolet automobiles during slack periods of the year and during lean years, Chevrolet could not depend upon discount houses or referral services to provide the active and aggressive sales efforts needed year in and year out.

On December 15, James M. Roche, then an executive vice president of General Motors, wrote to every General Motors dealer in the United States. He noted that the practices to which many were objecting *"in some instances* represent the establishment of a second and unauthorized sales outlet or location contrary to the provisions of the General Motors Dealers Selling Agreements" (italics added). Recipients of the letter were advised that General Motors proposed to have representatives discuss the matter with each of the dealers. General Motors instructed O'Connor and Roy Cash, regional manager for the Chevrolet Division, to carry on the personal discussions with the dealers.

General Motors personnel proceeded to telephone all area dealers, both to identify those associated with the discounters and to advise non-participants that General Motors had started to take action. The principal offenders were treated to unprecedented individual confrontations with Cash, the regional manager. The meetings were brief but wholly successful in obtaining from each dealer his agreement to abandon the practices in question. Some capitulated during the course of the four- or five-minute meeting or immediately thereafter.

One dealer abruptly terminated arrangements he had long maintained with two discount houses, despite the fact that one owed him $20,000 and the other $28,000. In the preceding four weeks the latter had reduced his indebtedness by $52,000 and could reasonably have been expected to erase it completely within a few weeks. The dealer anticipated that cancellation of the accounts would make these debts uncollectable. His fears were justified. The accounts

[4] Statement of General Motors' vice president in charge of distribution, quoted in *General Motors Brief* before the United States Supreme Court, October Term, 1965, p. 49.

were terminated, and the debts remained unpaid.

Another dealer, who met with the city sales manager for Chevrolet, put off his decision for a week "to make sure that the other dealers, or most of them, had stopped their business dealings with discount houses." Most of the dealers, however, left their meetings with the impression that every dealer who had been doing business with a discount house or referral service would soon quit.

This was precisely the impression General Motors had intended to implant. As was explained in an inter-office memorandum to the general sales manager of the Chevrolet Division, "[All dealers were talked to] in order that every dealer with whom the subject was discussed would know that a similar discussion was being held with all other dealers so that if certain dealers should elect to discontinue their cooperation with a discount house, we might be able to discourage some other dealer who might be solicited from starting the practice." Unanimity was not obtained without reference to the ultimate power of General Motors, though. Wilbur Newman, a dealer, said that regional manager Cash related a story about handling children, "I can tell them to stop something. If they don't do it . . . I can knock their teeth down their throats." The relevance of the story was not lost upon Newman; he ceased dealing with the discounters.

IV

By mid-January General Motors had elicited from each dealer a promise not to do business with the discounters, but the company did not expect that all dealers would voluntarily live up to their promises. It had already planned to ask some firms to police the actions of their fellow dealers. This plan was dropped, however, in favor of a joint effort between General Motors, the three defendant associations, and a number of individual dealers.

On December 15, 1960, the three dealer associations met and appointed a joint committee to study the situation and to keep in touch with Chevrolet's O'Connor as they worked together to eliminate the sales to discounters. What auto men feared most was the possibility of huge auto discount houses in which Chevrolets, Fords, Plymouths, Ramblers, and other makes might sit side by side, each with the price clearly labeled. A single attendant at the door could collect the customers' money as they drove out with their new cars. Sales could be made without benefit of a sales pitch that one car was better than another and, what was worse from the manufacturers' point of view, without the discounter even caring what kind of car was sold.

Early in 1961, the three associations agreed jointly to finance the "shopping" of the discounters to make sure that no Chevrolet dealer continued to supply them with cars. Each of the associations contributed $5,000, and a professional investigator was hired. He was instructed to try to purchase new Chevrolets from the suspect outlets, to tape record the transactions, if any, and to gather all the necessary documentary evidence, which the associations would then lay "at the doorstep of Chevrolet." These joint associational activities were both preceded and supplemented by similar "shopping" activities by individual dealers and by the defendant, Losor Chevrolet Dealers Association.

General Motors collaborated with the policing activities. Zone manager O'Connor and a subordinate, Jere Faust, actively solicited the help of individual dealers in uncovering violations. Armed with information of violations obtained from the dealers or their associations, O'Connor or members of his staff would ask the offending dealer to come in and talk. The dealer then was confronted with the car purchased by the "shopper," the documents of sale, and in most cases a tape recording of the transaction. In every instance, the embarrassed dealer repurchased the car, sometimes at a substantial loss, and promised to stop such sales.[5] At the direction of O'Connor or a subordinate, the checks with which the cars were repurchased were made payable to an attorney acting jointly for the three defendant associations.

O'Connor argued that on no occasion did he "force" a dealer to repurchase; he merely made the opportunity available. Dealers thought he did much more. One told of an invitation to meet the assistant zone manager for the Chevrolet Division to talk about discount sales: "He specified a sum of money which I was to bring with me when I came down and saw him . . . I kept the appointment and brought a cashier's check. I knew when I came down to Los Angeles that I was going to repurchase an automobile. . . ." Another dealer, upon being confronted with evidence that one of his cars had been purchased through a referral service, not only bought it back (without questioning the correctness of the price exacted) but also fired the salesman responsible though only a few weeks earlier this man had been commended by the Chevrolet Division as the "number one fleet salesman" in the 11-state Pacific region.

By the Spring of 1961 the campaign to eliminate the discounters from commerce in new Chevrolet cars was a success. Sales through the discount outlets had come to a halt. Not until a federal grand jury commenced an inquiry into the activities of General Motors and the dealer associations did any Chevrolet dealers resume their business association with the discounters.

V

On the basis of these facts, the Justice Department initiated criminal proceedings against General Motors and its dealers. A federal grand jury in the Southern District of California returned an indictment. The government argued as follows:

> The business logic of sales through discount houses refutes the argument that . . . [discount sales endanger] the franchise system. Suppose that General Motors sold its Chevrolet automobiles at a single price to both its franchised dealers and discount houses. In that event, there probably would be a substantial adverse impact upon the franchised dealers. They would be compelled to compete on equal terms with sellers who had no service obligations, were not tied to a single manufacturer, did not have to invest in very costly showroom facilities, and might be stronger and more diversified merchandisers. But General Motors does not distribute in that fashion. Discount outlets that desire to carry automobiles cannot obtain them from General Motors; their only source is the franchised dealer. Hence, the franchised dealer has a substantial built-in cost advantage over competing discount outlets which offsets his higher overhead. He buys at the manufacturer's price, while the discount house must price at a level reflecting a profit for the dealer. The dealer's profit is part of the discounter's—but not, of course, the dealer's—cost. The franchised dealer has an additional advantage *vis-à-vis* the discount house: The consumer would presumably prefer to patronize an authorized dealer, conveniently located, and well-stocked with parts and trained personnel, rather than a discount house—so long as the dealer is reasonably competitive in price.

[5] One of O'Connor's Zone Office subordinates described in testimony one such confrontation of a dealer with the tape recording as follows:

Q. When the tape recording was concluded, did Mr. Cashman [the dealer] appear at all embarrassed to you?
A. I would say so, yes, sir.
Q. So that, after playing this tape recording to which you have testified Mr. Cashman appeared embarrassed, no doubt you asked him a question, did you not?
A. I believe that I did. I believe I asked him if he wished to buy the car back.
Q. And what did he say to you, Mr. Thompson?
A. As I recall, he said he certainly did.
Q. And Mr. Thompson, did you expect him to say, "No"?
A. No, I don't think I did, no sir.

Brief for the United States, before the Supreme Court of the United States, No. 46, October Term, 1965, p. 16.

This means that sales through discount houses are likely to reach substantial proportions only in places where, and at times when, the franchise system fails to produce reasonably competitive results, and retail prices and profit margins of the franchised dealers are out of line or excessive. If prices and margins are reasonably low, there is unlikely to be enough "water" in them to permit (1) the franchised dealer to sell at the discount price and still make a profit, (2) the discounter to undersell competing franchised dealers in his areas, *and* (3) the discounter to recover his selling costs and a commission on the transaction. Unless all three conditions are fulfilled, selling through discount houses makes no business sense; where all three conditions are fulfilled, the chances are that retail profits and prices reflect the absence of vigorous competition. In other words, as the facts of this case demonstrate eloquently, selling through discount houses is likely to arise only in response to a failure of the franchise system, and its natural tendency is not to undermine the system, but, rather, by breaking the artificial price-and-profit level, to restore the system to competitive functioning. It is a safety valve, protecting rather than impairing efficient distribution of automobiles to the consuming public.

The Los Angeles experience tends to confirm that the franchise system would not be impaired by discount house selling. Although some 2,000 Chevrolets were sold in 1960 through Los Angeles area discount houses. no dealer in that area went out of business, General Motors conceded that there was no "impairment in the franchise system at that time," and the company was unable to show that any dealer was affected in any way that differed from the usual impact upon a merchant of vigorous competition by his rivals. Moreover, since dealers selling through discount houses charged discount house customers, there is no reason to assume the complaining dealers could not meet the "discount" price in their own places of business.

VI

In the trial, the defendants were found not guilty. Judge Thurmond Clarke reasoned that each defendant and alleged co-conspirator acted to promote his own self-interest; that General Motors, as well as the defendant associations and their members, had a lawful interest in securing compliance with the "location clause" and in thus protecting the franchise system of distributing automobiles—business arrangements that the court considered lawful and proper; and that in seeking to vindicate these interests the defendants and their alleged co-conspirators entered into no "agreements" among themselves, although they may have engaged in "parallel action." Judge Clarke also observed:

> There is no evidence in the record that . . . economic pressure and not self-interest precipitated the decision of the dealers. Indeed, termination of discount operations was encumbent upon the dealers, under the provision of the franchise contract which prohibits a dealer from establishing a second location, without the consent of General Motors. That the defendants did not stress the contractual clause at every opportunity does not mean that defendants put little stock in it. On the contrary, the record is replete with testimony that General Motors, through its officials, tries to reason and confer with its dealers as partners and not as antagonists. Similarly, there is nothing to show that the Dealers Associations did any more than to try to point out what was thought to be in the best interests of the dealers. . . .
>
> No reasonable juror could find beyond a reasonable doubt that termination of sales through discount houses unreasonably lessened and restrained competition. The record shows that dealers do compete in their pricing of new cars. The record further discloses that General Motors Corporation reasonably believes that franchise dealers are better representatives of the Corporation than discount houses for the reason that discount houses and referral services have no special or continuing interest in the well being of General Motors, offer no service facilities, and operate entirely free of any control by General Motors.
>
> In applying the antitrust laws . . . a bal-

ance must be struck . . . Business has, or should have, the right to merchandise a product in a manner that the particular manufacturer determines to be the most feasible and the most competitive. Indeed, I believe that the best way to further the interest of the consumer is to allow business, large and small, to avail itself of the free enterprise system with as little Government interference as possible. This court feels, therefore, that its decision protects both the interests of the public and the interests of business.

In its broader aspects, the case presents this question: . . . Should the Government, through the antitrust laws, compel General Motors to adopt the discount houses and with them, a method of merchandising not of General Motors' choosing? The court thinks not.[6]

VII

The case was then brought before the Supreme Court of the United States. In April, 1966, the Supreme Court reversed the finding of the lower court. Justice Fortas declared:

We have here a classic conspiracy in restraint of trade: joint, collaborative action by dealers, the defendant associations, and General Motors to eliminate a class of competitors by terminating business dealings between them and a minority of Chevrolet dealers and to deprive franchised dealers of their freedom to deal through discounters if they so choose. Against this fact of unlawful combination, the "location clause" is of no avail. Whatever General Motors might or might not lawfully have done to enforce individual Dealer Selling Agreements by action within the borders of those agreements and the relationship which each defines, is beside the point. And, because the action taken constitutes a combination or conspiracy, it is not necessary to consider what might be the legitimate interest of a dealer in securing compliance by others with the "location clause," or the lawfulness of action a dealer might individually take to vindicate this interest. . . .

Neither individual dealers nor the associations acted independently or separately. The dealers collaborated, through the associations and otherwise, among themselves and with General Motors, both to enlist the aid of General Motors and to enforce dealers' promises to forsake the discounters. The associations explicitly entered into a joint venture to assist General Motors in policing the dealers' promises, and their joint proffer to aid was accepted and utilized by General Motors. . . .

General Motors sought to elicit from each dealer agreements, substantially interrelated and interdependent, that none of them would do business with the discounters. These agreements were hammered out in meetings between nonconforming dealers and officials of General Motors' Chevrolet Division, and in telephone conversations with other dealers. It was acknowledged from the beginning that substantial unanimity would be essential if the agreements were to be forthcoming. And once the agreements were secured, General Motors both solicited and employed the assistance of its alleged co-conspirators in helping to police them. What resulted was a fabric interwoven by many strands of joint action to eliminate the discounters from participation in the market, to inhibit the free choice of franchised dealers to select their own methods of trade and to provide multilateral surveillance and enforcement. This process for achieving and enforcing the desired objective can by no stretch of the imagination be described as "unilateral" or merely "parallel."

There can be no doubt that the effect of the combination or conspiracy here was to restrain trade and commerce within the meaning of the Sherman Act. Elimination, by joint collaborative action, of discounters from access to the market is a *per se* violation of the Act. . . .

The protection of price competition from conspiratorial restraint is an object of special solicitude under the antitrust laws. We cannot respect that solicitude by closing our eyes to the effect upon price competition of the removal from the market, by combination or conspiracy, of a class of traders. Nor

[6] United States v. General Motors Corporation, 216 F. Supp. 362 (1963) 365.

do we propose to construe the Sherman Act to prohibit conspiracies to fix prices at which competitors may sell, but to allow conspiracies or combinations to put competitors out of business entirely.

Accordingly, we reverse and remand to the United States District Court for the Southern District of California in order that it may fashion appropriate equitable relief.

VIII

The day after the Supreme Court announced its decision, Frederic G. Donner, General Motor's board chairman, announced:

> We are disappointed and concerned by the ruling. . . . We have not had the opportunity to study the opinion and therefore cannot comment upon its possible effect on the operation of the franchise system of distribution in the automobile industry.[7]

Other interested businessmen commented more freely. A spokesman for Chrysler Corporation said that "the ruling . . . is a setback to the auto industry in its efforts to serve the public through the franchised dealer system."[8] Robin L. Farkas, president of the car rental division of Alexander's Department Stores praised the decision, however. He said that his company had wanted for some time to set up automobile discount supermarkets to sell all makes of cars. "I feel very confident we could find a variety of dealers of each make who would be very happy to get the extra volume at a lower mark-up." He estimated that Alexander's could save the consumer $160 on a standard automobile and up to $1,000 on a large car.[9] The sales manager of Spielman Motor Sales Company in Brooklyn, New York, commented that he and other dealers would do business with discounters so long as it made economic sense. "We've been selling Chevrolets to discount dealers all along. We'll go on selling just as long as the discount dealers want to buy."[10]

[7] *New York Times,* April 29, 1966.

[8] *Ibid.*

[9] *Ibid.*

[10] *Wall Street Journal,* April 29, 1966.

QUESTIONS

The Organization and the Right of Livelihood

1. Prepare a defense or challenge to the decisions of the Supreme Court in these two cases, basing your argument in large part upon a demonstration of the consistency of the Court's arguments or the lack of it.
2. Outline the pro and con arguments for a debate on the question, RESOLVED: In the Senn and General Motors cases the Supreme Court ignored the public interest as well as the interests of the individual.
3. Find illustrations in these cases of the rights and interests of individuals that organizations protect and enhance and also ones that they limit and injure.
4. For what reasons might the Wisconsin legislature and the U.S. Congress have encouraged unions in the 1930's at the expense of individual workers and businessmen? What circumstances might cause the state and federal legislatures similarly to favor the rights of large corporations over those of individual businessmen and employees?
5. To what extent did the Tile Layers Protective Union allow consumers to express their interest in the dispute with Senn? To what extent did General Motors allow consumers to express their interests in the dispute with the discounters and franchise dealers?
6. In what situations may one person destroy the livelihood and property values

of another without due process of law? Carefully consider the activities allowed and encouraged in the free, competitive market.

7. What distinguishes the methods used by General Motors to secure compliance with its policies from those used by the Tile Layers union? How effective were the union's tactics in Milwaukee in 1935? How effective might they have been in an anti-union town in the South?

8. Do you agree with Justice Butler that the Tile Layers union misrepresented the facts about Senn? Analyze the meaning of "unfair" in giving your answer.

9. What, if any, useful public purposes were the franchised dealers and discounters serving? In what ways can an automobile firm better serve the public if it eliminates the discounters? Upon what basis can one judge which provides more service to the public?

chapter **10**

THE INDIVIDUAL IN THE LARGE ORGANIZATION

Theoreticians of the classical liberal state regard the contract that an individual may freely make or refuse as having been an important instrument in freeing men from the restraints of inherited status and in safeguarding them against other forms of repression. Under the aegis of the liberal state and within the bounds of the competitive market, each individual had the opportunity fully to exploit his abilities and talents; he could contract to buy the labor of others or to sell his own labor at the most advantageous terms he could find. Whatever a man possessed, it was of little value, according to classical doctrine, if he did not enjoy free access to the market; his ability to protect himself or to improve his condition depended upon the contractual relationships he was able to establish for himself.

In earlier chapters we noted how restrictions upon the growth of industrial organizations in the United States gave way to pragmatic approval. As these corporate organizations increased in size and number, their managers were increasingly able to disregard the interests of individual workers because no competitive labor market operated well enough to allow employees to secure contract terms that would safeguard them.

To counter management's arbitrary exercise of power over their work lives, workers insisted upon the right to combine. This solution was at best a temporary one; the unions they formed grew in membership, established vast bureaucracies of their own, and in turn began to threaten the liberties and interests of their members. Through the Taft-Hartley Act of 1947 and again through the Landrum-Griffin Act of 1959 Congress attempted to protect the individual rights of workers by strengthening democratic procedures within unions. The stronger that democracy was within unions, the better, it was hoped, unions would protect workers' rights within the employing corporations.[1]

[1] For all practical purposes the public has gotten around the restrictions against applying antitrust laws to trade unions by demanding piecemeal legislation that would remedy one or another of the alleged abuses of union power. Americans have thus sidestepped the point that since labor is not a commodity it cannot be regulated by laws calculated to preserve the freedom of movement of goods, via healthy competition, in interstate commerce. Such logic, of course, was the constitutional basis for antitrust legislation.

If most employees were to belong to unions, legislation encouraging democracy in unions and, through them, in corporations, might conceivably provide the protection of individual rights and interests that the liberal state had promised. Today, however, less than a quarter of the labor force is actually enrolled in unions or covered by collectively bargained agreements. Moreover, the less organized category of white-collar workers is growing much faster than the blue-collar group; since 1956, white-collar employees have outnumbered blue-collar workers. Within the general white-collar category, the group that is increasing its numbers most rapidly is formed by the workers at the top of the occupational list, the professional and technical employees, who increased their numbers by about three and one-half times between 1950 and 1966. Totalling over 9 million, they are over two and one-half times more numerous than the unskilled manual workers, greater in numbers than the skilled workers, and two-thirds the number of semi-skilled manual workers. Most of these professional and technical employees work for profit or non-profit corporations where they practice their often exotic and esoteric specialties ranging from oceanography to cryoscopy.

How can white-collar employees protect themselves from the arbitrary demands and orders of the organizations for which they work? The classic liberal answer is to trust in "the competitive force of the free market"; if an employee feels disadvantaged he can seek employment elsewhere. This is the same answer given to blue-collar workers when the courts disallowed child labor laws, wage arbitration, minimum wages, shorter hours for women, and safety legislation in coal mines and elsewhere. American industrial workers did not accept that answer because they knew that the market too often provided no viable alternative to their current jobs. At the present time, many white-collar workers are beginning to feel that coercive restrictions are being imposed upon them even as their market avenues of escape are being closed off; how they will react only time can tell.

Instances of the apparent coercion of white-collar workers are beginning to attract public attention as corporations sometimes sacrifice the interests of employees—even high ranking executives—to protect the image or reputation of the organization. Consider the case of J. M. Shea, Jr., a senior vice president and director of the American Petrofina Company, an oil company that operates a network of 500 gas stations in Dallas, Texas.

Shea wrote an article for a national magazine in 1964, deploring the fact that he and other businessmen had remained silent while Dallas "allowed the fanatic fringe to intimidate the whole town." [2] Even though moderation might not have prevented the assassination of President John F. Kennedy by a Marxist, he wrote afterward, it certainly would have dampened the raucous prelude and angry aftermath to the shooting. Shea's comments raised a furor in Dallas; a campaign urging customers to turn in their Petrofina credit cards was begun against his employer. Though the company's sales actually rose during the campaign, some of its service stations did lose customers because of it. The nervous company officials demanded, Shea announced, that he promise "never to comment publicly without formally clearing each word in advance and in writing. The issue was not *what* I said, but whether I could say anything at all." Shea submitted his resignation from the company, explaining "The company policy reached beyond

[2] J. M. Shea, Jr., "Memo From A Dallas Citizen," *Look,* March 24, 1964, p. 90.

business into personal belief. I would have been promising never to exercise the right and responsibility of a citizen." [3] Petrofina's management then withdrew the demand it had made upon Shea. He was told that since he had involved the company in an unfortunate episode, he would be asked to go away for a year on a company scholarship to the Harvard business school. Shea refused, insisting that the company was merely trying to disguise an imposition of censorship.

Other business executives viewed the matter differently. "I draw all my income from this company," said the operations boss of a competing oil firm. "I consider that part of my compensation covers the things I give up. It's part of my obligation not to do anything that might hurt the company." Though this is hardly a statement that a person actively concerned with civil liberties would be apt to applaud, it is at least a worldly and voluntary acceptance of self-censorship. But the oil executive moved to a more questionable position when he went on, "Anyway, that's how I justify expecting the same thing from the people who work for me. We have a sort of unwritten agreement that they clear with me." This man asked not to be identified, which is hardly surprising, since his subordinates might well have a very different conception of what their agreement was with him.

The conflict between the putative interests of the corporation and an individual's conscience was resolved by another Texas business executive:

> Shea's an adult, and he has to take the consequences of his actions. Nobody put him in jail for free speech, and the Constitution does not protect your job. As an officer, you can't separate yourself from the company, and the company has a right to protect itself if you embarrass it. Shea gave his company reason to doubt his judgment in situations he would confront some other time.[4]

To doubt an executive's judgment, this manager seems to say, is to raise a fundamental question about the one characteristic which distinguishes the able and competent business executive from citizens who are socially responsible.

One cannot deny that corporations have images that are worth something to protect; the issue is only what costs can justifiably be incurred for this purpose. Although jobs are not protected by the Constitution, neither are corporate images. Should corporations be permitted to preserve their investment in an image by depriving individuals of their investment in a job that carries with it respect and protection? When we consider job specialties that are in general demand, so that alternative jobs are available to the workers in a competitive market that appreciates talent and ability, the present law seems practically sufficient, even though the long-range implications of allowing easy censorship of citizens by employers are disturbing for a democracy. A more serious problem is raised when corporate penalties are imposed upon employees whose positions are high enough to concern image-conscious managers but not high enough to make it easy for them to find another job, or whose skills are otherwise so specialized that alternative employment is difficult to obtain.

The plight of the individual employee is real; on the other hand, the needs of the organization cannot be ignored. If consumers do not choose to patronize a firm whose employees advocate civil rights or denounce "fanatic minorities," the organization is hurt, and so are all the individuals that own it, belong to it as

[3] T. George Harris, "Memo About a Dallas Citizen," *Look,* August 11, 1964, p. 64.
[4] Harris, *op. cit.,* p. 47.

members, or work for it. In many situations where the interests of an organization and its individual members clash, the courts are called upon to find the balance between them. The court must begin by examining the nature of the relationship between the organization and each individual involved. This task is made more complicated to whatever degree the contract between employer and employee is implicit rather than explicit. Even the existence of a written, carefully constructed contract, is not a complete solution. In the dispute between Olga Zdanok and the Glidden Company, beginning on page 253, a written contract existed, but the parties read it differently, and both based their interpretations on legal principles.

Such contradictory claims arising under the terms of a particular contract between an employer and his employees often require that we turn to judges to establish priorities among the deadlocked principles. Determinations emerging from a particular case survive it, however, and often come by accretion to be law. Such law is judge-made, but it is law nonetheless. In a series of cases involving arbitration clauses in labor–management agreements, the Supreme Court has sought to reverse the development of legal rigidity in dealing with the employment relationship as defined by collective bargaining agreements. Speaking for the majority in the Warrior case, Justice Douglas argued that employers and employees need to resolve many of their disputes through voluntary arbitration proceedings that are not fettered by legal rules and established precedents.[5] His argument was based on two considerations. First, he recognized that judges often have great difficulty in smoking out the real issues in industrial disputes, especially since many of the cases they must consider are frivolous or trumped-up for bargaining purposes and brought before them mainly as a function of the internal politics of corporate and union leadership.[6] Second, Justice Douglas recognized that arbitrators perform functions that are not normal to the courts and even fashion judgments that "may indeed be foreign to the competence of the courts" but that are nonetheless exceedingly useful to the parties involved in a dispute.

In the Warrior case, Justice Douglas suggested that the freely established, voluntary process of settling disputes over the rights and interests of organizations and their employees is at "the very heart of industrial self government." For him, voluntary arbitration is "the means of solving the unforeseeable in a bargaining relationship by molding a system of private law." He described the arbitrator's great advantage over the judge in these cases as follows:

> The labor arbitrator's source of law is not confined to the express provisions of the contract, as the industrial common law—the practices of the industry and the shop—is equally a part of the collective bargaining agreement although not expressed in it. The labor arbitrator is usually chosen because of the parties' confidence in his knowledge of the common law of the shop and their trust in his personal agreement to bring to bear considerations which are not expressed in the contract as criteria

[5] United Steelworkers of America v. Warrior & Gulf Navigation Company, 363 U.S. 574 (1960); *cf.* also United Steelworkers of America v. American Manufacturing Company, 363 U.S. 564 (1960); United Steelworkers of America v. Enterprise Wheel and Car Corporation, 363 U.S. 593 (1960).

[6] For a description of these activities see J. W. Kuhn, *Bargaining in Grievance Settlement* (New York: Columbia University Press, 1961).

for judgment. The parties expect that his judgment of a particular grievance will reflect not only what the contract says but, insofar as the collective bargaining agreement permits, such factors as the effect upon productivity of a particular result, its consequence to morale of the shop, his judgment whether tensions will be heightened or diminished. For the parties' objective in using the arbitration process is primarily to further their common goal of uninterrupted production under the agreement to make the agreement serve their specialized needs. *The ablest judge cannot be expected to bring the same experience and competence to bear upon the determination of a grievance, because he cannot be similarly informed.*[7]

Justice Douglas in effect called for the formal recognition of a new system of industrial jurisprudence based on an *agreement;* he played down the *contractual* nature of collective bargaining, and stressed the point that clashing interests are better handled without recourse to the formal law of contracts. Unlike buyers and sellers in the stockmarket or many spouses in a divorce proceeding, the parties to a labor agreement must work together after a legal decision has been handed down. Therefore, it might perhaps be better for employees and employers to work out flexible, reasonable adjustments of their disputes through private, voluntary adjudication than through the legally binding, precedent-making decisions of an arm of government.

Should Justice Douglas' logic prevail, a new stage in a historical progression could result; having already moved from "status to contract," employers and employees may go on "from contract to agreement." Whether or not this step would be beneficial is not entirely clear. It would seem to extend the reach of democracy and practicality in the work place; both are in the American tradition. Certainly, choices in some instances have to be made between supporting a principle and pragmatically resolving a problem. However, Douglas' opinion does not specify what the operative criteria are for making such pragmatic choices or how one is to determine the hierarchy of principles and priorities among equity and efficiency, reasonableness and rightness, private law and public law, individual rights and organizational rights.

The roles of contractual principles and pragmatic flexibility in the relationship between industrial organizations and their individual members may be summarized as follows: If the rights of either party are to be protected, it is important that stable principles, based on established legal concepts, define the relationship of organizations and their constituents. Contract law, it would appear, may offer just the needed corpus of doctrine. On the other hand, however, regarding the relationship between organizations and their members as strictly contractual gives rise to a growing legalism that tends to create fixed rights and intractable positions, ill-suited to the need for flexibility and adaptability in meeting industrial change. Excessive legalism undoes much of the value of the historical shift from status to contract, for it causes the parties in a cooperative venture to be preoccupied with their own advantage rather than with solutions to common problems.

The four cases that follow are concerned both with the methods currently employed in resolving disputes between large industrial organizations and their individual members and with the justice of the solutions that are reached. The

[7] United Steelworkers of America v. Warrior & Gulf Navigation Company, *op. cit.* Italics added.

first pair of cases is especially concerned with discovering the meaning of "due process" as it applies to such disputes; the second pair stresses the seriousness and intractability of some of the conflicts that arise.

Due Process Within Corporations and Unions

NEWBERG OF CHRYSLER

Early in 1960 the Chrysler Corporation was an unhappy corporate family. Chrysler had been having financial difficulties, and its share of the car market had declined during the post-war period from 25 per cent to about 11 per cent in 1959. By 1960 many of the stockholders were dissatisfied enough to threaten a fight for a radical change in corporate leadership. Sol A. Dann, a Detroit lawyer who owned 5,100 shares of the company's stock and who had lost more than $150,000 because of its drop in value on the stock exchange, spearheaded the stockholders' revolt. Dann collected as much evidence as he could about the leadership at Chrysler and then charged it with mismanagement.

I

As part of his campaign, Dann wrote letters to management officials at Chrysler, fellow stockholders, and the Securities and Exchange Commission, and he visited Chrysler headquarters at Highland Park, Michigan. At the general stockholders' meeting in April, 1960, Dann charged management with nepotism, favoritism, misconduct, payola, bribery, reckless disregard for the rights of stockholders, perpetuating itself in office by block balloting, and producing $100 million losses along with "two-bit dividends." Chrysler's president, Lester ("Tex") Colbert, replied to these charges:

> In view of Mr. Dann's statements, I would like to tell this meeting that I do not own now, nor have I ever owned, any interests by way of stockholdings or otherwise in any of our vendors or suppliers of materials, and furthermore, no member of my family owns an interest by way of stockholdings or otherwise in any of our vendors or suppliers of materials.
>
> To the best of my knowledge, none of the officers of this company nor any member of their families owns any interest by way of stockholdings or otherwise in any of our vendors or suppliers of materials that is in any way improper.[1]

Before the meeting Colbert had instructed his top executives to sell immediately any stock they might have in Chrysler's suppliers.

At the time of the stockholders' meeting, William C. Newberg had been with Chrysler for 27 years. He had come to the company in 1933 and had followed Tex Colbert up the chain of command of the Dodge Division. Newberg was known as "Colbert's boy," yet he coveted Colbert's position for himself, and many people familiar with corporate politics had expected that Colbert would eventually yield the presidency to him. This happened just nine days after the stormy stockholders' session, for on April 28, 1960, Chrysler's board of directors met and placed Newberg in the presidency. The directors also appointed Colbert as chairman of the board, a position that had been open since K. T. Keller resigned in 1956. There were hints at the time that these new appointments might have been influenced by the activities of Dann and other disgruntled stockholders, but they were also thought to be the results of maneuvering by the ambitious Newberg.

President Newberg soon showed that he was concerned with Chrysler's high costs in purchasing, and he proposed a systematic

[1] *Fortune,* 62 (November, 1960), 135.

search for economies. Two weeks after assuming office he told his executives that the cost cutters would not "be tender about anyone's feelings and not . . . worry about long-established personal relationships among any members of the Chrysler management." Newberg did not stay in office long enough to do much cost cutting, however. On June 30, within nine weeks of his appointment, the board of directors fired him and reinstated Colbert as president. The company publicly explained this dismissal as a result of "differences of opinion on certain corporate policies."

II

Newberg's removal actually came about, at least in part, because of an investigation ordered by the Chrysler Corporation. With other stockholders, Sol Dann had continued to charge company officials with embarrassing, as well as detrimental, dereliction of responsibility. Letters sent to Chrysler's directors early in 1960 had claimed that various officials of the company were involved in conflict-of-interest situations. Deciding that they had better know the facts of the case, the directors asked the company's law firm of Kelley, Dyre, Newhall, and Maginnes to make a quiet investigation. The lawyers were assisted by the company's auditors, Touche, Ross, Bailey, and Smart. The investigators studied the records of companies in which Newberg had held an interest and other papers and documents that Newberg himself willingly supplied. They discovered a number of situations involving Newberg and several other officers among the 36 investigated that the board of directors found disconcerting and troubling.

The investigators reported that Jack Minor, Director of Marketing for the Plymouth-DeSoto-Valiant Division, was a Director of the Taxi-Ad Company, which placed ads for Chrysler products on the backs of taxicabs. The company had been organized in 1952, before Minor joined Chrysler, but since then Minor and his associates had made an annual profit of about $25,000 from that company's operations. Minor was also found to have an interest in two other related firms. On August 31, 1960, the board fired him, too. He protested his dismissal, arguing that Chrysler officials not only had known of his other activities but had approved of them.

Another discovery of the investigators was that in 1940, Chrysler's president, K. T. Keller, and his brother had organized the firm of National Automotive Fibres, Inc. (NAFI). Suppliers who wanted to sell parts or materials to Chrysler were told to submit their bids to NAFI, which purchased the goods, shipped them directly to Chrysler plants, and collected a 5 per cent commission. The investigators concluded that as a result of this practice Chrysler was forced to purchase inferior parts and materials and was pressured to acquire automotive fabrics from NAFI, thus excluding other potential suppliers.

Several parallel situations involving other officers came to light. Robert T. Keller, a Chrysler vice president and K. T.'s son, assumed control in 1955 of Therm-Rite, a company in which other Chrysler executives had interests. Chrysler purchased welding gas from Therm-Rite at a cost greatly in excess of the market price, and other Chrysler suppliers were induced to do business with Therm-Rite. Rinehart S. Bright, a Chrysler vice president, seemed to have "induced" a man named Harry D. Hirsch to buy control of C. M. Hall Lamp Company, a manufacturer of auto headlights, in 1957. Shortly thereafter, Hall Lamp became the exclusive supplier of headlights for Chrysler and, in return, Hirsch gave Bright and his family 13,000 shares of Hall Lamp stock. Paul C. Ackerman, another vice president, was found to have acquired an interest in a company that provided sample auto bodies; there was evidence that he had used his position to channel business to this company and that he had accepted gratuities from a company that had used his influence to secure a contract with Chrysler.

As for William Newberg in particular, the investigators concentrated their attention on two areas of his activities. In the first, Newberg and vice president R. P. Laughna had apparently reallocated Chrysler's contracts with haul-away companies. The two men allegedly awarded the contract for hauling new cars to the Great Lakes Forwarding Company, owned by a close friend and neighbor of Newberg. The investigators found further that the company that had previously handled a large portion of Chrysler's haul-away business, the Metropolitan Convey Corporation, was eventually forced to sell its equipment to Great Lakes at distress prices.

A second special situation involved Newberg and his partner-neighbor, Ben Stone. In a suit brought by Chrysler, the two men were charged with having taken unfair advantage of Newberg's position and influence. Stone and Newberg were said to have set up a new firm, Press Products, Inc., with Newberg taking half the stock and Stone and his wife the other half. The firm produced automotive parts, including door hinges, deck lid (trunk) hinges, and hood hinges. Press Products supposedly was able to secure orders from Chrysler, its only customer, through the influence and assistance of Newberg. After selling Press Products in 1955, the Stones and Newberg were said to have organized the Bonan Company, which manufactured door trim panels for Chrysler and supplied no other customers. The company was sold to Allen Industries in 1958 and was renamed the Sango Company. In June, 1959, Newberg agreed to sell his stock in Sango to the Stones for an undisclosed price.

III

After studying the investigators' report, the directors issued a statement on July 31, 1960, charging that Newberg had violated his trust to Chrysler:

> In his capacity as an officer and director of Chrysler and as an officer and employee of the Dodge Division, said William C. Newberg occupied the position of a fiduciary with respect to Chrysler and its shareholders and at all times owed Chrysler the fiduciary obligations and responsibilities attendant upon his various positions including, among others, the duty of undivided loyalty to Chrysler.[2]

The board's statement also noted that "Chrysler will receive from Mr. Newberg profits in excess of $450,000 made by him from interests in vendor companies."

On August 18, 1960, Chrysler announced the appointment of the law firm of Dewey, Ballantine, Bushby, Palmer, and Wood to review the work of the investigators. The highly respected law firm was headed by Thomas E. Dewey, a former governor of New York and twice candidate for President of the United States. The review was to determine the adequacy, scope, and extent of the previous investigation conducted by Chrysler's own law firm. To supervise the review by the Dewey firm, a four-man committee chosen from the non-management directors of the company was appointed. The board of directors made public in October, 1960, both the report of the first investigation by the Kelley firm and the Dewey firm's report. Despite the questionable outside investments and activities of some of the company's executives, neither report found any wrong-doing or illegality. Neither report unequivocably charged that "conflict-of-interest" had been involved, since the investigators could not define the term clearly. The Dewey report confirmed the Kelley findings:

> There is no evidence and no reason to believe that any of the executives, members of their families, or close relatives at any time during the past ten years owned stock interest in Chrysler suppliers of a nature or under circumstances conflicting with their duties to the interests of the Corporation.[3]

[2] *Ibid.*, p. 135.
[3] *Ibid.*, p. 133.

Whether this clearance covered the officers recently dismissed as well as the then-current officers was not clear. Bright, Ackerman, and Laughna were still holding office, however. The Dewey report went on to explain that while some Chrysler executives did hold stock in supplier companies, the reviewers were unable to assert that mere ownership of stock in a supplier was, in itself, a conflict of interest.

> The size and the nature of the holding, the circumstances under which it was acquired, whether it was known and allowed by Chrysler, the amount of business done between the supplier and Chrysler, and other considerations ought to be taken into account.[4]

Though Mr. Newberg seemed to have been exonerated by the investigating firms, and though other executives who had invested in supplying firms retained their positions with the corporation, he was not reinstated.

[4] *Ibid.*, p. 287.

THE IAM SHOP STEWARDS

In October, 1956, A. J. Hayes, the president of the International Association of Machinists, appointed P. L. Siemiller, his general vice president, administrator of the 2,600-member Tool and Die Makers Lodge 113 in Chicago, Illinois. Later he expelled two active members from this local and suspended the right of a third to hold office for a year. Union officials said that the reason for these actions was dissension among the members of the lodge. According to sources in the Chicago local, the three men disciplined had been active in a reform group that wanted to investigate the financial "hanky-panky" of the local president.[1]

I

Marion Ciepley and Irwin Rappaport, the two men expelled from the IAM by Hayes, were long-standing members of Lodge 113; Rappaport had joined in 1951 and Ciepley in 1941. Both men had been in the tool and die business for over 20 years and earned top wages—Ciepley $3.30 an hour as a tool and die maker, and Rappaport $3.25 an hour as a toolroom machinist. Both men were shop stewards, Rappaport at Sunbeam and Ciepley at Hotpoint; both were active in their union and regularly attended union meetings.

In 1955, a reform group in Lodge 113 led by Ciepley and Rappaport had charged that the financial affairs of the local were not being properly conducted. The group accused local union officials of raising their own salaries without the authorization of the local members; they also charged that the books of the lodge had not been properly audited and that funds were being mismanaged. In reply, some of the lodge members accused Ciepley and Rappaport of being "Reds" out to make trouble for American unionism. Actually, the two men were members of the Socialist Party–Social Democratic Federation; they were self-educated radicals, and no ties to the Communists were ever found. (When the House Un-American Activities Committee came to Chicago in May, 1959, to investigate Communists in unions, this defense of the union officers' fiscal integrity was heard again; as the Chicago *Tribune* put it, the IAM wished to give its full cooperation to the Committee because for some time it had been "fighting an expensive and bitter battle with left-wing elements trying to take over locals representing tool and die makers.")

The reform group's charges of financial

[1] Paul Jacobs, "Mr. Hayes Settles a Local Disturbance," *Reporter* (April 2, 1959), pp. 18–21; and Robert Repas, *A Tale of Two Expulsions* (New York: privately printed, 1961).

mismanagement brought a request from the lodge officers for an examination by an auditor from IAM headquarters. His report to the membership, delivered June 8, 1956, upheld most of the charges made by the reformers. Dues stamps had been mishandled, the financial secretary was keeping thousands of dollars of lodge funds in his personal bank account, and no proper accounting had ever been made of strike funds collected during 1955–56. The auditor recommended bookkeeping changes and said: "If the officers involved with bookkeeping do not follow through with this, I would think it time for the lodge to consider making some changes in officers at your next election."

The reformers spread word of the auditor's findings by distributing handbills among the members. Shortly thereafter the reform group was able to secure the two-thirds vote necessary to make a number of changes in the bylaws. Believing that the reformers would win the next election of local officers, the lodge's business agents resigned, and most took managerial positions with private companies.

II

As a result of the resignations in Lodge 113, President Hayes suspended the lodge's charter on October 22 and appointed Siemiller to act as administrator. The lodge's bylaws were also suspended and the election of new officers was postponed indefinitely.

Siemiller's first act was to prohibit all partisan publications and all caucus meetings. He felt that union members should keep their troubles behind closed doors and that whatever problems existed were of concern to the union alone. Hayes had made his views clear earlier when he wrote to Rappaport:

> I am convinced beyond any doubt that the handbills distributed by the so-called "Committee to Save Lodge 113" certainly are not serving the best interests of this organization. I have already received reports that these handbills which advertise a controversy within our organization have fallen into the hands of employers and other labor unions in the Chicago area. I want you and all others to know that whoever is responsible for the publication and distribution of these handbills certainly is violating one of the basic concepts of trade unionism and one of the fundamental policies of our organization.

Rappaport replied to Hayes:

> As far as I know no "basic concepts of trade unionism" have been violated either by me or my friends. We are merely concerned with exercising our fundamental democratic right to freedom of speech and of the press in order to acquaint our union brothers with the serious situation confronting our Local Lodge.

In March, 1957, Siemiller drafted new bylaws to replace the suspended set enacted by the reformers. They were designed to put a damper on internal factional fights; they increased the term of office of the business agents from one to four years, outlawed the right of members to circulate petitions relating to union business without prior approval of the IAM executive board of the lodge, and in a new provision required that the "business" handled in shop meetings be confined to matters affecting the shop involved and not include any item that was properly a lodge matter.

In an initial vote the new bylaws were defeated two to one. After some minor changes Siemiller put them up for a vote again. He suggested that unless they were approved, the trusteeship would not be lifted; if they were approved, the suspension of the lodge charter would be lifted within 30 days. The members were persuaded to accept the changes, which then went into effect in mid-December, 1957. Hayes did not remove the lodge from trusteeship within the specified period, however.

In February, 1958, Lodge 113 was allowed to elect its officers, giving some hope to members that Hayes would lift the suspension before long. Ciepley ran for president and Rappaport for business representative. Siemiller helped organize another group of candidates under the name of the "All-American Slate." Sixty per cent of the membership voted, electing 11 All-American candidates and 9 reformers to the 20 positions open. Rappaport was defeated by a vote of 793 to 727, but it appeared that Ciepley had been elected by a vote of 765 to 763. At this juncture, the administrator ordered a recount. Siemiller ordered two absentee ballots to be counted which he said had been received at the Lodge office in time but had not been delivered to the tellers. Two more ballots were found in one of the ballot boxes used for a separate but simultaneous vote of the Grand Lodge (the international union). All four votes went for Ciepley's opponent. The retally thus showed that Ciepley was defeated by 767 to 765. Ciepley appealed the recount to Hayes but was denied.

After the election and the acceptance of the new bylaws, dissension and arguments continued in Lodge 113. Hayes, still dissatisfied with the situation, decided he had no choice but to suspend all regular meetings. Since the members could no longer formally meet, they could not secure a vote to request a lifting of the suspension. The reformers decided to try another tack; they circulated a petition asking the IAM Executive Council to remove the administrator and to give back to the Lodge its full powers. The petition received 900 signatures, one-third of the membership employed in shops under contract. On October 27, 1959, five days before the reformers filed the petition at the international's offices, Siemiller gave notice to Rappaport that he had seven days to show why he should not be removed as a shop steward at Sunbeam. Several days later Siemiller notified Ciepley that he, too, was to be removed from his position as steward at Hotpoint. The charge against both was the same:

> You . . . are causing a petition to be circulated for signature among the membership. . . . You . . . did knowingly and willfully violate this section of the By-Laws (Article IV, Section 3) by causing such petition to be circulated and advocating the membership to become signatories to this petition.

Both denied the charges, but they were suspended from the union. Furthermore, Ciepley was fired by Hotpoint; since he no longer enjoyed the superseniority of a steward, management was free to lay him off when work slowed down. He was not rehired.

III

New and different charges against Rappaport and Ciepley were now brought by the International. At the Illinois convention of the AFL–CIO in October, 1958, Ciepley and Rappaport had introduced a resolution calling for the establishment of public review boards and the limiting of local trusteeships to six months. Lodge 113's president protested the resolution, and later Rappaport and Ciepley were involved in an altercation with an IAM special representative, whom they denounced as a "slugger and a thug." They then asked the convention also to take a stand against physical violence, but the request was ignored.

After the convention George Christenson, an attorney employed by the Machinists, charged Rappaport and Ciepley with disregard of union rules and procedures. Under the new bylaws that Siemiller had persuaded the Lodge to accept

> any member . . . found guilty of causing any petition related to Union business to be circulated among the membership, except petitions for a Special Meeting of the Lodge, without the express approval of the Executive Board or the Lodge in prior session, or any member found guilty of conveying unauthorized Union information to the management of any shop or circulating printed or written material detrimental to the best interests of the IAM shall be subject to fine

or expulsion or both as may be determined by the Lodge.

To avoid a trial by Lodge 113, Hayes appointed a special trial committee of three Grand Lodge officials to hear the case. This was not the normal procedure for handling charges of this nature. Usually such a case would be brought before a committee of lodge members, which would report its findings back to the full membership, which would decide what punishment, if any, to levy. However, the IAM constitution gave the International president the right to appoint a special trial committee, which could report directly to him and whose verdict he could accept or reject. Under the terms of this special procedure, the defendants could appeal Hayes' decision to the union's executive council; the council's decision could then be appealed to the Appeals and Grievance Committee of the convention of the Grand Lodge, held every four years. The executive committee appoints members of the Appeals Committee, and the men whose cases are being heard are not allowed to be present at the hearings.

The trial committee heard the charges, and on February 4, 1959, made to Hayes recommendations that he never revealed. Hayes told Ciepley and Rappaport that he was "rejecting and striking from the record . . . the Trial Committee's Report and Recommendations, and in my determination of these matters, I shall consider for purposes of my decision, the transcripts, exhibits and evidence produced at . . . [the] trial." He thus ignored the findings of his own trial committee, apparently because they did not suit the judgment he had already reached about the two stewards. Hayes found both guilty on all counts and ordered their expulsion from the union. In March the two men appealed the decision to the Executive Council but were rejected. At the next convention of the Grand Lodge in September, 1960, they took their case to the Appeals and Grievance Committee but to no avail.

During the long wait for their appeal to be processed Ciepley and Rappaport were kept out of the union and were classed as expelled members. Ciepley permanently lost his job at Hotpoint after a layoff; furthermore, he claimed that he had been fired from new jobs because the lodge administrator advised the companies' personnel directors not to keep him. The union denied this charge. The employers for whom Ciepley worked after he lost his Hotpoint job said that the lodge administrator had called them to report on his background but "had not necessarily recommended firing him."

Rappaport continued on his job at Sunbeam, protected by the Taft-Hartley law. When the union went on strike in March, 1961, Rappaport went out too. The union lost the strike, and the company refused to rehire Rappaport, arguing in a case before the NLRB that he had disrupted Lodge 113. Apparently the company was as pleased as the union to see the fighting shop steward go.

QUESTIONS

Due Process Within Corporations and Unions

1. What reasons are there, if any, to argue that protection against arbitrary treatment of members by officers is more desirable in unions than in business corporations? Is it more important to protect business managers against arbitrary treatment by stockholders than to protect union leaders against arbitrary treatment by union members?

2. Will more protection of individuals in large organizations tend mainly to encourage lax work and incompetence or will it encourage independence of thought, frankness, and responsible action? Upon what do you base your answer?

3. "Newberg was the fall guy, sure! But they had to have a scapegoat for all their sins. It's tough, but that's the game, and he was around long enough to know it." This comment was offered by a long-time employee of Chrysler; from what you know of the situation at Chrysler and of business practices in general, why do you agree or disagree?

4. "Look, if a bank teller was seen around race tracks every weekend, do you think he'd keep his job long? Hayes had his union's reputation to look out for; those guys [Ciepley and Rappaport] were hurting the whole union, so I don't blame him." This is the comment of a business agent in a building trades union on the struggle within Lodge 113. Explain why you agree or disagree with this evaluation.

5. Write a short definition of "conflict of interest" that would apply both to managers in a large manufacturing corporation and to officers of a large union. Make explicit why the conflict exists and why it must be avoided.

6. What responsibility did the Chrysler board of directors have before, during, and after the Newberg incident? How well did they fulfill it before and during the incident?

7. Did Newberg and the shop stewards receive the protection of "due process" in their respective ordeals? Define "due process" as you would apply it in non-governmental organizations and then note what, if any, procedures were lacking in the handling of the Newberg and the shop steward cases.

Status, Contract, and Beyond

ZDANOK v. GLIDDEN

Early in 1957 the board of directors of the Glidden Company decided that the Durkee Famous Foods Division should discontinue operations at its Elmhurst plant near New York City and establish a new plant at Bethlehem, Pennsylvania. The company had operated a plant at Elmhurst, New York, since 1929, manufacturing among other things coconut products, spices, and condiments. The company leased the plant at Bethlehem on May 6, 1957, and notified its Elmhurst employees 10 days later that operations would be discontinued within several months.

I

Though the notification was unwelcome, it did not come as a surprise to the plant workers. In 1953, the Glidden management had begun a review of its operations, examining them for possible improvements to increase profitability. It found that the Elmhurst plant was a marginal contributor to the company; the building was an old four-story and basement structure that required an inefficient work flow, and the equipment in it was also old and outdated. A further consideration was that the Elmhurst location forced Glidden to pay certain freight penalties on vegetable oils shipped to and from the plant. The managers decided to move the operations.

As the first stage of the planned shift, in October, 1956, Glidden transferred all vegetable-oil refining operations from Elmhurst to its large vegetable-oil refinery in Louisville, Kentucky. Of the 40 employees laid off, plant-wide seniority allowed 30 of them to be rehired almost immediately. They transferred to other departments and bumped less senior workers to lower jobs. Ten of the 40 did lose their jobs, however, and, as the vice president in charge of personnel, Mr. Weeks, was later to testify, the union made no claims at the time for severance pay, nor did it argue that the displaced workers were entitled to transfer to Louisville.

During the earlier 1955 bargaining session Weeks had told Mr. Crotty, the representative of General Warehousemen's Union, Local 852, International Brotherhood of Teamsters, that the plant might be closed; he advised the union "that the continuing increase in labor costs at Elmhurst threatened the continuance of that operation." The union's response to this was to add severance pay to its wage proposal, but the company refused to grant it. According to Mr. Groves, assistant to Glidden's vice president for personnel, Crotty had recognized the possibility of a shutdown of the Elmhurst plant even earlier, telling him in 1953 that the union intended to "get it while the getting was good." In March, 1957, as soon as the workers and local union leaders heard about the Board's decision to close down the Elmhurst plant, Crotty approached Weeks to discuss the problems that a shutdown would cause for the workers. He mentioned specifically employment opportunities and severance pay.

At a meeting in June, shortly after the company had officially notified the workers of the closing, Crotty "wanted to know," Weeks reported, if Glidden "wouldn't give some kind of seniority" at Bethlehem. Weeks replied that the company could not allow Elmhurst employees to transfer their seniority to the new Bethlehem plant. The workers there might organize another union (as they did, choosing the United Steel Workers union), and the company would be bound to bargain with that union on the kind and application of work rules. Under law the choice of a union is the workers' prerogative, and theirs only; thus the company did not want to appear to influence this selection by transferring to the new installation a large bloc of workers belonging to one particular union. Important in the managers' thinking was the experience they had already had with moving employees from one location to another. Some time earlier they had transferred several salaried employees from a large city into the Pennsylvania Dutch country, only to find that after several months the employees resigned to return to their original homes.

II

The union rejected the company's arguments, and on July 9, 1957, formally requested in a letter "that the Company enter into negotiations pertaining to a severance pay allowance for these employees and [to a demand that] the Company . . . give these employees first option on employment at its new plant in Pennsylvania." The union pointed out that it had the legal right "to insist upon negotiations with respect to severance pay." In early August, union and management representatives met again to discuss the problems of closing. According to Weeks, he refused to grant severance pay after the union men had asked for it. He added that the union counsel

> also brought up this question of seniority and requested we grant some seniority or preference to employees who might go to Bethlehem. He did not indicate there was any claim under the contract; in fact, he said there wasn't, as Mr. Crotty also told me that there was nothing under the contract that would require us to do it, but he thought we ought to give some consideration to the people who went to Bethlehem.[1]

At a still later meeting attended by Weeks' assistant, a union representative stated

> that they had been advised by their counsel that they had no right to employment opportunities at Bethlehem or to severance pay but they wished the company to negotiate on these provisions. . . .

The union's counsel had not participated in the negotiations of 1955 when the agreement was drawn up, nor had he taken any

[1] This and following quotes have been taken from briefs of the parties and other court documents.

part in those of 1953. There was no evidence presented in court that he had particular knowledge of the background of the labor agreement.

On September 16, 1957, the company gave written notice to the union that it would terminate the collective bargaining agreement at its expiration date, November 30, 1957. The terms of the agreement stated that it would be automatically renewed unless either party gave 60 days' notice of termination. On a number of occasions the two parties had not completed negotiations by expiration time, and the old agreement continued in force. The first agreement, for example, was signed January 6, 1951, but it was effective from December 1, 1950, continuing for two years. The last negotiations were completed March 13, 1956, but covered the period from December 1, 1955, to November 30, 1957.

When notified of the company's desire to terminate the agreement, the union asked that the 250 workers it represented at Elmhurst be offered jobs at Bethlehem. The company officials refused the request, and the union then turned to the New York State Board of Mediation, asking it to arbitrate "the refusal of the company to offer its present employees employment at its new plant." Glidden declined to consent to arbitration, arguing "that transfer of the employees was not within the specific terms of the agreement and hence was not arbitrable." The company noted further that it had never simply refused to offer its Elmhurst employees work at Bethlehem; it would give fair consideration to any such application. Glidden did not offer to receive applications for Bethlehem jobs at Elmhurst, however; workers wanting employment at Bethlehem would have to apply in that city.

III

After its notice to the union that it was closing the Elmhurst plant, Glidden began to reduce production there and to move some of its machinery and equipment to the new plant in Bethlehem. The move continued throughout October, November, and December. About 75 per cent of the machinery used in the coconut processing and packaging operations was taken to the Bethlehem plant, and approximately 25 per cent of the machinery used in various grinding, filling, and packaging operations was moved.

Newly hired employees at the Bethlehem plant performed duties similar to those that had been carried out at the Elmhurst plant. However, the company had installed a considerable number of new machines in addition to the ones moved from Elmhurst, for the new plant was considerably more modern and efficient than the old. Many of the duties performed by certain categories of workers at Elmhurst were incorporated into other and sometimes new job classifications, but none of the new jobs required new skills that would have been difficult for any of the old employees to have acquired quickly.

As production closed down at Elmhurst, employees were laid off, in order of seniority wherever possible. The personnel office offered to help those laid off find other work in the metropolitan New York area. Some 120 job openings at comparable wage rates and appropriate skill levels were found for which workers could apply. The company also brought in representatives of the New York State Employment Service to conduct placement interviews, and it gave employees reasonable time off to look for jobs on their own. It also attempted to sell the plant to other food processors, so that employees might continue to work at that location, but apparently no buyer was found. Every employee received vacation pay even though he might have quit before his turn for layoffs arrived or even if he had not worked the 125 days required for drawing vacation pay. Some 69 employees were eligible for vested rights under the Pension Plan and were assured that the benefits of over $300,000 to which they were entitled would not be jeopardized.

Two workers applied for jobs at Bethlehem and were accepted. Only one of them actually went to work there, however, and he did not receive any credit for seniority accrued at the Elmhurst plant. New jobs were not readily available for all the laid-off workers, of course, and without severance pay some faced a difficult situation. Many of them were too old for other companies to accept as new employees.

IV

Unable to get any satisfaction from the company in the handling of seniority claims, the officials of Local 852 decided to proceed with arbitration. On October 23, 1957, they served notice on the company that pursuant to section 1458-a of the New York Civil Practice Act and the terms of their collective bargaining agreement they would ask an arbitrator to decide

> whether the collective bargaining agreement is being breached by the employer in the removal of its plant from the City of New York and by failing to offer each employee continued employment with full seniority.

Glidden moved in the Supreme Court of New York, Queens County,[2] to stay arbitration upon the ground that the disputes were not arbitrable under the agreement, the relevant provision of which read:

> Any question, grievance or dispute arising out of and involving the interpretation and application of the specific terms of this Agreement . . . shall, at the request of either party, be referred to the New York State Mediation Board of Arbitration.

[2] The company took its case to the state court to stop the union's appeal to arbitration. The later court actions were those initiated in the federal courts by a number of the workers. The New York Supreme Court did not participate, of course, in any of the federal court decisions, since it is a state court.

The court granted the company's motion, ruling that the issues tendered for arbitration did not "arise out of the specific terms" of the agreement. In the supporting opinion the court stated:

> In the case at bar the Union has not been able to point to any specific term or provision in the collective bargaining agreement in question or by reference to the welfare, pension and group insurance plans which are part of this record, requiring Glidden to continue operations at Elmhurst or to continue the employment of any employee for any period of time, certainly not beyond the expiration date of the agreement, or to offer to each employee employment with full seniority after the discontinuance of such operations, or as an alternative severance pay, or in any way dealing with alleged property rights for employees whose employment has been terminated by Glidden's discontinuance in good faith of its operations at Elmhurst. . . .
>
> [N]o provision was made in the collective bargaining agreement relating to the continuance or discontinuance of operations at Elmhurst; for the continuance of employment of the employees covered by the said agreement for any period of time other than the expiration date thereof, nor requiring the company to offer to each employee continued employment with full seniority in the event of discontinuance. It cannot, therefore, be said that the disputes the Union claims to have with Glidden are referable to arbitration under a clause which requires arbitration only with respect to *"specific terms"* of a collective bargaining agreement. . . .
>
> It follows that Glidden's motion to stay arbitration must be granted, whatever other remedies the Union may have with respect to the alleged disputes.[3]

V

Since the union had not been able to protect the workers' claims through arbitration, the workers decided to sue for relief in the

[3] Matter of General Warehousemen's Union, 1958, 172 N.Y.S. 2d, 678; 682; 683–84.

federal district court.[4] Five of the more senior Elmhurst workers—Olga Zdanok, John Zacharezyk, Mary A. Hackett (who died the next year), Quitman Williams, and Marcelle Kreischer—brought suit against Glidden for ignoring employment rights that, they argued, survived the terminated agreement. Their ages ranged from 43 to 61 years, and their length of service with Glidden at Elmhurst from 10 to 25 years. They conceded that the agreement governing employment relationships at the Elmhurst plant had been terminated on November 30, 1957, and that the company had fully complied with all statutory and contractual requirements. They also declined to challenge the company's right to close the Elmhurst plant and to open a new one in Bethlehem or to impugn its good faith in actually doing so. The sole issue raised was the scope and significance of the seniority provisions of the agreement.

The workers maintained that an implied condition of the bargain between the union and the company was that the seniority rights created by the agreement would survive the termination date. When the ambiguities and gaps in the agreement were studied in the context of the long-term employment relationship existing between the parties, they argued, the survival of seniority rights emerged as an implied part of the bargain. They asked only that the agreement be applied in a manner consistent with the intent of the parties in a situation for which no specific provision was made. To meet the continuing obligations imposed by the surviving seniority provisions, they contended, the company was required to offer the workers employment at Bethlehem of the kind their seniority status would have given them at Elmhurst. The failure of the company to make such an offer deprived the workers not only of their right to continued employment but also of their interest in fringe benefits arising from their pensions,[5] group life insurance,[6] and welfare plan.[7]

Glidden argued that no one could reasonably find in the terms of the agreement or in the prior relationship of the parties any implied understanding that seniority rights could survive the agreement. Rather, seniority ratings acquired at Elmhurst and the benefits secured by them derived from, and depended upon, an agreement expressly confined in scope and application to terms and conditions of employment at the plant at Elmhurst. Therefore, upon cessation of operations and lawful termination of the agreement the workers' seniority rights ceased to exist along with employment. In short, the company maintained that since

[4] Suits for breach of contract may be brought under Section 301 of the Labor–Management (Taft-Hartley) Act of 1947.

[5] Pursuant to the terms of the contract, the employees were entitled to benefits under the Retirement Plan for Hourly Employees so long as they complied with the necessary conditions of the Plan. The Plan provided for benefits to be paid employees retiring at age 65 and to employees who reached 55 years of age while still employed, had 15 years of credited service, and were retired as totally and permanently disabled. Vested rights to retirement benefits at age 65 were acquired after the employee reached age 45 and had 15 years of credited service with the company. The Plan covered regular hourly employees at the various plants throughout the United States where it was in effect.

[6] There was no reference in the contract to the company's Group Life Insurance Plan. However, on a voluntary basis, the company made its employees in the Elmhurst plant eligible under the plan after six consecutive months of employment. Insurance coverage was continued for 31 days after the employee's termination of employment.

[7] Under the contract the company was required to pay 4.5¢ an hour per employee or a maximum of $1.80 per employee per week into the Union Welfare Fund during the term of the contract. This requirement was amended December 1, 1956, so that the company was required to pay 8.55¢ per hour per employee or a maximum of $3.42 per employee per week for the remainder of the term of the contract. The company had no control or responsibility for the administration of the Union Welfare Plan other than to make the payments.

the two parties never bargained for transferable seniority rights, the implication that such rights were designed to outlive the life of the plant and the agreement was without foundation.

District Judge Palmieri heard the arguments in the first case in 1960 and found for the defendant company.[8] His opinion included the following analysis:

> Under the seniority system in effect at Elmhurst, employees were to be laid off in reverse order of plant seniority and recalled in inverse order of layoff. In instances of continuous layoff, the seniority of an employee with less than five years' employment was to terminate after two years' continuous layoff; for employees with more than five years' service seniority was to be terminated at the end of three years. If seniority had been terminated by reason of continuous layoff, a former employee would still be entitled to preference before new employees were hired.[9] Plaintiffs [the workers] point out that their employment was terminated by defendant [the company] shortly before the expiration date of the contract. Therefore, they assert that their rights to three-year retention of seniority and indefinite preferential rehiring had accrued while the contract was fully effective. In other words, plaintiffs view the termination of their employment as a layoff due to curtailment of production and claim that their accrued three-year seniority retention rights entitled them to resume work when operations commenced in Bethlehem.
>
> Whether the agreement should be understood to assure to plaintiffs retained seniority rights had operations continued at Elmhurst after the collective bargaining agreement expired would present a troublesome question of construction. . . . However, it is unnecessary to determine whether plaintiffs are correct in asserting that the expired agreement continued to afford recall rights to employees or whether, as defendant urges, all recall rights terminated when the period of agreement came to an end. For the critical issue is not whether plaintiffs' seniority retention rights accrued during the effective period of the collective bargaining agreement and survived its termination, but whether the unit to which their rights could attach extended beyond the Elmhurst plant. It is not enough for plaintiffs to establish that if Elmhurst operations had continued, their seniority status would have survived termination of the collective bargaining agreement. In order to recover, plaintiffs must also show that the governing seniority system gave them the right to "follow their work" to the new plant.
>
> I find nothing in the record to warrant the conclusion urged by plaintiffs as to the unlimited geographic scope of their seniority rights. Wide variations exist in seniority systems used in industry . . . . With respect to the unit covered, an entire multi-plant company or district may be made subject to the same system, or the system may be limited to a particular plant, department or occupation. Under the circumstances presented here—the situation of the contracting parties,[10] their description of the subject of their

[8] 185 F. Supp. 441; 446–49.

[9] The seniority system outlined in the text had been in effect continuously since December 1, 1949, the effective date of the first collective bargaining agreement between the Glidden Company and Local 852. The relevant seniority provisions of the agreement between Local 852 and Glidden were as follows:

6A. Seniority shall be terminated for the following reasons:
- (1) An employee quits voluntarily
- (2) An employee is discharged for cause
- (3) An employee fails to acknowledge within two days a notice to report for work
- (4) An employee fails to return to work within three days after being notified to report to work.

B. In instances of continuous layoff, seniority shall be terminated after:
- (1) An employee with less than five years' continuous employment at the time his layoff began is on a continuous layoff of two years; or
- (2) An employee with more than five years' continuous employment at the time his layoff began is on a continuous layoff for three years.

C. Employees whose seniority is terminated due to continuous layoffs shall receive first preference for employment before new employees are hired.

[10] At the hearing, plaintiffs' counsel conceded that even if all the 160-odd employees at the

agreement[11] and the absence of any prior history as to transferred seniority rights—I have concluded that the parties' bargain and understanding were limited to seniority rights at the Elmhurst plant.

The agreement between Glidden and Local 852 refers to plant and department seniority but no reference is made to the extension of the unit contingent upon events such as plant abandonment, transfer, merger or consolidation of operations. However, agreements containing provisions for extension of the area in which seniority rights may be exercised are not uncommon. Since such provisions are tailored to meet the needs of particular enterprises, they vary considerably in form and content. For example, they may be limited to a specific time period, to new plants only, or to employees laid off as a result of total plant closing. In view of the alternative techniques which might be employed to deal with the issue of interplant seniority, it would be unreasonable to expect a court to imply a general understanding between the parties as to the extent of the seniority unit when no evidence has been offered as to negotiations on the subject or an established course of practice on the part of the employer.

Contrary to plaintiffs' contention, the collective bargaining agreement does not become illusory if its provisions are held to relate to a single existing plant. This is not the case of an employer who has abandoned the specified plant and transferred operations to a new location in order to circumvent contractual or statutory requirements. Where, as here, the Board of Directors' decision to relocate is based on an exercise of business judgment in good faith, the employer's obligation to deal fairly and honestly with its employees is satisfied.[12] In sum, under the circumstances presented in this case, where no relevant limitation on the employer's freedom of action is found in the agreement or the prior conduct of the parties, no policy of New York law or our national labor laws requires the employer to preserve for its employees seniority status acquired under an expired agreement covering a closed plant.

Accordingly, it is my conclusion that plaintiffs have failed to prove facts which would entitle them to the relief sought.

VI

Having lost before the district court, the workers took their case to the Second Circuit Court of Appeals. Here they received a more favorable hearing. Judge Madden, writing for the majority, delivered the opinion:

> The defendant [Glidden] . . . contends that because the collective bargaining agreement contained provisions for the arbitration of disputes, the plaintiffs [workers] are not entitled to individually enforce their rights under the agreement. In the instant case, as we have seen, the Supreme Court of New York has held that the dispute with which this suit is concerned is not covered by the arbitration provision of the agreement. The plaintiffs have not, therefore, entrusted to their union representative the rights which they now seek to enforce.
>
> As to the merits of the plaintiffs' claims,

Elmhurst plant had accepted employment at Bethlehem, Local 852 could not continue as accredited bargaining representative.

[11] The agreement is entitled: "Agreement between Durkee Famous Foods, Division of the Glidden Company, No. 23—Elmhurst, New York, and General Warehousemen's Union, Local 852 of the International Brotherhood of Teamsters, Chauffeurs, and Warehousemen. December 1, 1955 to November 30, 1957.

Its preamble reads: "This Agreement Made and Entered into at New York, New York, by and between the Glidden Company, Durkee Famous Foods Division, for and on behalf of its plant facilities located at Corona Avenue and 94th Street, Elmhurst, Long Island, New York, hereinafter referred to as "the company," and General Warehousemen's Union, Local 852 affiliated with The International Brotherhood of Teamsters, Chauffeurs, Warehousemen and Helpers of America, AFL–CIO, hereinafter referred to as "the union."

[12] In urging that they had been deprived of rights under the Retirement Plan, Group Life Insurance Plan, and Union Welfare Plan, the workers did not rely upon any provision contained in special agreements setting up the plans. Rather, they asserted that they had been deprived of rights under each of the plans by reason of the company's alleged breach of seniority provisions of the agreement.

the defendant takes the bold position that the collective bargaining contract conferred upon the employees no rights which survived the contract. It says . . . :

> Even if the Elmhurst operations had continued but the collective bargaining agreement had expired, the seniority status of plaintiffs would not have survived the termination of that agreement. For it is only by reason of existing provisions in the agreement that provisions relating to the seniority have any application. When such provisions no longer exist, seniority no longer exists.

The defendant may have assumed this bold and uncompromising position because it feels uneasy about Judge Palmieri's having based his decision solely upon the geographical shift of the plaintiff's factory operations. We discuss that problem later herein.

We think the defendant's language, quoted above, is not supportable. Suppose an employee has completed five years of service in October, 1957. Under the seniority provision of the collective bargaining agreement, he thinks that he has earned, and acquired, by continuous service, valuable insurance against unemployment; that by reason of having worked continuously for this company longer than many of his fellow workmen, he could not be laid off unless the lay-off cut deep into the working force; that even if he should be reached in a layoff, he would be sure to be re-employed if at any time within three years after the layoff his name should be reached on the seniority list, for re-employment. As we have seen, the defendant's position is that the employee had not acquired any such rights.

Rights embodied in a collective bargaining contract negotiated by a union "insure to the direct benefit of employees and may be the subject of a cause of action." . . . If one has in October a right to demand performance of the corresponding obligation at any relevant time within a period of three years, it would be strange if the other contracting party could unilaterally terminate the right at the end of three weeks. Of course, the employee owning the right, or his authorized union agent, could bargain away the employee's right. Nothing of that kind occurred in the instant case.

At the time the Elmhurst employees were discharged, those who had reached the age of 65 and had otherwise satisfied the conditions prescribed in the collective bargaining agreement for receiving retired pay, were placed on the defendant's retired list and have been and are currently receiving their retired pay. Similarly, those who had reached the age of 55, or who had become permanently disabled in the service of the defendant, and had had 15 years of employment with the defendant, are receiving their retired pay. Those who had 15 years of service and had reached the age of 45 at the time of their discharge were advised by the defendant that they had vested rights to retirement benefits and would begin to receive payments when they reached the age of 65.

These rights to retired pay, though their realization will extend far into the future, and though they arise solely and only out of the terms of the union agreement with the defendant, have been treated as "vested" rights and are being voluntarily honored by the defendant. This was, we suppose, because the employees had earned these rights by compliance with the terms of the contract, and the fact that the contract was not renewed, and that other workmen in the future might think the plaintiff employees had, by the same token, "earned" their valuable unemployment insurance, and that their rights in it were "vested" and could not be unilaterally annulled.

We think, then, that if the plaintiff had continued to operate the Elmhurst plant, without a renewal of the union contract, or had reopened it after it had been closed for a time, the employees would have been entitled to re-employment, with seniority. This brings us to the issue which Judge Palmieri in the District Court, found to be the critical issue, i.e., whether the unit to which the employees' rights attached "extended beyond the Elmhurst plant." He held that the rights were not enforceable except in the Elmhurst plant, and therefore denied recovery. With deference, we disagree with this conclusion.

The union contract, in its preamble, recited that it was made by the defendant company

> "for and on behalf of its plant facilities located at Corona Avenue and 94th Street, Elmhurst, Long Island, New York."

If this narrow geographical description is treated as setting fixed boundaries upon the scope of the contract, difficulties immediately arise. If the plant moved from 94th Street to 93rd Street in Elmhurst, an active structure of valuable legal rights would tumble down. *A fortiori* if the plant moved to a site a few miles or a good many miles away, the consequence would be the same. But one would be obliged to wonder why so catastrophic a consequence should follow a mere change in physical location. And it would be hard to conjure up a reason why it should. Rather it would seem that the recital in the contract would be analogous to the *descriptio personae* familiar to the law in various situations.

A rational construction of the contract would seem to require that the statement of location was nothing more than a reference to the then existing situation, and had none of the vital significance which the defendant would attach to it. Contracts must, in all fairness, be construed *ut res magis valeat quam pereat*. If not, the reasonable expectations of the parties are sacrificed of sheer verbalism.

In the instant case the plant was, of course, not moved from 94th Street to 93rd Street in Elmhurst, nor from Elmhurst to another town within commuting distance of the then residences of the employees. It was moved to a city in another state. The fact does not seem to us to be decisive. It would, of course, have confronted the employees with troublesome problems. They would have had to decide whether the advantages of continued employment with this employer, the right to which they had earned in Elmhurst, were sufficient to induce them to make so considerable a move. It is probable that many of them would not have made the move. Those to whom the defendant had offered employment in Bethlehem, who did not accept the offer, would have, in effect, resigned their seniority and the rights that accompanied continued employment.

We can see no expense of embarrassment to the defendant which would have resulted from its adopting the more rational, not to say humane, construction of its contract. The plaintiffs were, so far as appears, competent and satisfactory employees. They had long since completed the period of probation prescribed in the union contract. It would seem that they would have been at least as useful employees as newly hired applicants. The defendant's Bethlehem plant was a new plant. There could not have been an existing union representative or a collective bargaining agreement there at the time the plant was opened.

In the circumstances, no detriment to the defendant would have resulted from a recognition by the defendant of rights in its employees corresponding with their reasonable expectations. In that situation, a construction of the contract which would disappoint those expectations would be irrational and destructive.

It follows from what we have said that the plaintiffs were entitled to be employed at the defendant's Bethlehem plant, with the seniority and re-employment rights which they had acquired at the Elmhurst plant. The refusal of the defendant to recognize that entitlement was a breach of contract, and the plaintiffs are entitled to recover the damages which that breach has caused them.

The plaintiffs allege in their complaint that they have been "deprived of employment by the defendant," as a result of the defendant's conduct recited above. That is an adequate allegation that they would have accepted employment at Bethlehem if it had been offered to them on the terms to which they were entitled. Proof of this allegation may well fall short of complete conviction, but the trier of fact will not penalize the plaintiffs on account of the uncertainty which has been caused by the defendant's conduct.

Whatever pension rights would have been earned by employment at Bethlehem, if it had been accepted, must be recognized by the defendant.

Since the case will be remanded, we leave to the District Court consideration of the right of recovery, if any, in connection with the welfare plan and the group insurance plans which were included in the union agreement. . . . *Reversed and Remanded.*

VII

Chief Justice Lumbard dissented, arguing in part as follows:

It is immaterial to the resolution of the question before us that the employment of competent and satisfactory employees is suddenly terminated, or even that the employer has acted ungenerously, as indeed it has. We are called upon to construe the contract upon which the parties agreed and not to substitute for it one with more humane or less destructive terms. . . .

[I]t is not uncommon for the parties to extend beyond a single plant the area in which seniority rights are to apply. Surely unions are now fully of age and are able to protect themselves and their members at the bargaining table. The consequences of dismissing the plaintiffs' case might indeed be unfortunate and even "catastrophic" from their point of view, but it is hardly "irrational and destructive" for a court to leave the parties as they are if they have never seen fit to provide otherwise.[13]

[13] 288 Federal Reporter, 2nd Series, 99–115 (2 Cir. 1961).

The case of Zdanok v. Glidden continued its long trek through the courts. Upon the announcement of Judge Madden's opinion favoring the five original plaintiffs, 157 other workers laid off at Elmhurst also sued Glidden. The company appealed Madden's decision to the Supreme Court of the United States, which decided against the company on a narrow technical point irrelevant to the problem of vested seniority rights that survive a labor agreement. The workers then sued in the District Court of Southern New York for redress of the damages done them. Judge Palmieri, who had heard the case originally in 1960, bowed to the decision of the Court of Appeals and found for the workers. The company brought its case before the Second Circuit Court of Appeals again, but its appeal was not sustained. On July 9, 1965, final orders dismissing the case were entered by the U.S. District Court for the Southern District of New York.

DUPONT v. HIRSCH

While leafing through a chemical engineering bulletin in October, 1962, Donald E. Hirsch of the DuPont Chemical Company came upon a recruiting advertisement and paused to examine it. The ad was of the specialized, technical kind most readers almost automatically overlook, but Hirsch was deeply interested, and from his interest arose a court case of lasting significance for professional employees in the United States.

I

The advertisement sought a chemical engineer "who must have TiO_2 [titanium dioxide] experience" to fill the position of manager of Technical Services in a new plant. At DuPont, Donald Hirsch had been occupied in research and development of the chloride process for manufacturing titanium dioxide. Since the latter part of 1961 he had been a part of a group advising in the design of the company's third titanium plant, being built at Antioch, California.

During his last few years with DuPont, Hirsch had become dissatisfied with purely technical assignments and had sought a position with the managerial responsibilities for which he considered himself qualified. Meeting with no success in this, he gave up hope that DuPont would broaden the scope of his work as he desired and notified his superior that he had decided to look elsewhere for a job that would better meet his expectations. Between 1960 and 1962, Hirsch had applied for positions with more than 10 other companies, but his applications were turned down because his experience was limited to chloride assignments. He could not offer the type of background the other companies needed in their jobs. The position described in the chemical engineering bulletin thus seemed well worth following up.

The ad had been designed to attract applicants to American Potash & Chemical Corporation. In August this company had hired Ward J. Jenssen, Inc., a management consultant firm, to help find personnel to staff a new chloride process plant that would produce titanium dioxide. Since DuPont was the country's only successful commercial producer of titanium dioxide using the chloride process, Jenssen first placed an advertisement in a newspaper published in DuPont's headquarters city, the Wilmington *Evening Journal.* Hirsch did not see it, or if he did, he did not respond to it.

After Hirsch answered the advertisement in the bulletin but before he was invited for an interview, American Potash requested that he submit copies of any unexpired contract on patent agreements he might have made with DuPont. The company did not want to be party to any contract violation, and it wanted to be sure Hirsch would be free of any restrictions on inventions or discoveries he might make after leaving his job. Having complied with this request, Hirsch went to Los Angeles for an interview. He did not tell anyone at DuPont about his trip.

Before the interview, in accordance with established procedures, American Potash had Hirsch sign an agreement not to disclose confidential information or trade secrets of any other company for whom he had worked. The interview went well, and American Potash officials were impressed with Hirsch's qualifications. He had a doctorate in chemical engineering from the University of Pittsburgh, familiarity with the general problems of titanium dioxide, and best of all, long experience with the chloride process.

Hirsch found the job under discussion to be to his liking. He testified later that in the interview he assured himself that American Potash "wanted my skills and general knowledge and not DuPont's secrets and proprietary know-how." [1] The company officials made it clear that "they had their own [TiO_2] process which they had spent time and money developing." As manager of Plant Technical Services in the new plant, Hirsch was to be concerned with the activities in every department, though he would not be involved in the actual development of the TiO_2 process. Specifically, he was to exercise supervisory control of technical services in the new plant, whose function was to improve existing methods of operations, initiate studies and investigations, and direct engineers and technicians so that the plant might operate with the highest possible efficiency. The company officials stressed that his duties would concern "the management of men who operate an existing plant and process rather than the development of a new process."

Hirsch felt that he could not deny himself the opportunity to move into a managerial position that fitted his training, experience, and preference. The career advancement to a management position rather than any increase in income persuaded him to accept the offer; his new salary was about the same as the one he received at DuPont, taking into account bonuses and fringe benefits. Accordingly, on November 23, 1962, Hirsch advised DuPont of his decision to join American Potash. A DuPont attorney talked with him about his leaving, asking that he reconsider and stay on. Hirsch said later that "he was told in substance that DuPont was losing engineers as fast as they could hire them and something had to be done to stop it and that he might be used as an example in this case." He recalled that the attorney told him the actions to be taken would be very uncom-

[1] This quotation and all the others in the case are taken from the briefs filed by E. I. DuPont de Nemours Company and by American Potash & Chemical Corporation and Donald E. Hirsch with the Court of Chancery of the State of Delaware. The briefs were filed between May 12, 1963, and January 20, 1964.

fortable and could possibly go on for a long period of time.

After a weekend of thought, Hirsch decided to go through with the move. On Monday, November 26, he submitted his resignation from DuPont, to become effective the following day. On November 28 he signed an employment contract with American Potash; it contained a stipulation that he would not disclose or use any trade secrets of other companies in his new employment.

II

Hirsch's promises to protect his former employer's trade secrets did not reassure the officials of DuPont; instead, they decided to take immediate legal action to insure the integrity of their chloride process. On November 30, 1962, DuPont brought suit against Hirsch and American Potash in the Delaware Court of Chancery and sought an injunction to prevent the disclosure and use of trade secrets relating to the manufacture of titanium dioxide by the chloride process. Specifically, DuPont asked the court to enjoin Hirsch from working in the chloride process for American Potash and to forbid the company from employing Hirsch in that activity. Despite these legal maneuvers, in mid-December, 1962, Hirsch moved to California with his wife and four children to take up his position with Potash. He was assigned to the Trona Operations in work removed from that of titanium dioxide.

DuPont did not accuse Hirsch of either disclosing or intending to disclose any trade secrets, nor did it claim that American Potash had or would seek disclosure of any trade secret. Neither did it maintain that American Potash would use a trade secret were one disclosed to it. Nevertheless, DuPont maintained that disclosure was inevitable. DuPont's counsel argued, "It is 'inevitable' that trade secrets will be revealed and used since it is and will be impossible for the defendant Hirsch to serve the defendant [American Potash] in any capacity in connection with the construction, development or operation of the plant . . . without divulging or using plaintiff's trade secrets." Counsel pointed out that even if Hirsch said nothing he could give secrets away. "He cannot even work alone with his conscience, but will be required to carry on dialogues with others. Moreover, the character of such dialogues will be such that at times his silence or an assertion that he could not speak or act because of an ethical barrier would itself be revealing."

Hirsch had been a key member of an advising group helping to design DuPont's new titanium dioxide plant at Antioch, California. From this work as well as his earlier experience in research and development, Hirsch was intimately acquainted with all phases of the chloride process. It was the responsibility of the Antioch task force to conduct various plant tests, prepare basic data, and provide detailed assistance in the design and early operation of the new plant. Further, it was the responsibility of the task force to undertake necessary engineering development work at the site and incorporate into the Antioch operation all of DuPont's latest chloride process technology, including all past DuPont experience and improvements in the process acquired at its Edge Moor and Johnsonville operations. Hirsch was fully familiar with most, if not all, of DuPont's trade secrets involved in its chloride process; he testified that he probably knew "as much about DuPont's TiO_2 chloride process as anyone in DuPont except E. L. Cussler [the technical superintendent at the Edge Moor plant]."

The injury to DuPont from a loss of its trade secrets pertaining to the chloride process would have been serious. The company reported that it had developed its successful and efficient process only after engaging in extensive and continuous research and experimentation extending over many years at a cost in excess of $15 million. While certain features of the process were protected by patents issued to DuPont, other features were simply trade secrets and confidential information that the company had taken great effort to protect. Its precautions involved the installation of fencing around its plants, establishing a system of guards, restricting visitors, prohibiting sketches and photographs, and requiring all employees, suppliers, and other persons who necessarily came to the premises to agree in writing not to use or divulge any information concerning the process. DuPont's care in safeguarding its secrets not only protected its past investment in the process but also its competitive advantage over all other producers who used the less efficient sulfate process to manufacture titanium dioxide.

The last point in DuPont's argument was that without Hirsch's know-how and aid, American Potash did not have the necessary technical information required to operate a successful, full-scale chloride process. According to DuPont officials, although American Potash had already committed approximately $15 million to achieve a competitive position, in March, 1961, the company had concluded that it was necessary to request a license to use DuPont's patents and secrets for the chloride process. DuPont offered to license some of its patents but refused to grant any rights to its trade secrets. American Potash's interpretation of these negotiations with DuPont was that it had merely discussed with DuPont officials the company's licensing policy in the course of preparing a research survey on titanium dioxide and that nothing more serious could be deduced from the fact of the meeting.

Whatever the real motives of the American Potash negotiators may have been, DuPont officials feared that American Potash would now be tempted to try to find a short cut around the expensive roadblocks it had encountered. In order to make good the promises that American Potash managers had made to the stockholders for several years, to avoid further embarrassments because of delays and postponements, and to save the substantial investment the company had already made, DuPont suggested, "some ambitious person within American Potash—perhaps acting secretly even with respect to his own colleagues—may decide to get the benefit of some of Hirsch's information. . . ."

III

Hirsch and several American Potash officials replied to the DuPont charges by swearing without reservation that Hirsch could "fully discharge his responsibilities under his new employment contract without disclosing or using trade secrets." Further, American Potash claimed that it had no need of secrets or confidential information from Hirsch; he had been hired for his general experience and competence as a manager. The company also argued that DuPont officials had no way of knowing what information American Potash possessed about the chloride process. Finally, the company expressed doubt as to just how many of DuPont's secrets were really secret:

> During the last 15–20 years considerable knowledge regarding chloride processes for producing titanium dioxide has entered the public domain, principally because of the expiration of patents. During the same period there have been very significant technological advances made in the development of specialty chemical process equipment in this and allied fields. Knowledge of processing techniques now in the public domain and knowledge as to the uses and applications of equipment available to the public generally is part of the general knowledge and skills which defendant Hirsch properly may bring to his job.

For proof that it already possessed knowledge of a chloride process before hiring Hirsch, American Potash pointed out that it had joined with Laporte Industries, Ltd., of Great Britain in operating a small chloride pilot plant with a capacity of two tons a day. Laporte had designed and built a larger plant at Stallingborough, England, indicating that American Potash could build a large, commercial chloride-process plant in the United States with Laporte's aid. The chloride process had been mastered by other companies, too; the Cabot Corporation of Boston, for example, was constructing a titanium dioxide plant at Ashtabula, Ohio, that would use a chloride process. American Potash was thus unwilling to concede that everything Hirsch had learned at DuPont was a trade secret, and in its presentation to the court it tartly remarked that DuPont's "saying so does not make it so."

The burden of the argument made by Hirsch and American Potash was that DuPont was trying to protect itself against competition by restricting an employee's freedom of employment. The contract Hirsch made with DuPont contained no restriction on his later competing with the company or working for a competitor in a field involving trade secrets. In their argument before the court Hirsch and American Potash maintained that:

> [DuPont] is asking this court to write into its employment contract a restrictive covenant against competition, a covenant which, for obvious reasons, plaintiff [DuPont] was not willing to write in itself. Such a covenant would make it a most unattractive place for a young and energetic man to work, and its efforts in recruiting new personnel would suffer markedly were such a covenant present. However, nothing less than a restrictive covenant will afford plaintiff the relief it seeks from this Court. And even with such a restrictive covenant, it is highly doubtful whether plaintiff could obtain the injunction it seeks, for the books are replete with cases denying such relief even with the presence of a restrictive covenant . . . and yet plaintiff is attempting to convince this Court that it should be entitled to whatever advantages there might be in such a restrictive covenant and the relief which might be granted were such a covenant present, while fearful for competitive economic reasons, it refrains from inserting such a covenant in its boiler-plate employment application.

Since Hirsch's employment contract contained no restrictive covenant, his counsel maintained that the court could enjoin him only upon evidence of an existing violation or of a willful intent to violate either the contractual and/or common law prohibitions against disclosing and using another's trade secrets. Since no evidence had been shown of a violation or even of willful intent to violate, American Potash argued that no basis for an injunction existed. Only in extreme situations had courts enjoined a person's economic freedom in the past; care had to be taken that the court did not prevent a former employee from using his general skills and general knowledge learned in his prior employment. Equity provides protections for no more than those "ideas and information which rise to the character of 'trade secrets' as defined by the courts." The argument made for Hirsch maintained that:

> In balancing the equities between protecting business property and safeguarding an individual's economic liberty, the Court must favor the individual and follow a policy which encourages freedom over restriction of employment.
>
> In weighing these factors, it must be remembered that the knowledge and skill which is obtained through experience is not a trade secret, that sound public policy favors employees bettering themselves, and that employees may carry away and use the skill acquired during the course of an employment either in business for themselves or in the service of other employers.
>
> The employer must present a very strong case in order to secure relief by injunction; if his was the secret, his was the burden of guarding it and his is now the burden of proving that it was in fact a "trade secret" [Sun Dial Corp. v. Rideout].
>
> The Pennsylvania Supreme Court states this preference [Wexler v. Greenberg] where it upheld the "right of an individual to the unhampered pursuit of the occupations and the livelihoods for which he is best suited."

A good statement of the law which must be here applied was made [in another case] where an employer unsuccessfully sought to enjoin his prior employee from disclosing secrets to and working for a competitor:

Equity will to the fullest extent protect the property rights of employers in their trade secrets and otherwise, but public policy and natural justice require that equity should also be solicitous for the right inherent in all people, not fettered by negative covenants upon their part to the contrary, to follow any of the common occupations of life. Every individual possesses as a form of property the right to pursue any calling, business or profession he may choose. A former employee has the right to engage in a competitive business for himself and to enter into competition with his former employer even for the business of those who had formerly been the customers of his former employer, provided such competition is fairly and legally conducted . . ." [Continental Car-Na-Var Corp. v. Mosely].

On the one hand, an employee may not reveal the trade secrets of his former employer. On the other, a restriction placed on a former employee restraining him from pursuing his chosen occupation is contrary to public policy and void. . . . Defendants [Hirsch and American Potash] contend that the present relief sought would violate the second principle without even a proper showing of contravening the first. . . .

Certainly there exists in this case no more than an opportunity for disclosure and use. Since defendants are not charged with the possibility of intentional action, the only situation the Court may consider is that of an inadvertent, mistaken disclosure and use of trade secrets. In viewing such a case, the Court should keep two factors in mind. First, the persons who would be committing this careless inadvertence are highly educated and sophisticated men who are thoroughly trained in their field. Second, a trade secret to be so classified and protected by the Courts must be some very specialized and definable item. A vague concept or general method would not qualify. . . . Thus, it would seem highly unlikely that such knowledgeable men would by careless inadvertence reveal and use such a special and unique idea or process. It must be obvious that the knowledge in the titanium dioxide field which is possessed by defendant Hirsch includes non-proprietary information as well as proprietary secrets of plaintiff. If plaintiff [DuPont] fears that defendants will use and develop ideas from defendant Hirsch's non-proprietary general background and knowledge (not trade secrets) which he acquired from employment with plaintiff along with the alleged trade secrets, its fears are well justified, but from these fears the law provides no relief. . . .

IV

DuPont answered the arguments presented for Hirsch and American Potash by maintaining that it was not trying to prevent Hirsch from seeking employment elsewhere but only seeking to enjoin him from working for a competitor in an area sensitive to the disclosure of trade secrets.

[DuPont] does not seek to deprive Hirsch of his opportunity to earn a livelihood or to pursue his calling as a chemical engineer. The demand in industry for trained engineers such as Hirsch is great.[2] Indeed, in this case DuPont has not sought to prevent Hirsch from working for [American] Potash, as he is in fact doing under precisely the sort of injunctive order that DuPont seeks to have made permanent. . . .

DuPont insisted that it did not seek to stop Hirsch from using his "general" skills in competition with it. The company was perfectly content to have Hirsch continue to work for American Potash or for any

[2] Hirsch testified that he considered himself fully qualified to work (1) in industries involving metal chloride chemistry, high temperature processes, and corrosive chemicals; (2) in thermodynamics, his specialty as a graduate student; (3) in connection with high pressure equipment, because of his ability to analyze problems of a technical nature; (4) as a research director charged with conceiving and directing research projects relating to various inorganic chemicals, not including titanium dioxide.

other competitor, but it did want to prevent him from disclosing or using its trade secrets.

The DuPont argument observed that when Hirsch and American Potash quoted from Sun Dial Corp. v. Rideout in discussing the balance of equities between protecting business property and safeguarding individual liberty, they did not choose to cite the more apt statement of the higher court which reheard the case and granted injunctive relief for the protection of trade secrets.

> There is undoubtedly . . . an important policy which encourages employees to seek better jobs from other employers or to go into business for themselves. . . . But there is also a policy which is designed to protect employers against improper disclosures of information which their employees have received in confidence, and this policy may perhaps be receiving increased recognition in the light of the marked changes in the attitude of the law towards the need for commercial morality. Our judicial decisions have faithfully sought to vindicate both policies by preserving to employees their unfettered right to leave their employment and use elsewhere their acquired skill and knowledge of the trade generally as distinguished, however, from any trade secrets imparted to them in confidence and which they must continue to honor as such. . . .[3]

DuPont argued that if timely and meaningful protection of its property rights were to be provided it would have to be before the trade secrets were disclosed, whether willfully or inadvertently. If the company was required to wait until Hirsch actually disclosed or used the trade secrets involved in the chloride process, it would enjoy no effective protection at all. To lock the barn door after the horse has been stolen would be a frivolous remedy. Simply to forbid Hirsch from disclosing or using the trade secrets was not enough; he must be forbidden to work in that portion of the industrial field to which the trade secrets related.

After consideration of the facts of the case and the arguments of the parties, the court granted DuPont the injunction it sought. In a public statement issued in April, 1963, American Potash declared:

> More is at stake in this case than the career of one man or the right of the Company to hire qualified personnel and compete in a new field. Vital as these are, there is the larger question of whether one corporation, whatever its size and power, can enforce an industry-wide system of involuntary servitude for professional employees. . . . This question has overtones of long-term significance to all professional engineers and manufacturing industries in the United States.

Neither the company nor Hirsch appealed the decision of the state court, and it therefore stood as the legal and binding judgment of the dispute until May 5, 1967, when DuPont agreed to dismiss the suit and thus terminate the injunction against Hirsch. Officials of American Potash pointed out that further litigation seemed unwarranted, since its TiO_2 chloride process pigment plant had been producing specification material since the last quarter of 1965. Hirsch remained under obligation, however, not to divulge any of DuPont's trade secrets.

[3] Sun Dial Corp. v. Rideout, 16 N.J. 252, 108 A2d 442, 447 (1954).

QUESTIONS

Status, Contract, and Beyond

1. Compare and contrast the different conceptions of contract argued by Glidden and by DuPont. Which conception is best suited to an individualistic, competitive economy?
2. If you were a union organizer, which case would present you with a situa-

tion that would offer the greater opportunity to "sell" a union to the employees and why?

3. If you wished to weaken unions, which case offers the better opportunity to separate the interests of the workers from those of the union and why?

4. A legal scholar declared that decisions such as those made by the courts in these two cases were moving our society backward—away from a society based on contract to one based on status. What evidence in these cases supports the statement? What evidence in the cases counters it?

5. In a case similar to Hirsch's but which happened a year earlier, an engineer left a job in the spacesuit division of Goodrich to take a similar job with International Latex, and was quoted as saying, "Loyalty and ethics have their price; insofar as I am concerned, International Latex is paying the price." Should loyalty and ethics have a price? What, if anything, do they have to do with changing jobs from one American company to another?

6. If a company calculated it could more profitably operate in another, distant location than in its present one, should loyalty to its employees or the community be a consideration in deciding whether or not to move? Should ethics be a consideration? Explain your answers.

7. For whom is seniority a worthwhile, valuable interest? For workers only? Why is it an attractive method of discriminating among people despite its obvious shortcomings?

8. List the evidence that indicates Hirsch was a "key member" of DuPont's technical staff concerned with the production of titanium dioxide through the chloride process. List the evidence that suggests he was not a "key member." Which list is more persuasive?

9. A scholar once wrote that court decisions

> are often more solicitous of the privileges and immunities of corporations than of people. . . . A corporation is a creature of the state. It enjoys numerous valuable privileges, all of them conferred by the state. I know of no philosophic, economic or legal reason for supposing it enjoys or ought automatically to enjoy the rights of natural men. . . . The Government has a responsibility to protect the economic interests of natural persons against these exercises of market power. The time and place to defend human liberties are when the liberties of humans are at stake.

Can this statement be used accurately to criticize the effect of the court's decision to grant DuPont an injunction limiting Hirsch?

10. Does Judge Madden's decision imply that the Glidden company has no alternative but to offer jobs at Bethlehem to every worker laid off at Elmhurst who has enough seniority? How would you recommend that the company deal with the workers so as to minimize costs but also to comply with the legal ruling?

11. How would advocates of a competitive product market justify extending legal protection to trade secrets, thus creating a limited form of government-protected monopoly? How would they defend the court's decision to grant DuPont's request for the injunction?

12. Judge Madden's decision in the Zdanok case recognized that workers, as individuals and not as union members, had job rights that survived the contract; his decision also mentioned several different ways these rights might be extinguished. Considering the realities of individual workers' bargaining power,

what substantial rights did the workers gain in the Zdanok v. Glidden case? What substantial rights did the union gain?

13. Try to devise an arrangement by which the property claims of companies and the right of workers to maximize their potential may be most profitably reconciled and the public interest served in such a conflict as was present in the dispute between DuPont and Hirsch.

14. The National Labor Relations Board and the courts have long held that parties bargaining with each other do not have to agree. If they reach an impasse, one or the other may proceed with whatever settlement it can unilaterally impose. In the light of this principle, what effect do you think the court's decision had upon the Glidden Company?

chapter **11**

EQUALITY OF INDIVIDUAL AND CORPORATE OPPORTUNITY UNDER LAW

Americans may not be unique in their enthusiasm for simple formulations of their beliefs and values, but they possess a truly remarkable capacity for holding firmly to such formulations while resolutely pursuing a contradictory course of behavior. Such at least is the conclusion of a succession of foreign observers—among them Harriet Martineau, Alexis de Tocqueville, Andre Siegfried, and Gunnar Myrdal—who thought they discovered wide discrepancies between our beliefs and practices as well as a penchant in our ideology for "moralistic denial."

Consider the faith of Americans in the importance of "individualism." In one of the worst years of the Great Depression Herbert Hoover wrote:

> While I can make no claim for having introduced the term "rugged individualism," I should be proud to have invented it. It has been used by American leaders for over a half century in eulogy of those God-fearing men and women of honesty whose stamina and character and fearless assertion of rights led them to make their own way in life.[1]

This passage must have seemed somewhat naive to the third of all American workers who, through no obvious faults of their own, were unemployed when the late President wrote it, and it could seem almost as naive today in the era of the organization man; nevertheless, it probably strikes a responsive chord in most of us. Perhaps there has been, as Daniel Bell argues, "an end to ideology," but few Americans are yet prepared to relegate individualism to the museum of ideas.[2] Though self-made men and Horatio Alger heroes may be "more conspicuous in history books" than in American history,[3] Americans still respond

[1] Herbert Hoover, *The Challenge to Liberty* (New York: Charles Scribner's Sons, 1934), pp. 54–55. On October 22, 1928, President Hoover used the phrase "rugged individualism" in a campaign speech in New York to describe "the American system."
[2] E. Wight Bakke, in a study of the unemployed during the depression, reported that most of his respondents blamed themselves and assigned relatively little blame to "the system" in their assessment of their circumstances; see *The Unemployed Worker*, The Institute of Human Relations (New Haven: Yale University Press, 1940), pp. 92–130.
[3] William Miller, "Historians and the Business Elite," *Journal of Economic History*, 4 (November, 1949), 286–305. See also Mabel Newcomer, *The Big Business Executive* (New York: Columbia University Press, 1955); William Miller, ed., *Men in Business* (Cambridge: Harvard University Press, 1952); W. Lloyd Warner and J. Abegglen, *Big*

to political rhetoric, economic theorizing, and social commentary that stress individualism as an important factor in America's development and as a reason for giving respectful admiration to our captains of industry. Popular faith in the value of individualism is also reflected in America's preoccupation with "helping people to help themselves," with "motivating the poor," and with "preserving individual incentives."

Individualism is highly praised in America, yet bureaucracy, which often requires that the individual be treated impersonally and even as a simple cog in a machine, has become in many respects our way of life. Efficiency, which we value as highly as individualism, regularly demands that certain organizational needs take precedence over the rights of individuals. We have already examined some of the situations where the interests of individuals must give way to the requirements of union strength, corporate popularity, or industrial harmony; we have also noted that the personnel policies of many business firms are designed to induce cooperation and collaboration by heightening group consciousness and making all employees members of a team. Collective behavior of this sort hardly seems consistent with the individualistic ethic we proclaim.

Perhaps the inconsistency between belief and practice is not as sharp as it seems. Indeed, if one examines the data on social mobility and considers the differing success of those who enjoy similar benefits, such as those provided by "G.I. Bills" for education, and the advantage enjoyed because of birth into the prosperous middle class, we find there are many individuals who go faster, go farther, and do better than others. After all, a society allows considerable scope to individuals when an ex-haberdasher or a Texas schoolteacher can win the Presidency. These examples probably would not reassure Messrs. Shaw, Newberg, or Hirsch, Mrs. Benson, or the IAM shop stewards, however. Their personal experiences may tell us a good deal more of the inability of individuals to make the "fearless assertions" to which President Hoover made reference than they do of the success individuals enjoy in making "their own way."

Before the average American finds himself caught up in the bureaucratic web of our unions, corporations, and associations he must survive innumerable tests of personal endurance and many lonely trials requiring him to make independent, individual judgments. Most Americans are reared in what sociologists call "nuclear families"; they do not have the support, aid, and comfort of the "extended kinship groups" found in pre-industrial lands around the world. Geographic mobility and the considerable distances from one labor market to the next in America conspire against our having a system, such as many more "primitive" peoples enjoy, that automatically assures children the solicitous attention of close relatives. Instead, the care of American children is the object of a bargaining relationship among parents, babysitters, and entrepreneurial nursery school operators, which often leaves the individual child feeling unprotected and on his own. This feeling is likely to be strengthened once the child is in school, for he immediately finds himself examined, graded, and matriculated through a series of highly competitive, individualistic educational programs. The strategic choice that confronts the individual as he approaches the end of his schooling—

Business Leaders in America (New York: Harper & Row, 1955); and S. Keller, "The Social Origins and Career Lines of Three Generations of American Business Leaders," unpublished Ph.D. dissertation (New York: Columbia University, 1953).

whether or not to attend college, and which college, if any, to apply to—is also a problem that he must resolve completely by himself.

Once an individual's education is ended, he must find a job. Job seeking in the poorly structured American labor market is itself a trying test in applied individualism. Most young people find their jobs in an extremely haphazard fashion through friends or classified ads; any connections that exist between the training they have received in school and the job opportunities that confront them are left to the resources of their own imaginations to discover.[4] Allowing young people to make judgments about the nature and extent of their schooling, to estimate the requirements of various jobs, and to find jobs for themselves without the support of stable, persuasive social conventions and definitions is to preserve much room for individualism indeed.

Even on their jobs within big bureaucratic organizations Americans are able to display a certain individuality. Workers can bargain inventively with foremen and superintendents for valuable work rules despite corporate regulations and union contracts that forbid this, business executives with political knowledge of how the Defense Department operates can make handsome profits from providing new and exotic materials for missiles, or a daring entrepreneur may even ride high for a time while selling for millions of dollars interests in non-existent salad oil.[5] A definition of individualism that makes no room for such expressions as these is too narrow.

While the bureaucracy of large organizations and individualism are thus not wholly incompatible, there are grounds for concern about individual rights in an age of big organizations. Behind the slogans of American ideology stands a genuine commitment to the dignity and rights of individuals. Our society does not guarantee anyone that all his claims will be fulfilled, but it does intend each

[4] Arthur Stinchcombe recently examined a troubled California high school and found that the students were rebellious and dissatisfied because they did not understand what relevance, if any, their education would have to the rest of their lives; see Stinchcombe's *Rebellion in a High School* (Chicago: Quadrangle Books, 1964). Without making the relevance or purposes of education any clearer, American society has continued to upgrade the educational requirements for work; this trend puzzles many young people, for they are aware that job tasks have not been upgraded nearly as much as educational requirements; see Abraham Jaffe and Walter Adams, "Educational Attainment and Technology," *Statistical News,* New York Chapter of the American Statistical Association, 16 (December, 1964), 2; and Ivar Berg, *Educational Requirements for Work,* Columbia University Conservation of Human Resources Project and Center for Urban Education. In preparation, 1967.

[5] Judges and businessmen, at least, appear to know and admire an able and highly individualistic man when they meet one. Thus Judge Wortendyke, who presided in the scandalous 1965 "Salad Oil Case" in which Tino DeAngelis was tried (and convicted) for perpetrating a $150 million swindle, gave a "glowing" account of DeAngelis' business acumen and said, "You, yourself, Mr. DeAngelis, have exemplified what can be achieved with only a little backing and influence, by courage and vision. . . ." The judge was reported to have cited this success in business as proof that we have a workable democracy.

Something of the same attitude may have been held by DeAngelis' victimized backers, though their admiration for him was perhaps rooted in even rockier soil. It was rumored in financial circles that DeAngelis was involved with the *Cosa Nostra.* Said an official of one of the major companies that extended credit to DeAngelis (with imaginary salad oil as collateral): "If he were backed by that kind of money, we would have known that he was good for all that he owed us." N. C. Miller, *The Great Salad Oil Swindle* (New York: Coward-McCann, 1965), p. 243.

citizen to have the right to make his claims and express his individuality free from any restraint of status. America has joined in the progression from status to contract; it has developed in the direction of an ideal society in which men are measured by their personal achievements and in which their rights are secured by universal legal criteria rather than by concession or *noblesse oblige.*

Unfortunately, although the importance of inherited status has declined in America, a strong tendency remains to ascribe status to a person on the basis of his organizational ties. Of particular significance in defining such status is the organization through which the individual is obliged to earn his livelihood. Insofar as organizations do not in fact enjoy equality before the law, the equality of their individual members must be impaired. Historically, we know that judges, legislators, and public opinion have sometimes favored certain organizations and their members over others, even when little or no rational basis to justify any distinction could be discerned. The following cases pose the question of the extent to which we continue to make judgments on the basis of ascribed position and fail to consider individuals and their actions for what they are in themselves.

The Equal Treatment of Organizations

DISCLOSURE IN UNIONS

By the end of World War II union membership in the United States had grown to over 15 million persons, and many observers felt that unions were now so large and powerful that legislation was needed to make union leaders more responsible to the public, to their members, and to other workers in the shop. The two main pieces of legislation to result from this sentiment were the Labor-Management Relations Act (the Taft-Hartley Act) of 1947 and the Labor-Management Reporting and Disclosure Act (the Landrum-Griffin Act) of 1959.

I

Through the Taft-Hartley Act, Congress attempted to protect employees, the public, and management from irresponsible union action. The new labor law included provisions that prohibited the closed shop; allowed the union shop only with the approval of a majority of the workers concerned; provided employers freedom to speak to their employees about union representation as long as their expression "contains no threat of reprisal or force or promise of benefit"; denied workers who had struck for higher wages the right to vote in representational elections if the employer was able to hire enough new workers to take the strikers' jobs; gave strike-breakers equal protection with strikers; spelled out in great detail the mutual requirements to bargain in good faith; allowed bargaining between individuals and their employer if the resulting terms were no worse than those in the collective agreement; made unions liable in court for non-performance of the agreement; and allowed workers to vote on acceptance of a firm's last offer in an emergency strike situation.

Insofar as the Taft-Hartley Act was an attempt to strengthen the right of workers to resist unionization and to bargain individually for themselves, it miscarried. In over 90 per cent of the union-shop elections, for example, workers overwhelmingly voted for compulsory membership; as a consequence the union shop spread rapidly across the nation, and in 1951 Congress quietly repealed the Act's union-shop provision. Furthermore, in emergency strikes where workers voted on the employer's last offer, huge majorities regularly supported the union and rejected the offered terms. In general, workers indicated that they favored unions and collective bargaining; they rejected almost every "opportunity" provided by the Act to escape from their "labor bosses."

Despite the workers' proven acceptance of unionism—or because of it—many people complained that unions needed to govern themselves much better than they were doing. Loose handling of finances, kickbacks, bribes, extortion, and embezzlement were reported to be all too common in a few unions. Racketeering had appeared in the longshore industry in the Port of New York and among several Teamsters locals throughout the country; critics pointed out that gangsters had won control in 1934 of the Theatrical Stage Employees and the Moving Picture Machine Operators and that George Scalise, head of the Building Service Employees' International Union, had been jailed for embezzlement in 1941. It was well known among students of labor that the Hod Carriers had held no convention for 30 years, though membership increased from 13,000 to 230,000 during that time, and that the Tobacco Workers went for nearly 40 years without a convention, calling one finally only at the order of a court. Since the Taft-Hartley Act had not directly attempted to remedy such abuses of internal union government, many union critics and even union supporters argued that new regulations should be enacted.

II

Early in 1957, Senator John L. McClellan became chairman of a Select Committee set up to probe more deeply into some evidence of racketeering and corruption that Robert F. Kennedy had incidentally uncovered in another investigation. The hearings of the McClellan committee revealed more unsavory activities and shady dealings among unions than even labor leaders realized existed. One of the most publicized revelations involved Dave Beck, president of the International Brotherhood of Teamsters, the country's largest union.

Through a labor relations counselor in Chicago, Nate Shefferman, Beck had spent $85,000 of union funds for personal purchases. He charged the bills to the Teamsters Public Relations Account, and a partial list of his purchases includes such assorted goods as fancy undershirts, golf balls and clubs, sheets and pillow cases, 21 pairs of nylon stockings, 5 dozen diapers, rugs, a gun, a bow tie, a boat, and a radio. He had also conspired with Shefferman to make large profits in selling land to the union for its elaborate and expensive marble and glass headquarters building in Washington, D.C. An audit of the union's books revealed that Beck had improved and maintained his Seattle estate with union funds. The total, about $150,000, was merely borrowed, Beck said, though no proper or accurate accounting was ever made. After the investigation began, he authorized the union to buy the estate for $163,000 and then arranged for the union to accord him free use of it. Beck's taste for money was so keen that he defrauded the widow of one of his best friends. As a trustee of a memorial fund to benefit the widow, he used $71,000 to buy from the union mortgages whose value actually totaled $60,000; he and a larcenous partner split the profit of $11,000. Further investigations suggested that a number of Teamsters officials were as bad, if not worse, than their president; testimony was heard concerning illegal activity in at least 40 locals of the union.[1]

The McClellan committee turned up evidence of corruption in several other unions besides the Teamsters. The unions that received the most attention were neither large nor important; among them were the Allied Industrial Workers, the Laundry Workers, the Bakery and Confectionery Workers, and

[1] For further details of Beck's affairs, see Robert F. Kennedy, *The Enemy Within* (New York: Harper & Row, 1960).

the Distillery and Wine Workers. Almost without exception, the union and management corruption discovered had flourished in industries where firms were relatively small, where competition was severe, and where the labor force was highly mobile. Senator Wayne Morse pointed out that "although these improper activities [of the investigated unions] were shocking, they were confined to a small fraction of the unions comprising organized labor." [2] Nevertheless, according to Senator Pat McNamara, who served on the committee, the investigators proceeded to generalize on the basis of limited findings and gave the false impression that the entire labor movement was corrupt.[3]

The AFL–CIO had begun to try to root out corruption prior to the McClellan hearings. In 1956 and 1957 it adopted a series of six codes of ethical practices and, after investigating illegal and improper practices expelled a number of unions, including the Teamsters, for not abiding by the codes. This effort at self-policing was easily overlooked, however, as the press and a chorus of public officials demanded that new, comprehensive legislation be drawn up to put an end to "labor corruption and racketeering." Spurred by the popular outcry, Congress began the consideration of regulations that would keep union officers from hiding their personal dealings and make them reveal all financial transactions of unions. The legislation that emerged was the Labor-Management Reporting and Disclosure Act. The act's declaration of purpose begins:

> Congress finds that, in the public interest . . . it is essential that labor organizations, employers, and their officials adhere to the highest standards of responsibility and ethical conduct in administering the affairs of their organizations, particularly as they affect labor–management relations. Congress further finds, from recent investigations in the labor and management fields, that there have been a number of instances of breach of trust, corruption, disregard of the rights of individual employees, and other failures to observe high standards of responsibility and ethical conduct which require further and supplementary legislation that will afford necessary protection of the rights and interests of employees and the public generally as they relate to the activities of labor organizations, employers, labor relations consultants, and their officers and representatives.

Certain provisions of the Act as finally passed establish rules and requirements designed to make democratic procedures always available to union members; other provisions require unions to report annually and in detail on their financial affairs to the Secretary of Labor. Unions must report their strike funds, reserves, cash, and other assets and their debts, mortgages, and other liabilities. They must provide full information about dues, special levies, initiation charges, fees for work permits and transfer papers (authorized changes of membership from one local to another), interest and dividend income, and all other receipts, and they must account for all such disbursements as salaries, administrative expenses, professional fees, contributions, and strike benefits. Unions must also report any loans larger than $250 made to officers, employees, or members of a union, and any loan to a business enterprise. These reports were to be submitted by all the 42,000 local unions, the 2,475 intermediate bodies —city-wide councils, joint boards, and district offices—and the 260 national unions; the information they furnish the Secretary of Labor is made available to the public, and any person may inspect or examine the data contained in the reports upon making a reasonable request to the Secretary.

[2] *Symposium on LMDRA* [Labor-Management Reporting and Disclosure Act], Ralph Slovenko, ed. (Baton Rouge, La.: Claitor's Bookstore, 1961), p. 97.

[3] *Interim Report of the Select Committee on Improper Activities in the Labor or Management Field,* Senate Report 1417, 85th Cong., 2nd Sess., 1958, pp. 454–62.

III

The reporting and disclosure section of the new act was thoroughly debated in Congress before it was approved. Those who favored it argued that union members should have access to all union records and that since the public had a decided interest in union affairs it, too, had a right to know how unions raised and spent their money and what their financial strength was. Those who opposed the disclosure provisions contended that those could harm the unions because employers would examine the data and learn a great deal about a particular union's willingness and ability to "take strikes"; a valuable basis of union strategy thus would be undermined.

Senator John F. Kennedy of Massachusetts appreciated the injury that full disclosure could inflict upon unions and proposed a compromise. He introduced a bill that would require labor organizations to submit financial reports to and for the exclusive use of the Secretary of Labor. Thus, union records would be subject to scrutiny by a public official, but they would not necessarily be revealed to those who might desire to use them to injure unions. During the debate on the bill Senator Barry Goldwater of Arizona offered the following amendment to Kennedy's initial proposal:

> Every labor organization required to submit a report under this title shall make available copies of such reports to each of its members and shall permit such members to examine the books, records, and accounts of such transactions as were or may be necessary to prepare or verify the reports required by [this Act].
>
> The Secretary shall by regulation prescribe the form and manner for making such reports available to such members, and the time, place, circumstances, and conditions under which such books, records and accounts may be examined by such members.[4]

[4] *Congressional Record,* 105 (April 23, 1959), 6520.

Goldwater argued for his amendment, saying:

> [My addition] would require the union to make copies of the reports available to each of the members and permit the members to examine the basic records upon which the report is based. The Secretary would be given the authority to issue regulations governing the time, place, and so forth, whereby such records may be examined by the members.
>
> The [Kennedy] bill purports to insure honesty in union officials by requiring the union to make the report available to all the members. But does it? Let us see how this provision works out in actual practice. The union files the reports and gives copies to all its members. The member reads the report and comes across a particular statement about which he has some doubt. . . . The union officer is perfectly within his rights to refuse a member access to the basic records according to the [Kennedy] bill. . . .
>
> The only person authorized under the bill to inspect the basic books and records is the Secretary of Labor. With literally thousands of union reports streaming in on him, the only way that he can determine the truth or falsity of these reports is to resort to a "spot check" of some of them.[5]

Senator Goldwater went on to say that he was afraid that under the Kennedy disclosure provision it would take the Labor and Justice departments a long time to find defects and that "about two years after the horse has run down the road with a load of money on his back the barn door will be closed."

Senator Kennedy asked whether a shareholder in a corporation is permitted to examine company books. Senator Goldwater replied:

> I do not think we can in this case make a direct comparison between a corporation and a union. Let us compare the union with the American Legion, or some organization for the mutual benefit of its members. That is

[5] *Ibid.*

what a union organization really is. Certainly in organizations such as that the members have access to the books at any time, and to the detail in the books.

In a corporation, one of the reasons why a stockholder does not have access in every case to the details, such as the checkbooks, etc., is that it would result in the giving away of corporate secrets. There is no profit-making included in the union organization, so there is no danger of giving any secrets away.[6]

And Senator Kennedy replied:

In order really to protect the interest of union members in a genuine way, the bill provides for a very full reporting of all financial transactions of the union. The reports would be made to the Secretary of Labor. They would be sworn to. If information were omitted or misstated, that would constitute a crime. The Secretary must make the information available to union members in the way he thinks best to carry out the purposes of the act.

The Senator from Arizona would change all that, and provide every union member—some of whom may be engaged in harassing activities, or may be extremely interested on behalf of employers, [with] the right to examine all the files and data of a union.

A union is not the American Legion. It is organized for the purpose of protecting the economic rights of its members. It is given special privileges and rights by the Federal Government, and certain duties are imposed upon it.

I would object to a corporation being compelled to give every shareholder a list of all its customers and the prices it is quoting, and all letters of information it receives on any matter in any of the books of the corporation.

This provision and the bill itself protect the rights of union members in a far more satisfactory and genuine manner than would the amendment of the Senator from Arizona. In my opinion his amendment could open up opportunities for harassment, and in some cases the disintegration of unions. In my opinion it is not intended to protect the financial rights of responsible union members.[7]

Senator Goldwater retorted that a corporation is an organization in which a person can invest or not according to his will; a union, however, is an organization to which a man must belong if he wants to work. According to Goldwater, if a man is not happy with the corporation he can sell his stock, but if a man withdraws from a union, he is in effect quitting his job. (Loss of job follows loss of membership only under the union shop, of course.)

Union officials protested the Goldwater amendment and made clear their opposition to the detailed reporting procedures required elsewhere in the bill. Since 70 per cent of all union locals had receipts of less than $10,000 a year, the records that would have to be kept, and the work of filling out the reports, would prove to be a serious burden. No more than 1,700 locals, 4 per cent of the total, had incomes of over $100,000 a year, and less than a third of the *national* unions had incomes of more than $500,000 a year. Union leaders feared that employers opposed to unions would find the information reported helpful in disrupting organizing campaigns and that established unions would be forced to lay too many of their cards face up on the bargaining table, with an obvious weakening of their bargaining strength.

Union spokesmen also objected to the legislation on the grounds that it would permit dissident members or workers in the pay of employers to harass them. As finally approved, the act allowed members to bring suit in connection with alleged violations of its other requirements; those bringing suit could ask for injunctions under several provisions, and proof of violations could bring fines and imprisonment to the union leaders responsible. In some cases, members could sue for recovery of damages as well. In the face of these formidable sanctions, union officials foresaw the possibility of

[6] *Ibid.*, p. 6521.

[7] *Ibid.*

severe consequences for even innocent errors. Beyond that, they believed that Congress was treating them and their unions with presumptive suspicion not at all warranted by their record. The provisions of the new act would continue to magnify public mistrust of all unions.

IV

The Goldwater amendment was not approved in its original form, although the Senate did accept a modified version of it. On April 30, 1959, as a final version of the entire Reporting and Disclosure bill was awaiting congressional approval, Senator Morse read into the *Congressional Record* a comment by Walter Lippmann on the purpose to be served by the bill:

> The overriding national interest is that a bill should be passed which establishes the principle, as does the Senate bill, that there is a public interest in the internal management of the labor union, and that the right to regulate them is legally recognized and universally acceptable.[8]

Later, when asked to comment on the new act, Professor Otto Kahn-Freund of the London School of Economics said that from a foreigner's point of view it raised questions that he thought Americans ought to consider:

> Why is it that so many people are so sensitive and so anxious to protect the workers where internal trade union law is under discussion, and so insensitive to similar phenomena in the sphere of labor-management relations? Is this a question for the psychologist or is it one for the sociologist? It certainly is a question for a lawyer.[9]

[8] *Congressional Record,* 105 (April 30, 1959), 6320.

[9] Slovenko, *op. cit.,* p. 309.

DISCLOSURE IN THE STEEL INDUSTRY

Steel is a basic industry; its economic performance and the wage and price decisions of its managers affect the whole economy. And since steel is a major component in most consumer durables, its price affects the final prices of many other goods. Prices and wages in the steel industry also often establish patterns that are followed by the rest of the economy. In the early 1960's, the President and many Congressmen were especially concerned that inflationary price and wage increases in the steel industry not adversely affect wage and price stability throughout the country. When most of the steel companies suddenly raised their prices in April, 1962, therefore, it was not surprising that the government sought to bring various types of pressure to bear on the companies. One type of pressure consisted in the demand that steel executives disclose the internal cost data upon which their pricing decisions were ostensibly based.

I

Shortly after the price rise of April, 1962, President Kennedy declared in a speech that raising steel prices at the time was not in the public interest because it would increase defense expenditures and also "make it more difficult for American goods to compete in foreign markets, more difficult to withstand competition from foreign imports, and thus more difficult to improve our balance of payments position and stem the flow of gold." [1] Most Democrats and many Republicans in Congress supported the President's stand.

In the midst of this steel-price furor, Senator Estes Kefauver of Tennessee, Chairman of the Senate Antimonopoly Subcommittee (a subsidiary of the Senate Judiciary

[1] *Kennedy and the Press,* Harold W. Chase and Allen H. Lerman, eds. (New York: Thomas Y. Crowell Company, 1965), p. 223.

Committee) decided that his subcommittee should investigate the basis for steel price policies and the way in which these policies were formulated. He also wanted to explore the effect upon the public welfare of the price increase. Kefauver was suspicious of large corporations and was a strong advocate of rigorous enforcement of the antitrust laws. In the tradition of Justice Brandeis, who had denounced the acceptance of "the evils attendant upon the free and unrestricted use of the corporate mechanism as if these evils were the inescapable price of civilized life and, hence, to be borne with resignation," [2] Kefauver believed that the large size of corporations gave them an influence in the economy and society that could be injurious. Brandeis had observed, "Through size, corporations, once merely an efficient tool employed by individuals in the conduct of private business, have become an institution—an institution which has brought such concentration of economic power that so-called private corporations are sometimes able to dominate the state." [3] To prevent corporate domination of government policy, or what was as bad, corporate actions that nullified or undid government programs, Kefauver believed that corporate officials should publicly and responsibly justify their major decisions and activities before Congress. The attempt of the steel companies to raise prices when the government was trying to avoid inflation made him doubt that steel officials were acting responsibly.

To secure data and information that would allow some understanding of the needs of the steel companies and their economic position, Kefauver subpoenaed production-cost records of 12 major steel producers for the years 1954–61. A subpoena issued by a congressional committee is much the same as a request to answer questions under oath before a congressional body; failure to comply can lead to citation for contempt of Congress and prosecution in federal court by the U.S. Attorney General. Kefauver said that the subcommittee's purpose in asking for production cost data was an attempt to solve two problems that lie at the heart of the monopoly issue: the extent and use of monopoly power in the steel industry, and the relationship that exists between size and efficiency.

Senator Kefauver told the steel managers that this data would not be allowed to become public information, for he recognized that release of some of the data might harm the steel companies. Cost data was to be submitted to the government's General Accounting Office, as had been done in earlier investigations of the banking and automobile industries. Percentage figures were to be compiled and used in groupings so that the costs of any individual company would not be disclosed.

II

The antimonopoly subcommittee's subpoenas required that all the relevant production cost data be submitted to the General Accounting Office by August 15, 1962. Eight of the 12 steel companies complied,[4] although their officials protested that the subcommittee did not have the right to demand the data. Steel officials argued that if they divulged the data they would give away company secrets. On August 13, John F. Smith, Jr., president of Inland Steel, wrote to Senator Kefauver.

> I do wish to make it clear that the action which Inland is taking is not meant to be construed as a recognition of any right on the part of your committee to require production of the information which we are prepared to furnish.

[2] Liggett v. Lee, 288 U.S. 517 (1933) 548.
[3] *Ibid.,* p. 565.

[4] The eight companies complying with the subpoenas were United States Steel, Jones & Laughlin, Youngstown Sheet and Tube, Inland Steel, Kaiser, Colorado Fuel and Iron, Wheeling Steel, and McLaughlin. The four companies refusing to comply were Bethlehem, Armco, National, and Republic.

Inland not only questions the right of your Committee to issue these subpoenas, but also considers them to be ill-advised.

We believe that cost data can serve no proper or useful function in the investigation which your Committee has been authorized to undertake. Costs, and particularly the costs of any given company at any given time, may play only a limited part in determining prices which competition and the laws of supply and demand either force or permit a company to charge.

Cost data is misleading for the further reason that it has no bearing upon the ratio of profits to capital investment, which is the only significant measurement of the profits of a company or industry.[5]

On August 22, 1962, the Antimonopoly Subcommittee voted to issue "second-chance subpoenas" to the four companies whose officials had failed to comply with the initial requests. The new subpoenas were served on the companies and on the chief executive officers of the companies as well. Meanwhile, officials of the eight companies who had complied were advised by Kefauver to hold their records until the dispute was settled.

On August 30, the chief executives of the four reluctant companies notified Kefauver that they would not appear before the subcommittee on the following day in accordance with the subcommittee request. They stated that there was no reason for them to appear since they were not going to turn over the data, their lawyers having advised them not to recognize the subpoena. They further stated that to do so would "prejudice our attempt to secure a final determination of [the subpoena's] propriety and validity."

On the afternoon of August 30, Kefauver telegraphed the executives:

> Regardless of the expression of your intention not to comply with the subpoena directed to you, the subpoena commands your personal appearance before the Subcommittee on Anti-Trust and Monopoly in session August 31, 1962, at 10 A.M., then and there to make compliances. As Chairman of the Subcommittee, I shall consider your failure to do so as contempt under the subpoena.[6]

The steel executives did not appear, and the companies produced no data. The subcommittee then voted on September 2, by a 5 to 3 margin on straight party lines, to initiate contempt proceedings. The Senate Judiciary Committee held a full hearing the following week to consider the subcommittee's proposal.

III

Thomas Patten, president of Republic Steel, testified on behalf of the defendants. He discussed with the full committee the competitive pressures brought to bear upon American firms by foreign steelmakers who were cutting into traditional markets at home and abroad. This rising competition and increasing costs had forced some companies to cut their dividends in the second quarter of 1962, he pointed out, while other firms did not earn enough to cover their declared dividends. Under such conditions the companies could not afford to let out cost information. If the officials of another company knew the items with which a competitor was having cost problems, they could gear their firm's sales and price campaigns accordingly and take away the competitor's business.

Senator Kefauver wondered why the steel companies had not hesitated to submit cost data during the second world war when they had sought reductions in wage increases. Mr. Patten replied that wartime conditions were not competitive. Patten rejected the proposal to combine the firms' data and use percentages on the grounds that given the relevant percentages and base figures, any statisticians could calculate the actual data without much difficulty. He also argued that disclosure of information would expose American producers to "unfair competition by foreign producers," and he ex-

[5] *New York Times,* August 18, 1962.

[6] *Ibid.,* August 31, 1962.

pressed his doubt that the data sought were pertinent to the subcommittee's lawmaking function.

On September 25, the Senate Judiciary Committee voted, 10 to 5, to reject the Antimonopoly Subcommittee's contempt citation. Four Southern Senators joined with the six Republicans on the Committee to defeat the resolution. The five Democratic members of the Antimonopoly Subcommittee who had voted for the original citation voted for the contempt citation. The Judiciary Committee vote ended the quest for the cost data, and prevented the question of contempt from coming before the Senate as a whole.

QUESTIONS

The Equal Treatment of Organizations

1. Under what conditions can one expect union leaders and company officials to find it difficult to "adhere to the highest standard of responsibility and ethical conduct in administering the affairs of their organizations"?

2. Evaluate the arguments of John F. Smith, Jr., president of Inland Steel, and of Thomas Patten, president of Republic Steel, that they should not be required to reveal company cost data. Do their arguments support or contradict each other?

3. Evaluate Senator Goldwater's arguments in favor of secrecy for corporate financial records and disclosure for union finances. Evaluate Senator Kennedy's arguments.

4. Does Congress insist upon more public and detailed financial accounting for unions than for corporations? How are the annual reports of corporations and the financial statements prepared for stockholders comparable to the reports required of unions?

5. Prepare a list of reasons why Congress should and should not regulate the internal financial affairs of corporations in as much detail as it regulates those of unions.

6. A student wrote after reading these two cases, "The issue is easily resolved. The market regulates business firms and ultimately makes them responsible to the public. Unions, however, are outside the market; only government rules and laws will keep them responsible." Explain why you would agree or disagree.

7. How would you answer Professor Kahn-Freund's first question? In what ways, if any, are employees protected against corrupt or abusive employers if no union is present?

The Equal Treatment of Individuals

UNITED STATES v. RE, et al.

The job of the stock-exchange specialist is to maintain, at trading posts on the stock-exchange floor, orderly and fair markets in the stocks assigned to him. He achieves this by following closely a few stocks and, at the appropriate moments, buying or selling them in quantities calculated to offset sharp, short-term fluctuations. The specialist serves a dual function—as a broker who handles orders for other brokers and as a dealer who buys and sells stocks for his own account.

I

Realizing the ambiguous position of the specialist as both broker and dealer, Congress included a number of restrictions on his activities when it passed the Securities Exchange Act of 1934. By the terms of the Act the specialist is forbidden to effect any transaction as a broker except upon receiving a market or limited-price order—orders that entail no discretion.[1] He is also specifically prohibited from revealing the information on his "book" to any but officials of the stock exchange or the Securities and Exchange Commission. As a dealer, he is prohibited from making any transactions for his own account other than those that are properly part of his actions taken to maintain a fair and orderly market.[2] The law further prohibits any transactions calculated to raise or depress stock prices for the purpose of inducing the purchase or sale of such stocks by others.[3] In short, the purpose of the specialist is neither to incite a spark of interest in an undecided investor nor to cause a new investment decision to be made but to see that the investment decision already made and the orders already placed are handled in the "fairest, most orderly and most continuous" manner.[4]

Of the 1,366 persons and firms that in 1963 were members of the New York Stock Exchange (and so able to transact business on the exchange floor), 360 were specialists. At the American Stock Exchange, 159 of the 499 members were specialists. The specialists thus clearly constitute an important segment of the traders in the market at the two main exchanges at any time. An extensive study of the New York Stock Exchange made by the Securities and Exchange Commission in 1963[5] disclosed no widespread abuses or patterns of illegality among the specialists, but from time to time events have demonstrated the potential for abuse inherent in the specialist system and have led some observers to favor "automating the specialists"—that is, performing their work with the aid of computers to make it impersonal and subject to close supervision. One of the most startling of these events was the scandal that came to light in the late 1950's involving Jerry A. Re and his son Gerald F., both specialists on the American Stock Exchange.[6]

II

Jerry Re had been a member of the American Stock Exchange for over 40 years, and his son Gerald had been a member of the same Exchange for over 17 years; together they functioned as specialists in various stocks traded on the American Exchange. While they held these responsible positions, they participated in what later became known as the Swan-Finch conspiracy.

The mastermind of the conspiracy was Lowell M. Birrell, a young lawyer turned big-time swindler and financial conspirator. Following his favorite technique of acquiring control of a company and then watering its stock, on May 17, 1954, Birrell acquired control of the Swan-Finch Oil Corporation, a New York company with an authorized capitalization of 16,000 shares of common stock. Seven months later, he convinced its board of directors to increase the authorized common stock to 1,000,000 shares; on September 15, 1955, Birrell got the board to approve a three-for-one split, bringing the capitalization to 3,000,000 shares.[7] Birrell

[1] 15 U.S.C., No. 78 (b).

[2] Securities and Exchange Commission, *Staff Report on Organization, Management and Regulation of the Conduct of Members of the American Stock Exchange* (Washington: Government Printing Office, 1962), p. 22.

[3] 15 U.S.C., No. 78(a) (2).

[4] Securities and Exchange Commission, *Report of the Special Study of the Securities Markets* (Washington: Government Printing Office, 1963), pp. 78–82 and 162.

[5] *Ibid.*

[6] United States v. Re, *et al.,* U.S. District Court, Southern District of New York, No. 62 Cr. 307.

[7] U.S. Court of Appeals, Southern District of New York, "Indictment," *Brief for the Appellant,* Docket No. 28526, p. 23a.

managed to acquire approximately 50,000 shares of Swan-Finch stock issued prior to the split and 1,700,000 shares issued after it, for a grand total of 1,850,000 shares. His next step was to make arrangements to offer his shares to the public. He also used these shares as collateral for loans on which he subsequently defaulted.[8]

The participation of Jerry and Gerald Re in the Birrell conspiracy was unmistakable. The Res and Birrell had first done business together in the mid-1940's when the Res were specialists in, and Birrell the principle stockholder of, the Calude Neon Corporation. Soon after Birrell's acquisition of control of Swan-Finch, he and Jerry Re took the necessary steps to assure that the two Res would be appointed as the specialists for Swan-Finch. And in July, 1954, the Res were able to put the company on their books.[9] The Res then became instrumental in rigging the price of the Swan-Finch stock on the American Stock Exchange to encourage sales, and in addition they publicly distributed approximately 600,000 shares of unregistered Swan-Finch stock through a complex of 21 brokerage accounts in various names controlled by them.

As disclosed in their trial, the Res used a variety of devices to manipulate the price of the Swan-Finch stock. They and their friends engaged in a series of purchases of the stock on the American Stock Exchange, and they persuaded others to do likewise. They also persuaded many persons who already held shares not to sell them on the American Stock Exchange. The continued buying and decline in offers to sell that resulted naturally raised the price of the stock and made it appear to be an increasingly attractive investment to the public. When stockholders did insist on selling, the Res purchased their shares privately to prevent news of the sales from spreading. The two specialists disposed of the shares they acquired in a series of sales outside the Exchange in order to keep the listed price at a high level.

These devices had the net effect of causing a series of price jumps for Swan-Finch. Before the Res became specialists in Swan-Finch it was an inactive stock. One week after the Res took over the book, the trading volume increased about 20 times while the price rose by 27 per cent. Within five months, the stock shot up from $15 a share to a high of $38.[10]

The Res and Birrell were in contact daily. The Res managed to sell to the public some 600,000 of Birrell's shares through their own accounts and by arrangements with the brokerage accounts of others; for example, they were responsible for the sales of more than 400,000 shares through Batkin and Company, Baruch Brothers and Company, Phoenix Securities Corporation, I. F. Stillman and Company, L. J. Mack and Company, and Steven Randall and Company.[11] Furthermore, in making the offer and sale of the Swan-Finch stock, the Res made fraudulent and misleading statements concerning the financial condition and performance of the Swan-Finch Oil Corporation and the value and the market price of the stock.[12] Birrell handsomely compensated the Res for their services; the evidence at the trial indicated that they netted more than $1,000,000 for their "assistance."

III

Between April 2, 1957, and March 22, 1960, the Grand Jury of the Southern Dis-

[8] When bankruptcy proceedings were in process for Swan-Finch, the trustees reported that the Company had no assets.

[9] Unlisted stocks were traded like listed stocks, but they did not have to comply with the reporting requirements and other provisons of the Securities Exchange Act of 1934. Swan-Finch's trading privileges were based on 15 U.S.C., No. 78 1(f) (1), which permitted the continuation of the privileges of the stocks that enjoyed them as of March 1, 1934. U.S. Court of Appeals, 2nd Circuit, *Brief for the U.S.*, Docket No. 28526, p. 18.

[10] *Ibid.*, p. 19.

[11] *Brief for the Appellant,* pp. 25a–27b.

[12] *Ibid.*

trict of New York filed charges against the Res and others on eight counts of conspiracy and other illegal activities. Among the charges were violations of federal statutes by selling unregistered stocks on the American Stock Exchange, conspiracy to peg and fix stock prices, and false testimony. The case dragged through the courts for about six years. Finally, on July 11, 1963, all defendants were convicted in a jury trial. Before pronouncing the sentence, the presiding justice, Judge Bonsal, said "No doubt it is a fact that the leader in these operations was Lowell A. Birrell; but he is beyond the reach of this court at this time [having fled to Brazil]." Addressing Jerry Re he added, "But in the eyes of the jury, you were guilty of the things you did. It seems to me that as a specialist, you . . . betrayed the American Stock Exchange and its governors, who had entrusted you with a quasi-judicial responsibility." For their complicity in the conspiracy the judge sentenced each of the Res to three years in prison; he suspended two and one-half years of each sentence, however, so they were to serve only six months. They were also fined $15,000 each.

Speaking for the senior Re, attorney Harris A. Steinberg complained that several other securities dealers had admitted that they had sold some unregistered Swan-Finch stock but were not prosecuted. He declared further that the Res were made "the goats" for the looseness of market operations that the Securities and Exchange Commission wanted to attack and that they were used by the government "to shrive the community guilt." [13]

[13] *Wall Street Journal,* September 11, 1963.

UNITED STATES v. MAX DAVIS

In recent years, the money pouring into employee retirement benefit plans has become a mighty flood. At the end of 1964, private pension funds had assets of $77,-200,000,000 and were increasing at the rate of over $7 billion annually. Nearly 2.5 million beneficiaries were receiving payments and over 17 million employees were estimated to be covered by such plans. Many pension funds are administered solely by the corporations whose employees they serve; others are run by unions and employers together, and some are administered by unions alone. The pension fund assets that unions handle or help administer make up about $5 billion of the total, although precise figures are not available.

I

With the Taft-Hartley Act of 1947, Congress instituted some regulation of employee trust funds, limiting them to certain purposes and requiring certain forms of administration to protect the rights of the workers covered. Enforcing these legal restrictions and safeguarding the funds against misuse is not easy, however. There are thousands of funds, large and small; most are managed by expert, competent trustees, but some are in the hands of men whose honesty, sense of responsibility, and ability leave much to be desired. One such trustee was Max Davis, the secretary-treasurer of Local 10, Independent Brotherhood of Production, Maintenance, and Operating Employees, a New York union with some 500 members. On September 12, 1963, Davis was found guilty of embezzling money from his union's welfare pension fund.

According to testimony at his trial, Max Davis withdrew $16,500 from the pension fund of Local 10 on February 7, 1963. Davis declared that he had only been following orders. The president of the local, he said, was confined with an illness and had told him to make a withdrawal in the following way: He was to make out two

$10,000 checks against the union's account at the Chemical Bank and deposit them with the Amalgamated Bank; then he was to cash checks for the amounts of $10,000 and $6,500 and turn the money over to the president. Davis testified that he did exactly as he had been instructed.[1]

Shortly after Davis had completed these transactions, federal government officials became suspicious of the management of the welfare fund. All unions must submit reports and records of their financial condition to the Department of Labor, and in the preliminary examination of Local 10's reports several discrepancies were discovered that led government officials to believe that they should look more closely at the local's financial records and statements. Preparatory to a careful and detailed examination, a subpoena for Local 10's records was issued. In response, Davis removed the pertinent papers from the union's files and burned them in an incinerator. On February 11, 1963, he left for California with his paramour, Marcia Pickerell. For four months he lived in Los Angeles under the assumed name of Max Froshman. The FBI was asked to help locate him as a suspected embezzler, and it began a diligent search throughout the country. On June 11, 1963, an agent apprehended him in San Diego; he was arrested and returned to New York for trial.

[1] United States v. Davis, 63 Cr. 19174, Stenographic Minutes, August 9, 1963, U.S. Southern District Court of New York.

A grand jury heard the case against Davis and charged him with having embezzled $16,500 from the union's employee welfare benefit fund and also with having removed and destroyed the subpoenaed union records. On September 12, 1963, in the U.S. Southern District Court of New York, Davis was found guilty on all counts. Judge John M. Cannella sentenced him to five years in prison and a fine of $25,000.

II

After Judge Cannella read his verdict, Harold Baer, Jr., the prosecuting attorney, commented:

> It is said indeed that throughout this entire investigation, not a single one of the members of the Union communicated their concern to this office or came to the aid of the Government. It is this apathy [among the rank and file] which in a very real way contributes to the commission of crimes such as this. . . . This [corrupt] element in the labor movement is comparatively small; unfortunately, it is growing. It is fast becoming a recognized and accepted area for the fast buck—it is taking its place along with gambling and narcotics as a bona fide racket.

QUESTIONS

The Equal Treatment of Individuals

1. Compare the crimes of the Res and of Davis; contrast the penalties imposed after they were found guilty. What explanations can you suggest for the difference in treatment?

2. Why did the Res' case take six years to complete but the Davis case only three months?

3. The attorney who prosecuted Davis complained that no union members helped the government in its case against Davis. Similar complaints were made by government officials that Teamster members did not help in the more highly publicized prosecution of James Hoffa, the convicted president of the Teamsters Union. Might union members have reason to be suspicious of the impartiality of the law and thus reluctant to aid it?

4. The attorney for the Res complained that many security dealers had engaged in the same activities his clients had and suggested that it was unfair to prosecute only the Res. What answer would you give him?

5. If one paraphrased the remarks of the prosecuting attorney about the implications of the Davis case and applied them to business and members of the business community, would it be a fair charge? Why? Was it a fair charge against unions and their members?

section **5**

AN INDUSTRIAL WORLD

Until recent years we Americans were content to accept what seemed to be an obvious validation of our business system: it works. With the disturbing exception of the Great Depression of the 1930's, it had produced wealth, provided jobs, and promised opportunities for our citizens in an abundance unmatched in all history or by any other existing system. Per capita income had risen by about 20 per cent a decade—a six-fold increase since the Civil War. If the same rate of increase were to continue for another 100 years, income would be 38 times that received in the 1860's. Such wealth and output stagger the imagination when considered from the perspective of several centuries, but to most Americans the growing productiveness of the industrial system seemed perfectly natural, and they comfortably trusted it to continue as bountifully in the future as it had in the past.

We recognized that America's natural wealth contributed greatly to the system, but the basic source of its success was, we assumed, the special relationships of our citizens to each other, to the organizations that governed their work lives, and to the state. An individualism that allowed workers and employers freely to pursue private interests supplied the business system with the essential ingredient that called forth and enlisted all the resources and abilities necessary for a productive, progressive industrial society.

In the 1950's the nation's unexamined assumptions about the source of its business success and the easy confidence that it would always continue were called into question by two events. First, the newly independent countries and the economically poorer nations began to awaken to the promise of industrialism, and many of them looked to the United States for advice and aid in their attempts to transform their economies and societies. To discover the keys to economic prosperity, we began to examine our own experience, seeking to understand how our industrial business system was built, what its prerequisites had been, and why it evolved as it did. Foreign businessmen and government officials visited our factories and watched workers operate machines of the latest design; American researchers, managers, and trade unionists traveled around the world, inspecting the beginning efforts to industrialize elsewhere. Many of the conclusions reached as a result of these initial investigations were of slight value.

For example, the president of United States Steel, serving on a government mission to several underdeveloped countries, advised the Burmese to adopt "free enterprise" if they wished to industrialize as the United States had.

Simply mentioning "free enterprise" was not an adequate explanation of how we attained our successful industrial development. Foreigners and perceptive Americans alike could and did pertinently ask, "How free and enterprising is the free enterprise carried on in the United States? How independent, self-reliant, and private are American businessmen? How devoted are Americans to the individualism they proclaim, and what exactly do Americans mean by individualism?" The earlier sections of this book indicated that these questions have no simple answers. Much of our business is conducted by large organizations; while their freedom to operate may be legally justified by the same arguments used in the eighteenth and early nineteenth centuries to justify personal liberty, they clearly do not behave like private individual entrepreneurs. As Section 2 suggested, it is because business organizations are so large and influential today that the very distinction between public and private interests is becoming increasingly blurred. The character of the economic units operating in the market has changed accordingly; equally changed, as indicated in Section 3, is the market mechanism itself. Though the market is a device of great usefulness to us, we do not accept its decisions uncritically or maintain it in the pure, simple form suggested by early economists. As for the individual Americans who use and hopefully benefit from our economic system, most of the cases in Section 4 suggest that in an important part of our lives, the time we spend at work, we are willing to subordinate individualism to the needs of our organizations. Legislators, judges, arbitrators, and union and business leaders often seem convinced that individualism is not truly compatible with free enterprise, since all too often it interferes with successful (efficient) operations.

The changing situation in the less developed countries was one event that encouraged us to scrutinize and reassess the values, performance, and problems of our modern business society; a second event was the post–World War II rise of the Soviet Union. The Russians' early success in harnessing nuclear power in 1949 and their mastery of the technique of the hydrogen bomb soon thereafter indicated that a new and effective industrial power had emerged under a system that Americans had long thought would make such an occurrence unlikely, if not impossible. The orbiting of Sputnik I, man's first artificial satellite, in 1957 indicated that the U.S.S.R. could and would contest the industrial preeminence of the United States. At the Twenty-first Congress of the Communist Party two years later, Chairman Khrushchev made the challenge explicit; he declared that "the Soviet Union intends to outstrip the United States economically."

The problem of continuing our industrial development at a pace rapid enough to insure military superiority in the world and a thriving, fully employed economy at home—all the while maintaining the values we believe make life worthwhile—quickly became a major issue in politics and economics. How was it possible that a nation that allowed neither free enterprise nor democracy and that denounced individualism as an evil had become the world's second greatest industrial power and could boast of an economy that at the time seemed to be growing faster than our own? In what ways was the Soviet Union different from—and in what ways like—the United States? In response to the Soviet challenge, American businessmen, scholars, government officials, and countless other individuals sought to improve their understanding of the sources and essential mechanisms of industrialism. This effort at self-analysis, like the effort growing out of our need to help less developed nations, has not yet resulted in a satisfactory new theory to explain the operations of our business system, but it has enabled us to clear away many false ideas.

chapter **12**

IDEOLOGY AND BUSINESS PRACTICE

The dominant economic theories and business ideologies of the United States and of the Soviet Union are clearly quite different; what is less obvious is the significance of the difference. Jawaharlal Nehru, the late prime minister of India, maintained that industrial development had made the Soviet Union and the United States more alike than different; he was more impressed, he said, with the similarities he observed in the two countries than with the distinction each claimed for itself. Several French scholars have gone further and claimed that industrial technology has pressed the Russian and American societies into the same mold, making life in the two countries almost indistinguishable.

Foreign observers are not the only ones to observe that the requirements of industrialism are causing societies in different countries increasingly to resemble each other. In a study entitled *Industrialism and Industrial Man,*[1] four eminent American economists examined the evolutionary paths followed by the more developed countries, such as the United States and the Soviet Union, and currently being followed by such developing nations as Brazil and India. They concluded that despite differences in national ideology, the more industrialized nations become, the more that "social systems will be reasonably uniform around the world as compared with today's situation." [2] They suggested that the industrial society of the U.S.S.R. is likely to become more like that of the United States; at the same time, the society of the United States is also responding to the demands of technology and the forces of progress by changing its traditional forms of organization and ideology.

Ideological conflict over social arrangements in each country will fade, they assert, for it

> can get in the way not only of progress but even current production. [As realists, the people within each country] may even drop their ideological inheritance in favor of a new pragmatism . . . [for] industrial society must be administered, and the administrators become increasingly benevolent and increasingly skilled. They learn to respond where response is required, to anticipate the inevitable. The benevolent

[1] Clark Kerr, John T. Dunlop, Frederick H. Harbison, and Charles A. Meyers (Cambridge: Harvard University Press, 1960).
[2] *Ibid.,* p. 296.

political bureaucracy and the benevolent economic oligarchy are matched with the tolerant mass.[3]

The view that industrialism entails specific organizational forms may seem comforting insofar as it can really assure us that the rest of the countries of the world are on the way to becoming modified versions of our own society. It is disturbing, however, in that it assumes we are a tolerant mass, satisfied to be governed by political bureaucrats and economic oligopolists; moreover, it too quickly and too easily assigns a small, insignificant role to ideas and values.

Of course, the influence of technology upon social forms has been studied thoroughly, especially in connection with the ideas of Karl Marx. He argued that the mode of production (the pattern of ownership that prevails in a society) determines a people's ideas, ideology, politics, and law. This assertion was useful in drawing attention to one important influence on social forms, but it was also misleading: Marx too readily excluded other sources of behavior. Ideas and values drawn from nontechnical, nonindustrial sources may be forceful and more or less autonomous stimulators of human activity, even guiding technology itself into any one of numerous possible alternative forms. History provides many cases in which the influence of technology was not decisive. For example, the same agricultural and commercial technology was common to both Sparta and Athens, but the two societies were remarkably different. Agricultural techniques in seventeenth-century England, Russia, and China were not nearly as different as were their societies. There may be no more reason for thinking that similar industrial technologies of the future will produce like social arrangements among different countries than did similar agricultural technologies of the past.

In comparing nations or societies, one should specify exactly what characteristic, activity, or process is being compared; then one must distinguish between apparent or superficial and real or essential differences. In the sphere of politics, for example, the government of Great Britain formally is quite unlike that of the United States, but most observers feel that its monarchical trappings are not enough to cause British and American democracy to differ in kind. Both are fundamentally alike in that the governors and lawmakers are responsible to the electorate. The government of the Soviet Union on the other hand, has some of the trappings of a democracy—periodic elections and a parliament of representatives—but few would take these forms for the substance of democracy.[4]

In the following cases the reader should try to discover ways in which American business is like and unlike Russian business. An examination of ideology may lead to one conclusion and an examination of practice may support a quite different judgment. And in the case of political forms, we need to look behind the prevailing stereotypes for the substance of our economic differences and similarities. Traditionally, we have assumed that the market is an alternative to government control of economic life and a means of fostering private over public enterprise. However, as Professor Charles E. Lindblom has pointed out, the market mechanism can serve a governmentally directed, centrally planned, or dictatorial economy as well as a laissez faire, free enterprise system.[5]

[3] *Ibid.*, p. 283.

[4] Of course, "form" should not always be designated as "mere form." The forms and procedures through which men accomplish similar purposes may be exceedingly important. As the aphorism has it, "one man's red tape is another man's due process."

[5] Charles E. Lindblom, "The Rediscovery of the Market," *The Public Interest,* Summer, 1966, pp. 100–101.

There can be no doubt that the American business system is different from the Russian system; we also confidently believe that it is better. It may well be, however, that the superiority of the American system, and therefore its best justification, does not lie in such changeable market characteristics as competition, profitability, or efficiency, but rather in the goals we seek and the values we express through the particular use we make of the market.

National Uses of Economic Power

THE SOVIET OIL OFFENSIVE

At the Arab Petroleum Congress in late 1960 the Soviet delegation made plain its government's intentions of once again becoming a major exporter of oil to western markets. E. P. Gurov, spokesman for the delegation and chairman of Soyuzneftexport, the Soviet oil export trust, pointed out that during the decade 1925–35, Russia had supplied 14.3 per cent of all the oil imported by west European countries, and during 1930–33, its share had reached 19 per cent. By 1956–59, however, Soviet oil exports accounted for only 4.4 per cent of the same countries' imports. Gurov declared that the U.S.S.R. wanted a "legal place among petroleum exporting nations . . . [and desired] to exercise its right to compete freely in the world market." [1]

I

Gurov's declaration at the Arab Petroleum Congress did not represent a wholly new departure in Soviet trade policy. Nikita Khrushchev had long urged increased trade between the Soviet Union and the West. Speaking to an audience of Western businessmen in 1959 at the Leipzig Trade Fair, Khrushchev declared that such trade could only be good for the capitalist countries:

> As a representative of Soviet business circles [I can tell you that it] is of advantage to you to conduct extensive trade with us, because it is advantageous for your countries to use your industries to capacity, to reduce unemployment, and to obtain normal income and profits. If you do not understand this today, you will understand it tomorrow, and you will enter into comprehensive economic relations with Socialist countries.[2]

Increased trade may or may not have had as much advantage for the West as Khrushchev declared, but there was no doubt that increased oil exports were greatly to the advantage of the U.S.S.R.

During Stalin's rule Soviet planners had based industrialization almost exclusively on coal, a policy shaped by the assumed "necessity to develop local energy resources wherever possible." The result was an extraordinarily heavy investment in coal mining and an underutilization of petroleum, which seems all the more remarkable in view of the extent of Soviet oil resources. Between 1932 and 1937 proved reserves of oil in the U.S.S.R. increased at a rate of 8.7 per cent, 2.6 times as fast as the growth of oil production. Proved and apparent reserves grew at a rate of 30 per cent a year. (During a comparable period in the United States production increased twice as fast as reserves.) [3] Soviet geologists estimated in the late 1930's that the U.S.S.R. contained two-thirds of the then known oil reserves,

[1] *Business International,* December 16, 1960, p. 8.

[2] Samuel Pisar, *A New Look At Trade Policy Toward the Communist Bloc,* prepared for the Subcommittee on Foreign Economic Policy of the Joint Economic Committee (Washington: Government Printing Office, 1961), p. 13.

[3] *New Directions in the Soviet Economy,* Part II-A, Economic Performance, Subcommittee on Foreign Economic Policy of the Joint Economic Committee (Washington: Government Printing Office, 1966), p. 217.

and in 1960 American experts estimated that the total reserves of the U.S.S.R. were currently twice those of the United States.

After Stalin's death in 1953 and Khrushchev's rise to power in 1955 the Soviet government began to exploit its petroleum resources more fully, raising the contribution of petroleum to total output of energy fuel from 17.4 per cent in 1950 to 34.8 per cent in 1963. Oil from newly developed fields in the Ural–Volga area in 1955–57 and additional new drilling in Uzbekistan and Kazakhstan in 1960–62 more than kept pace with expanding domestic and export needs. By 1960 the U.S.S.R. had outstripped Venezuela as the world's second largest producer of crude oil; its production was 148 million tons, four times the 1950 level. By 1964 production had increased another 40 per cent to 220 million tons. Yearly growth in production has ranged from nearly 8 per cent to over 10 per cent; in the United States the rate has varied between 1.8 per cent and 2.1 per cent.[4]

Had even greater use of oil been made, the U.S.S.R. would have saved significantly on capital requirements in the mining, iron and steel, and railroad industries. Belatedly Soviet planners realized that the rate of investment in petroleum needed to be sharply increased. One of the high priority programs in the modernization of Soviet industry during the 1950's was accordingly the conversion of the national economy from a coal to a more efficient petroleum-natural gas base.

Before the new fuels could be used extensively by Soviet industry they had to be transported from the fields to the industrial areas. Soviet planners ran into severe difficulties in this respect; the railroad system was already overburdened and could not support any substantial addition in oil traffic. Truck transportation was not a feasible alternative, for the highway network in the U.S.S.R. is rudimentary. Pipelines had to be constructed, which in turn required either an investment in plants and equipment to make large diameter pipe or the importation of pipe from abroad. Since the country's metallurgical industry was not able to increase its capacity sufficiently to meet the new demands of the oil industry, the Soviet Union turned to the West as a source for steel pipe, pumps, and valves. To pay for these vital supplies the Soviets offered oil, which in turn required the construction of more pipelines to shipping points so that oil could be sent abroad and hence made necessary the acquisition of more pipe. The process seemed to be a case of pulling one's self up by one's bootstraps, a difficult maneuver.

By 1955 the Soviet Union had become a net oil exporter; in that year it shipped a meager 8 million tons. By 1959 it was able to ship 25.3 million tons, and by 1961 33 million tons, nearly one-fifth of its oil production, and enough to supply about 8 per cent of the oil needs of the Western importing countries. By the mid-1960's oil exports were earning the U.S.S.R. the equivalent of about a billion dollars a year, almost a third of the revenues coming to it from Western Europe. Oil had become the country's principal earner of foreign currency.

The U.S.S.R.'s first opportunity to sell oil to the West in significant quantities came during the Suez crisis of 1956–57 when oil movements from the Middle East were temporarily interrupted. The sales that resulted were limited by the Soviet's lack of adequate transportation facilities, but they served notice of a serious intent to penetrate free world's oil markets and actually marked the beginning of real competition with Western private oil enterprise. In the years that followed the Suez crisis, sales of Soviet oil steadily increased. By 1960 Western oil men had become seriously alarmed, and they have seen little in the statistics of international oil shipments to give them peace of mind since then. Between 1960

[4] *World Petroleum Report,* 1958–65. (This is a quarterly supplement to the magazine *World Petroleum.* The particular data used here was given in the annual March 15 supplements.)

and 1964, Italy, West Germany, and Finland raised their imports of Soviet oil by 27 per cent; several less developed countries raised their imports even more. The United Arab Republic, Morocco, and Brazil increased their imports of Soviet oil by more than 89 per cent in only three years, 1962–64.[5] The statistics for 1966 showed that Soviet bloc oil exports to the non-Communist world were continuing to expand.[6]

One of the fears of Western oil men was that the Soviet exports were displacing oil from non-Communist sources, even though West European demand for oil products was rising rapidly; another, more serious fear was that the Soviet exports were disrupting a well-established oil pricing system. If their phenomenal rate of increase of the past decade were maintained for another 10 years, Soviet sales would be a major and troublesome force with which all private firms would have to contend.

II

Soyuzneftexport's pricing policies disturbed Western oil men more than did the volume of oil it exported. One complaint was that the agency appeared to be cutting prices where competition existed in order to penetrate the market and to be running loss leaders to attract buyers. In 1957 Soyuzneftexport offered crude oil on the international market at $2.06 a barrel when Middle East oil was priced at $2.79 a barrel. In November, 1960, it sold crude oil to Italy at $1.00 a barrel at Black Sea ports; after processing in Italian refineries, this oil could be marketed at a price about one-third lower than Middle East oil similarly refined.[7] The American Petroleum Institute pointed out to critics of the Soviet sales to Italy that the price was probably a secondary concern in the arrangement; the U.S.S.R. was exchanging a surplus commodity, its crude oil, for significant quantities of steel pipe, an item in desperately short supply in the U.S.S.R. and essential for an expansion of the vital pipeline system.[8]

Western oilmen also accused the Soviets of charging premium prices where buyers had little choice of competing brands. In 1959, for example, the U.S.S.R. charged its satellites 88.1 rubles per metric ton for crude oil and 158.2 rubles for petroleum products. Comparable products were sold to the West for the equivalent of 55.2 rubles and 75.8 rubles respectively.[9] Students of Soviet trade pointed out that the satellites paid for the oil with low quality goods, however, so that the higher prices they paid for oil may have been more apparent than real.

The Soviet Union's offer of oil was especially attractive to countries that had been dependent upon a single supplier. Competition usually provides a buyer more opportunity than does monopoly. Tailoring its sales policies to the circumstances of its customers, Soyuzneftexport was willing to accept payment in various goods and raw materials, such as sugar from Cuba, or even in soft local currencies, such as Indian rupees and Egyptian pounds. The easy credit terms that the U.S.S.R. made available also proved to be a valuable inducement to various countries, developed and undeveloped alike.

The competitive tactics employed by Soyuzneftexport are illustrated by the Soviet oil campaigns in Pakistan, Ceylon, and Italy. In Pakistan, seven American and British oil companies had been prospecting since 1947, with negligible results. When the Western firms wound up their explora-

[5] Pisar, *op. cit.*, p. 930; and *The Times Review of Industry* [London], 1961, p. 41.
[6] *Wall Street Journal,* November 9, 1966.
[7] Halford L. Hoskins, *Problems Raised by the Soviet Oil Offensive,* prepared for the Committee on the Judiciary of the U.S. Senate (Washington: Government Printing Office, 1962), p. 4.

[8] Robert E. Ebel, *The Petroleum Industry of the Soviet Union* (Washington: The American Petroleum Institute, 1961), p. 155.
[9] *Ibid.*

tions in late 1960, the U.S.S.R. offered to continue the search for oil. The Soviets promised to conduct an extensive geological survey financed by a low-interest loan of $35 million, to be repaid over a 17-year period; if oil were found, it would all belong to Pakistan (the Western agreements had allowed Pakistan only a 25 per cent interest in any discoveries). Pakistan accepted the Russian proposal, and the final arrangements were concluded in January, 1962.[10]

While the U.S.S.R. was negotiating with Pakistan, it was working out an oil deal with Ceylon. The Soviets offered to sell oil at three-quarters current market prices and to accept Ceylonese rupees on six-month credit as payment. Two major international oil companies, Standard-Vacuum and Caltex, controlled all of Ceylon's oil trade, and their officials did not enjoy the prospect of losing a part of it to the Russians. They succeeded in having strong protests issued by both the British and American governments but to no avail, for in June, 1961, the Ceylonese Parliament established a tax-exempt, state-owned corporation to import and distribute oil, with the power to fix prices and acquire any property required for such purposes.[11] Later that year the new corporation entered into a long-term contract calling for the importation of 275,000 metric tons of oil annually from the U.S.S.R. In early 1962 the fears of British and American oilmen were realized; the Ceylonese oil corporation took over 108 of the 175 gasoline stations owned by the Western oil companies without offering any compensation.

In retaliation for the confiscation of the gasoline stations, the United States suspended all foreign aid to Ceylon. The Ceylonese government then imposed price ceilings on imported petroleum products; they were slightly above the Soviet prices but well below posted international prices. Spokesmen for the western companies refused to accept the new price limits, arguing that the Soviet oil was being brought in at far below regular commercial rates. The managing director of Caltex said, "This is really an economic war between East and West, and it's gone far beyond the point of private companies' being able to fight it on their own." [12] Finally, in June, 1965, Ceylon agreed to pay the oil companies a total of $11.6 million over five years as compensation for the assets confiscated. However, by that time the Soviet Union was shipping 828,000 metric tons of oil a year to Ceylon, and contracts for 1966 called for it to ship 869,000 tons, three times the amount sold under the initial contract.

The largest purchaser of Soviet oil outside the Communist bloc has been Italy. In 1963 Italy received from the Russians shipments valued at $89.7 million that amounted to about 20 per cent of its total oil supplies. A 1962 report prepared for the Senate Committee on the Judiciary noted several effects of the large and still growing Italian imports from the U.S.S.R.:

> Until recent years Italy's needs for oil fuels were supplied largely by the international oil companies operating in the Middle East. The companies' operations in Italy included the construction of refineries and the development of distribution facilities for the local marketing of oil products throughout the country. This sphere of company operations is being restricted step by step, owing to measures taken by a corporate arm of the state itself. With the oil and gas from Italy's domestic fields and extensive petroleum imports from the U.S.S.R., this agency, a corporation called Ente Nazionale Indocarburi (ENI), a state-owned fuel trust now embracing some 75 other corporate bodies operating in many fields, is in process of eliminating such foreign business enterprise within Italy as may profitably be displaced. ENI, moreover, has become a principal channel through which Soviet oil, often in camouflaged form, is distributed elsewhere in Europe and the non-Communist world.[13]

[10] Hoskins, *op. cit.,* p. 5.
[11] *Ibid.,* p. 7.

[12] Washington *Post,* May 14, 1962.
[13] *Ibid.,* p. 11.

In late 1960 and early 1961 the Italian government and the Soviet Union signed contracts obligating the U.S.S.R. to supply 30 million barrels of oil a year, in return for which Italy was to ship large-diameter-pipe and pumps to Russia. Western oil companies issued statements protesting these arrangements, and the governments of several Western nations expressed their dismay to the Italian government over the terms of the sales to and from the U.S.S.R. In August, 1962, the Italian government announced a new policy of limiting Soviet oil to 16 per cent of its total imports. Nine months later, in April, 1963, Esso, the largest American-based oil company, and ENI signed a five-year pact which called for delivery of a total of 80 million barrels of crude oil at prices representing about a 20 per cent discount. Payment for this oil was to be made largely in equipment and machinery produced by Italian state-owned industries. Agreement to such a barter arrangement was a major change in policy for Esso; it was clearly a response to the Soviet competition and gave more consideration to Italian interests than ever before. Not only did Italy get its oil for a lower price, it also was allowed to make payment in the way that it found most favorable.

Spokesmen for ENI announced that Italy was going to continue its policy of pursuing cheaper energy, and also noted that "ENI did not want to be identified with 'Western oil companies' or . . . [be] dependent on them." [14] On November 15, 1963, the Soviet press announced a new and intensified oil export drive to help finance the expansion of the Soviet chemical industry, and at the same time ENI and the Soyuzneftexport announced the signing of a $400 million, six-year pact. Under its terms, the Soviet Union was to deliver 25 million tons of crude oil in exchange for synthetic rubber, plastics, chemical products, machinery, fiber goods, and "fixtures" for chemical and petroleum plants. The price at which the oil was offered was less than Esso had asked earlier in the year. ENI claimed that the transaction would help Italy's balance of payments and help her increase her trade with countries in the Communist bloc that were eager to buy Western goods.

[14] *New York Times,* April 27, 1963.

III

A number of Western businessmen and government officials saw something akin to a military offensive in the Soviet oil competition. George Getty II, president of the Tidewater Oil Company, proposed that the United States exempt American petroleum companies from antitrust penalties so that they could combine and better compete with the U.S.S.R. George Reed, chairman of the Texas Gulf Producing Company, suggested the formation of an "economic NATO" which would set limits on Soviet imports. And Senator Mike Monroney of Oklahoma, declaring that oil had become a principal weapon in an economic war between the United States and the U.S.S.R., proposed that the oil industry be given more tax allowances to aid in meeting the Soviet challenge.[15]

American companies had already used various tactics to block Soviet oil from world markets. When the U.S.S.R. first began exporting oil after World War II, the Western oil companies realized that the shortage of Soviet tankers made the Russians vulnerable, and they tried to prohibit the leasing of tankers to them. Standard Oil of New Jersey proposed in July, 1960, and again in April, 1962, that the American

[15] In July, 1961, the European Common Market executive commission had proposed a limit of 250,000 barrels a day on the importation of Soviet oil. In March, 1962, the EEC Assembly also urged the adoption of a policy of restricting imports of fuels from "nations which could not guarantee long-term stability of supply." Italy strongly opposed these proposals, and the Common Market adopted neither. See also *Journal of Commerce,* June 5, 1961; *New York Times,* June 22, 1961, and November 14, 1961; and Hoskins, *op. cit.,* p. 13.

Maritime Association establish a blacklist barring from the American oil import trade vessels that had carried Soviet crude.[16] When the blacklist was initiated, however, it had little effect, because about 10 per cent of the total tanker tonnage owned by Western firms was idle at the time, and shippers were more interested in carrying oil—anyone's oil—for some profit than in foregoing income to help out fellow capitalists. Furthermore, the Soviet Union moved quickly to strengthen its tanker fleet. Taking advantage of the financially depressed condition of West European shipyards, the U.S.S.R. ordered over three dozen new tankers, most of them from Finland, Germany, and Japan. In 1963, after France vetoed Britain's membership in the Common Market, Britain also agreed to build tankers for the Soviet Union, in exchange for oil. By the end of 1964, the U.S.S.R. had the world's tenth largest tanker fleet with 2.6 per cent of the world's tanker tonnage. It also had the fourth largest number of tankers on order, 51, which when delivered would raise its capacity by 50 per cent.[17] Most of these new ships were small, however, designed for use on the Baltic and Mediterranean seas.

The American companies also attempted to hinder the fulfillment of the Soviet Union's pipeline program. The primary project in this program, which was begun in 1958 and scheduled for completion early in the 1960's, was the "Friendship Pipeline," a 40-inch pipe that would transport oil from the Ural–Volga fields to the Baltic and Black seas and to Poland, Czechoslovakia, and Hungary. Late in 1962, the United States persuaded the NATO Council to put a ban on exports of large pipe to the Soviet Union. The Americans argued that large size pipe was a strategic good, and the completion of the Friendship Pipeline would expedite the delivery of fuel to Soviet armies in Eastern Germany.

[16] Hoskins, *op. cit.*, p. 3.
[17] *World Petroleum Report,* March 15, 1965, p. 23.

The government of the U.S.S.R. strongly protested the NATO ban; Premier Khrushchev denounced it as a result of "crude pressure" by the United States. He assured the world that the Soviet Union would complete its pipeline by itself, and ridiculed the American contention that the pipeline was a strategic good:

> Of course anything you want can be classified as strategic material, even buttons, because they can be sewed to a soldier's pants. The soldier will not wear pants without buttons, otherwise he will have to hold them up with his hands. And what will he then do with his weapons? . . . If one thinks in this vein, then buttons are the most strategic of materials.[18]

Responding to the NATO resolution, the government of West Germany asked its steel companies to cancel a $40 million order for pipe for the Soviet Union. Despite severe political repercussions within the governing coalition, West Germany enforced the ban. Much to the chagrin of the Americans, however, the British government then allowed its steel companies to take orders for about 40 per cent of the tonnage of pipe that the German firms had been forbidden to deliver. Thus, in spite of the American attempts to hinder the Soviet pipelaying program, nothing more was accomplished than a delay of a few months. The Friendship Pipeline was completed in the fall of 1964.

IV

A number of Americans were critical of their government's response to the Soviet oil competition. The *New York Times* argued that the government was in fact protecting American firms against price-cutting rather than meeting the real Soviet challenge, its rapid rate of economic growth.[19] The *Economist* maintained that a major source of the downward pressure

[18] *New York Times,* March 2, 1963.
[19] *Ibid.,* April 13, 1963.

on world prices was the restrictions on imports imposed by the United States. Because they were unable to sell in the world's biggest oil market, companies had to sell their oil elsewhere, getting rid of the world surplus at lower prices than otherwise would prevail.[20]

Experts in oil economics pointed out that the price instability of recent years had not been so much the result of any Soviet oil offensive as it was the consequence of the breakdown of a producers' cartel as a result of pressures from West European governments and the governments of the producing countries in the Middle East. Both had good reason to encourage independent companies to enter the trade; the European countries looked for price cuts while the Middle Eastern countries hoped for high prices and a larger share of the profits. Consequently, in the 10 years from 1954 to 1964 the share of the export market held by the seven major Western companies—Standard Oil of New Jersey, Royal Dutch Shell, Gulf, Texaco, British Petroleum, Socony Mobil, and Standard Oil of California—decreased from 90 per cent to below 70 per cent.[21]

Other commentators pointed out that in selling its oil, the Soviet Union was probably trying to maximize the net return on its whole national industrial effort. The country needed capital equipment and other goods from the West to develop its own industry most effectively. It may well be cheaper for the Soviet to produce oil and sell it abroad for machinery and goods than to keep its oil and attempt to produce the needed machinery itself; under present conditions oil could even be expected to enjoy a declining marginal cost in the Soviet Union.

Not everyone agreed that the Russian competition in oil was merely a matter of economics. Senator Kenneth Keating of New York was of the opinion that the Soviet Union's oil was being used as a weapon in the Cold War:

> Sold at prices determined by political rather than economic considerations, accompanied by propaganda, technicians, and all the prerequisites of a Communist marketing system, and designed to undermine the commercial activities of the free enterprise system, Soviet oil has already begun to injure the West. Unless steps are undertaken now, the onrush of Soviet oil over the next 5 to 10 years may seriously undermine the economic independence of Western Europe and the future of private enterprise in the underdeveloped countries.[22]

The report of a subcommittee of the Senate Committee on the Judiciary issued in 1962 took very much the same view:

> In the first place, Soviet oil is a commodity entirely under government control and consequently can be employed in the interest of the state in any manner deemed useful by the heads of government. The economic profit motive, while undoubtedly present in all engagements entered into with respect to oil supply or provision of technical services relating to oil exploration, production, refining or transport, invariably has been subordinated to whatever ulterior purposes have been components of Communist state policy. This has given the Soyuzneftexport an inestimable advantage in competing with private enterprise as represented by the major oil companies inasmuch as these are compelled to operate at a profit in order to continue to exist. There have been limits, therefore, to the extent to which the majors [the big international oil companies] have been able to trim prices to meet the Soviet challenge and even the reluctance of governments in the free and uncommitted world to deal with the U.S.S.R. for political or ideological reasons in an increasing number of instances has not equaled the need for obtaining oil fuels, on which their economies and even their security measures are dependent, at the most favorable prices available.[23]

[20] Gilbert Burck, "The Boiling World of Oil," *Fortune,* 71 (February, 1965), 127.

[21] *Economist,* July 16, 1960, pp. 195–96.

[22] Hoskins, *op. cit.,* p. viii.

[23] Hoskins, *op. cit.,* p. 4.

FREE ENTERPRISE IN THE OIL INDUSTRY

Private, profit-making American companies produce and sell some $8 billion of domestic crude oil a year drawn from about 563,000 oil wells in 30 states. Several dozen big, integrated companies and about 7,000 "independent" firms make up the petroleum industry, which is one of the largest industries in the United States. The annual capital expenditures of these companies usually amount to nearly one-quarter of all private American investment.[1] Petroleum technology requires exceedingly high capitalization; assets per employee averaged almost $78,000 in 1964, half again as large as the next highest industry, and 4.5 times the median for all industry.

I

The American petroleum industry has performed remarkably well, in the opinion of industry spokesmen, for it has supplied ever increasing quantities of petroleum to meet the basic fuel needs of the country. In 1900 it provided 64 million barrels of domestic crude oil; by 1964 its production reached 2.8 billion barrels, 27 per cent of the world's output of crude petroleum. Moreover, the same spokesmen maintain, the industry has provided this vast amount of oil at low cost to the consumer; prices of gasoline have hardly changed due to industry action in nearly 40 years. The industry also takes credit for having made an inestimably great contribution to national defense by helping to conserve existing supplies and expanding reserves through exploration and discovery. In all, the spokesmen conclude, the industry has performed well; it is a good example of free enterprise at work. Private firms have assumed the risky task of satisfying their consumers, and proof of their success lies in the profits that they have made over the years.[2]

Successful as it may have been under the private enterprise system, from time to time the petroleum industry has had problems so serious that the federal government has had to take a hand. First the government acted to break up monopoly, and later it tried to contain the destructive effects of rampant competition. The monopoly problem arose after 1899 when John D. Rockefeller and his associates merged 400 companies into an oil empire, the Standard Oil Company of New Jersey, which by 1904 dominated the industry. It probably controlled 84 per cent of domestic sales and a higher proportion of refined petroleum exports. Rockefeller's managerial genius and the economies of scale certainly contributed to the company's success, but his ruthless pursuit of competitive advantage was what insured it. By denying sources and markets for oil to independent pipeline companies, making crude oil prohibitively expensive to independent refineries, and using predatory local price cutting, Standard Oil drove many of its competitors out of business. Several customers and surviving firms sued the company, accusing it of "unfair" competition, unreasonable restraint of trade, and attempting to monopolize the industry. When they were unsuccessful in these private suits, they sought government aid. In 1911, the efforts of the government were successful, for the Supreme Court ordered the dissolution of the company.

In the following two decades the companies spawned by the breakup of the former Standard Oil empire slowly and gradually

[1] Joel B. Dirlam, "The Petroleum Industry," in Walter Adams, ed., *The Structure of American Industry,* 3rd ed. (New York: Macmillan, 1961), p. 278.

[2] See John H. Lichtblau and Dillard P. Spriggs, *Energy Policy and Competition* (New York: Petroleum Industry Foundation, 1961), and the *Tipro Reporter,* published by the Texas Independent Producers and Royalty Owners Association.

evolved into competitors. More competitors also appeared as new oil fields were discovered in Texas and California, and the soaring sales of automobiles opened a wider market for motor fuel.

After 1929 the whole crude oil industry was staggered by two events, each of which compounded the difficulties caused by the other: the onset of the Great Depression reduced the demand for gasoline and put heavy pressure on prices; and the vast new East Texas oil field that opened in 1930 flooded the market with crude oil. Prices soon collapsed, and the industry was thrown into turmoil. By July, 1930, crude oil in East Texas had dropped from $1 a barrel to 18¢; later the price reached a low of 10¢ a barrel!

II

Faced by such desperate conditions as these, the governor of Texas called out the militia to enforce production regulations. His ability to take this step can be traced back to World War I, when state and federal officials had become concerned about the conservation of oil because of its assumed scarcity and importance for military uses. In 1924 President Coolidge established a Federal Oil Conservation Board with both governmental and industry members; it encouraged several of the states to develop conservation programs, and under its aegis the concept of proration took shape. The wild, unregulated exploitation of the East Texas field during the oil crisis in the early 1930's prompted the state and federal governments to use their conservation programs as devices to stabilize the market as well as to guard a vital national resource that was thought to be in limited supply.

Texas, the primary oil-producing state, charged its Railroad Commission with the responsibility of setting production quotas for each oil well. Louisiana, Oklahoma, Kansas, New Mexico, and Arizona adopted similar procedures. Each state restricted its total monthly production to the estimated market demand for crude oil; the total was then prorated among the wells as the monthly "allowable," each well's fair share of production. While this procedure helps eliminate some wasteful practices, it obviously also can help to maintain prices and reduce the risks of production. When the commissioners estimate the demand for crude oil in a month in order to set a quota, they necessarily have a specific price in mind, since demand varies with price.

To make state regulation effective, the federal government enacted the Connelly "Hot-Oil" law in 1935. This law prohibited and subjected to confiscation any oil shipped in interstate commerce produced in violation of a state's proration orders. Congress also authorized the states to form an Interstate Compact to Preserve Oil and Gas. Through this compact, state officials have been able to coordinate their oil regulations and price controlling activities. In effect the federal legislation allowed the industry, through state regulatory bodies, to fix prices in a way that would have been unlawful through a trade association or cartel.

Since state authorities historically have fixed monthly allowable production of crude oil on a *per well* basis, they have encouraged drilling more wells than needed. The more wells a producer had on his claim, the more oil he could pump out. In Texas alone, probably more than half the 194,000 wells are superfluous. They were drilled not because they were needed to get oil out of an underground pool more effectively or efficiently but simply to get more allowables. Their low production helps keep the average flow of oil from all American wells down to 13 barrels a day. The resources wasted in drilling unnecessary wells run into millions. One expert estimates that in all the oil states the industry recently has been spending as much as $1 billion a year on superfluous new wells.

By drilling unneeded wells, the oil industry has raised its costs. The excess wells are featherbedded once they are in production, and few produce at their optimum flow. To keep the supply of oil down to demand at the going price, the Texas Railroad Commission has limited allowable production to as little as one day out of three. This means that the cost per barrel of oil produced is pushed still higher, of course, for a well's overhead is spread over a third of its possible production.

The Texas Railroad Commission does not prorate "stripper" wells and wells that are involved in secondary recovery.[3] Were the number of such wells insignificant, the Commission's policy would be easier to understand, but in fact they are so numerous that they produce a third as much as the optimum yield of the prorated wells. In the month of November, 1963, Texas produced 2.8 million barrels of crude oil; 1.1 million of the total came from strippers. The prorated wells in Texas at the time could have produced nearly 3.2 million barrels had they not been restricted. Proration has created the strange situation where a flush well, capable of producing 1,000 barrels of oil a day, is allowed to produce only 8 barrels while a nearby stripper produces 10. Writing in *Fortune,* Gilbert Burck sarcastically remarks that this practice "makes about as much economic sense as paying a man $500 to till a plot with a total output worth $50.[4] Professor M. A. Adelman estimates that stripper wells and overdrilling may cost the American oil industry, and ultimately the consumers, some $2.5 billion more than the worth of the oil they recover.

[3] A stripper well is a marginal well whose production barely covers costs at prevailing prices. Most require their oil to be pumped out. About two-thirds of all U.S. wells are strippers; they furnish about one-fifth of the total U.S. production, averaging less than four barrels a day. See Dirlam in Adams, *op. cit.,* p. 284. Secondary recovery is securing oil from a well that has ceased to produce by injecting water in the surrounding oil rock strata and driving the remaining oil to the well from which it can be pumped.

[4] "U.S. Oil: A Giant Caught in its own Web," *Fortune,* 71 (April, 1965), 116.

III

Throughout the 1930's and 1940's the American oil industry was quite satisfied with its government sponsored "conservation" program. The market for crude oil was reasonably managed—at least it served the reasonable expectations of investors in the industry. As more and more new foreign fields began supplying oil to the world market after World War II, however, cheap, imported crude increasingly competed with the domestic product. By 1954 it was equal to more than 10 per cent of oil produced in the United States and by 1958 14 per cent. Domestic oil producers argued that it was desirable to restrict imports—to insure a strong industry at home in the interests of national security and conservation, of course. In 1955 a Presidential Cabinet Committee recommended that the oil companies voluntarily limit their imports of crude oil and residual fuel oil to the ratios of imports to domestic crude production that had existed in 1954. The companies gave general formal assent to the limitation.

During the Suez crisis of 1956 the federal government encouraged the states to increase production allowables so that American oil would be available to meet the demands of Western Europe. When the Suez canal reopened in 1957 domestic production had to be cut back again, for not only did European demand disappear, but the international companies were anxious to bring in the cheaper foreign oil. Imports, which had averaged 900,000 barrels a day in 1950, climbed to 1.6 million a day in 1958; the difference between productive capacity and allowables for the domestic producers was over 2 million barrels a day and continued to grow. By 1960 production in the Texas fields had declined from 15 days of pumping a month in 1956 to 8 days. Independent oilmen complained that the international companies were using the state commissions to keep supplies low at home and domestic crude prices up. By recommending low allowables in key production states and then importing cheap foreign oil to fill the gap in supplies, they were enhancing their profits at the expense of the smaller domestic companies.

Since the voluntary import limitations scheme instituted in 1955 did not work, President Eisenhower ordered mandatory quotas in 1959. The Trade Agreements Act of 1955 gave him authority to regulate imports when they "threatened the national security," and he and his advisors concluded that national security, as well as the profits of the thousands of independent producers, was indeed at stake. Neither the independent oilmen nor the managers of the international companies were happy with the result of the administration's action, however. M. J. Rathbone, a former president of the American Petroleum Institute (API), a trade association dominated by the large companies, and also a past president of Standard Oil of New Jersey, told his industry colleagues in 1960:

> We are not running our business in what businessmen would consider an intelligent fashion. . . . This could very well lead to demands for some sort of government regulation. God forbid that it should, but I feel somehow that we invite it when we present such a disorderly picture.[5]

The managers of the international companies found the quotas to be anti–big business, for they were set on a sliding scale that permitted smaller firms to satisfy a greater proportion of their needs through imports. Since the quotas were distributed equally, without regard for the amount of oil actually imported in the past, many small companies sold their import licenses to the large companies, pocketing profits of about a dollar a barrel.

The domestic companies noted that despite the mandatory curbs imposed in 1959, imports of crude oil continued to rise in the following years. Exempted imports from Canada and Mexico almost doubled between 1959 and 1962, and more than doubled again by 1964. The Texas Independent Producers and Royalty Association, a conservative trade group that speaks for small independent producers, protested against the rising volume of imports and at the same time rejected the argument that such protests showed that domestic companies were inefficient and acting to restrain competition. The Association stated:

> Anyone with a modicum of understanding of the American free enterprise system should realize that the kind of "efficiency" [promised by importers of crude oil] can only come at the expense of property rights and the destruction of most of our nation's less-economical producing wells. . . .
>
> But let us hope that those within industry and those in government who understand the industry, will stop implying that we can compete with foreign oil by becoming more "efficient." Nothing that we could do short of abandoning all but the most flush, newest oil production in America would enable us to compete, particularly in light of the highly-favored tax treatment accorded the foreign production of American companies.
>
> If the objective is to preserve a virile home industry, there must be some degree of protection against imports. If our objective is to maximize "efficiency," we can "solve" the import problem through the single expedient by permitting the destruction of our "inefficient" producers—and thereby creating a need for more imports.[6]

The issue facing the oil industry, the Association's *Reporter* maintained, should not be characterized as efficiency versus inefficiency but as monopoly versus free enterprise. To illustrate the advantages enjoyed by the international producers, the magazine singled out Gulf Oil's efficient monopoly in Kuwait. In 1961 Gulf produced 180,000 barrels of crude oil a day from about 14,000 wells in Texas, accounting for 7 per cent

[5] *New York Times,* November 14, 1961. Apparently Rathbone feared *new* government regulations, for the industry was used to and lived under many already.

[6] *New York Times,* March 12, 1959.

of the state's output. In the same year the company, through the Kuwait Oil Company, took 825,000 barrels a day from only 184 wells in Kuwait, 50 per cent of Kuwait's total output. Gulf's Texas wells averaged 12.8 barrels a day, while each Kuwait well averaged almost 4,500 barrels. The enormous advantage in producing cheap oil abroad provided Gulf and other similarly situated international producers with the means to increase their dominance in the U.S. market, threatening the small producer and his ability to compete.[7]

Under the Kennedy administration the restrictions on oil imports were made tighter than before. In 1962 imported oil was limited to 12.5 per cent of domestic oil, and Canadian and Mexican imports were to be deducted from the total imports allowed. The Johnson administration continued the restrictions, though it attempted to adjust them to the benefit of the smaller producers.

IV

Shortly after he took office, President Johnson decided to transfer authority over national policy from his office to the Department of the Interior in order to lessen the political dangers that would arise in dealing with the "rich and powerful oil lobby . . . which has long managed to win preferential treatment in Washington," as an editorial in the *New York Times* put it. The editorial went on to observe, however, that

> oil is so important that however much the President tries to extricate himself, he cannot avoid becoming embroiled in formulating policy. The disposition of import quotas affects our diplomatic relations, our foreign trade policy, our aid program, and the level of domestic production. . . . [Since] he must in the long run shoulder the responsibilities for the oil policies of his administration anyway, [the formulation of oil policy] is an unavoidable obligation [of the President].[8]

[7] The details of the argument are presented in *Tipro Reporter,* February, 1962, pp. 13–20.

[8] *New York Times,* December 19, 1963, p. 32.

National oil policy is a subject in which many citizens besides the President have an interest. A commission appointed by President Kennedy to investigate government policy in oil concluded that the price of crude oil produced in the United States averaged about $1 a barrel higher than it would if the industry were subject to genuine competition. The commission contended that government policy allows and encourages the oil industry to follow a pricing policy that increases the cost of petroleum production to the nation by at least $3.5 billion a year, or nearly $20 for every person in the country. This cost does not take into account the value of tax revenues lost to the nation as a result of tax concessions granted to the oil industry; the depletion allowance alone benefits the industry by about $1 billion a year.

In 1926 Congress granted oil producers a depletion allowance of 27.5 per cent of gross revenue from production (or 50 per cent of net income before depletion, whichever is smaller), arguing that oil in the ground is a capital asset and should be depreciated as such. According to a study made by Senator Paul Douglas, the results of the depletion allowance are that companies make large deductions from their income, thus reducing their taxes significantly. In the period 1945–54, 27 domestic oil companies with before-tax incomes of $3.25 billion paid taxes of only $562 million, or 17 per cent of net income; the effective rate for other kinds of business enterprises was nearly 50 per cent. A study of the 1954 records of 24 large oil companies revealed that they paid an effective tax rate of 22.6 per cent on net revenue, compared to 48.1 per cent for all industry. In 1957 the Humble Oil Company paid but $17 million in income tax on a net income of $193 million before taxes; and Continental, which netted $51 million, paid taxes of only $4.55 million. According to the Secretary of the Treasury in 1951,[9] the tax

[9] Robert Engler, *The Politics of Oil* (New York: Macmillan, 1961), p. 161.

provision in effect allows oil companies to double count the same capital charge, reducing tax liabilities on income of many million dollars.

Despite these figures, Richard Gonzales of the Humble Oil Company has argued that the incidence of taxation on petroleum is in fact much higher than for other industries, and he draws attention to the special taxes that only the petroleum industry has to pay, such as the 5 per cent–10 per cent state output taxes on crude petroleum and the state and federal gasoline taxes. Gonzales concluded that the total tax burden on large integrated petroleum companies is roughly 22 per cent of gross revenue, compared to a little over 5 per cent for all other manufacturing concerns. As for the justification for depletion allowances, Gonzales believes that the depletion law has played an important part in the growth of the American economy. It has encouraged the development of ample supplies of gas and oil that permit these goods to be sold at reasonable prices and that have played a vital role in national security. This achievement has not been due to any advantage America holds over other nations in petroleum resources but rather "has been due to individual initiative and enterprise and to tax laws which have encouraged risk taking and investment in exploration and drilling." [10]

V

American tax laws provide the oil producers with even more benefits for their overseas operations than for their domestic production. Taxes incurred abroad can be written off directly against American tax obligations, though local and state taxes within the U.S. must be counted as business expenses to be subtracted from gross income before taxes are calculated.

[10] Richard J. Gonzales, "Taxation of Petroleum," a talk before the Fifth Annual Meeting of the Colorado Petroleum Council, Colorado Springs, Colorado, June 12, 1964.

The federal government has helped oil companies establish advantageous arrangements with foreign countries, and in the process it has sometimes seemed more concerned with the interests of the private companies than with the collection of taxes. In 1950, for example, representatives of the State Department and the Internal Revenue Service helped Saudi Arabia officials rewrite that nation's tax laws. An existing 50-50 profit-sharing program between Saudi Arabia and Aramco (an international oil company owned by Standard of California, Texaco, Standard of New Jersey, and Socony Mobil) was replaced with a new scheme splitting gross revenues approximately into a 35 per cent income tax and 15 per cent government royalty for Saudi Arabia and a 50 per cent share for the company. In 1956 Aramco grossed $744 million; under the new arrangement Saudi Arabia received $80 million in royalties and $200 million in income taxes, no American income tax was paid, and Aramco distributed profits of $280 million to its four owners. If Saudi Arabia's 50 per cent share had been paid exclusively as a royalty, as before, the United States Treasury would have been over $100 million richer.[11]

The federal government has often aided American oil companies in their overseas activities in other ways than by favorable tax treatment. After Mexico seized the assets of foreign oil companies in 1938, for example, the American government ordered a boycott of Mexican oil. The State Department has also frequently applied pressure to help American companies gain footholds in foreign fields. Some of the Department's methods in winning concessions of this sort were described in a 1944 departmental memorandum on U.S. foreign policy on petroleum. Referring to the Gulf Oil Company, the memorandum noted that in 1931 only a British company was permitted to obtain a concession in Kuwait, adding: "The Department of State's reaction to this

[11] Engler, *op. cit.,* p. 224.

information was prompt and on December 3, 1931, instructions were sent to the Embassy in London to make representations with a view to obtaining equal treatment for American firms. . . . After long negotiations, a concession was granted to [Gulf] in 1934. . . . Otherwise this oil might now be wholly British held." The concession thus obtained for (Gulf) turned out to be the world's richest oil prize.[12] In 1953 when Iranian oil was being re-introduced into international markets, the American government also insisted that the British and Iranian governments give a 5 per cent share to a group of eight American companies.

Overall American public policy in the oil industry has resulted, industry spokesman think, in

> the encouragement of competition between the various fuel industries. This, of course, is in keeping with the overall free enterprise orientation of the American economy. . . . Competition and the consumers' freedom of choice are stimulated by antitrust laws. . . . These laws, and the body of judicial decisions which have been built up over decades of their enforcement, insure the continuity of competition.[13]

Other observers of the petroleum industry have come to very different conclusions. One scholar, who is intimately familiar with the industry and government policy, recently declared:

> If there is one thing clear about our domestic crude oil policy, it is that it has never been frankly explained to the citizens who pay the price, nor fully debated by the Congress that has enacted piecemeal the legislation under which production is restrained, imports restricted, and exploration tax-subsidized.[14]

[12] "U.S. Oil Import Policy and Monopoly," *Tipro Reporter,* January–February, 1962, p. 17.

[13] John H. Lichtblau and Dillard P. Spriggs, *Energy Policy and Competition* (Petroleum Industry Research Foundation, 1961), p. 29.

[14] Dirlan in Adams, *op. cit.,* p. 299.

QUESTIONS

National Uses of Economic Power

1. In his book *The American Economic Republic* (New York: Harcourt, Brace & World, 1963) Adolf A. Berle wrote:

I here suggest that there is no way of knowing whether any enterprise in the United States, taken by itself, makes or loses money, and that the utility or nonutility of the goods or services it produces or provides is not necessarily the factor determining the profit. I believe that the profit-and-loss statements made up at the end of the year really reflect whether the enterprise holds a favored or an unfortunate niche in the whole [political, social and economic] aggregate.

In what way does this statement accurately describe the situation in the American oil industry? In the Soviet oil industry?

2. A small independent oil producer testified, "The difference between the U.S.S.R. and the U.S.A. in the oil industry is the difference between monopoly and free enterprise."

Prepare a short, critical evaluation of this businessman's assertation. What values do you believe he probably attaches to "monopoly" and to "free enterprise"?

3. A student commented after reading a preliminary version of these cases that "the basic difference between the oil industry in the two countries is that in the United States it has to make profits but in the Soviet Union it can run at

a loss." Explain your agreement or disagreement with this opinion; consider the effect of government policy upon the profits of the American oil industry.

4. Explain which of the following opinions better describes the American position in the international oil competition with the Soviet Union:

a. Foreign trade and industrial production are state monopolies in the Soviet Union and both are wielded as important instruments of national policy, giving the U.S.S.R. a decided advantage in its competition with the U.S. in world markets.

b. Americans have never been limited by their ideology, but have often pragmatically combined government and private efforts to create flexible, effective means of furthering national interests. We underrate our abilities to meet the economic challenge of the Soviet Union, if we listen to what we say and ignore what we do.

5. What are the similarities and differences in the oil policies of the United States and the U.S.S.R.?

6. Explain why American businessmen, usually so quick to praise the free economy, are willing to fight competition from Soviet oil by an increased use of government controls and regulations.

7. Analyze the way the United States has used the production of a subsidized industry such as agriculture, shipping, or air transport, as an instrument to advance American policy. In what ways has the U.S. use of these products and services differed from the Soviet Union's uses of oil?

8. The economic law of comparative advantage in international trade states that a nation should determine which goods to produce not on the basis of their absolute cost but of their relative cost. What reason is there to believe that the Soviet Union enjoys a comparative advantage in the producing and selling of oil? If so, how does this fact affect your judgment of whether the U.S.S.R. is pursuing its oil policy for political or for economic reasons?

A 7
B 8
C 9
D 0
E 1
F 2
G 3
H 4
I 5